Global Financial Integration Thirty Years On

Early in the new millennium it appeared that a long period of financial crisis had come to an end, but the world now faces renewed and greater turmoil. This volume analyses the past three decades of global financial integration and governance and the recent collapse into crisis, offering a coherent and policy-relevant overview. State-of-the-art research from an interdisciplinary group of scholars illuminates the economic, political and social issues at the heart of devising an effective and legitimate financial system for the future. The chapters offer debate around a series of core themes which probe the ties between public and private actors and their consequences for outcomes for both developed markets and developing countries alike. The contributors argue that developing effective, legitimate financial governance requires enhancing public versus private authority through broader stakeholder representation, ensuring more acceptable policy outcomes.

GEOFFREY R. D. UNDERHILL is Chair in International Governance in the Department of Political Science at the University of Amsterdam.

JASPER BLOM is a Ph.D. candidate at the Amsterdam Institute for Social Science Research, University of Amsterdam.

DANIEL MÜGGE is Assistant Professor of International Political Economy in the Department of Political Science at the University of Amsterdam.

Global Financial Integration Thirty Years On
From Reform to Crisis

Edited by

Geoffrey R. D. Underhill
University of Amsterdam

Jasper Blom
University of Amsterdam

Daniel Mügge
University of Amsterdam

CAMBRIDGE UNIVERSITY PRESS
Cambridge, New York, Melbourne, Madrid, Cape Town,
Singapore, São Paulo, Delhi, Mexico City

Cambridge University Press
The Edinburgh Building, Cambridge CB2 8RU, UK

Published in the United States of America by Cambridge University Press, New York

www.cambridge.org
Information on this title: www.cambridge.org/9781107406902

© Cambridge University Press 2010

This publication is in copyright. Subject to statutory exception
and to the provisions of relevant collective licensing agreements,
no reproduction of any part may take place without the written
permission of Cambridge University Press.

First published 2010
First paperback edition 2012

A catalogue record for this publication is available from the British Library

Library of Congress Cataloguing in Publication Data
Global financial integration thirty years on : from reform to crisis /
  [edited by] Geoffrey R.D. Underhill, Jasper Blom, Daniel Mügge.
    p. cm.
  Includes bibliographical references and index.
  ISBN 978-0-521-19869-1
  1. International finance.   2. International economic integration.
  3. Financial crises–History–21st century.   I. Underhill, Geoffrey R. D.
  II. Blom, Jasper, 1978–   III. Mügge, Daniel.   IV. Title.
  HG3881.G5737 2010
  332´.042–dc22
  2010021892

ISBN 978-0-521-19869-1 Hardback
ISBN 978-1-107-40690-2 Paperback

Cambridge University Press has no responsibility for the persistence or
accuracy of URLs for external or third-party internet websites referred to in
this publication, and does not guarantee that any content on such websites is,
or will remain, accurate or appropriate.

Contents

List of figures	*page* viii
List of tables	x
Notes on contributors	xi
Preface	xiii
Acknowledgements	xv
List of abbreviations	xvii

Introduction: the challenges and prospects of global
financial integration   1
GEOFFREY R. D. UNDERHILL, JASPER BLOM AND
DANIEL MÜGGE

Part I History and context: input, output and the current architecture (whence it came)   23

1 Financial governance in historical perspective: lessons
from the 1920s   25
RANDALL GERMAIN

2 Between the storms: patterns in global financial governance,
2001–2007   42
ERIC HELLEINER AND STEFANO PAGLIARI

3 Deliberative international financial governance and apex
policy forums: where we are and where we should be headed   58
ANDREW BAKER

4 Finance, globalisation and economic development: the
role of institutions   74
DANNY CASSIMON, PANICOS DEMETRIADES AND
BJÖRN VAN CAMPENHOUT

v

vi   Contents

Part II Assessing the current financial architecture (how well does it work?)   93

5 Adopting international financial standards in Asia: convergence or divergence in the global political economy?   95
ANDREW WALTER

6 The political economy of Basel II in the international financial architecture   113
STIJN CLAESSENS AND GEOFFREY R. D. UNDERHILL

7 The catalytic approach to debt workout in practice: coordination failure between the IMF, the Paris Club and official creditors   134
EELKE DE JONG AND KOEN VAN DER VEER

8 Empirical evidence on the new international aid architecture   150
STIJN CLAESSENS, DANNY CASSIMON AND BJÖRN VAN CAMPENHOUT

9 Who governs and why? The making of a global anti-money laundering regime   172
ELENI TSINGOU

10 Brazil and Argentina in the global financial system: contrasting approaches to development and foreign debt   187
VICTOR KLAGSBRUNN

11 Global markets, national alliances and financial transformations in East Asia   204
XIAOKE ZHANG

Part III Does the future hold? Reactions to the current regime and prospects for progress (where is it going?)   221

12 Changing transatlantic financial regulatory relations at the turn of the millennium   223
ELLIOT POSNER

13 Monetary and financial cooperation in Asia: improving legitimacy and effectiveness?   241
HERIBERT DIETER

14 From microcredit to microfinance to inclusive finance: a response to global financial openness   256
BRIGITTE YOUNG

Contents   vii

15 Combating pro-cyclicality in the international financial architecture: towards development-friendly financial governance   270
JOSÉ OCAMPO AND STEPHANY GRIFFITH-JONES

16 Public interest, national diversity and global financial governance   287
GEOFFREY R. D. UNDERHILL AND XIAOKE ZHANG

Conclusion: whither global financial governance after the crisis?   304
DANIEL MÜGGE, JASPER BLOM AND
GEOFFREY R. D. UNDERHILL

References   316
Index   347

Figures

3.1	Continuum of deliberative equality	*page* 71
4.1	The complex dynamics of financial globalisation	83
4.2	(Appendix) Recursion diagram	90
5.1	The spectrum of compliance	99
5.2	Private sector compliance costs and third-party monitoring costs for different international standards	107
6.1	Number of countries which have a positive, neutral or negative spread change due to Basel II	128
6.2	Average spread change in basis points under Basel II	129
6.3	Internal and external ratings in the East Asian financial crisis	131
7.1	Estimating a country's financing gap	137
8.1	Bilateral net ODA transfers, 1970–2006	154
8.2	Responsiveness of aid to countries' income, policy, population and debt	159
8.3	Time-varying, donor-specific sensitivities for CPIA	161
8.4	Time-varying, donor-specific sensitivities for GDP	162
8.5	Time-varying, donor-specific sensitivities for population size	163
8.6	Time-varying, donor-specific sensitivities for debt outstanding disbursed	164
10.1	Current account balance as % of GDP	190
10.2	Trade balance selected developing countries in US$ billions – I	190
10.3	Trade balance selected developing countries in US$ billions – II	191
10.4	Effective real exchange rates	192
10.5	Brazil: international total reserves, total external debt and net external debt	198
10.6	Argentina: total external debt, 1995–2007	200
10.7	EMBI spread Argentina vs. global, 1998–2007	201

List of figures

10.8	EMBI spread Brazil vs. global, 1998–2007	201
14.1	Accessing financial markets: progressive stages for MFIs	266
15.1	Emerging market spreads on JP Morgan EMBI global and US high-yield bonds	274

Tables

4.1	Evolution of external flows to Sub-Saharan Africa and to other developing countries	*page* 81
5.1	Formal compliance with SDDS, IFRS and Basel I standards	98
5.2	Moody's weighted average long-term deposit ratings, bank financial strength ratings and average CARs, Asian and US banks, 2003	109
7.1	Official lending in countries with an IMF programme	141
7.2	Official financing and the catalytic effect of IMF programmes	142
8.1	Overview of the paradigm changes in the international aid architecture	152
8.2	Monitoring the Paris Declaration commitments: 2005 baseline and 2010 targets	165
8.3	Measures of aid quality and governance of bilateral donors	166
8.4	(Appendix) Fixed effects, random effects and Hausman-Taylor estimations	171
10.1	Brazil: external debt of central government	199
12.1	Empirical expectations of regulatory centralisation explanation	228
12.2	Transatlantic dispute management over time – the turning points	229
12.3	Transatlantic dispute management over time – EU centralisation	234
13.1	Total reserves minus gold of selected Asian economies	246

Contributors

ANDREW BAKER is Senior Lecturer in political economy at the School of Politics, International Studies and Philosophy, Queen's University, Belfast

JASPER BLOM is a Ph.D. candidate at the Amsterdam Institute for Social Science Research, University of Amsterdam

BJÖRN VAN CAMPENHOUT is a researcher assistant at the Institute of Development Policy and Management, University of Antwerp

DANNY CASSIMON is Senior Lecturer at the Institute of Development Policy and Management, University of Antwerp

STIJN CLAESSENS is Assistant Director of the Research Department at the International Monetary Fund and Professor of International Finance Policy at the Faculty of Economics, University of Amsterdam

PANICOS DEMETRIADES is Professor of Financial Economics at the Department of Economics, University of Leicester

HERIBERT DIETER is Senior Fellow at the German Institute for International and Security Affairs and Associate Fellow at the Centre for the Study of Globalisation and Regionalisation at Warwick University

RANDALL GERMAIN is Professor of Political Science at the Department of Political Science, Carleton University

STEPHANY GRIFFITH-JONES is Director of the Financial Markets Programme at the Institute for Policy Dialogue, Columbia University

ERIC HELLEINER is Professor, Department of Political Science, University of Waterloo

EELKE DE JONG is Professor of International Economics at the Nijmegen School of Management, Radboud University Nijmegen

xii Notes on contributors

VICTOR KLAGSBRUNN is Professor of Economics at the Department of Economics, Fluminense Federal University, São Paolo, Brazil

DANIEL MÜGGE is Assistant Professor of International Political Economy at the Department of Political Science, University of Amsterdam

JOSÉ OCAMPO is Professor in the Professional Practice of International and Public Affairs at the School of International and Public Affairs, Columbia University

STEFANO PAGLIARI is a Ph.D. candidate in the Global Governance programme at the Balsillie School of International Affairs, University of Waterloo

ELLIOT POSNER is Assistant Professor of Political Science at the Department of Political Science, Case Western Reserve University

ELENI TSINGOU is Research Fellow at the Centre for the Study of Globalisation and Regionalisation, University of Warwick

GEOFFREY R. D. UNDERHILL is Chair in International Governance at the Department of Political Science, University of Amsterdam

KOEN VAN DER VEER is a researcher at De Nederlandsche Bank and a Ph.D. candidate at the Department of Economics, Radboud University Nijmegen

ANDREW WALTER is Reader in International Political Economy at the Department of International Relations, London School of Economics and Political Science

BRIGITTE YOUNG is Professor of Political Science and International/ Comparative Political Economy at the Institute for Political Science, University of Münster

XIAOKE ZHANG is Associate Professor in Political Economy and Asian Studies at the School of Politics and International Relations, University of Nottingham

Preface

Producing a volume on financial governance just at the outbreak of the worst financial crisis since the Great Depression proved to be both a daunting and exciting task. While the onset of crisis raised the salience of work on financial governance considerably, both editors and contributors might be forgiven for a sense of exhaustion related to the hot pursuit of a moving target. This has meant that the purpose of the volume has evolved rather rapidly over the past three years. The volume began life as an analysis of the record and historical experience of the 'new international financial architecture' developed in the wake of the emerging market crises of the 1990s and early 2000s. The analysis yielded the conclusion that not all was functioning as effectively as the architects believed. The aim was to challenge the apparent complacency of the period of calm following the Argentine default, and to stimulate new thinking based on the understanding and reading of the evidence that all was not well and that fundamental flaws in global financial governance required urgent attention.

By August 2007, when an early version of the manuscript was ready and much of the research findings had been discussed in workshops, it became clear that the usual crisis rumblings but of unusual force were beginning deep below the fine edifice constructed by the architects. There was much discussion of these rumblings at a workshop devoted to the second full draft of the volume which assembled the contributors in Venice in May 2008, a sense of foreboding but not yet real understanding of what lay ahead. By the end of the summer 2008 the sense of foreboding had certainly increased as the manuscript was submitted for review. By early October the entire picture had changed so dramatically that the new circumstances raised questions about the viability of the project and the relevance of the manuscript to the rapidly evolving situation. The edifice of global finance had been brought down and the world was on the way to devoting an unprecedented ratio of annual GDP to rescuing the banks. By this time our tentative conclusion that something was amiss was clearly a no-brainer and we and the

xiv Preface

contributors wondered what on earth would happen next to the financial world and to our volume. As editors we chose path dependency and soldiered on.

We would like to thank one of the anonymous reviewers in particular for the encouraging and confident assessment that we did indeed have a story to tell and that the research which found its way into the chapters remained relevant if in obvious need of updating. The result must be judged by the reader, but we believe we have succeeded in adapting and updating the analysis and research findings of the chapters to yield an explanation of how the reforms which were the new financial architecture became an integral part of the problem which led to the outbreak of crisis. The contributions do so on a particularly broad scale, and our thanks to Cambridge University Press for supporting a project of such scope in this era of sound bites, summaries and opinionated blogging.

In this sense the volume is no straightforward look at the usual suspects in global financial markets and their governance, although these are there. This volume provides comprehensive coverage of the international financial system and its governance, from microfinance and aid architecture in relation to poverty relief and the problems of underdevelopment, to the money-laundering regime to the supervision of the world's most sophisticated and largest (and many still fragile) financial institutions. The volume provides a launch pad for debate and discussion of what should be done and in which direction the reform process should proceed, all based on original research by an interdisciplinary set of authors conscious of our shared critical yet constructive purpose. The volume begins with historical context and looks at the aims of financial reform in the 1990s through to the period of calm before the current crisis. The analysis of what was wrong with the new financial architecture is then employed to develop ideas on where reform should now be headed. In this sense the volume provides an interdisciplinary guide to the origins of the crisis and the governance issues which the post-crisis reform process must address. There had emerged over time a vision of market-based governance shared by the public and private sectors in international finance which failed to prevent the current calamity and to provide a financial order compatible with basic stability. These problems were far from resolved at the time of writing and it is not clear that sufficient political will exists to realise the necessary change going forward.

Acknowledgements

It is with great pleasure that we acknowledge those who have supported us in this project over the past three years. Our first and greatest debt is to the excellence of our contributors and their loyalty and patience in sticking with the effort to send the book to press. A few of the scholars who contribute to this volume first came into regular contact with each other many years ago, but a particular impetus in terms of original research findings was given to the project by the funding provided by the Economic and Research Council of the UK under its World Economy and Finance research programme. From 2005 it funded a project headed by Panicos Demetriades at the University of Leicester and including as partners the London School of Economics and Political Science and the University of Amsterdam ('National and International Aspects of Financial Development', award no. RES-156-25-0009). The regular series of workshops organised by Panicos and his team at Leicester were invaluable in terms of establishing working relationships across disciplinary boundaries and building confidence and collegiality among a number of the contributors presented here.

Further impetus was given by the European Commission's Framework Six research programme, which funded a major network of excellence also beginning in 2005 (GARNET, award no. 513330), headed by the University of Warwick with over forty partners across Europe. The contacts developed through the work package on global economic governance and market regulation (the coordination of which was shared by Geoffrey R. D. Underhill and Heribert Dieter) have proven invaluable. Once again a series of successful cross-disciplinary workshops brought scholars and policy practitioners together, directly contributing to some of the research found in these pages and particularly to connecting them to each other. GARNET funding in particular financed the May 2008 workshop in Venice, at the University of Warwick's Palazzo Pesaro-Papafava there, the workshop which yielded the second full draft of the manuscript and set it on course for peer review and publication. A final push was facilitated by yet another EU research grant, this time

xvi Acknowledgements

under the Framework Seven programme project PEGGED (Political and Economic Governance: the Global and European Dimensions, award no. SSH7-CT-2008-217559) and which began in the summer of 2008. Our research institute at the University of Amsterdam, the venerable Amsterdam School for Social Science Research (ASSR), provided logistical support and inspirational colleagues who participated and inspired us in this project. Our thanks go in particular to José Komen who manages the school so well. The School also financed four years of Ph.D. research for Daniel Mügge, now assistant professor at the Department of Political Science, hosted and financed workshops, and funded much occasional conference and other research-related travel over the years. Research funding for Jasper Blom was provided by the Netherlands Organisation for Scientific Research (NWO, grant no. 400-04-233), funding without which his contribution would not have been possible and then neither would this book. We are also grateful to De Nederlandsche Bank (central bank of the Netherlands), in particular Jan Brockmeijer who was long head of the Financial Stability Department and now fills the same function at the IMF, for its support for the major 2006 conference 'Global Financial and Monetary Governance: the EU and Emerging Market Economies', and for keeping us in touch with the real world of financial governance. Finally, we are indebted to Takeo David Hymans for his thorough edit of the entire book manuscript and compilation of the index. No doubt these acknowledgements have left someone out but we have done our best to cover the considerable ground required in expressing our heartfelt thanks.

We leave it to the reader to judge the result. Any remaining weaknesses in the final product are ours alone.

Abbreviations

ABF	Asian Bond Fund
ABMI	Asian Bond Market Initiative
AMF	Asian Monetary Fund
AML	Anti-Money Laundering
AREAER	Annual Report on Exchange Arrangements and Exchange Restrictions (IMF)
ASEAN	Association of South-East Asian Nations
B-I	Basel I (capital accord)
B-II	Basel II (capital accord)
BC	Basel Committee on Banking Supervision
BCP	Basel Core Principles for Effective Banking Supervision
BFSR	Bank Financial Strength Ratings (Moody's Investor Services)
BIS	Bank for International Settlements
CAC	Collective Action Clause
CAR	Capital to risk-weighted Assets Ratio (Capital Adequacy Ratio)
CCL	Contingent Credit Line (IMF)
CDI	Commitment to Development Index (Center for Global Development)
CDO	Collateralised Debt Obligation
CESR	Committee of European Securities Regulators
CFF	Compensatory Financial Facility (IMF)
CFT	Combating the Financing of Terrorism
CFTC	Commodities Futures Trading Commission
CMI	Chiang Mai Initiative
CPIA	Country Policy and Institutional Assessment (World Bank)
DAC	Development Assistance Committee (OECD)

xvii

xviii List of abbreviations

DPP	Democratic Progressive Party (Taiwan)
EC	European Commission
ECA	Export Credit Agency
ECU	European Currency Unit
EEA	Exchange Equalization Account (UK)
EFF	Extended Fund Facility (IMF)
EMEAP	Executives' Meeting of East Asia and Pacific Central Banks
EMU	Economic and Monetary Union (EU)
ER	External Rating
ERM	Exchange Rate Mechanism (EU)
ESF	Exogenous Shocks Facility (IMF)
FASB	Financial Accounting Standards Board
FATF	Financial Action Task Force
FCD	Financial Conglomerates Directive (European Commission)
FCL	Flexible Credit Line (IMF)
FESE	Federation of European Securities Exchanges
FinCEN	Financial Crimes Enforcement Network (US Treasury)
FoBF	Fund of Bond Funds (CMI)
FSAP	Financial Sector Assessment Programme (IMF/World Bank)
FSAP	Financial Services Action Plan (EU)
FSB	Financial Stability Board (formerly FSF)
FSCG	Financial Services Consumer Group (EU)
FSF	Financial Stability Forum
FSM	Financial Sector Masterplan (Malaysia)
GAAP	Generally Accepted Accounting Principles (US)
GDP	Gross Domestic Product
GFA	Global Financial Architecture
HIPC	Heavily Indebted Poor Country
IAASB	International Auditing and Assurance Standards Board
IAS	International Accounting Standards
IASB	International Accounting Standards Board
IASC	International Accounting Standards Committee
ICRG	International Country Risk Guide
IFF	International Finance Facility
IFIs	International Financial Institutions

IFRS	International Financial Reporting Standards
IIF	Institute of International Finance
IMF	International Monetary Fund
IOSCO	International Organisation of Securities Commissions
IR	Internal Rating
IRB	Internal Ratings Based
KLSE	Kuala Lumpur Stock Exchange
KMT	Kuomintang (Nationalist Party, Taiwan)
MAS	Monetary Authority of Singapore
MDB	Multilateral Development Bank
MDGs	Millennium Development Goals
MDRI	Multilateral Debt Reduction Initiative
MERCOSUR	*Mercado Común del Sur* (Southern Common Market)
MFIs	Microfinance Institutions
MiFID	Markets in Financial Instruments Directive (EU)
MSB	Money Service Business
NCCT	Non-Cooperative Countries and Territories (FATF)
NIFA	New International Financial Architecture
NPL	Non-Performing Loan
NYSE	New York Stock Exchange
ODA	Official Development Assistance
OECD	Organisation for Economic Cooperation and Development
OFAC	Office of Foreign Assets Control (US Treasury)
PAIF	Pan-Asia Bond Index Fund
PCAOB	Public Company Accounting Oversight Board
PCG	Principles of Corporate Governance (OECD)
PD	Paris Declaration (on Aid Effectiveness)
PRGF	Poverty Reduction and Growth Facility (IMF)
PRSP	Poverty Reduction Strategy Paper (IMF)
ROSC	Report on the Observance of Standards and Codes (IMF)
SBA	Stand-By Arrangement (IMF)
SDDS	Special Data Dissemination Standard
SDR	Special Drawing Right (IMF)

SDRM	Sovereign Debt Restructuring Mechanism
SEC	Securities and Exchange Commission (US)
SIA	Securities Industry Association (later SIFMA)
SIFMA	Securities Industry and Financial Markets Association
SME	Small and Medium-sized Enterprise
SOE	State-Owned Enterprise
TFP	Total Factor Productivity
TSE	Taipei Stock Exchange
UMNO	United Malay National Organisation
VaR	Value at Risk

Introduction: the challenges and prospects of global financial integration

Geoffrey R. D. Underhill, Jasper Blom and Daniel Mügge

The bitter winds of financial crisis have once again swept global markets, this time beginning at the core of the system, Wall Street. Whether blame be assigned to private greed, public policy lapses, or both, vast sums of public money and shareholder capital have been wiped out in the otherwise noble cause of preventing systemic breakdown. Vulnerable citizens once more count the costs to the real economy. As massive liquidity has been made available to private financial institutions on exceptionally permissive terms, it has been difficult not to notice the striking contrast with the management of earlier crises based in the emerging markets. When they were in the dock, the emphasis was on the conditionality of the terms of rescue; with Wall Street and the City in trouble, the terms of rescue have been much more open-ended.

As growing uncertainty combined with these apparent double standards, the crisis has reopened debate on the global financial architecture, public policy and regulation. Global financial integration and the governance of the global monetary and financial system stand at a crossroads after over thirty years of market-oriented cross-border integration and development preceded and indeed exacerbated a financial crisis on a scale not seen since the 1930s. This ongoing process of integration, regularly punctuated by crises and instability, raises analytical, normative and policy dilemmas which challenge our current understanding of financial and monetary governance. Many scholars argue that higher levels of economic integration require greater degrees of regional and global governance (e.g. Cerny 1995; Zürn 2004). Yet the relationships between economic integration, competitive market dynamics, international political cooperation and potentially new patterns of multilevel governance remain unclear as policy-makers face the difficult task of reform while still coping with the consequences of crisis.

While the capacity of the current global financial architecture to cope with monetary and financial challenges is once again in serious doubt, the future direction of reform remains uncertain. To complicate matters further, not only the capacity and efficiency, but also the *legitimacy* of contemporary governance arrangements is in question. The current pattern of member-state influence and voting rights in global and even some regional institutions does not (yet, despite the recent IMF quota reforms decided in October 2009) reflect the growing weight of emerging markets in the global economy, despite the costs these economies and their citizens have often paid for the system's volatility. At the same time, global and regional financial governance is characterised by the growing involvement of private actors in both the policy process and in governance, a trend which raises legitimacy questions of its own. In fact it appears that the close and growing involvement of private interests in governance is related to the unequal distribution of costs and benefits in the system, to the risks which accumulated under new forms of financial supervision, and to the way crisis management and bail-outs take place. Both these issues make for an unequal power structure in determining the future direction of global financial governance.

In what is a regrettable but seemingly persistent historical pattern, serious debate on the need for reform correlates closely with episodes of major and costly systemic crises. Perhaps more disturbingly, those crises which imposed relatively limited costs on the core economies of the global financial system generated rather less institutional overhaul than the damage they inflicted on emerging markets might justify. This failure to reform the system more thoroughly and with greater regard to the real nature of the risks inherent in contemporary financial market practice has much to do with the current state of affairs where even the citizens of developed economies are now paying a high price for financial system failure.

An earlier period of policy debate on a 'new international financial architecture' began with the global financial instability of the mid to late 1990s (notably the East Asian crisis). This debate and its limited reform measures came to an end early in the twenty-first century, despite the severe Argentine crisis of 2001–2. Many initiatives were then taken in the field of crisis prevention, with a focus on improving transparency in financial markets and macroeconomic governance (IMF Reports on the Observance of Standards and Codes or ROSCs). New consultative forums emerged as a response to the exclusion of emerging markets (G20) and the need for better overview and supervisory coordination of globally integrated markets (Financial Stability Forum or FSF – recently renamed and strengthened as the Financial Stability Board or FSB). Yet none of these bodies have real power to set rules for global financial governance; much may still lie with the major G7/G10 economies despite the new role for the G20 and the major emerging market countries therein. The one serious institutional innovation in the

Introduction: challenges and prospects

field of crisis resolution, the Sovereign Debt Restructuring Mechanism (SDRM), failed to materialise and was replaced by the incremental and voluntary Collective Action Clauses (CACs) and the non-binding private sector 'principles' promulgated by the Institute of International Finance (IIF 2006b). These and other private sector initiatives were as much an attempt to pre-empt public intervention as they were attempts to fill gaps in governance.

The subsequent 'period of calm', 2002–7, saw the consolidation of new forums for international cooperation and the beginnings of a new if questionable Basel capital standards regime. This period bred a sense of complacency that the new global financial architecture was working and was successfully preventing the outbreak of new major crises.[1] Nonetheless, less positive signs were visible to those who wished to see: capital flows to emerging markets and poorer developing countries remained volatile and unpredictable over time (World Bank 2006a). New market developments and players emerged around the explosion of asset securitisation and credit derivatives, private equity and sovereign wealth funds. Private indebtedness combined with asset bubbles in core economies grew, and global payments and exchange rate imbalances (especially around the US dollar) loomed ominously. While this potentially explosive mixture stored up by the market and public policy lapses was brought to the attention of policy-makers by a range of scholars, BIS and IMF reports, and some investors and market observers, the problems were largely ignored.[2]

If the series of emerging market crises underscored the vulnerability of these economies and their systemic importance, developments since August 2007 have shown that core countries in the global financial system are unexpectedly vulnerable to shocks, with yet greater systemic risks. The credit crunch not only demonstrated vulnerability in unexpected places; it showed that the apparently sound and stable financial architecture of the 'period of calm' was less successful than hoped. The most sophisticated of national financial systems were now at the eye of the storm. In these circumstances, the attention of policy-makers has unsurprisingly been absorbed by largely unilateral and ad hoc measures to prevent a further deepening of the crisis, so far with at least an eye on their possible cross-border impact. But it takes a limited degree of perspicacity to observe that the situation could benefit from higher degrees of cross-border cooperation. If the current pattern were to deteriorate

---

[1] The Argentine and Turkish crises in fact rumbled on for some time, as did the exchange rate aftershocks experienced by Brazil and other emerging market economies.
[2] See Nouriel Roubini's web-based Global EconoMonitor for an overview of warnings.

into competitive unilateralism the danger could escalate significantly. At the time of writing it is too early to tell which way governance will develop. International agreement is still elusive in spite – or maybe because – of the plethora of recommendations tabled by regulators, academics, market participants and politicians.

History may hold important lessons about future scenarios. A significant group of countries have responded to what they perceived as the unsatisfactory nature and extent of post Asian-crisis reform by decoupling themselves from the established institutions of the global financial architecture. They were essentially checking out of Hotel Capital Mobility as built by the global financial architects (Underhill 2007). While they *do* want capital inflows, they are determined never again to submit to the humiliation and intrusion of the conditionalities of the International Financial Institutions (IFIs). In the Asian region this entailed a huge build-up of currency reserves and the development of regional self-help agreements, a build-up that ironically was instrumental to the growth of the US asset bubble (Schwartz 2009). In Latin America, the same feeling translated into the early repayment of IMF loans by Argentina and Brazil and a number of electoral victories by leftwing governments with a clear anti-'Washington consensus' agenda. This seismic shift may yet impair international cooperation. The Fund's programmes have continued to play an important role in chronically indebted Sub-Saharan African countries, while there is little evidence that forty-plus years of IMF policies have been particularly favourable for growth and development (Vreeland 2003). Nor is the rapid growth of international capital flows associated with the post-Bretton Woods global financial architecture closely correlated to economic growth in non-industrial countries, as the (now former) chief economist of the IMF, Raghuram Rajan, among others recently concluded (Prasad *et al.* 2006). While the crisis means that the IMF is clearly 'back' and participating in the rescue of Iceland, Eastern European, Southern and other economies, suspicions of conditionality and policies of self-insurance through excessive international reserves in Asia and Latin America still remain in place.

This implies that eventually the focus must shift back to developing a cross-border framework for global financial governance that is more durable, effective and legitimate. The declining systemic 'weight' of the United States and the dollar and the inclusion of a greater diversity of private actors in a context of integrated financial markets all reinforce the need for new patterns of governance. The crisis and credit crunch remind us that policy issues born of financial integration combined with more traditional monetary questions such as the management of

Introduction: challenges and prospects

macro-payments and exchange rate imbalances present enduring and daunting challenges.

The focus of this volume therefore lies on the urgent revival of debate about the requirements of financial and monetary governance under conditions of cross-border market integration. How we understand the relationship between the evolution of markets and of the institutions of governance in the monetary and financial domain will be central to the contributions; a primary objective is to link scholarly analysis more effectively to the potential reform of governance. The volume frames the debate first in terms of both the *effectiveness* and the *legitimacy* of the current architecture and eventual reform. Two contrasting arguments are under scrutiny here. On the one hand, the literature traditionally points to a trade-off between the effectiveness of decision-making (particularly in crisis circumstances) and the incorporation of varying and possibly conflicting interests in a (more) democratic fashion (e.g. Dahl 1994). On the other hand, as argued in this Introduction and in several other chapters, a *lack* of inclusiveness may undermine the effectiveness of governance as few actors will accept the substantive outcomes of an exclusionary process and as the free competition of policy ideas is limited. To work, global rules will need to take heed of local conditions and hence require input from a wide variety of stakeholders. Simultaneously, a lack of inclusiveness may also undercut the legitimacy of governance, as authority serves only the constituencies involved in decision-making.

Although both effectiveness and inclusion may be seen as necessary sources of legitimacy in governance, much empirical scholarship continues to assess inclusion/legitimacy and effectiveness (to say nothing of market efficiency) independently of each other. In a plural system where emerging markets and developed economies vie for influence on increasingly equal terms, it becomes all the more important that reforms address the concerns of a wider range of stakeholders in global finance than has hitherto been the case, and that new and more effective patterns of governance are developed. This volume therefore places the relationships and tensions between decision-making effectiveness, substantive outcomes and legitimacy centre stage.

Scharpf (1999) has famously analysed legitimacy as comprising 'input-oriented legitimacy' (concerning the decision-making process) and 'output-oriented legitimacy' (concerning the substantive outcome of decision-making over time). The volume adopts this distinction between the input/process side and the output/substantive-outcomes side as a second way of framing the debate, but adapts it by observing that though input and output legitimacy can be distinguished for analytical purposes, in political practice they are ultimately two sides of the same coin: desirable 'policy output' depends on the voices heard on the input side of governance (Mügge 2010, in press; see also Underhill and Zhang in this volume). While the constituencies involved in and affected by financial market governance have potentially conflicting policy objectives and preferences, only a limited range of these constituencies have been included in policy-making at either the domestic or international levels. In this light, a range of chapters in this volume analyse the input or 'policy process' side and the issue of inclusion in decision-making. Others focus on the output side: substantive outcomes, their perceived effectiveness, and their impact on a range of stakeholders and constituencies. The aim is to draw attention to how the problem of inclusion on the input side contributes to a potential lack of legitimacy in outcomes on the output side by affecting the effectiveness and distributional outcomes of governance for the range of constituencies involved.

Within this framework, the volume draws attention to debates focusing on four crucial issues in financial governance. First, there is the question of the proper balance between private participation and interests in the policy process and the broader public good. Specifically, there is a debate among the contributors about whether the decision-making process at the national or international level might be characterised by policy capture on the input side, and how this might skew substantive outcomes on the output side. Second, the question of inclusion on the input side may be specifically raised in relation to developing countries, whose effective participation in decision-making is (effectiveness of recent reforms pending) at best indirect and most of whom arguably have less influence on policy than major private financial institutions in developed countries. On the output side, the system's distribution of costs and benefits is possibly skewed towards the developed economies and their powerful private financial institutions. Third, and mostly relevant to the output side, is the debate on the pressures exerted by the current architecture's norms in favour of financial integration and convergence among national financial systems, which constrain the 'policy space' (Rodrik 2007) available to developing and other economies in the system. Debates around all three of these issues directly concern the tensions between effectiveness and legitimacy, and lead to the fourth issue: because the legitimacy of the current financial architecture was in question even before it was properly established and functioning, it has over time generated *reactions* at national, regional and global levels, particularly in Asian and developing countries. These reactions focus on questions concerning substantive output-side issues

Introduction: challenges and prospects

as much as the input or process side. How such reactions should be assessed remains an open question until the current reforms under discussion (or those yet to come) have been effectively implemented: do they strengthen global financial governance? Or are they – consciously or not – potential obstacles to the difficult but necessary endeavour of finding global answers to the challenges of global markets?

The volume addresses these four issues first by analysing the historical context and emergence of the current financial architecture from the mid-1990s to the end of the emerging market crisis period in 2001–2. The next set of chapters looks at how well it works, assessing the input and output aspects of the financial architecture in relation to the first three issues outlined above. A final set of chapters focuses on reactions to perceived lapses in effectiveness and legitimacy and efforts at further reform.

Historical context

Since the emergence of the off-shore Eurocurrency markets in the late 1950s, the combination of cross-border financial market integration and the liberalisation of formerly repressed national financial systems following the collapse of the Bretton Woods system in 1971 has been one of the fundamental transformations of our time (Helleiner 1994) alongside the digital revolution and impending climate change. This turn towards the market in national economic policies marked the beginning of systemic change. The rapid spread of information technology coupled with policies to break down barriers among market segments and national financial systems has altered market structures. The widespread securitisation of transactions and the resulting de-segmentation of financial institutions have created complex and dynamic linkages between banking and public and private securities markets, including the rapidly growing derivatives segment. Capital account opening and the removal of exchange controls essentially erased the distinction between 'national' and 'off-shore' financial markets. The new system is characterised by a high degree of market-led adjustment, product innovation and capital mobility. These developments have vastly altered the financial and monetary rules of the game and have created a more challenging policy environment for governments and international institutions alike. The difficulties for developing and emerging market economies have been particularly marked.

Financial markets presuppose governance – a legal and macroeconomic order in which market and inflationary expectations and adjustment mechanisms among national currencies obey relatively consistent and predictable rules and norms. Most market agents seek calculable risk as opposed to uncertainty, a climate which is partially delivered by a regulatory and policy environment which allows them to form expectations for the medium and longer term. The assumption behind the emerging market-based system was that market processes would prove self-regulating and, in combination with flexible exchange rates, would generate more stability than the policy mistakes of the 1970s such as inflation, state bail-out and protection of lame duck industries, and growing budget deficits. This 'governance light' came to mean the pursuit of stable and market-friendly macroeconomic policies by governments, providing a positive investment climate as well as market and regulatory transparency at the national level. Private financial institutions and markets were largely left to themselves, under the implicit assumption that they would develop self-regulatory governance mechanisms where necessary. Market discipline would apply to state behaviour and fiscal and monetary policies too. For this last mechanism to work, once-separate national financial systems had to converge sufficiently in terms of regulatory policy and business practice (and therefore market expectations) so as to constitute a more or less contiguous market in the eyes of investors. Yet the degree of convergence in national policies and financial systems required for such a system to function never fully materialised, and is arguably unlikely to do so in the near future.

Some analysts have assumed that market forces would automatically induce policy and financial system convergence over time (Smith and Walter 2003). Others (Eichengreen 1999; Bryant 2003) have argued that the conditions for operating global markets could be consciously developed, but attention to stability and convergence of national policies was necessary. Of course there were also those who argued, on the basis of historical evidence, that financial markets and monetary systems are inherently unstable in the first place (Kindleberger 1982; Galbraith 1995; Strange 1998) so that they required the consistent intervention of political authorities. The persistent pattern of crises, exchange rate volatility and payments imbalances which accompanied the emergence of the market-based system seemed to give the latter the better part of the argument – unless and until the proper conditions for self-adjusting markets could be achieved.

The global 'system' of the early to mid-1990s was in fact a series of complex linkages facilitating high degrees of capital mobility among dissimilar national financial systems characterised by contrasting legal traditions and national policy styles (see e.g. Richardson 1982; Allen and Gale 2000). There were considerable differences in levels of national financial development, openness vs. repression, regulatory and legal traditions, and national monetary and exchange rate policy imperatives. The combination of these differences yielded high levels of 'dissonance' as capital moved rapidly across borders, responding to a bewildering array of signals under conditions of imperfect information. A host of collective action problems emerged as governments facing adjustment followed policies that made sense for them but not for the system as a whole. National institutional capacities to deal with these problems diverged widely, often worsening the situation in times of crisis. National financial reforms revealed themselves to be less than rational processes replete with unintended consequences. In fact, they were often highly political affairs in which special interests could write their own rules in narrow and effectively closed policy communities (Moran 1991; Underhill 1995; Coleman 1996; Zhang 2003b).

Governments faced domestic private constituencies and political imperatives as well as external pressures which were difficult either to ignore or to square with each other. Investors found themselves in financial environments about which they knew little and cared less (ubiquitous trader: 'we went into Latin America knowing nothing about it, and we came out of Latin America knowing nothing about it'). Investors seeking higher returns sent surges of capital in and out of small and shallow economies, which were often overwhelmed by the effects. The sense of helplessness among their governments was seldom relieved by the intervention of global institutions, the IMF in particular; conditionality imposed difficult adjustment processes, often presenting governments with political legitimacy problems.

Uncertainty appeared to have the edge over calculable risk, while pricing signals became difficult or impossible to read in such a way as to facilitate smooth adjustment. Crises with potentially systemic implications became a regular feature of the system. Following the surprise outbreak of the 1994–5 peso crisis in a Mexico which had undergone considerable adaptation to the new market-based order, the G7/G10 countries initiated reform of what became known as the 'international financial architecture' (Eichengreen 1999). These efforts were redoubled after the 1997–8 Asian crisis with the professed (but contested) aim of strengthening the weakest emerging market links in the system. Regulatory reform and convergence were encouraged through the promulgation of macroeconomic and regulatory standards and codes.

The tensions between global structures and national policy imperatives lay at the heart of the choices to be made (Underhill and Zhang 2003; Zhang 2003b). While the reforms emphasised adaptation of emerging market financial systems to developed country norms – with important consequences for their long-run development plans and prospects – evidence

10   *Geoffrey R. D. Underhill* et al.

accumulated that this approach was unlikely to achieve its objectives (Eichengreen and Hausmann 2005). Institutions responsible for crisis prevention and management such as the IMF experienced difficulties designing policies perceived as fair, applicable across national contexts, and distributionally balanced, while erstwhile emerging market economies became serious global financial players, clamouring for influence commensurate with their economic role and weight.

In the midst of this turbulent period, the IMF proposed a major public sector initiative to inject greater levels of predictability and burden sharing in post-crisis debt workouts. In short, the Sovereign Debt Restructuring Mechanism (SDRM, see Krueger 2001, 2002) was a modified form of bankruptcy procedure for countries in crisis. The proposal was defeated by a combination of intense private sector lobbying, related US-based opposition and the opposition of two key emerging market economies, Mexico and Brazil. The SDRM was succeeded by a voluntary private sector initiative developed and led by the powerful representative of the global banking industry, the Institute of International Finance (IIF 2006b). Collective Action Clauses (CACs) for debtors and bondholders, promoted by the G10, became the market standard.

'Governance light' and the market system of adjustment thus appeared to hold sway. The reform process as originally conceived was essentially complete, but the debate about the eventual nature of the global financial system and its governance clearly was not. The volatility associated with the US sub-prime mortgage market shows that the market continues to throw up instability, even in the most developed markets.

The current regime

The volume takes the 2002–7 period of calm as its starting point and focuses on the consolidation of the contemporary financial architecture and ongoing controversies about its legitimacy and effectiveness (Parts I and II) before turning to current crisis-period debates about further policy reform (Part III). In this way the volume (as mentioned) seeks to employ scholarly analysis in relation to potential new departures for the reform process.

The crises of the 1990s made it clear that financial regulation and monetary governance by national governments alone was increasingly ineffective; a market-based system strengthened by sound domestic regulation, better crisis prevention mechanisms, and better national macroeconomic policies and related international monitoring and coordination was billed as the solution. The 'new' international

Introduction: challenges and prospects

financial architecture focused on facilitating the free flow of capital across borders, preserving the same market-based characteristics that emerged in the 1980s and 1990s – also common to the rapid succession of crises from 1994 into the new millennium. Official policy has so far failed to ask whether net capital flows in such a system are indeed stable and positive for a diverse group of developing economies. IFIs, in particular the IMF, continued to focus on this 'orthodox' policy mix (though with perhaps somewhat greater forbearance in the current crisis trough). Thus far they have largely disregarded the pressure it puts on domestic political systems, including social expenditure (Nooruddin and Simmons 2006), especially where the democratic preferences of electorates confront the preferences of international investors and conditionality attached to IFI assistance. This contradiction was etched on the drama of the Argentinean debt workout. The question whether there is reliable empirical evidence to support the particular version of economic theory underpinning this supposedly effective governance pattern has come to the fore again during the current credit crunch. If the answer is no, should we try to change the facts? Or is it time to adapt the theory?

While strengthening governance and implementing sound national macroeconomic policies was a positive step, did this fully address the problem of financial and monetary instability in emerging markets? Many crisis victims had debt to GDP ratios, inflation records and current account balances which were entirely honourable compared to the performance of developed countries. To analyse the output legitimacy of the current governance pattern, we need to engage the debate on alternative theories, such as what Eichengreen and Hausmann referred to as 'original sin' – 'the inability of emerging markets to borrow abroad in their own currency' (Eichengreen and Hausmann 2005: 266). Eichengreen and Hausmann showed that developing country crises are not necessarily due to weak institutions or the lack of credibility of their fiscal and monetary policies. Those forced to borrow in foreign (hard) currencies face debt service volatility five times higher than developed economies (2005: 266). While the quality of governance and the credibility of policy varied greatly across developing countries, original sin was an almost universal feature (2005: 245), suggesting very weak correlation between institutional/policy reform and crisis prevention. Furthermore, can a governance pattern based on domestic adjustment truly be effective in the face of herd behaviour or irrational exuberance in global financial markets?

It is also clear that under the current architecture, despite the implementation of institutional and policy reforms, net private capital flows reach the developing world irregularly at best (World Bank 2006a: 180–7; Prasad *et al.* 2006). At the same time, total external debt loads remain high if unevenly distributed (World Bank 2006a: 193–9, 201–3). Where net capital flows are positive, they are also unevenly distributed to a few major emerging markets which often have weak institutions of governance and policies which are far from market-friendly (especially China, which receives the most by far). To be judged effective, the global financial architecture needs to accommodate these and other inherent difficulties of developing economies, given that these economies constitute most of the world's population. The answer cannot be limited to domestic adjustment, since it has become abundantly clear in the near-meltdown of September 2008 that financial crises and the resulting diminished growth prospects can stem from developed countries as well, and this was in turn inflicted on the developing world.

Reform of the financial architecture therefore remains problematic, particularly from the point of view of developing economies, which are under-represented in governing institutions compared to the OECD countries. The crisis points to weaknesses of the architecture from the point of view of developed countries as well. The system is arguably too inflexible to cater to economies at different levels of development, permitting national authorities insufficient room to manoeuvre as they seek to balance their international obligations with political and social pressures at home. This Introduction argues that enhancing the legitimacy of the output side requires confronting the norms, political underpinnings and distributional impact of the financial architecture, especially with respect to: (1) who has the power to decide, in whose interest; (2) the legitimacy of both decision-making processes and the policies which result; and (3) the links between the decision-making process and outcome. The other contributors debate these issues of input and output legitimacy and what to do about it throughout the volume.

Representation of actors and interests

Governance requires a modicum of consent by those affected by it, and participation in decision-making is an important element of legitimacy on the input side. Case research reveals a familiar pattern (Cohen 2003; Baker 2005a; Baker *et al.* 2005; Mügge 2006; Claessens *et al.* 2008): financial policy-making typically takes place in relatively closed policy communities in which central banks, finance ministries, regulatory agencies and their private sector interlocutors interact to determine the scope of the market, the terms of competition and the costs

Introduction: challenges and prospects

of supervision and regulation. While the decisions taken affect a broad range of interests in society, the preferences which underpin policy outcomes are the product of a close alliance of private actors and autonomous state agencies. Accountability remains limited. The public choice literature warns us that such arrangements run a persistent risk of policy capture.

Cross-border market integration has exacerbated the problem. The policies of developed countries have tended to facilitate further cross-border integration accompanied by 'governance light' with little of the legal and regulatory framework normally associated with functioning domestic financial markets. The growing technical complexity of global markets has also rendered public agencies dependent on the preferences of private agents and has contributed to the emergence of closed and transnational policy decision-making clubs. International level decision-making is yet further removed from traditional lines of democratic accountability; decisions at the international level have become dominated by these policy communities rooted in but increasingly detached from the G10 countries. This was manifested in the strong policy preference for a market-oriented financial architecture. More recently, crisis-stunned electorates have watched aghast as financiers departed ruined institutions saved at taxpayer expense with substantial bonus and severance benefits. Given this role of private actors, it is increasingly important to improve our understanding of the dynamics of private governance arrangements such as international accountancy standards and their relation to public (international) institutions.

Exclusionary decision-making also yields legitimacy problems on the output side. The frustration of many non-OECD countries with what they experience as ossified governance structures unresponsive to their needs and views (cf. Mahbubani 2008) has led them to seek alternatives for addressing policy problems, both unilaterally and in smaller or larger groupings. As mentioned, the major Asian members of the IMF have built virtually impregnable reserve fortresses against future crises and question a range of IFI policies. A series of elections in Latin America indicates considerable dissatisfaction with global economic integration and the policies that attend it. Debtors are turning to regional development banks where developing country influence over policy is greater. National or regional solutions to crises may be the future preference to avoid intrusive and inappropriate IMF and other IFI policy advice and conditionality.[3]

---

[3] As shall be seen, some chapters argue that national and regional solutions may prove more effective and legitimate over time.

14   *Geoffrey R. D. Underhill* et al.

The bottom line is that private actors, in particular large internationally active financial institutions, have more influence on financial architecture reform than developing country members of the Bretton Woods Institutions (though some contributors to this volume suggest that the danger is less than argued here). Those most successful at influencing decisions tend to derive the most benefit from them. Despite their pervasive influence on global supervisory and other standards, institutions such as the Basel Committee on Banking Supervision, Financial Stability Forum (FSF) and the International Accounting Standards Board either excluded non-G10 countries altogether or only included a few 'reliable' outsiders (Australia, Singapore and Hong Kong in the FSF). Even though the current crisis has led to changes on this front with the rising prominence of the G20 and the inclusion of all its members in the Basel Committee and the new Financial Stability Board (the successor to the FSF), the interactions of these forums with a select group of private financial institutions, represented for example by the IIF, are frequent and pervasive. The rules of the game are still established by developed countries and their major financial institutions, which benefit considerably and have learned to cope with the uncertainties of cross-border financial integration. Yet the functioning of the international financial architecture imposes serious costs on developed economies (Bhagwati 1998; Claessens *et al.* 2008), the poorest citizens of which often bear the brunt of adjustment in case of debt or financial crisis. This may well conflict with the widely hailed goal of poverty alleviation and the reduction of inequality (Wade 2004).[4]

There are thus serious questions to be asked about the institutional framework of global monetary and financial governance, the relation between national and other levels of governance, the norms which underpin policy and its implementation, and the interests which governance processes can and should represent. How might one enhance the legitimacy of the institutions of global governance, adjusting the policies of international institutions so as to enhance the capacity of national governments to achieve their aims and satisfy their key political constituencies? Who should be represented in the process and how? How and through what sorts of institutions, with what sorts of authority relative to national instances, should the tasks of global monetary and financial governance be achieved? What sorts of normative and political underpinnings are appropriate for a system which must cater to developing, emerging market and developed countries alike?

---

[4] Though once again, some contributions to this volume contend that the constraints of the system on policy space are not as great as argued here.

Institutional reform and innovation

So what is to be done? Given the apparent tension between effective and inclusive governance, how might institutions be further developed? One solution would be to return to national monetary and financial governance, though this would likely exacerbate policy problems for governments and may reverse the benefits of global financial integration. The point of course is to maximise the benefits while minimising the costs; regional or global governance helps to resolve collective action problems in the international system (Hveem 2006) and to provide the collective goods which states individually cannot ensure. As Zürn has argued, '... international institutions give back to national policy makers the capacity to deal effectively with denationalised economic structures. Seen thus, international institutions are not the problem, but part of the solution to the problems confronting democracy in the age of globalization' (Zürn 2004: 286). The question is how to engineer win-win situations and legitimate and efficient institutions which can implement policies appropriate to the diversity of the global monetary and financial system.

This will mean strengthening the voices of those who have thus far been disenfranchised. But it remains an open question whether giving more room to governments who have hitherto had little say is the only or, for that matter, the appropriate answer. From a practical point of view, the recent enhancement of the role of forums such as the G20 is clearly desirable (cf. Germain 2001); its membership could be expanded further, though this may conflict with decision-making efficiency. Strengthening the broad 'public interest' aspects of policy, particularly in view of recent publicly financed bail-outs of financial institutions, has also become an urgent priority. There may however be limits to how far governments can be expected to translate the interests of diverse societal actors into collectively binding rules (Thirkell-White 2004). From the perspective of social justice and equity, there remains tension between attempts to *include* governments which may themselves *exclude* the legitimate interests of considerable parts of the population. Even though this problem is most obvious in the case of autocratic regimes, democratic governments are not immune to serving the interests of a narrow group of societal actors.

The current system suffers from fragmentation and the proliferation of decision-making on national, regional and global levels. Intergovernmental forums (G7/8, G10, G20, G24); regional bodies such as the European Union (EU); new international forums and institutions with 'technical' functions, in particular policy domains such as the Financial Stability Board and the Basel Committee; a series of private regulatory initiatives; the Bretton Woods Institutions; multilateral development banks; and other existing regional and global institutions all have overlapping jurisdictions and responsibilities while the precise relationships between them remain unclear. While regional processes may more successfully combine manageability and political legitimacy, the global nature of risks and of contagion in the financial and monetary domain imply that at a certain point, institutions with responsibility for the system as a whole are required. In short, the locus of authority remains unclear in an increasingly multilevel system functionally fragmented along institutional lines. Thorough-going market integration requires systematic institutions of governance and the performance of some functions of domestic monetary and financial governance at the international level.

In addition, the institutions and decision-making processes of global monetary and financial governance are neither representative of the diversity of the countries in the global system, nor particularly inclusive (Underhill 2007; Underhill and Zhang 2008). Decision-making is dominated by G7/G10 countries, which can no longer justify their overwhelming influence simply by referring to their percentage of global GDP. Furthermore, limited voting reforms (IMF 2008b), which were decided in October 2009, still leave Belgium with more votes than Brazil. Moreover, the extent of the problem is deeper. Essentially, current reform debates concern integrating major emerging market economies – now substantial financial and monetary powers – into existing institutions. This of course is long overdue. Yet notions of representation in the current debate remain constrained to say the least, with the poorest countries falling through the cracks. The balance between the authority of such institutions and their membership also requires close attention: the growth in US payments imbalances went unchecked by international surveillance mechanisms. Reform discussions are addressing this issue but the outcome is not yet clear.

While focusing on their particular topics – and often taking issue with the arguments presented here – the contributors to this volume ask: what is the appropriate balance between public and private forms of authority in decision-making, rules-setting and enforcement? Who should shoulder the burden of crisis prevention and resolution? How might the international financial architecture be made more compatible with the specific aspirations of countries? To what extent must national authorities relinquish 'sovereign' control to benefit from greater stability? What role can or should regional cooperation play in monetary and financial governance in light of both effectiveness and

Introduction: challenges and prospects 17

legitimacy? What principles of representation do the requirements of legitimacy and effectiveness imply? What are the implications of the current regime for poverty and inequality across a wide range of societies? How can the economically disadvantaged best be represented in the international financial architecture, recognising that improving their development prospects is a principal aim of global financial governance?

Overview of the volume

The contributions – by economists, political economists and political scientists – are organised in three sections. The first section analyses the emergence of the current financial architecture. The subsequent set of chapters examines how well it works, assessing the input and output aspects of the financial architecture in relation to the three issues outlined above. A final set of chapters focuses on reactions to perceived lapses in effectiveness and legitimacy and efforts at further reform.

In the first section, Germain (Chapter 1) explores the parallels between the current junctures in global financial governance with earlier periods that were marked by a mismatch between globalised finance and relatively underdeveloped governance mechanisms. Experiences from the 1920s underscore both the inherently global nature of financial dynamics, which require global answers, and the need to keep policy sensitive to national economic imperatives and preferences. Helleiner and Pagliari (Chapter 2) lay out the most important trends in global financial governance since the turn of the millennium. A period of relative calm after the Argentinean debt default in 2001, they argue, has left the new international financial architecture a half-built house. While for example the G7 did less than promised to overhaul financial governance and make it more inclusive with respect to emerging markets, rule-setting in many domains was increasingly transferred to private or semi-private bodies. The authors thus shed light on the origins of an incoherent financial governance structure, the inadequacy of which has been thrown into sharp relief by the global credit crisis. Baker (Chapter 3) examines this institutional proliferation and functional specialisation in the global financial architecture further, arguing that it has led to the rise of 'apex policy forums'. These forums (most notably the G7 and G10) bring together senior financial policymakers from central banks and finance ministries and set the strategic priorities, agendas and normative parameters for the debate within the international forums of financial governance. He signals that the exclusive membership of these apex policy forums might lead to a skewed policy dialogue and hence to a less efficient and legitimate governance output. Shifting attention to the position of developing countries in the global financial architecture, the final chapter in the first section by Cassimon, Demetriades and Van Campenhout (Chapter 4) analyses the effects of financial development and integration on economic development. It shows that the financial system which has emerged over the past thirty years has a systemic flaw: low-quality institutions can hinder financial integration and thereby economic development. Yet the opposite holds as well: without financial integration and economic development, the quality of institutions is likely to remain low. This leaves developing countries at the risk of ending up at the margins of the global financial system, stuck in a vicious circle that effectively constitutes a 'financial globalisation trap'.

Part II of the volume assesses the current international financial architecture in the lead-up to the crisis of 2007–8. After the Asian crisis, the development and monitoring of international standards and codes was the main reform project implemented in the 'new' global financial architecture. Walter (Chapter 5) opens the second section by assessing the success of this regulatory reform project. He shows that although the quality of financial regulation in some emerging market countries has improved considerably since the late 1990s, there has not been a systematic convergence on western regulatory standards. Implementation of international standards and codes has in practice varied considerably across countries. In general, however, it has been gradual, limited and often superficial rather than substantive. In short, Walter argues, there is 'mock compliance'. This points to the complex and nuanced relationship between input and output legitimacy in the field of international standards and codes.

Taking one crucial case of such standards and codes, Claessens and Underhill (Chapter 6) investigate the new Basel capital accord, known as Basel II. From their analysis emerges a picture that sees deficiencies on the input side of governance translate into suboptimal policy output. Large financial corporations from OECD countries are shown to have had substantial influence over the redrafting of the Basel accord, especially as concerns the use of banks' own risk assessment models in the calculation of capital reserves they need to hold. The analysis shows that the application of the accord yields competitive advantages for these same banks, and it remains unlikely to cope well with the problems of systemic risk which recently proved so prevalent. In contrast, developing countries have had much less of a say in the design of new standards, even though, as the authors show, Basel II is likely to affect borrowing costs in emerging markets substantially, often to these

Introduction: challenges and prospects 19

countries' disadvantage. In particular, they are likely to face bigger cyclical swings in their cost of capital, something that matches badly with their need of steady capital flows to support economic development.

In Chapter 7 de Jong and van der Veer analyse a specific cornerstone of longstanding and still current IMF policy: the catalytic effect of IMF programmes on private financing. This catalytic effect turns out to be elusive, hampering the achievement of a proper balance of the burden of adjustment between the domestic public and private creditors. The authors therefore argue for a more coercive instrument of private sector involvement, and examine the usefulness of the existing Paris Club 'comparability of treatment' clause as such an instrument. Despite having some promise, in the end an instrument capable of encompassing all types of private capital flows is necessary to ensure structural improvements in a country's balance sheet.

Claessens, Cassimon and Van Campenhout (Chapter 8) turn the spotlight to developing countries again by analysing the effectiveness of improvements in the global aid architecture. These improvements have been codified into the 2005 Paris Declaration on Aid Effectiveness, a framework of concrete indicators and targets in the field of institutional quality in donor and recipient countries, harmonisation and alignment to be fulfilled by all signing (bilateral and multilateral) donors. The authors show that although there are overall increases in aid selectivity and the use of appropriate modalities, significant differences between donors remain. The authors suggest that the quality of donors' own institutional environments is an important explanatory factor for these differences, suggesting that the problem 'lies at home'. Low transparency and limited voice and accountability in donor countries, possibly combined with a perverse political economy, make donors deliver aid poorly.

Tsingou (Chapter 9) focuses on another element of the global financial architecture: the Anti-Money Laundering (AML) regime. She underlines the importance of the AML regime to global financial markets as a whole. This regime appears to constrain capital mobility, contrary to the continuing financial integration over the past decades. The regime grows from policy-makers' feeling that they must be seen to be taking robust action to address a diverse set of public policy goals which are often in tension with each other: criminal justice and security issues, but also relieving financial centres in member countries of the OECD from the competitive pressures of offshore finance. As a side effect, the regime shapes private sector practices in a way which can consolidate and strengthen the position of the largest global financial players. In sum, then, in spite of the regime's ambitions, its achievements remain

20   *Geoffrey R. D. Underhill* et al.

modest while many of its side effects raise serious concerns about its functioning, efficiency and legitimacy.

Both the chapters by Klagsbrunn (Chapter 10) and Zhang (Chapter 11) compare the experiences of different emerging markets under conditions of globalising financial markets and the attendant pressures IFIs have often exerted on them for financial reform. Klagsbrunn contrasts Argentina's experience of recent years with that of Brazil. Both countries faced similar problems with respect to external debt and exchange rates but found highly divergent answers. Whereas Brazil largely stuck by Washington Consensus-inspired policy guidelines, Argentina famously defaulted on its debt. With the benefit of hindsight it becomes clear, however, that neither route was necessarily more advantageous; in any case Argentina's unorthodox choice of debt default did not put it at a long-term disadvantage to Brazil. While this chapter can be read as an encouragement to emerging markets to become more daring in defending national economic imperatives when dealing with financial crises, it also shows how a perceived unresponsiveness of the IMF in particular to national economic interests pushed both Argentina and Brazil down policy routes that were suboptimal. In that way, Klagsbrunn's analysis underlines the potentially superior policy output of governance institutions that also score higher on the input side than current arrangements.

Zhang's findings resonate with Klagsbrunn, in particular as concerns the 'policy space' that also emerging market governments retain – quite in contrast to popular assertions that global finance may constitute a policy straightjacket for countries. His analysis of financial market transformation in Thailand and Taiwan during the past two decades shows how policy outcomes result from a complex mix of international and domestic factors. He cautions against a view that sees financial liberalisation as a one-way route that inevitably leads countries towards a common financial market model as they climb the ladder of financial development. If global financial governance is to be successful and legitimate, it needs to be cognisant of the continuing divergence of financial market models and the national political idiosyncrasies that underpin them.

The chapters in the third section aim to provide policy suggestions and avenues for further reform, by focusing on contemporary reactions to perceived lapses in effectiveness and legitimacy. Posner (Chapter 12) starts by arguing that a new transatlantic policy community is emerging, where the preferences of US officials may no longer prevail but a genuine Euro-American regulatory condominium has emerged. This has increased the influence of the European voice in global financial

Introduction: challenges and prospects 21

governance, and is a result of the development of a regional polity, the EU. This has considerable significance for the ongoing post-crisis reform process: US preferences will be attenuated by this pattern of cooperation, enhancing coordination, yet the combined EU-US voice will remain powerful. A key remaining question concerns which interests, what *range* of interests, the transatlantic policy community will choose to represent, if as a community it continues to function.

Dieter (Chapter 13) shifts the attention to East and Southeast Asia while equally examining financial regionalism and its potential tension with global governance. To say the least, the Asian financial crisis has catalysed regional developments and attempts at cooperation, most prominently in and around the ASEAN forum, but also through the Chiang Mai Initiative and for example to develop regional bond markets. Dieter shows how not only the crisis of the late 1990s itself, but also the perceived lack of legitimacy of global financial governance arrangements spurred these developments. Two questions follow immediately: what does the future hold for regional cooperation in the region, and is it a reason for concern? One of the main obstacles for further progress, Dieter argues, is a potential rivalry between China and Japan for regional leadership. In line with analyses in the preceding chapters, it seems clear that for effective global financial governance, such regional developments can form a sensible complement to truly global mechanisms, but they are unlikely to be an effective replacement for them.

Young (Chapter 14) analyses new departures in global finance on a quite different level. Tracing the evolution of microfinance from microcredit, its predecessor, she places microfinance in the broader global aid architecture. The alleged shortcomings of more heavy-handed state involvement in transfer payments combined with debt and financial crisis provided the driving force behind the 'microfinance revolution'. It is noteworthy that large financial corporations have discovered financial services for 'the poor' as a new domain in which to do business. On the one hand, this seems to hold promises for local development, which has often floundered in the absence of basic financial infrastructure. On the other hand, multinational banks that engage in microfinance see such activities as a business investment like any other; should the results disappoint, the provision of microfinance might thus cease as quickly as it had begun. It therefore remains for the future to show just how much of a role microfinance can play as one plank in the broader fight against poverty through financial system developments.

Ocampo and Griffith-Jones (Chapter 15) also explore the compatibility of financial agents' private interests with broader public goals

22 *Geoffrey R. D. Underhill* et al.

in financial markets and development. They analyse the problem of pro-cyclical credit extension, which makes credit abundant when the economy is doing well but sees it curtailed just when the riding gets rough and borrowers may be in particular need of funds to weather the storm. How can developing countries in particular gain access to funding that is not only less sensitive to the periodic ups and downs in economic activity, but may even support efforts to counterbalance them? There clearly is a role to be played for public authorities and lenders in this domain, but Ocampo and Griffith-Jones also explore more market-based mechanisms such as sovereign bonds that have repayments indexed to GDP growth of the country in question. In any case, addressing pro-cyclicality in lending emerges as a crucial challenge to a global financial system that is more in tune with developing countries' economic objectives and is currently also an important topic in policy debates.

The final empirical chapter of this volume by Underhill and Zhang (Chapter 16) returns to a theme that has also stood central in this Introduction: how should we think about the relationship between input and output legitimacy and what does that imply for the future of global financial governance? Their analysis underlines the need to think of the two as complementary rather than competing: participation of hitherto under-represented stakeholders not only increases the latter's acceptance of policy output. It also provides input that is crucial to make governance 'work'. Global financial governance that remains insensitive to the concerns of, for example, developing country governments is bound to flounder on the mismatch between global prescriptions and local realities. Their chapter can therefore be read as an encouragement to put stakeholder input central when contemplating avenues for future governance reform. The Conclusion ties the main arguments of the volume together and links the discussion to recent developments following the credit crunch. It drives home a point that resonates throughout the volume as a whole in a variety of ways: many policy-makers and academics have ignored questions of legitimacy in global financial governance at their own peril. It is time for that to change.

Part I

History and context: input, output and the current architecture (whence it came)

1 Financial governance in historical perspective: lessons from the 1920s

Randall Germain

> Out of the ruins of the Old World, cornerstones of the New can be seen to emerge: economic collaboration of governments *and* the liberty to organize national life at will.
> (Polanyi 1944/1957: 254, italics in original)

Introduction: financial governance in history

What are the central dynamics associated with financial governance today? How should we understand the historical development of financial governance and what, if any, lessons do previous historical eras hold for those preoccupied with today's issues? These are the questions which animate this chapter, explored within the framework of the contradictory pressures of national accountability and international capital mobility. Today, as in the past, those who regulate financial institutions and their activities work within parameters that pull them in two often-conflicting directions. On the one hand, they must strike a compromise between enforcing adequate prudential safeguards on institutions active within their jurisdictions without unduly constraining them in their international activities. Here lines of accountability are primarily national, albeit with significant international spillover effects. On the other hand, they must be wary of the trade-offs between maintaining their economy's satisfactory access to global financial resources and unduly amplifying its vulnerability to external shocks, which is the corollary of such openness. While this trade-off has long existed, its precise balance in terms of perceived 'policy space' has changed over time.

The principal benefit of looking at this trade-off historically is twofold: (1) to recognise its historical evolution; and (2) to consider the

---

I would like to thank the editors of this volume and a range of discussants where earlier drafts of this paper were presented for valuable feedback. My research has received support from the Economic and Social Research Council of the UK and the Social Sciences and Humanities Research Council of Canada.

26   *Randall Germain*

parallels and discontinuities between past and present in order to better evaluate current trajectories. The interwar period, and especially the 1920s, stands as a testament to the pitfalls of outsourcing responsibility for the organisation of the world's monetary and financial system to independent central banks (cf. Ahamed 2009). Governments digested this lesson over the 1930s and put into effect their responses in the early post-World War II years. The result was the relative subordination of central banks to governments (through ministries of finance), and of capital mobility to domestic economic considerations. John Ruggie (1982) astutely labelled this the 'compromise of embedded liberalism': after World War II, political authorities privileged the stability of the national economy within the context of strengthened state authority, embedding international liberalism within the national welfare state.

Ruggie's famous term was itself built on the spirit of an earlier insight, developed by Karl Polanyi during the darkest days of World War II. Polanyi (1944/1957) argued that the attempt to isolate and insulate the self-regulating market was a utopian enterprise that unsurprisingly prompted a societal backlash – he called it a *double movement*. Fascism and socialism were political manifestations of this backlash, alongside democratically inspired efforts to reform liberal capitalism. Polanyi's chief insight, picked up by Ruggie, was that a new balance was being fashioned, one that refused to subordinate the national economy and policy autonomy to international pressures. His historical narrative thus announced that the 1920s were an inherently conservative decade and the 1930s a revolutionary one.

But if we examine the history of financial governance, this conclusion is suspect in at least two important ways. First, the history of the 1920s provides an example of innovations that confirm a powerful recurrent theme in financial governance: financial crises have always drawn public authorities further into regulatory initiatives as a significant part of the solution, and this deepened involvement hardens into a new baseline for future governance activities. Second, financial governance has increasingly acquired an international dimension that serves to anchor and support national-level financial regulation. Together, these two lessons turn part of Polanyi's insight on its head: while it may be that markets require careful government oversight to operate on a sound and stable basis, this oversight needs to be solidly supported by an international infrastructure that bears a striking relationship to what many now call 'global governance'.

These lessons support the framework of trade-offs identified by Underhill, Blom and Mügge in this volume's Introduction, further clarified by Helleiner and Pagliari in Chapter 2. The trade-offs involved in organising governance create tension between national and international pressures which have been articulated and mediated differently throughout the twentieth century. In particular, the balance that governments must strike between direct national accountability and internationalised competencies is determined by the distribution of benefits they receive and the costs associated with supporting internationalised governance mechanisms. The rethink of financial governance that the 2007–8 credit crisis has prompted is precisely a recalibration of these benefits and costs in light of the dramatic failure of national level regulation in the USA.

In what follows, I establish a narrative of financial governance that highlights this national/international trade-off. I then use this narrative to outline the important parallels and discontinuities between the contemporary period and the interwar era. My principal argument is that financial governance works best when robust international institutions support strong national authorities. If financial governance is to be adequate to the tasks set for it by the global financial system, it will need to adhere to this national/international formula. Like the world of the 1920s, states today require strong and active international institutions if they are to adequately and legitimately govern internationally active financial institutions.

Financial governance and the interwar period

Defining finance, much less governance, is a complex affair. For reasons to do with the social nature of finance, I will assume for the purposes of this chapter that by finance I mean financial networks, or more specifically networks of financial institutions, and that it is these which are the objects of governance. Furthermore, I will also assume that by governance I mean publicly sanctioned decision-making, whether by public or private authorities (or a combination of both). Financial governance thus refers primarily to publicly sanctioned decision-making directed towards establishing the framework of rules by which and through which financial institutions undertake and organise financial transactions within and across borders. This framework can be formulated along a continuum that runs from the national to the international.[1]

---

[1] The assumptions in this paragraph require a monograph to sustain. I have explored them elsewhere (Germain 2004, 2007) but it must be acknowledged that there is a lively debate about each assumption. For good overview volumes, see Cutler *et al.* (1999) and Andrews *et al.* (2002).

28   *Randall Germain*

Historically, finance has been governed or regulated largely by national authorities. This is because the early modern roots of financial governance lie in the long drawn-out struggles of competing national authorities to subject financial actors to their needs and demands. But as nation-states became increasingly consolidated across Europe during the seventeenth to nineteenth centuries, and as their growing organisational capacities, self-confidence and imperial ambitions enabled them to stamp their authority on their economies and even their monies, financial institutions ultimately had to adapt to the exigencies of the new political world of modern sovereignty. In short, financial systems developed in Europe under the parallel dominance of increasingly powerful *nation*-states and increasingly centralised *national* economies. The chief dynamics propelling financial governance, in other words, were national in scope (Börn 1977/1983; Braudel 1979/1982; Kindleberger 1984/1993; Gilbert and Helleiner 1999).

At the same time, although the modern era was dominated by the consolidation and then imperial expansion of national economies, a distinct and growing layer of economic activity could be identified as global in scope by the middle of the nineteenth century. The most visible financial dimension of this layer of activity was associated with what Karl Polanyi (1944/1957) identified as *hauté finance*, the internationally oriented finance houses that comprised the pinnacle of the world's increasingly interlinked financial systems. The activities of these finance houses – for example the Rothschilds of London, the Morgans of New York, Lazard Fréres of Paris and the Mendelssohns of Berlin – concentrated in a very few hands the bulk of international financial transactions, thereby centralising the operational dynamics of the world's financial systems at the global level.

It was the high degree of centralisation that enabled this credit system to be governed to the extent that it was. Governance worked at two levels. Most importantly, governance was exercised diffusely through the operation of a set of linked world markets mainly centred in London (Brown 1940; Williams 1963). London-based financial institutions organised development finance for the nineteenth-century equivalent of 'emerging markets' on an unprecedented scale. Capital poured out of London destined for India, Australia, South America, South Africa, Canada and the USA, financing the construction of railroads, ports and factories as well as government operations (Feis 1930/1964; Thomas 1967). As a result of the dominance of London-based private financial institutions over global flows of capital, it was their practices and norms that provided the global financial system with 'governance' or what Paul Langley (2002: 27–9) calls 'world credit practices'. Global finance came to be associated with

Financial governance in historical perspective 29

how these institutions operated, and what we would today call 'best practice' came to be symbolised by their 'gentlemanly' codes of conduct (Cassis 1987). Underhill, Blom and Mügge (this volume) would see this as the determination of public goods by private interests.

The second level through which governance was exercised during this time was central bank interaction. The nineteenth century was an era of nominally 'private' central banks; governments conceded to them enormous latitude in managing the external value of national currencies, relatively unconstrained by domestic political considerations. It thus fell to central banks – primarily those of the United Kingdom, Germany and France since the USA did not establish its central bank until 1913 – to assist each other in their attempts to support their currencies and contain banking crises (Kindleberger 1984/1993). This they could do precisely because of the high degree of centralisation in the global financial system, with London at the apex and Paris, Berlin, Amsterdam and other Continental financial centres playing a subordinate but supportive role. Central bank cooperation in this environment could work with markets because of the symbiotic relationship which these (private) banks had with other leading financial institutions (Eichengreen 1996).

The key here was the high degree of centralisation in the global financial system; without this degree of centralisation, central bank cooperation would have been rudderless and impotent, as was demonstrated during the turbulent interwar years. This critical point is made by Marc Flandreau (1997), who argues persuasively that central bank cooperation under the nineteenth-century gold standard was fitful, sporadic and above all never institutionalised. Indeed, Flandreau points out that as often as not, cooperation occurred in spite of the jealousies and animosities of leading central bankers, who acted on their own individual interests rather than out of a genuine sense of collective responsibility or belief in the so-called 'rules of the game'.

The highly centralised and finely calibrated pre-1914 financial system fell apart with the onset of hostilities in August 1914, with only a vestige of the old trans-Atlantic linkages surviving to fund the Allied war effort (Brown 1940). After the war, financial markets could not be seamlessly reconstructed along their pre-war lines, and the 1930s witnessed an almost total collapse of international financial transactions (Helleiner 1994; Germain 1997). Underlying the inability to reconstruct a global financial system was, as many argue (Kindleberger 1973; Block 1977), an international power vacuum in which no single state could take a leading political role to re-establish a properly functioning global economy (much less a monetary and financial system).

30   *Randall Germain*

At the same time, states desperately searching for ways to reconstitute a vanished international political economy embarked on a number of startlingly innovative practices that were to bear fruit only after World War II. These innovations are canvassed below on two levels. Nationally, states asserted increased control over their economies as the interwar period wore on: currency manipulation became evident, capital controls were experimented with, and trade became increasingly subject to government aims and objectives. But it was in the international arena where the most interesting innovations occurred. International cooperation was deepened, with new institutions emerging to address issues associated with cooperation between states. Although these innovations had significant deficiencies, their revolutionary character should not be obscured.

National level innovations

Innovations in financial governance at the national level took three main forms: (1) in the practices associated with how governments managed their public debt; (2) in central bank operations; and (3) in jurisdictional developments. With respect to how governments managed their (growing) debt, innovation was largely concentrated in the types of government paper used to finance it. In the UK and the USA, treasury bills of various durations became common, ushering in a period of increased government control over interest rates through money market operations. Prior to World War I, most government finances revolved around increasing revenue – mostly provided by customs duties and taxes levied on land, commerce and income – and issuing long-term debt. Issuing debt of widely different maturities was a startling innovation during wartime, as much for the additional revenue it raised as for the enhanced control over the money supply it promised. Both the UK Treasury and the Federal Reserve Board in the USA, for example, began open market operations during the early 1920s, and this development revolutionised the way in which interest rates and liquidity within the financial system could be set and managed (Moggridge 1972; Balderston 1989). Monetary policy thus became much easier to fine-tune during this period and allowed state authorities a firmer grip on the activities of private sector financial institutions.

The second important national-level innovation concerned central bank operations. The 1920s mark the first great wave of central bank expansion in the twentieth century. Many countries that had heretofore done without them created their own, whether due to the achievement of colonial self-government, the break-up of multinational empires, or

Financial governance in historical perspective 31

simply due to the exigencies of national development (Flandreau *et al.* 2003; Helleiner 2003). Whatever the cause, central banks were established across much of central and eastern Europe, Latin America and Asia, and one of their chief tasks was to establish modern standards of financial governance. For many of these countries, this was an innovation of the first order.

The final national-level innovation comprised a new 'sectoralisation' of financial governance in which different parts of the financial system became subject to specific, often statutorily independent, regulatory agencies. This occurred most notably in the USA in the wake of the stock market's collapse. The speculative excesses of the 1920s and the consequences of the 1929 crash led directly to government oversight over stock exchange regulation with the creation of the Securities and Exchange Commission. The Glass-Steagall and McFadden Acts, which among other things separated investment from commercial banking, confined branch banking within state lines and introduced deposit insurance, were also enacted during this period (Garten 1997; Russell 2008). Although these initiatives were not all replicated outside of the USA, it marked the beginning of the trend towards 'sectoralisation' within financial regulation.

In addition to these important innovations, states themselves continued to refine their objectives and mechanisms for intervening in the operation of foreign exchange and capital markets. With the suspension of currency convertibility by all of the belligerent nations in 1914, governments became increasingly adept at intervening in foreign exchange markets to manage their currency's exchange rate. The tools at their disposal were sharpened considerably as the interwar period wore on. Particularly noteworthy was the introduction during the early 1930s of exchange stabilisation funds which allowed governments to manage exchange rates more effectively.[2] Whereas responsibility for currencies prior to 1914 was the almost exclusive preserve of central banks, it was now recognised as an integral responsibility of governments.

Similar recognition occurred in the area of capital account openness, where the interwar years witnessed an intensification of government involvement in controlling and directing capital movements (Helleiner

---

[2] The UK Exchange Equalization Account (EEA) was formed in 1932, while the US Exchange Stabilization Fund began operations in 1934. In the case of the UK, the EEA was used to help manage the sterling area in the 1930s (Drummond 1981). Important also, but in a different way, were the efforts made by fascist governments to control their citizens' international transactions. In Germany's case, this resulted in the construction of an elaborate machinery to control transactions with its central and eastern European neighbours (Neal 1979).

32   *Randall Germain*

1994; Eichengreen 1996). Governments had of course long been part of the capital movement equation (cf. Feis 1930/1964); the difference after the end of World War I was that governments became formally and explicitly involved in mediating the impact of capital mobility on their economy's financial health. This concern was deepened in light of the jarring effects of the 1931 financial crisis and the Depression, when central banks proved incapable of maintaining the postwar monetary and financial system.

International level innovations

Innovations in financial governance at the national level had their counterparts at the international level. Three developments are especially noteworthy during this period: the extension of the nineteenth-century conference system to international economic issues; the deepening of public international financial networks to help steer the global economy; and the creation of a primitive international institutional capacity to assist in the coordination and facilitation of international transactions. Together, these developments constituted the wellsprings of a public infrastructure to support financial governance at the international level. We may therefore identify them as the first hesitant steps towards the emergence of a genuinely international system of financial governance.

The first development – the extension of the nineteenth-century conference system into the economic realm – was initially the least successful. On one level, the conferences held in Brussels in 1920, Genoa in 1922 and Geneva in 1927 to chart the re-establishment of the international gold standard and restore international trade must ultimately be judged as failures, simply because the gold standard itself so clearly failed (Clay 1957). However, the lasting importance of these conferences can perhaps be discerned in their unstated but widely accepted premise: that governments had a crucial role to play in managing international exchange rates within agreed upon rules. We might also consider the failed London Economic Conference of 1933 to fall into this category. Convened to consider an international response to the Depression, it foundered on American President Franklin Roosevelt's affirmation just prior to its commencement that any actions taken to address the parlous economic circumstances must focus on the raising of domestic prices. By privileging national over international responses to the worldwide economic crisis, Roosevelt's actions provided weight to the growing recognition that governments had to shoulder an increased set of responsibilities for the operation of financial and monetary affairs.

It was, as Barry Eichengreen (1992) rightly argues, the first necessary step to combat the deflationary consequences of the gold standard.

What these conferences all acknowledged in different ways was the increasingly important role played by governments in guiding and otherwise regulating economic activity both within and beyond their borders. It introduced the element of negotiation and bargaining over economic issues on a multilateral basis into the international realm, and by doing so set the stage for the complex negotiations that took place at Bretton Woods in 1944. Far from being abject failures, the economic conferences of this period offered important learning markers for governments; they helped to recalibrate the calculated costs associated with the trade-offs between national and international pressures (Pauly 1997).

Economic diplomacy, however, was only part of the process of deepening the involvement of public authorities in matters relating to financial governance. Another dimension of this process during the 1920s could be seen in the strengthening of links between European central banks and the newly established Federal Reserve Board in the USA. During the early years of the Federal Reserve System, the New York Fed's first president – Benjamin Strong – worked especially hard to cement these ties. Strong had a clear grasp of the importance of the US financial system to the world's financial flows, and participated vigorously with his European counterparts – especially Montagu Norman of the Bank of England, but also Emile Moreau of the Banque de France, and eventually Hjalmar Schacht of the German Reichsbank – in facilitating cooperative monetary policies that would not undermine global financial stability (Clay 1957; Chandler 1958; Clarke 1967). The early successes that Strong is often credited with, however, were severely impaired by his premature death in 1928 and the onset of the Depression after the 1929 New York stock market crash.

Nevertheless, even the Depression, with all of its attendant contractions and inward orientations, could not sever completely the international connections and networks built up over the 1920s. Although private capital markets were for all practical purposes moribund after 1931, bankers in New York, London, Amsterdam and Paris continued to travel and meet regularly, as did government and League of Nations officials (Toniolo 2005). The search for suitable economic arrangements led both towards the development of regional solutions (such as the strengthening of the gold, dollar and sterling blocs) and towards interregional or perhaps better 'international' arrangements such as the Tri-Partite Agreement between France, Britain and the USA in 1936 over managing the franc/sterling/dollar exchange rate (Drummond

34   *Randall Germain*

1979). Despite the increased economic nationalism of the interwar period, financial and monetary affairs were never completely detached from an international trajectory, even if their cross-border connections were stunted during the 1930s.

The involvement of public authorities in the international organisation of credit is also evident in the final dimension of international innovations during the interwar period: the creation of an incipient international institutional capacity to oversee or facilitate the operation of a rebuilt and refashioned postwar international economy. These included the creation of an Agent General for Reparations Payments in 1924 to oversee amended German reparations payments arising out of the Dawes Plan; the growth of an economic oversight capability within the League of Nations; and the creation of the Bank for International Settlements (BIS) in 1930. Each of these initiatives was a direct response to the vexed question of how to reconcile war debts and reparations with postwar economic and political realities, and each involved public authorities in the active management of the machinery of a growing international economic infrastructure.

The Agent General for Reparations Payments was created as an essential component of the Dawes Plan. This was the proposal by the Commission of the same name convened to find a way out of the fiasco of the French and Belgian occupation of the Ruhr consequent to Germany's decision to discontinue reparations payments in 1922. The Dawes Plan promised to re-establish German reparations payments by floating a large international loan to be used by Germany to support its currency – which had been eviscerated by hyperinflation (McNeil 1986). The novelty of the Agent General's office lay precisely in institutionalising a decision-making capacity to which others would have to submit, and which ideally would be insulated from the political machinations of both the French and Germans. It also required an American to serve as Agent General, and produced an intense search for an appropriate individual involving heated negotiations between governments, central bankers and especially New York financiers (Jones 1977).

The Agent General had the power to alter Germany's reparations payments in light of changing economic circumstances. This power was most pertinent to Germany, of course, but others too could and did have their expected payments changed unilaterally by Seymour Parker Gilbert, the young American who ultimately became the first Agent General. The granting of this power to the Agent General was most importantly an admission that the political decision to extract reparations needed to take into account Germany's capacity to pay, and that the victors were not entitled to make that decision unilaterally. Of course

Financial governance in historical perspective

there were other important dynamics that made the creation of the Agent General's office attractive, such as the need to somehow insulate the issue of reparations from the toxic effects of Franco-German rivalry, and of the pressing requirement that American private capital be made available to Europe but without official American government guarantees (McNeil 1986). In terms of economic governance, the creation of the Agent General's office should be seen as an important milestone, not only in assembling the required machinery to make international transactions workable, but also in establishing the principle that the vulnerable or weak have an important stake in the construction of the apparatus of decision-making.

The Bank for International Settlements had a similar point of origin. It was part of the recommendation of the Young Plan, produced by an international commission with the mandate to break the reparations impasse that once again threatened to strangle international financial flows after 1928. The innovation of the BIS was that it enabled payments to be made through a neutral third party in a manner designed to minimise upheavals in foreign exchange markets. It also had as an explicit part of its mandate the fostering of cooperative relations among the world's central banks (Simmons 1993; Toniolo 2005).

The BIS of course failed spectacularly to alter the twin trajectories of economic depression and financial chaos unleashed over the 1929–31 period. Perhaps, as Barry Eichengreen (1992: 263–4) argues, it was doomed by American abstention and fatally undermined by being charged with *both* facilitating reparations and forging a common monetary outlook. Or, alternatively, it (along with most governments) was simply overwhelmed by the scale of the unfolding disaster.[3] The BIS was new, untried, light on resources, and working in an environment characterised by relatively ponderous personal communications. To expect more of this new institution in such a situation might be asking more than could legitimately be demanded.

At the same time, the creation of the BIS affirmed, alongside these other developments, the importance of the international dimension of public responsibility in the face of seemingly intractable economic tensions. It was an admission by experts that cooperation requires an international institutional infrastructure beyond what markets could provide; some sort of publicly sanctioned support was needed for such machinery to come into effect. We can therefore see in the creation of the BIS another step in the long road to erecting a world financial

---

[3] This is closer to Gianni Toniolo's (2005) argument, which is much more sympathetic than Eichengreen's to the economic predicament into which the BIS was inserted in 1930.

36 *Randall Germain*

system supported by adequate public authority organised at least in part internationally. It was a small and incomplete step to be sure, but it nonetheless pointed in the right direction.

The final innovation in financial governance at the international level concerns the economic activities of the League of Nations. These were spread over a number of committees (the Economic Committee; the Financial Committee; the Economic Intelligence Unit; the Economic, Financial and Transit Department; and the Economic and Financial Organization). While the record of these committees, departments and organisations is decidedly mixed (Eichengreen 1992; Clavin 1996; Pauly 1997), their work established important principles concerning the achievement of multilateral oversight, the creation and maintenance of a necessary international machinery, and the kinds of ideas that should or ought to inform sound economic policy. Ultimately such an institutional capacity could not lead where governments and private sector forces feared to tread. Yet by establishing the general utility of international institutional capacity for cooperative activity, the League's economic activities offered another important learning marker for governments in later years.

As the above discussion indicates, the key dynamics driving innovation in financial governance during the 1920s were both national in origin and international in delivery. Governments laboured to regain control over their finances in the face of reconstruction burdens and the commitments entailed in working to re-establish a viable system through which international payments could be conducted. They also followed international practices in establishing and/or strengthening their central banks. At the same time, governments were engaged in a desperate search for international arrangements that could resolve the conundrum of inter-allied wartime debts and reparations within the context of what almost everyone thought should be a return to some form of international gold standard. Although these efforts ultimately failed, they provided much of the groundwork for the Bretton Woods negotiations which eventually followed (Pauly 1997; Toniolo 2005).

Looking back from the present: discontinuities and parallels

The point of historical comparison is to probe for similarities and differences between the past and the present. In terms of discontinuities, the most important difference between the 1920s and the contemporary period is illustrated by the then overwhelming dominance of Europe and the European powers in the world political economy. Europe in the

1920s provided the principal cipher or prism for financial issues despite the weight of the USA in world economic and monetary affairs. In contrast, the world political economy today is globalised, perhaps to an unprecedented extent. It is the USA and emerging markets – principally those in Asia – which act as the central cipher for financial and monetary affairs. Beyond this, it is important to note that whereas the interwar period fell prey to competing national solutions and eventually the shadow of war, the contemporary period is mostly free of large-scale conflict. Contemporary public policy has certainly proven vastly different and international cooperation far more effective in the management of the current crisis than in the interwar period. While war between major powers is not unthinkable, interstate war on a global scale is currently beyond the realm of reasoned hypothesis. Lessons concerning policy and the need for institutions of financial governance were indeed learned, though not sufficiently well to prevent the current crisis from emerging in the first place.

In terms of parallels, both periods are marked by significant and ongoing change in the nature of wealth creation and the structural determinants of financial governance. Shifts in the form and geography of wealth creation are central to both eras. In the interwar period, electrification, the internal combustion engine and Fordism or mass production transformed how wealth was created, while the invention and spread of mass consumption and consumer credit spread that wealth in new and significant ways. Today, the steady onslaught of the knowledge economy together with the evolving international division of labour are transforming how wealth is created and where and to whom it is connected.

Politically, both periods have seen tremendous changes in the nature of the state's involvement in economy and society, together with significant movement in the international balance of power. At the close of World War I, three empires (Russia, Germany and Austro-Hungary) had disintegrated, one (Ottoman) was teetering, and two (Britain and France) faced new and intense strains. Today, we have lived through the end of the Cold War, the disintegration of the Soviet Union and the peaceful dissolution and/or creation of several states. In both periods, financial governance occurs in a fragmented and decentralised international political environment.

But the most significant parallel lies in the powerful nature of the global pressures driving the modalities and mechanisms of financial governance. The key pressures here are associated with capital mobility. The dynamics of privatisation, deregulation and securitisation today frame nearly all debates about financial governance, along with the conduct and behaviour of financial institutions. Helleiner and Pagliari (this volume) call this the 'standards-surveillance-compliance regime'. Financial governance is about containing, leveraging and enabling liberalisation and its attendant consequences. During the interwar period this was also the case, with one important caveat: efforts to organise financial governance beyond the nation-state during the 1920s were geared towards re-establishing the conditions that would make capital more rather than less mobile, while efforts during the 1930s were heavily geared in the reverse direction. But in both cases it was the mobility of capital that was the wellspring and chief target of policy.

This common wellspring helps to account for the peculiar global origins of major policy innovations during the interwar period. Institutional innovations such as the Agent General for Reparations, the League's Economic and Financial Organization and the BIS were global in scope, insofar as their membership was drawn from systemically significant actors and the ideas underpinning them were global in origin. Central bank cooperation during the mid-1920s spanned the Atlantic, as did the negotiations leading up to the Tri-Partite Agreement of 1936, even if that arrangement reinforced rather than undermined regional developments. In short, efforts to improve financial governance responded to and reflected globally oriented dynamics during the interwar period, including the turn towards regionalism during the 1930s.

In this context, perhaps the most worrying parallel between the interwar period – especially the 1920s – and the contemporary period is precisely the reluctance of governments to support and/or extend the international infrastructure which so significantly supports domestic initiatives to govern financial networks and activities. In the 1920s governments were determined to return control over monetary and financial policy to central banks. This might have been a sustainable policy if at the same time governments had provided central banks with sufficient resources to support one another during moments of crisis such as in 1931. They did not, however, and governments complicated the mix by engaging in forms of diplomacy that reflected the strangulated state of international relations after World War I. This refusal or inability both to bring central banks fully into *national* political structures and to build an appropriate *international* infrastructure doomed the interwar period to monetary and financial turmoil. The times called for clear leadership, but little was provided.

Put differently, if sustainable and legitimate financial governance requires a balancing between national and international imperatives, then contemporary institutions have clearly and for some time been in need of further strengthening and recalibration. Jacqueline Best (2003) has argued that financial governance in the one to two decades preceding the credit crisis was characterised by an attempt to re-embed liberalism – but this time very different from the embedded liberalism Ruggie (1982) identified. The project of a 'new international financial architecture' claimed to serve national economic interests by unleashing the beneficial forces of internationalised capital markets while, so went the argument, containing crisis, mainly through market transparency. In this top-down re-embedding of global finance there was little scope for national policy autonomy, nor was there a recognition of legitimate national policy objectives that might be at odds with a global governing consensus. In short, global cooperation ahead of the credit crisis was no longer a complement to national policy-making, safeguarding the efficacy of the latter – it was a substitute, with national authorities relegated to implementing a globally agreed 'best practice'.

History teaches us that such an imbalance between national control and international cooperation and governance is potentially unsustainable. Certainly among the OECD countries, cooperation addressing the recent crisis has worked fairly well. Negative externalities as those associated with the management of the Great Depression – the infamous beggar-thy-neighbour policies – have largely been avoided. Unlike in 1931, complete financial meltdown has been avoided, and that is no mean achievement. The real test for international cooperation will come later on, however. The current strategy of delaying policy adaptation through sky-high public deficits is not sustainable. In one form or another, the costs associated with the crisis will have to be paid, and it will be then that we will be able to assess whether the current mix of international governance and (what is left of) national policy autonomy to address domestic problems in idiosyncratic ways will be successful. Only then will governments have to make hard choices about sticking to the internationally embedded orthodoxy versus seeking a national route. Then the present order, which puts such a premium on international cooperation, may emerge as one that is unable to accommodate legitimate national concerns, and one that misses both the conceptual frameworks and the institutions to preserve international financial openness while enabling governments to find national answers to painful reductions of public debt that, in one way or another, will have to happen in the future. In short, politics will catch up with financial governance eventually, and it may again be that the top-down global financial order will founder on the bottom-up demands that national governments and societies will place on it.

Our knowledge of economies and financial systems today is a good deal more advanced than during the early years of the twentieth century.

40   *Randall Germain*

However, the political mistakes and miscues in evidence during the interwar period are again threatening to surface. While the threat of global war may be slight, the scale, degree and depth of international political change are today unremitting. The challenge posed to the prevailing financial power structure by the rise of emerging market economies such as China, India and Russia risks complicating the coordination of international relations necessary to extend the international infrastructure of governance in ways demanded by the increasingly integrated nature of global financial and monetary transactions. Even worse, among governments with the greatest stake in sound structures of international financial governance, a predisposition to cede authority to independent central banks and to parcel out the regulatory patchwork to statutorily independent organisations and committees threatens to undercut the very political support they will need to reassert public control over global financial networks and activities. The demands associated with creating and extending a sustainable international infrastructure seem to have been trumped by the narrow dictates of private gain and licence and the preference given to facilitating international capital mobility.

Conclusion: insights and lessons

The interwar years provide two valuable learning markers or insights for contemporary policy-makers. The first insight is that the organisation and dynamics of finance are inherently global in scope. Although a regional arc of finance may be identified, the dynamics that drive financial transactions and which inform financial institutions are predominantly global. This is in part due to the fungibility of money and credit, and in part to the array of possibilities opened up by technological innovation. But more fundamentally, it arises out of the way in which credit networks have been organised historically: they have always leaned towards a global formulation. Where these dynamics compel public authorities to respond, their response may sometimes take a regional form, but only when compatible with pre-existing global pressures. Thus the use of formal and informal imperial preferences in the 1930s as a way of insulating metropolitan economies from withering international competition, or the more recent development of EU-wide financial standards and a single currency to foster a European capital market: in both cases, developments were shaped in significant ways by global pressures (Drummond 1979; Henning 1994). While reactions to these pressures may take national or regional forms, the pressures themselves always contain a global element.

This leads to the second insight. Liberalism and all of the supposed benefits that flow from it demand a robust global public infrastructure that works to support national goals. The trade-off between national accountability and internationalised competencies cannot be out of balance for long. In each phase of globalisation from the early nineteenth century up to the present, public authorities have become progressively more involved in financial governance in order to make financial systems more effective, stable and efficient. Effective and legitimate national financial governance demands that public authorities exercise their responsibilities in a manner consonant with the arc of their financial institutions' transactions. Since the early years of the twentieth century, financial governance has been necessarily global in scope and national in execution.

A historical perspective can thus provide a window onto unfolding and dramatic social transformations that touch the economic, political and ultimately social organisation of the world. In Karl Polanyi's (1944/1957: 4) arresting phrase, historical explanations do not provide a 'convincing sequence of outstanding events, but an explanation of their trajectory in terms of human institutions'. In the case of financial governance, a historical perspective provides the key insight that strong national states buttressed by strong and well-embedded international institutions have historically been the most viable means of creating effective, efficient and legitimate governance mechanisms. This insight also suggests that the current tensions between G7 states and emerging market economies over the global constitution of financial governance is unlikely to end soon, as the axes of conflict run directly through the vexed question of how strong and active states are to construct strong and active international institutions.

2 Between the storms: patterns in global financial governance, 2001–2007

Eric Helleiner and Stefano Pagliari

Global financial governance is marked by a paradox: while financial markets are among the fastest evolving economic activities, their governance is most often reactive rather than forward-looking. As the previous chapter (Germain) in this volume confirmed, dramatic changes in the patterns of global financial governance are most often triggered by major financial crises which politicise the regulatory debate and pressure policy-makers to react. But once the storm has passed, both public authorities and private actors tend to be affected by what Reinhart and Rogoff (2008) have called the 'this time is different syndrome'. Confidence is restored and complacency sets in until a new storm breaks out, opening a new cycle in the governance of financial markets.

Recent experience has been no exception. Between 1994 and 2001, the world financial system was shaken by a series of major crises emanating from 'emerging markets', most notably Mexico in 1994, East Asia in 1997–8 and Argentina in 2001. These crises prompted the leading financial powers of the G7 to launch a set of ambitious regulatory and institutional reforms to create a 'new international financial architecture' (NIFA). This reform agenda has been well-documented elsewhere (e.g. Eichengreen 1999; Kenen 2001) though post-2001 results have received less attention. After briefly outlining the NIFA project, we highlight in this chapter how the absence of serious international crises between 2001 and 2007 weakened the urgency of this reform agenda for G7 governments and scaled back the level of ambition, yielding greater reliance on market-based governance mechanisms.

However, the NIFA project was not just weakened by G7 complacency. Equally important were the reactions of many developing and emerging countries' governments who had learned a different set of lessons from the crises. Emerging markets' governments were much

For their helpful comments, we thank the editors, the anonymous reviewers, Andrew Baker and all the other participants in the May 2008 Venice workshop.

42

Patterns in financial governance 43

more inclined to blame international financial markets – as well as the G7-dominated IMF – for the crises and they subsequently worked to bolster their autonomy from these external pressures. The result of these trends was a rather incoherent system of global financial governance in the 2001–7 period, with public authorities in different parts of the world working in different directions. In the final section of this chapter we suggest that the new financial storm that broke out in the USA in 2007 signals a turning point in global financial governance. Despite its contradictory trends, the 2001–7 period was unified by its common reference to the 1994–2001 crises. There is now a new reference point and the distinct features of the present crisis are prompting different kinds of political responses and opening a new cycle in the governance of financial markets.

The G7 push for a new international financial architecture

The content of the NIFA project reflected the lessons that many G7 policy-makers drew from the emerging market crises of 1994–2001. The dominant G7 view – particularly in the USA – was that the roots of crisis lay in the inadequate domestic institutions and policies in emerging countries, rather than in the instability of international financial markets.[1] Consistent with this diagnosis, G7 policy-makers urged these countries to increase the transparency of their domestic financial systems and upgrade their regulatory and supervisory systems in relation to Western practices. The instrument to promote this project became the formulation and global dissemination of a common set of international best practice standards and codes (Walter 2008: chapter 1). These were defined by the then UK Chancellor of the Exchequer Gordon Brown (2001) as the 'new rules of the game ... not incidental to the financial architecture for the new global economy: they are the financial architecture for the new global economy'.

This 'standards and codes' agenda took off in the aftermath of the Mexican crisis in 1994, which was blamed on the Mexican government's excessive borrowing and macroeconomic policies. The lead-up to the crisis was seen to be aggravated by lack of data on Mexico's financial position; the IMF thus responded to a request from the G7 by developing in 1996 the 'Special Data Dissemination Standard'. This was

---

[1] This view was not universal among G7 policy-makers. Top Japanese officials, for example, were more inclined to blame the markets for the East Asian crisis, and the content of their proposal for an Asian Monetary Fund in 1998 – discussed later in this chapter – reflected this view.

followed by codes of good practice on transparency for fiscal, monetary and financial policies in 1998 and 1999. When new financial crises broke out in 1997 in East Asian countries, many of whose macroeconomic fundamentals appeared relatively sound, the G7 expanded the agenda to microeconomic factors. East Asian countries had been left exposed to the instabilities of international financial markets because of their 'sins of omission', such as lax supervision and prudential regulation of the financial sector, and their 'sins of commission', such as the opaque relations between corporations, banks and the government (so called 'crony capitalism') (Corsetti *et al.* 1998; Haggard 2000). Codes of best practices were thus developed in a broader range of financial areas including banking, securities, insurance, accounting and auditing standards; corporate governance; and payment systems regulation. The expansion of the agenda created demands for 'transparency about transparency'. In 1999 the IMF and World Bank began assessing countries' observance of certain internationally recognised standards and codes within their Article IV Consultations. They also introduced a new 'Financial Sector Assessment Programme' (FSAP) and began compiling 'Reports on the Observance of Standards and Codes' (ROSCs).

In order to strengthen the institutional basis of this 'standards-surveillance-compliance' regime (Wade 2007), the G7 launched the Financial Stability Forum (FSF) at the Cologne Summit in 1999. The FSF tried to rectify the lack of coordination among financial regulators by bringing together for the first time the treasuries, central banks and supervisory agencies of the G7 countries (with the later inclusion of Australia, the Netherlands, Singapore, the Hong Kong Monetary Authority, and more recently Switzerland[2]), as well as representatives from the major international financial institutions and standard-setting bodies. The G7 also sought to strengthen the legitimacy of the NIFA by reaching out to emerging countries' officials through the creation of a Group of 20, an informal forum that included finance ministers and central bankers from the G7 as well as countries in Asia (China, India, Indonesia, South Korea, Russia), Africa (South Africa), the Middle East (Turkey, Saudi Arabia), Latin America (Mexico, Brazil, Argentina) and Australia.[3] The membership of the BIS was also expanded after 1996 from thirty-six to fifty-five members, while representative offices were opened in Hong Kong (1998) for the Asia and Pacific region and Mexico City (2002) for the Americas.

---

[2] At the April 2009 G20 summit, the FSF was replaced by the Financial Stability Board with a wider membership including the European Commission, Spain and the remaining G20 countries.

[3] The G20 has since become a full-blown summit replacing the G7 as responsible for global economic management issues and cooperation.

It was not just emerging markets governments that were blamed for the crises of the 1990s. Many G7 countries also criticised their own practice of bailing out private international investors by providing ever-larger rescue packages, primarily via the IMF (see Chapter 7 by de Jong and van der Veer). When Latin American governments threatened to default on loans to the largest Western banks in the early 1980s, international bail-outs had seemed more justified because of the clear risk of a meltdown in the international financial system. But as financial flows to emerging markets shifted from bank loans to bond finance, this rationale made less sense since defaults to thousands of individual Western bondholders posed less systemic risk. After the US Treasury and the IMF directed $50 billion in official financing to Mexico – the largest package in the history of the Fund – these bail-outs began to be described as part of the problem rather than the solution. They appeared to create 'moral hazard' at the international level by simply rewarding investors for their poor investment choices at taxpayers' expense.

When the IMF was called upon again during the East Asian crises of 1997–8, the criticism of bail-outs became even more intense and the G7 began to press private sector creditors to assume more of the burden. The 'bailing in' of private investors began during the South Korean crisis of 1998 and several subsequent crises in Ecuador, Pakistan and Ukraine in 1999–2000, when the IMF pushed investors to accept debt restructuring at the outset of debt crises (Blustein 2001, 2005). The new policy was then implemented much more dramatically during the Argentine crisis. As Argentina headed for crisis in late 2001, the IMF refused to extend new loans, a move that helped to trigger the country's massive default. The IMF and G7 then made clear that they would do little to protect the interests of private holders of Argentine bonds during the latter's subsequent negotiations with the Argentine government (Helleiner 2005; Taylor 2007).

The G7 also explored new ways of institutionalising the 'bailing in' of private investors. In 1996, a report from the G10 recommended that collective action clauses (CACs) could be written into international bond contracts. These clauses provided a framework for restructuring negotiations between bondholders and debtors by replacing bondholder contract unanimity requirements with qualified majority voting, and restrictions on the ability of individual creditors to sue debtors or demand full repayment. When this recommendation was largely ignored by investors, attention soon focused on the creation of a more formal international bankruptcy mechanism. In a high-profile speech in November 2001 (one month before the Argentine default), the IMF's deputy managing director Anne Krueger backed this idea, proposing

46 *Eric Helleiner and Stefano Pagliari*

a new IMF-led Sovereign Debt Restructuring Mechanism (SDRM) (Helleiner 2009b).

G7 complacency and the push for market-based forms of governance

The Argentine crisis in 2001 was a turning point in the G7 attitude towards the reform of the international financial architecture. Although the 2001–7 period continued to be plagued by asset bubbles in several markets and growing global imbalances, there were no more major international financial shocks generated in emerging markets during this period. Unlike the East Asian crisis – the effects of which spread to Brazil, Russia and, ultimately, to the USA with the collapse-rescue of the hedge fund Long Term Capital Management (LTCM) in 1998 – the Argentine default was followed by a marked decline in international contagion. The decoupling of spreads between Argentine bonds and neighbouring countries' debt was presented as evidence of the success of the initiatives undertaken in the previous years. The then Undersecretary of the US Treasury John Taylor (2007) argued that greater transparency had enabled investors to anticipate the events in Argentina and had prevented the disorderly winding down of positions from other emerging countries that followed the Russian government's default in 1998. At the same time, the absence of a bail-out of foreign investors during the Argentine crisis was seen to have sent an important signal to the markets, limiting moral hazard for the future.

These considerations and the absence of further major financial crises in emerging markets meant the NIFA dropped down the G7's priority list, generating a certain degree of complacency. While references to the need to 'strengthen financial stability' and implement standards and codes were a quasi-mantra in G7 summit statements at the end of the 1990s, they ceded their place after 2001 to other issues such as the fight against money laundering and terrorist financing, international debt relief and fluctuations in oil prices and exchange rates. The 9/11 terrorist attacks led the new US administration to prioritise security issues over global economic reforms (see Tsingou, Chapter 9 in this volume), while major regulatory initiatives within G7 countries emerged more at the national level in reaction to domestic scandals (e.g. the Sarbanes-Oxley Act of 2002 in the aftermath of the Enron and WorldCom scandals).

The restored confidence in the stability of the markets encouraged G7 officials to give greater emphasis to market-based forms of governance and to delegate regulatory functions to the private sector. The trend was apparent, for example, in the debate that followed Krueger's 2001 proposal to create an SDRM. Some G7 policy-makers, particularly those in the Bush administration, soon argued that this 'statutory' approach was too ambitious and bureaucratic, and their opposition – along with that of leading emerging markets' governments (see below) – forced the IMF to drop the proposal by 2003. Instead, G7 policy-makers threw their weight behind the more market-oriented CAC approach to debt restructuring and worked hard to encourage market actors to embrace CACs as a market norm. At the end of 2002, only 30 per cent of sovereign bonds issued by emerging markets had CACs; by the first half of 2005, the figure was close to 100 per cent (Helleiner 2009b).

The G7 also supported the creation of a private sector voluntary code of conduct to govern future debt-restructuring processes that had been promoted as an alternative to the SDRM by the leading lobby group of international banks, the Institute of International Finance (IIF). The code was designed to influence the behaviour of both investors and debtor governments with respect to information sharing and transparency, debtor-creditor dialogue and cooperation, good faith actions in debt restructurings, and equal treatment of all investors in case of defaults. In late 2004 the IIF succeeded in securing the code's endorsement by four key emerging countries (Brazil, Mexico, Turkey and South Korea) and the International Primary Market Association representing debt underwriters. The USA and many other G7 governments openly welcomed this initiative, as did the G20 as a whole; over thirty other countries soon backed the code. The code's implementation and further development continues to be promoted by the IIF, which for this purpose has established a secretariat and several advisory bodies comprised of private sector representatives, and government officials and ex-officials (IIF 2006b; Helleiner 2009b).

Other standards and codes of best practices set by private market actors were endorsed by the G7 and the FSF, and brought within the perimeter of the international financial regulatory architecture. While the East Asian financial crisis and the collapse of the US hedge fund LTCM brought the regulation of hedge funds onto the international regulatory agenda, the FSF repeatedly refrained from recommending direct regulation of these investment vehicles (FSF 2000a, 2007) and the G7 welcomed the voluntary codes of best practices drafted by hedge fund groups. The Financial Stability Forum also endorsed the international accounting and auditing standards set out by two other private groups, the International Accounting Standards Board (IASB) and the International Auditing and Assurance Standards Board (IAASB). The influence of the IASB was further bolstered by the European Union's decision to require all companies listed on a European stock exchange since 2005 to publish their consolidated financial statements according to its reporting standards. There are now more than a hundred countries worldwide that allow or require listed companies to adopt these accounting standards, and the USA has announced its intention to converge.

The G7 preference for more market-based or private forms of regulation was apparent in other areas as well. In the field of international bank regulation, the new 'Basel II' Agreement, published in 2004, still required internationally active banks to hold capital equal to at least 8 per cent of risk-weighted assets. But it allowed the most sophisticated financial institutions to use their own internal models and databases to self-assess their risk exposure. Commercial credit rating agencies (e.g. Moody's, Standard & Poor's) were also given a semi-regulatory role, as the less sophisticated banks could now weight the risk of their sovereign and corporate exposure according to their ratings (Claessens and Underhill, Chapter 6 in this volume). Moreover, the Basel II agreement even elevated 'market discipline' to one of its three pillars of regulation, alongside formal capital requirements and supervision. This was representative of a broader trend which culminated in this period of shifting part of the responsibility for regulating and monitoring markets from the hands of regulators into the hands of private investors themselves. Increasingly, international regulatory agreements requested private and public actors to disclose more information regarding their activities, explicitly relying on the discipline imposed by financial markets to support the goals set by international standards and codes.

Some analysts interpreted the growing significance of these private governance mechanisms and their capacity to replace or prevent the emergence of public regulation as evidence of a dramatic shift in power in the global financial realm away from states. However, those arguments underestimate the role played by public authorities in encouraging this trend. In some cases, the G7 and international regulatory bodies actively triggered the emergence of market-based governance mechanisms by delegating regulatory functions or threatening more stringent public intervention. More frequently, public authorities strengthened and legitimised pre-existing private initiatives by exercising their 'power of endorsement' (Baker, Chapter 3 in this volume). Therefore, even when they were not directly created by public authorities, it is more accurate to see market-based governance mechanisms as taking place within the 'shadow of the state' (Scharpf 1997; Ronit and Schneider 1999).

Why did the leading financial powers deliberately encourage the shift of regulatory authority to the private sector? As discussed in the Introduction to this volume, the close correspondence in this period between policy outcomes and the preferences of the private sector could be interpreted as an example of 'policy capture'. In this period, public authorities were indeed permeable to the influence of private actors, and the benefits and legitimacy of this involvement were not openly questioned (Tsingou 2007). However, the 'regulatory capture' interpretation needs to appreciate how the legitimacy of market-based governance mechanisms rested on a specific historical context, and how the delegation of regulatory responsibilities to markets remained under the threat of being reversed when this context changed (Pauly 2002). In a period of renewed financial stability and diminished demand for heavy-handed public regulation, public authorities found market-based governance mechanisms attractive tools to help them to 'walk a fine line between stability and competitiveness', as Singer (2007: 23) describes the regulators' dilemma. Especially in the USA, public authorities have seen the involvement of private actors as a viable solution to govern the markets without imposing traditional 'command-and-control' forms of regulation, often depicted as too burdensome for the competitiveness of their domestic financial industry.

Underlying the proximity of interests between public authorities and private actors in favour of market-based governance mechanisms was a benign view of financial markets, which were seen as capable of governing themselves and ultimately acting in the public interest once the kind of government intervention that had contributed to the crises of 1994–2001 was corrected. This faith was particularly strong among Bush administration officials who came to power in 2001. Many of them had been highly critical of IMF bail-outs on moral hazard grounds, with some, such as Taylor, going so far as to advocate the abolition of the IMF before assuming office (Helleiner 2005). In their view, markets were best at understanding and pricing risk while government intervention was usually inefficient and distorting. Indeed, in retrospect it appears that the period of relative financial stability between 2001 and 2007 created the conditions for increased reliance on market-based governance mechanisms rather than the other way around, as Taylor had argued. As will be discussed in more detail in the final section of this chapter, when the period of financial stability ended in 2007, the shadow of the state quickly loomed much larger on market-based governance mechanisms, and regulators did not hesitate to assume regulatory roles that had previously been delegated to the markets.

Emerging market government reactions

Beyond G7 complacency and changing priorities, emerging countries' reactions to the NIFA agenda also undermined this initiative. Unlike G7 governments, many emerging countries were more inclined to see the roots of the 1994–2001 crises (see Armijo 2001) in the fickleness and irrationality of international financial markets than in crony capitalism or inadequate domestic financial regulations. From this perspective, the crises demonstrated very plainly the severe economic costs that could result from overdependence on such markets. The crises also highlighted these countries' vulnerability to Western and IMF influence. During the East Asian crisis, the IMF imposed extensive conditionalities that went well beyond the standard programmes and generated widespread opposition. At best, IMF advice was deemed inappropriate and blamed for worsening the crisis in many countries. At worst, many saw behind its intervention a 'Wall Street-IMF-Treasury Complex' trying to use the crisis to promote its strategic and economic goals in the region (Wade and Veneroso 1998). The IMF's reputation was undermined further by the Argentine economic collapse of late 2001 (see Chapter 10 by Klagsbrunn). Argentina had been under the ten-year watchful eye of the IMF and was widely seen as one of its 'star pupils' in the region throughout the 1990s.

Many emerging market governments thus saw themselves much more as victims of external forces than as actors to be blamed for crises, and concluded that they needed to protect their national autonomy more carefully from overdependence on international financial markets and external influence. This made them sceptical of key elements in the G7 agenda for a NIFA, particularly the G7-led initiative to develop standards and codes as benchmarks to evaluate the soundness of their financial systems. What were presented by the G7 as international best practices derived from the experience of Western countries, and in particular the predominance of American and British regulators. The G24 – the main intergovernmental group of developing countries in international financial affairs – expressed concerns about the implementation costs for countries with limited human and financial resources, as well as the appropriateness of a 'one-size-fits-all' approach in countries at varying stages of development and coming from different traditions. Deeper resentment arose from the asymmetry between the obligations on public institutions in emerging markets and the private sector in northern markets (Mohammed 2003). The asymmetry in the agenda was not surprising since emerging countries had been given little say in the development of its content. With the relative exception of IOSCO, emerging market economies lacked adequate representation in standard-setting bodies. The only authorities from emerging countries represented in the newly created FSF were Singapore and the Hong Kong Monetary Authority, while emerging markets' governments have much less voice than the G7 in the IMF and were not represented at all as full members in the decision-making committee of the Basel Committee (see Delonis 2004).

Reactions to the G7 standards and codes project took various forms (Thirkell-White 2007). Through the G24, emerging markets' governments successfully resisted G7 attempts to include adherence to standards and codes among the conditions attached to regular IMF loans. While countries did accept voluntary monitoring by the IMF and World Bank through ROSCs and the FSAP, they reserved the right to block the publication of results. Faced with this resistance, the G7 hoped the ROSCs would at least encourage financial markets to discipline non-compliant countries; the markets, however, generally failed to perform this role. Moreover, Andrew Walter (Chapter 5 in this volume) highlights how many countries engaged in 'mock compliance' of various standards and codes, particularly those which were hardest to monitor and costly for the private sector, such as accounting and corporate governance.

Some emerging markets' governments also played a role in defeating the SDRM proposal in 2001–3. Part of their opposition stemmed from their fear that an international bankruptcy court might increase the costs of international borrowing. Mexico and Brazil in particular highlighted this concern. But these countries were also wary of granting new powers to the G7-dominated IMF to interfere in their policy-making autonomy. To make debt restructuring more orderly, they preferred to minimise external constraints on their behaviour by backing the more limited initiatives of introducing CACs and the voluntary code of conduct (Helleiner 2009b).

In addition to resisting G7 initiatives, many emerging countries took more proactive steps to boost their policy autonomy. The temporary introduction of capital controls by the Malaysian government at the height of the East Asian crisis was not replicated elsewhere. However, emerging countries pursued a different strategy to shield against future international financial instability: the accumulation of foreign exchange reserves. By 2007 the sums involved had become massive, particularly in the East Asian region, further fuelling the build-up of 'global imbalances' and feeding the bubble mounting in the American economy through a sustained inflow of cheap credit (Wolf 2008).

Large-scales reserve accumulation enabled emerging countries not just to protect themselves from speculative attacks (and thus check out of Underhill's 'Hotel Capital Mobility') but also to reduce their dependence on the IMF. Many countries – including some of the IMF's largest borrowers such as Brazil, Argentina and Indonesia – paid off their IMF loans early and suggested their intention not to borrow from the Fund again. These moves have been portrayed locally as a kind of boycott of, or declaration of independence from, the G7-dominated financial institution (Helleiner and Momani 2008).

While boosting national autonomy, the 'self-insurance' of reserves accumulation has been costly when the reserves are held conservatively in low-earning assets such as US Treasury bills. As a result, some countries with large reserves have begun investing them more aggressively in global markets through the creation of 'sovereign wealth funds'. This trend has worried the USA and some other OECD governments who fear that the growing influence of these funds may increasingly 'politicise' global financial markets (Helleiner 2009a). In this way, emerging markets governments' quest for policy autonomy increasingly had systemic consequences.

This is not the only way in which emerging countries have begun to transform the international financial order in more proactive ways. In East Asia, the 1997–8 crisis encouraged region-wide initiatives to create alternative financial arrangements to provide an additional layer of protection against external influences. To this end, the ASEAN countries, along with Japan, China and South Korea, launched the Chiang Mai Initiative (CMI) in 2000 (see Dieter, Chapter 13 in this volume), creating a set of bilateral swap arrangements among the region's monetary authorities. As initially implemented, the CMI posed little challenge to the IMF's role in the region as governments requesting more than 10 per cent of its funds had to have IMF programmes in place. But the threshold was raised to 20 per cent in 2005, while in 2008 participants agreed to 'multilateralise' the CMI by creating a self-managed multilateral reserve pool governed by a single agreement. The 'multilateralisation' of the CMI and its expansion to at least $80 billion are thus moving financial cooperation in East Asia closer to the $100 billion Asian Monetary Fund (AMF) controversially proposed by Japan – and opposed by the USA – in 1997 at the height of the East Asian crisis (ASEAN+3 2008).

Dissatisfaction with the IMF in Latin America also generated interest in regional financial arrangements. One such arrangement is the Banco del Sur, created in 2007 by Argentina, Bolivia, Brazil, Ecuador, Paraguay and Uruguay. Unsurprisingly, the Banco was promoted

Patterns in financial governance 53

most actively by those most critical of the Fund, including Venezuelan President Hugo Chavez and Ecuador's Rafael Correa as well as Argentine President Nestor Kirchner whose tough and successful bargaining with the IMF in 2003–5 did much to undermine the IMF's powerful image in the region. In the early stages of planning, advocates had hoped the Banco would provide both long-term development loans and short-term balance of payments financing in ways that allowed Latin American countries to reduce their dependence on both the World Bank and IMF. These ambitions, however, were watered down considerably, particularly by Brazil, and the final agreement commits the Banco to use its $7 billion initial capital only for long-term development lending. Although not a challenge to the Fund, the creation of this institution marks another way in which many developing countries moved from the position of 'rule-takers' into 'rule-makers' in the international financial realm (Sohn 2005).

From the calm to a new storm

In sum, the post-2001 period saw the emergence of two trends in global financial governance. In G7 policy-making circles, the relative calm generated a certain degree of complacency and encouraged greater reliance on market-driven governance mechanisms. In many emerging countries, the distinct lessons drawn from the crises of 1994–2001 led governments to bolster their autonomy from external pressures, pursuing initiatives often in contrast with those promoted by the G7.

Although these trends were often contradictory, they both contributed to weaken the NIFA project, particularly the development and implementation of the 'standards and codes' agenda. The design of new international standards and codes clearly lost the momentum it had right after the East Asian crisis, while the implementation of existing ones remained uneven. Compliance gaps were not limited to emerging countries, as described in the previous section, but they applied even to some of the same G7 countries that were the main promoters of the NIFA. Although the USA supported mandatory participation in the review process (Walter 2008), it released only two ROSCs and did not announce its first FSAP evaluation until 2008, *after* the crisis in the US domestic financial system had began.[4] For this reason, the IMF Managing Director Dominique Strauss-Kahn rejected in 2008 the accusations that the IMF had failed to spot the weaknesses in the US financial system 'owing to the fact that our main instrument to make

---

[4] For the latter see www.treas.gov/press/releases/hp838.htm.

54   *Eric Helleiner and Stefano Pagliari*

that kind of supervision was not used in this country' (*Reuters* 2008). Germany also failed to publish a ROSC until 2003 (Schneider 2003).

In addition to undermining the NIFA project, the two post-2001 trends also worked to marginalise the IMF. From the perspective of many US and G7 policy-makers, the IMF was an overly bureaucratic institution, too committed to bail-out lending. At the same time, many emerging markets' governments saw its conditionality as overbearing and its operations too dominated by G7 governments and free market ideology. The reforms undertaken by the IMF to address these criticisms in the 2001–7 period, including a timid step to increase the voting power of under-represented emerging and developing countries, did not succeed in cultivating new enthusiasm for the institution. At the same time, and compounding its difficulties, the IMF suffered an internal financial crisis because its lending – and thus the interest it earns on its loans – rapidly shrunk with the build-up of reserves in many emerging countries, the early repayment of debts by its main borrowers and the absence of major crises (Torres 2007; Helleiner and Momani 2008).

With the benefit of hindsight, then, the period 2001–7 will be remembered not only for its relative financial stability but also for having been characterised by a rather incoherent system of global financial governance with public authorities in industrialised countries and emerging countries working in separate directions. With the former set of countries increasingly relying on market-based governance mechanisms, and the latter working to bolster their autonomy from the vagaries of financial markets, the new international financial architecture never fully emerged. At the same time, the IMF suffered one of its most difficult moments.

Each of these trends might well have endured were it not for the sudden outbreak of a new international financial crisis starting in 2007. The crisis shook off the complacency of the 2001–7 period and sharply refocused the attention of public authorities on issues of financial stability. While calls for a 'new international financial architecture' once again captured the headlines, the crisis has not pushed policy-makers to bring to completion the reforms initiated after the crises of the late 1990s. On the contrary, the distinct features of the present crisis prompted different kinds of political responses from those that characterised the NIFA. The NIFA had been informed by the view that the roots of the crises of the 1990s laid in inadequate domestic institutions and policies in emerging countries, and it consequently placed emphasis on the need to address government failures. The consensus among policy-makers from both industrialised and emerging countries is that the post-2007 crisis is the result of market failures as much as government failures. Equally important, the NIFA had urged emerging markets to upgrade their regulatory and supervisory systems in relation to western practices, assuming they would be the most likely cause of a future crisis. The epicentre of the post-2007 crisis, however, is not in an emerging country but at the very core of the global financial system.

In our view, these differences make the crisis a turning point in the evolution of global financial governance, opening a different cycle from the one that emerged from the crises of the 1990s. Within the G7 itself, the crisis has prompted public authorities to reconsider the confidence placed in the kinds of market-based governance mechanisms that became so popular in the previous decade. After the emerging market crises of the 1990s, many G7 countries had warned against the moral hazard generated by the bail-out of private investors and preached the need to scale back the intervention of public authorities. The post-2007 crisis has forced the same countries to dramatically extend the reach of their action in the governance of financial markets as never before. As governments from G7 countries have employed unprecedented amounts of taxpayers' money to bail out domestic financial institutions, new actors have entered the regulatory debate calling for tighter public regulation and questioning the hands-off approach that characterised the previous decade.

Moreover, the very private market actors that were assigned formal regulatory roles – private banks, credit rating agencies, accountants, hedge funds – suddenly appear undeserving of the trust placed in them. Banks' internal risk models, a second input in Pillar I of the Basel II Accord, have been proven flawed, especially during periods of crisis. Credit rating agencies are now criticised for having failed to understand the risks posed by the securitisation of poor-quality US mortgages, and for being subject to multiple conflicts of interests. Fair value accounting practices such as those supported by the IASB, as well as the activities of hedge funds, have been blamed for deepening the crisis by creating strong pro-cyclical effects in periods of disorderly financial markets. More generally, the crisis has shaken the benign view of financial markets as capable of governing themselves that informed the NIFA.

The more financial issues become politicised and the greater the loss of trust in market mechanisms, the larger the shadow of the state looms over market-based governance mechanisms – and the more likely is a return of the state in the governance of financial markets. Signs of this shift can be found in the initial reaction of the G20 to the global financial crisis. Regulators have endorsed for the first time the regulation of markets that had previously been left self-regulated such as hedge funds and derivatives. They have assumed the task of enforcing compliance with the international standards for credit rating agencies, whereas they had been content to delegate enforcement to voluntary efforts and market pressures before the recent crisis. They have created a monitoring body comprised of public authorities to oversee the private International Accounting Standards Board. While it is premature to draw definitive conclusions, the new cycle in global financial governance opened by the new financial crisis is much less likely to rely on market-based forms of governance than the 2001–7 phase described in this chapter.

Another result of the recent crisis is that the legitimacy of the G7-led standards and codes project has been undermined elsewhere in the world. The crisis has raised serious questions about Anglo-American financial governance as a model to emulate. The very officials from G7 countries who lectured emerging countries on the inadequacy of their financial regulation now find themselves subject to the same criticism from emerging countries.

The crisis of legitimacy of the NIFA threatens to accelerate the decentralising trends in global financial governance that were becoming apparent in the years before the crisis. Already during the Basel II negotiations, Asian countries frustrated by lack of attention for their concerns were considering the creation of an alternative 'Asian Basel' system (Walter 2008: 181). In the initial phase of the crisis, these kinds of proposals have gained an even more sympathetic hearing, as witnessed by the Japanese proposal in May 2008 to create an Asian version of the FSF (now FSB). Similarly, the crisis has boosted the appetite of some European countries for strengthening financial governance mechanisms at the regional level.

The crisis has also confirmed the lessons learned by developing countries during the financial crises of the 1990s about the costs associated with openness to international markets. Those countries that had accumulated large-scale foreign exchange reserves in the previous period were rewarded, as they were able to partially shield themselves from the global spillovers of the US-originated financial storm. Many of those that had not been able to afford this luxury, however, now found themselves forced to seek financial assistance from the IMF. In response, the G20 leaders in April 2009 tripled the resources of the IMF, thereby throwing an unexpected life jacket to the Fund. At the same time, they committed to reform its mandate, scope and governance, signalling another potential departure of global financial governance from the direction taken in the 2001–7 period: the strengthening of its institutional foundations.

Most importantly, G20 leaders have pledged to reform these institutional foundations by giving greater voice and representation to emerging and developing countries within the Fund and beyond. With the G20's encouragement, the key international regulatory bodies (FSF (now FSB), Basel Committee, IOSCO's Technical Committee, the Committee on Payment and Settlement Systems and IASB) expanded their membership in early 2009 to include more systematically important developing countries.[5] Moreover, while the agenda for international reforms was set by the G7 after the emerging markets' crises of the 1990s, the more representative G20 has taken the lead from the autumn of 2008 onwards. The crisis has thus created the conditions for an increase in the representativeness and 'input legitimacy' of the global financial governance regime.

It is still premature to draw conclusions about whether this process of institutional reform will tame the decentralising trends in global financial governance, or to what extent the global financial crisis will change the relation between public authorities and private market actors in the governance of financial markets. What is certain, however, is that the era described in the first two sections of this chapter has ended. Global financial governance in the era of relative calm between the storms was characterised by many diverse trends but was unified by the fact that all the actors involved had the common reference point of the crises of 1994–2001. The initiatives undertaken in response to those crises have left an important legacy as the world rides through a new set of financial storms. But the specific crises that triggered those initiatives are now an increasingly distant memory to those charting the trajectory of global financial governance today.

---

[5] The Financial Stability Forum (now renamed Financial Stability Board) has expanded its membership to include all G20 countries (Spain and the European Commission were also included). IOSCO invited Brazil, India and China to join its Technical Committee, while the membership of the Basel Committee was expanded to include also Argentina, Australia, Brazil, China, Hong Kong SAR, India, Indonesia, Mexico, Russia, Saudi Arabia, Singapore, South Africa, South Korea and Turkey. Also the Committee of Payment and Settlement Systems expanded its membership to include Australia, Brazil, China, India, Mexico, Russia, Saudi Arabia, South Africa and South Korea. The IASB also guaranteed geographical diversity on its Board for the first time in a manner that guaranteed developing country representation.

3 Deliberative international financial governance and apex policy forums: where we are and where we should be headed

Andrew Baker

Over the last thirty years the evolution of the global financial architecture (GFA) has been characterised by twin processes of institutional proliferation and functional specialism (Porter 2003; Baker 2005, 2009). Today, numerous bodies, institutions, committees and groups clutter the stage of global financial governance; most oversee a specific sector of the financial services industry or perform a niche functional task or responsibility. In the midst of this landscape, we have witnessed the emergence of 'apex policy forums'.[1] Apex policy forums bring together the most senior national figures from national finance ministries and central banks, to engage in processes of recurrent informal deliberation with the intention of formulating international consensus. The defining feature of apex policy forums is their quest to oversee and set strategic priorities, agendas and normative parameters for the entire institutional complex of global financial governance (Germain 2004; Baker 2009). These forums play a crucial role in contemporary global financial governance and include the G7 and, since 1999, the G20 (see Chapter 2 by Helleiner and Pagliari).[2]

This chapter examines two issues. First, it analyses the workings of the input side of the GFA by critically examining the role of apex policy

---

[1] The term apex policy forum is not my own, but is enjoying increasingly wide usage in Washington IFI and G-group circles. I first encountered the term while working in February 2008 as an expert consultant for the United Arab Emirates Ministry of Finance and Industry and the Islamic Development Bank, on a proposal to establish an 'International Islamic Finance Apex Policy Forum', although the definition of an apex forum used to inform those discussions was derived from my own work (Baker 2006, 2009).

[2] One could claim that regional groupings perform an apex role within a particular geographical territory, but my focus in this chapter is on those groupings with pretensions to a global reach and with a specific deliberative focus – the G7 and the G20. I am not going to discuss the activities of the Financial Stability Forum (now the Financial Stability Board) as its activities are of a more detailed technical nature rather than the setting of normative parameters, priorities and agendas, which I take to be the function of apex policy forums (Baker 2009).

58

Deliberative financial governance and policy forums 59

forums, asking how they operate, what they do, how important they are, and how input relates to the policies promulgated on the output side and the broader legitimacy of financial governance. The focus here is largely on the 2002–7 period of 'calm' though some reference is made to immediate post-Asian crisis architectural debates (see Chapter 2 by Helleiner and Pagliari). Second, this chapter reflects upon how apex policy forums might be made more inclusive, benefiting a wider range of constituents and interested parties. These two issues relate directly to two debates identified in this volume's Introduction: on the balance between public and private authority, and on the possible tensions between inclusion and effectiveness in global financial governance. This chapter argues that there is a clear causal relationship between input and output. In this case, the exclusive membership of apex policy forums has to date restricted the range of arguments and perspectives heard during the course of deliberation, with the effect of limiting the range of information considered in the evaluation of policy options, leading to the adoption of inferior policies due to a skewed and ideationally biased process. In other words, a restricted input process causes inefficient and flawed outputs based on errors of judgement in policy-making, as evident in the failure to identify or address the problems that resulted in the recent 2007–9 global financial crisis.

The chapter has three sections. The first introduces apex policy forums and how they operate. The second examines their track record by focusing on three issues: the setting of key normative parameters and objectives for global financial governance; the track record of the international financial standards and codes agenda; and the relationship of apex policy forums to private financial sector interests. The chapter's third section highlights the problems of existing apex policy forums stemming from their restricted membership and the group dynamics this may produce. It then discusses the legitimacy gains that would be derived from creating a more heterogeneous deliberative process than the existing G7/G20 finance ministry and central bank groupings, and forwards proposals for reconfiguring existing apex policy forums.

The emergence and powers of apex policy forums

Apex policy forums, as considered in this chapter, bring senior finance ministry and central bank officials together from self-selecting groups of systemically significant countries. Crucially, here we are concerned with those policy forums that operate at the very highest levels of national officialdom. They have a global perspective, or remit, and seek to define priorities, directing, steering and framing work conducted elsewhere,

60   *Andrew Baker*

rather than undertaking substantive work themselves. Finance ministers and central bank governors are supported in their activities by their 'deputies' – usually the head of the international affairs division in the case of finance ministries, or the deputy governor in the case of central banks. Deliberations result in statements or communiqués designed to convey a sense of consensus on priorities, agendas and broad policy orientation to national authorities, markets, the financial press, and to an array of other more specialist bodies and committees that make up the current global financial architecture: the IMF, World Bank, Basel Committee, IOSCO, the Joint Forum, the Financial Stability Forum (FSF) – now renamed the Financial Stability Board – and the Financial Action Task Force. We will not consider leaders' summits directly in this chapter because their interest in financial governance is somewhat sporadic and they most frequently take their lead from the ongoing work of the finance ministries and central banks.

The two most prominent apex policy forums are the G7 and the G20. The current financial crisis has ushered in a period of flux. After spending ten years in the shadow of the G7, the G20 now appears to be emerging as the premier apex policy forum, although long-term patterns remain to be deciphered. Where financial and monetary governance is concerned 'G' groups can be traced back to the creation of the G10 in 1962, but the mandate and function of the 'G' groups has shifted over time. Today, relatively little of their discussion concerns the coordination of domestic macroeconomic policies or exchange rates (Bergsten and Henning 1996; Webb 2005; Baker 2005b). Instead, they are increasingly engaged in crafting normative consensus about what the global financial system should look like, how it should function and which values should inform its overall operation and organisation. This involves framing the conduct of global financial governance by diffusing objectives and priorities to other relevant bodies and determining the terms and content of financial governance discourse and debates. For example, a practitioner involved in the early years of the G20 reported that the group was implicitly given a mandate to facilitate agreement on international and domestic action, institutional arrangements to prevent and resolve crises, to prevent a backlash against globalisation by promoting its benefits, and building consensus on key financial issues that would facilitate decision-making in other institutions such as the IMF and World Bank (Rubio-Marquez 2009). This is a politically significant and contentious role as apex policy forums essentially define how global financial governance challenges are to be understood and defined and, most crucially, who has a legitimate right to participate in key debates.

Unfortunately, because the 'G' groups have no formal, legal mandate or functions, it is difficult to be precise about the nature and extent of their power or how that relates to the individual power of their national members. Nevertheless, it is possible to identify three distinct but overlapping forms of power enjoyed by existing apex policy forums. The first is the power of veto, which essentially amounts to a capacity to stop certain things from happening. For example, the IMF's proposal to create a Sovereign Debt Restructuring Mechanism (SDRM) required the approval of member countries to adjust the IMF's articles of agreement. Once the G7 finance ministries and central banks rejected the SDRM proposal, its adoption became impossible. Likewise, if leading finance ministries and central banks rejected a proposal for a loan, it would not be further discussed by the IMF's Board of Directors (Woods 2001). In short, apex policy forums set the parameters within which wider multilateral institutions operate, and provide the political support necessary for their survival. Without the approval of leading figures from national finance ministries and central banks, very little in global financial governance can happen. Proposals that are collectively opposed by G7 or G20 members are effectively vetoed or rejected.

The second power is the power of instigation. Apex policy forums initiate proposals and set broad agendas and priorities for the wider institutional complex of global financial governance. Many of the more specialist regulatory committees and bodies within the global financial system are staffed by less senior officials from finance ministries, central banks and or semi-autonomous regulatory agencies. This gives apex policy forums, operating as they do at the most senior level, significant directional capacity. Strategic meetings of senior figures from finance ministries and central banks catalyse the bureaucratic and technical capabilities of their respective institutions. Finance ministers and central bank governors urge their bureaucracies to work together to share findings, experience and information (albeit within the context of agreed normative objectives). Sometimes this extends to the finance ministers and central bank governors asking certain bodies to conduct work on their behalf and report back. At other times they simply seek to steer the priorities and procedures of institutions such as the IMF.

The third form of power is the power of endorsement. This involves official approval of the findings of more specialist committees and bodies that produce technical reports such as the Basel Committee, IOSCO, the FSB and the IMF. Although apex policy forums are selective in their endorsements, they rarely contest or reject the technical detail within the reports produced by these specialist bodies (the SDRM proposal is a notable exception). Experience suggests that if the proposals of specialist

62   *Andrew Baker*

bodies are to enjoy political authority, the approval of apex policy forums is essential. One of the most interesting patterns to emerge from the current crisis is that due to its sheer complexity, there appears to be a shifting balance between the power of instigation and the power of endorsement, with the G20 and G7 becoming increasingly dependent on the work of bodies such as the FSB, IOSCO and the Basel Committee, while engaging in considerably less instigation of their own proposals than was the case in the period immediately after the Asian financial crisis. The long-term implications of this for institutional power relations in the global financial architecture remain to be seen.

In short, the power of apex policy forums is complex, subtle and multi-faceted. They are as much about catalysing developments elsewhere, and formulating and endorsing approaches and ideas, as they are about arriving at detailed proposals and decisions in their own right. They seek to raise consciousness, set agendas, create networks and 'light fires under civil servants and bureaucrats' (Hodges 1998) and to give a sense of urgency to their ongoing work. To the untrained eye, the G7 and the G20 may appear little more than talking shops. But as apex policy forums, they have increasingly important directional functions. Their agenda-setting and norm-framing role within the wider global financial architecture could therefore be formally acknowledged and lines of accountability usefully specified, especially in the context of a growing dependence on an increasingly specialist differentiated, technical governance machinery (Porter 2003).

The track record thus far

Strategic objectives and normative judgements

Apex policy forums seek consensus on strategic objectives for global financial governance, which in turn creates parameters within which debates proceed. In this respect, much of the discussion that takes place at G7 and G20 gatherings, at least at the level of deputies, takes the form of knowledge generation – or, more precisely, knowledge affirmation – in which existing preferences and beliefs are reaffirmed by themed debates and research reports highlighting key targets, principles, objectives and governance challenges. This was certainly a salient pattern during the 2002–7 period of relative financial 'calm' and complacency described by Helleiner and Pagliari in Chapter 2, during which apex policy forums displayed political and normative leadership that effectively endorsed and reinforced a neoliberal model of finance based on an Anglo-American-centric view of the world.

Apex policy forum statements represent reference points for governance and are designed to inform, influence and guide the activities of other actors. This is far from a neutral or value-free process, and powerful social and political influences appear to shape and frame this process of knowledge generation and definition. Recent G20 experience provides a good example of this. In 2004, the G20 deputies held a workshop on the development of capital markets. The transcripts of the workshop revealed broad normative agreement on the desirability of disciplined macroeconomic policies (strongest), carefully sequenced financial liberalisation to produce complete capital account liberalisation, and improved implementation of international codes and standards (G20 2004). Unusually, outsiders were invited to present papers. In each case they were professional economists working within the above normative parameters. The only private/civil society representative was an economist from the Institute of International Finance (IIF) representing the largest international banks. Papers were presented in an academic style, but discussant comments by G20 officials and follow-up discussion largely concurred with the findings and theories of the specialist presenters. Significant dissent and disagreement appeared to be almost entirely absent. Essentially, debate occurred in isolation from perspectives outside the forum's normative parameters, while input from societal actors was restricted to one interest association sympathetic to the intellectual train of debate. While anecdotal, the occurrence is not atypical and suggests that apex policy forums have been characterised by relatively isolated and consensual forms of deliberation. Notably, there is a strong tendency for the deputies and a number of ministers and governors to have strong social bonds, based on a similar shared academic background and training revolving around neoclassical economics.[3]

---

[3] For example, during 1996, eight out of fourteen national officials comprising the G7 deputies were Ph.D. economists. The remaining six had a postgraduate qualification (masters level) in economics or finance. In all emerging markets comprising the G20, with the exception of Russia, either the central bank governor or the finance minister had spent some time studying economics or finance in either the United States or the United Kingdom. Of the eleven finance ministers currently representing the G20 emerging markets, five have a masters and/or Ph.D. in economics from a US university, while two have MBAs from US universities. Of the eleven central bank governors in the G20, three have economics qualifications from UK universities and six have postgraduate qualifications from US universities in finance and economics. Only the Russian and Chinese central bank governors were entirely educated locally. The Chinese finance minister was formerly employed by the US Treasury Department; the Brazilian finance minister has held council positions in two US universities and has run a Boston-based bank; and the Turkish finance minister has spent two years as a consultant in a Chicago-based securities firm. An education, training and background

64 *Andrew Baker*

Furthermore, there seemed to be group pressure to conform, with participants appearing unwilling to too openly dissent from the majority, or mean, position. In this respect, the context in which debates take place (input) appears to have a powerful influence on the resulting consensus (output). Even the Chinese central bank deputy, Ruogu Li, acting as discussant for Ronald McKinnon's paper on the appropriate sequencing of financial liberalisation at the 2004 workshop, stressed that China was gradually moving towards relaxing restrictions on capital account transactions, broadly in accordance with the so-called McKinnon order (McKinnon 1993; G20 2004). Li took the issues raised in prior discussion by McKinnon – including the normative desirability of capital account liberalisation – as given, and applied this to the (very particular) Chinese experience, documenting progress on the road to capital account liberalisation. The entire debate was structured around the McKinnon reform sequence most likely to result in successful capital account liberalisation.[4] The workshop went on to strongly endorse a process of sequencing – a route map to capital account liberalisation.

But it is far from clear that steady progress towards capital account liberalisation is in the interests of the Chinese financial system; indeed, the government recently felt obliged to *tighten* restrictions in response to growing turbulence in the world's leading capital markets. Thus for most of the last decade, the G20 collectively has appeared to be more pro-capital account liberalisation than the sum of its members' individual preferences might lead us to expect. Until very recently, capital account liberalisation, and financial openness more generally, have been seen as inherently normatively desirable. This has been underpinned by a faith in the efficiency of private financial market forces, and their ability to perform best, when free from regulatory and state interference, enabling them to reach rational decisions and price their own risk, in the most efficient fashion possible, and in turn generate wealth and growth. It was from such assumptions or premises that all debate proceeded, despite much empirical evidence that increased financial openness does not always contribute to, and can often hamper,

---

in Anglo-American finance and economics, generally of a neoclassical orientation, is the common shared background of officials involved in the 'G' groups. Empirical studies suggest that training provides an effective proxy for the beliefs officials hold (Chwieroth 2007).

[4] The precise order of sequencing advocated by the G20 is taken from Stanford economist Ronald McKinnon's work, 'the McKinnon Order': first establish sound macroeconomic policies; then liberalise domestic financial markets while maintaining prudential supervision and regulation; then eliminate restrictions on capital movements starting with the liberalisation of long-term flows, eventually leading to complete capital account liberalisation (G20 2004: 2).

economic development (Prasad *et al.* 2006; Rodrik and Subramanian 2009; Cassimon, Demetriades and Van Campenhout, this volume).

The G7 complacency referred to by Helleiner and Pagliari in Chapter 2 of this volume is deeply rooted in the social, political and intellectual dynamics of apex policy forum decision-making mechanisms, and stretches back beyond the 2002–7 period. In this respect, certain perspectives and arguments have not received a fair hearing and are excluded from deliberation, while other assumptions and normative priorities have simply been taken as given. This was apparent during the architectural debates after the Asian crisis when proposals forwarded by what Armijo has referred to as a 'financial stabilisation' camp – which generally looked to more interventionist measures to restrict the speed and volume of speculative financial flows – were largely overlooked (Armijo 2001). Notably, a UN report that viewed capital controls as permanent safeguards rather than instruments to be abolished was all but ignored in the G7 and G20 (UN 1999; Culpepper 2003). Further evidence of a process of 'ideational screening' within apex policy forums came with the rejection of the SDRM proposal (based on payment standstill and judicial arbitration) on 12 April 2003, in favour of inserting more market-friendly, voluntary Collective Action Clauses (CACs) into sovereign bonds (G7 2003) – a position later echoed by the G20 (2003). While the full story of the politics behind the rejection of the SDRM remains to be told, it confirms a general pattern of intellectual bias against market interventionist proposals in current apex policy forums. There is therefore much to suggest, that what political theorist Cass Sunstein has called a skewed 'limited argument pool' involving ideational bias, creating powerful conformist affects (Sunstein 2002), have been evident in the functioning of both the G7 and the G20. As we shall see with the standards and codes agenda, there are good reasons to be concerned when limited argument pools become too ensconced.

The standards and codes agenda

The implementation of the twelve standards and codes – launched by the G7 and G22 (the precursor of the G20) following the Asian financial crisis as the centrepiece of the global financial architecture proposals – has had limited success (Thirkell-White 2007; Walter, this volume). The G24 group of developing countries has raised concerns about the costs of implementation, the lack of adequate technical assistance and their appropriateness in particular national contexts. This in turn has been reflected in the poor implementation record of many developing countries (Thirkell-White 2007: 27). I would argue that these problems are directly related to the restricted input process (the limited argument pool) which has constrained debate in apex policy forums, and has allowed flawed intellectual assumptions to reign unopposed, resulting in the adoption of questionable outputs (standards and codes).

The standards and codes agenda assumed financial crises have their roots, not in the nature of financial markets (which are assumed to be efficient and rational) but in poor-quality information and concealed data – that is a lack of transparency. Enhanced transparency is therefore the solution. Financial markets will discipline national government policies as investors use the increased availability of data on the structure and state of economies to rationally evaluate where to invest so as to maximise returns; reckless national policies would thus be punished by investors withdrawing their money. But problems with these assumptions throw the whole standards and codes agenda as a route to financial stability into question.

Most notably, there appears to be little market awareness of the standards and codes, or of the country Reports on the Observance of Standards and Codes (ROSCs) published by the IMF and the World Bank; and they are used somewhat sparingly in credit assessment (Thirkell-White 2007). World Bank officials working on ROSCs quickly realised that their principal audience was not international investors and financial market participants as envisaged by apex forum transparency advocates, but national regulatory authorities and the individual executives of corporations in assessed countries.[5] The standards and codes agenda can hardly be expected to realise its objective of preventing future financial crises if market participants are not using them to guide investment decisions in a significant fashion. In this context, standards and codes begin to look like empty vessels as devices for disciplining developing country governments (Walter, this volume).

Furthermore, contrary to the assumptions of the transparency agenda, the process of how financial markets react to data is unclear and uncertain. Different investors and analysts have different interpretations and reach different judgements (Thirkell-White 2007). Some empirical work suggests that markets rely on mutual guesswork, rumour, reputation, perception and analysis of the behaviour of other traders and investors as much as reasoned evaluation of data (Pilbeam 2001). Ultimately, there is little empirical evidence to show that markets rationally evaluate data as the transparency perspective

---

[5] Confidential interview with World Bank official, 13 April 2007.

would propose, and plenty of evidence to suggest that they use a narrow and unrepresentative range of data (Mosley 2003). The transparency perspective of the G7 and G20, however, denies such possibilities. Indeed, the transparency agenda may be predestined to fail precisely because it discounts such possibilities. Standards and codes emerged as the panacea in international financial governance precisely because a narrow and contestable view of financial markets was allowed to go unchallenged and generated proposals based on assumptions for which there was little empirical verification. Furthermore, reigning neoliberal, Anglo-American premises resulted in an unevenness and asymmetry in the way in which the standards and codes were applied. It was assumed that transparency and market discipline was greatest in those countries with the most developed and sophisticated financial markets, that were most unhindered by state intervention and regulation and which represented the greatest degrees of market freedom – the United States and the United Kingdom – and that therefore these countries had little need to participate in ROSCs and Financial Sector Assessment Programmes (FSAPs). In other words, reigning assumptions and mindsets in contemporary 'G' groups, were partly responsible for the uneven coverage of multilateral financial surveillance launched after Asia, contributing to the sense of complacency, which meant that problems within the edifice of Anglo-American finance remained concealed, and/or ignored.

Why has the transparency perspective reigned unchallenged within apex policy forums? One of the reasons, this chapter argues, lies in the institutional design of current apex policy forums and the limited argument pools and social pressures this design has generated. It is entirely possible that Anglo-American perspectives were able to dominate due to the position of economic strength of the United States and the United Kingdom and the apparent structural power of the City of London and Wall Street as engines of growth for the world economy, but suspicions remain that there have been many intellectual sympathisers to this perspective within finance ministries and central banks from across the G20.

At the same time, however, there is evidence to suggest that emerging markets have been less vocal in the G20 than in other settings, indicating that some group dynamic may be at work. Research has shown that G20 communiqués have largely endorsed the G7 position on standards and codes, but this is less straightforward than it might first appear (Martinez-Diaz 2009). A US Treasury official, for example, noted that while governors and ministers in the G20 had no objections to standards and codes, some of the same countries represented

68 *Andrew Baker*

by different officials then raised all kinds of problems in the executive board of the IMF (Martinez-Diaz 2009). This raises the prospect that the informal collegiate deliberations of the G20 may have had an inhibiting effect on participants, while the more formal IMF setting allowed pre-prepared objections to be raised. Collective G20 support for standards and codes thus appears stronger than individual states' preferences would indicate, suggesting that G20 may not have acted as an effective vehicle for articulating the interests and concerns of developing countries and emerging markets, at least in the finance ministry and central bank setting. Concerns remain that because finance ministry and central bank officials tend to evaluate one another in terms of their professional technical expertise and competence, the question of peer credibility may have created a reluctance to depart from the normative parameters of a limited neoliberal argument pool. This chapter forwards the proposition that restricting apex policy forums to informal, collegiate exchanges between a limited number of finance ministry and central bank officials has created powerful conformist and consensual pressures that further consolidated officials' intellectual inclinations and instincts, contributing to the financial complacency of the 2000s.

Ideas, private financial market interests and power differentials

One of the recurring themes of this volume is the public-private balance in the global financial system, and whether the global financial architecture has been captured by private market interests. The relationship of private interests to apex policy forums is far from clear-cut. During the Asian financial crisis, for example, there was relatively little formal lobbying of the US Treasury by commercial concerns (Robertson 2007; Baker 2008). US firms were not the main beneficiaries of market opening and restructuring in Asia, yet such measures were still applauded by the Treasury for ideological reasons, reflecting officials' intellectual inclinations and formal training (Robertson 2007, Baker 2008). Many finance ministry and central bank officials regard themselves as technicians searching for the correct answers. They may generally pay little attention to outside interests, though they are most likely to listen to large-scale internationally active banks and bodies such as the IIF. Crucially, however, the interests of such bodies in the activities of apex policy forums remain somewhat sporadic, coalescing around issues that might have a direct effect on day-to-day market operations such as the SDRM proposal, and on the content and detail of the macroprudential regulation agenda emerging from the current crisis, which private actors will no doubt seek to minimise and dilute, through national lobbying and expert contributions to the reports and recommendations of bodies such as the FSB, IOSCO and Basel. Clearly apex policy forums have had a track record of defending and promoting the broad Anglo-American consensus of the last twenty to thirty years, and with major banks and financial institutions having found this consensus favourable to their activities, their incentive to get involved in proactive lobbying campaigns has been minimal.

Ultimately, dominant concepts in contemporary financial governance such as transparency and credibility have been favoured by G7 and G20 officials because they resonated with their own intellectual beliefs and prejudices. In both the United States and the United Kingdom, there is some evidence of a revolving door operating between regulatory agencies, the Treasury departments, the central banks and prominent Wall Street and City of London private financial institutions. However, this practice is primarily the result of a prevailing mindset, which has prioritised the attainment of credibility with private market actors as the guiding rationale for all financial and monetary policy, and has supposedly necessitated the export of individuals with market expertise and sensitivity into the policy community (Baker 2005; Hall 2008). As I have argued elsewhere the most important single factor accounting for this situation has been the dominance of those ideas about finance that advocate the importance of credibility and transparency, and result in a structurally asymmetric 'confidence game' between public and private authorities in which the balance is very much tilted in the favour of the latter (Baker 2008). However, these ideas are not prominent in the world's leading finance ministries and central banks, most notably the US Treasury and in apex policy forums, simply because they reflect the preferences of large Wall Street banks and investment firms, or because the Treasury simply acts on behalf of Wall Street, but because there has been a genuine intellectual faith in these ideas among senior officials, which has often run beyond the limits of economic science, and at times has come to resemble an ideology, or mindset (Stiglitz 2002). Internationally active financial interests do enjoy privileged status in the deliberations of apex policy forums, but this is primarily the result of ideational bias and a skewed argument pool, stemming from the membership and composition of these forums and the ideational and institutional culture of their constituent agencies, rather than from any explicit political control of the agenda by private market interests.

70   *Andrew Baker*

Where should we be headed?

Current apex policy forums are therefore problematic because they gather groups of officials with similar intellectual inclinations into close-knit, informal and collegiate environments. This leads not only to the strengthening of prior inclinations and the screening-out of alternatives, but also to environments that favour conformity and complacency in a crisis-prone sector, which would benefit from more critical analysis. As we have seen in the operation of current apex policy forums, policy-makers in such contexts begin to privilege the normative elements of economic theory over its explanatory elements, elevating normative judgements to the status of 'singular truths' (Best 2003; Grabel 2003). Political theorists have identified this phenomenon in the context of other deliberating groups and have warned of the dangers of 'enclave deliberation' (Sunstein 2002).

Enclave deliberation refers to deliberation among like-minded people who spend much of their time in isolated enclaves without sustained exposure to competing views, with the result that they only hear echoes of their own voices (Sunstein 2002). Setting aside concerns about exclusion and legitimacy, concerns have been raised about the greater likelihood of error. 'When group discussion tends to lead people to more strongly held versions of the same view with which they began, and when social influences and limited argument pools are responsible, there is little reason for great confidence in the effects of deliberation' (Sunstein 2002: 188). The biggest single danger of enclave deliberation is that certain policy stances come to be favoured not because of their merits, but because of social dynamics and the limited nature of the arguments and positions considered in the course of deliberation, resulting in the adoption of inferior policy. In particular, errors can occur when individuals isolated from others draw on a limited skewed argument pool, because flawed assumptions will go unchallenged and alternative perspectives will be unheard. We have seen how this applied in the case of the standards and codes agenda, and how stabilisation-type proposals have struggled to receive a fair hearing. In such instances, limited input processes directly damage output efficiency and legitimacy evident in the failure to spot or respond to the looming financial crisis in developed countries and Anglo-American markets.

Ideally, outputs should be the result of learning and the critical consideration of a range of evidence. Policy-makers should therefore avoid insulating themselves from views that may turn out to be right, or at least informative (Sunstein 2002). According to Sunstein, 'what is necessary is not to allow every view to be heard, but to ensure that no single view is so widely heard, and reinforced, that people are unable to

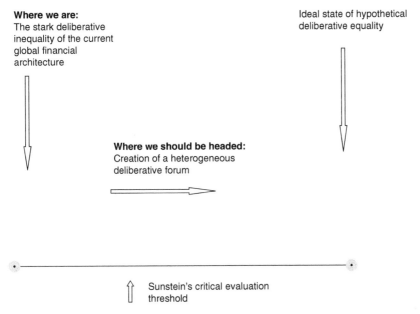

Figure 3.1. Continuum of deliberative equality

engage in a critical evaluation of the reasonable competitors' (Sunstein 2002: 193). Current apex policy forums are not meeting this minimum threshold; as a result the current global financial architecture is characterised by stark deliberative inequality (see Figure 3.1).

As apex policy forums increasingly set priorities for the entire global financial architecture and reach normative judgements about what the global financial system should look like and what values should underpin it, issues of representation and contestation in its forums have become more important. While the defence that narrow technical questions are most appropriately dealt with by a limited number of experts has some merit, this hardly applies when broad normative judgements on underlying values, priorities and parameters are the order of the day. Normative judgements about what a desirable global financial system should look like, how it should be organised, and for what purposes, should be arrived at through open debate among as wide a range of interested parties as possible. As apex policy forums increasingly do precisely this in the field of international finance, it is important to formally acknowledge this role and define it with a clear mandate. Formally acknowledging that these forums are engaged in normative oversight and agenda-setting activities would make the current form of enclave deliberation much harder to defend.

72   *Andrew Baker*

Work on deliberation has consistently found that heterogeneous groups generally produce better judgements because they consider more information and perspectives in the course of their deliberations (Fishkin 1995; Sunstein 2002; Bohman 2006). There is thus a very strong case, on both epistemic as well as legitimacy grounds, to make 'G' group apex policy forums more heterogeneous in composition. One pressing issue is how to ensure voices from the more interventionist financial stabilisation perspective receive genuine consideration. This would introduce debate over the desirability of complete capital account liberalisation (from which all 'G' group deliberation has proceeded for most of the last decade), and subject the assumptions of the transparency perspective on market decision-making to greater critical scrutiny.

To address the ideational inertia that results from the deliberative inequality of current apex policy forums arrangements, the existing finance ministry-central bank monopoly needs to be challenged. Interestingly, given the evidence and argument presented in this chapter, the recent G20 leaders summits appear to have resulted in emerging markets developing a more distinctively vocal and assertive position than has been the case in the finance ministers and central bankers process. Consequently, recent G20 leaders' communiqués have expressed support for something resembling a more interventionist top-down, rules-based form of macroprudential regulation, even if, for the time being, this remains light on detail. In relation to future financial apex policy forums, I would advocate building on this development by creating a multi-agency forum including some representatives from industry, housing, labour, welfare and development ministries (with a quota on the number of finance ministries and central bank representatives allowed to attend and each state allocated one representative only) from a mix of systemically significant developed and developing countries, so as to set normative priorities and agendas in global financial governance. A UN representation would also ensure a greater hearing for stabilisation-type proposals. Likewise, debate would be broadened by the inclusion of two or three renowned academic economists, particularly those more critical of financial orthodoxy. While such a forum need not go beyond thirty or forty representatives, it should broaden representation and include voices that are currently excluded – particularly if it were given a clearly defined oversight and agenda setting-mandate.[6] In

---

[6] A separate forum of finance ministries and central banks could continue to discuss exchange rate and current account imbalances. I do not expect that this argument in favour of a more heterogeneous forum would easily be accepted by finance ministries and central banks, but it is my contention that existing exclusive arrangements have

Deliberative financial governance and policy forums

this sense, broadening inputs into the deliberative and decision-making process offers the prospect of improving the quality of subsequent outputs.

Conclusion

What we should be aiming for is a less consensual and less socially and intellectually homogenous set of institutional arrangements than we currently see in apex policy forums. More heterogeneous forums that at least attempted to realise some degree of deliberative equality (Slaughter 2004) would constitute a reasonable first step towards achieving a more inclusive, socially aware and progressive system of global financial governance. Such a move would at least ensure that Sunstein's threshold – of no single view being so widely heard, and reinforced, that people were unable to engage in a critical evaluation of the reasonable alternatives – could be crossed (see Figure 3.1). Ultimately, active efforts to include a broader range of intellectual perspectives in apex policy forums would challenge the kind of G7 complacency described by Helleiner and Pagliari (in Chapter 2 of this volume) by subjecting governance proposals and initiatives to a greater degree of critical scrutiny. In this respect, debates on the future reform of the global financial architecture need to appreciate that input and output legitimacy (Scharpf 1999), as the editors of this volume suggest, are often two sides of the same coin.

resulted in the institutionalisation of a restrictive myopic mindset, which has contributed to the current crisis.

4 Finance, globalisation and economic development: the role of institutions

Danny Cassimon, Panicos Demetriades and Björn Van Campenhout

Introduction

As discussed in the introductory chapter of this volume (Underhill, Blom and Mügge), across-the-board G7/G10 and IFI pressure for increased capital mobility and capital account openness has been a central feature of the (new) global financial architecture, a policy prescription which a wide range of developing countries have adopted. This chapter critically examines the relationship between financial integration/openness and financial development and, in turn, economic development. In doing so, it evaluates the effectiveness of this input side push towards financial openness to produce (as its output) successful economic development in developing countries.

The belief in the virtues of capital mobility – and the determination with which it is translated into policy advice at the global level (see Baker's chapter in this volume) – is grounded in standard theoretical economic analysis. In theory, financial development should be good for growth as it allows for the efficient mobilisation of savings for productive investments. Furthermore, the development of banks and other financial intermediaries increases the average productivity of capital by reducing problems of adverse selection and moral hazard. Financial openness should enhance financial development, while standard neoclassical growth theory also predicts huge gains for developing countries from financial market integration. Differences in the capital-labour ratio provide scope for increased efficiency in the global allocation of capital. Furthermore, there is scope for improved international risk-sharing and capital deepening. Promoting (capital account) openness thus became one of the core elements, not only of the new global financial architecture of the 1980s, but of the broader economic reform agenda termed the (original) Washington Consensus.

This work has been supported by the UK ERSC under its World Economy and Finance (WEF) Programme, *National and International Aspects of Financial Development*, Award RES-156–25-0009.

The basic argument that financial openness and global financial integration promote economic development has only very recently begun to be challenged.[1] Drawing on an extensive literature, we review the most recent empirical findings and qualify this basic argument – especially in the case of poorer developing countries – by drawing attention to the role of institutions. More precisely, this chapter challenges the presumed virtues of capital openness (and the effective working of the current global financial architecture) to the extent that it leads to a bifurcated world in which poorer countries – despite major efforts to increase (capital account) openness – risk entrapment in a vicious and self-perpetuating cycle of low financial integration–financial development–economic development. In essence, countries may find themselves in a 'financial globalisation trap'.

While numerous studies confirm that the development of financial systems and especially banks can have a positive effect on economic growth, the evidence suggests the relationship can vary considerably across countries. The relationship exhibits reverse causality in many countries, while non-linearities have been established which indicate – alarmingly – that the finance-growth relationship is at its weakest in the poorest countries. The evidence is even less robust in the case of financial integration, where results seem to depend on its definition. Here again, it has often been argued that the relationship is not linear: for certain groups of countries (typically the poorer ones), there is no relationship between cross-border financial integration and economic development. Worse, some have argued that increased financial integration has raised volatility for these countries. In both cases, a critical reading of the available empirical evidence leads us to the importance of the institutional framework for financial and economic development.

Simultaneously, one observes divergent degrees of (de facto) financial integration among groups of countries at various levels of development, a divergence which continues despite converging degrees of (de jure) capital account openness. This divergence is addressed through the so-called Lucas paradox (Lucas 1990): why are observed capital flows so small compared to (theoretically) predicted flows? Again, we examine the most important explanations put forward to explain the relationship between financial integration and economic development. For both financial development and financial market integration, the quality of institutions once again appears to matter.

---

[1] Enthusiasm for financial openness became somewhat qualified following the mid to late 1990s period of global instability; qualifications focused mainly on the sequencing and speed of openness reforms.

76   *Danny Cassimon* et al.

We will examine how the dynamic relationships between financial globalisation, financial development and (possibly endogenously evolving) institutions affect the evolution of financial integration over time. When the absence of financial integration, and the absence of any positive effect of integration on development, is primarily explained by the low quality of institutions – and institutional quality is not enhanced by greater financial integration – we may be witnessing a feedback mechanism that leads to an economy, caught in a vicious circle, remaining on the margins of the global financial system at low levels of development, similar to the conditional convergence found in poverty traps.

Acknowledgement of this systemic flaw has profound consequences for the current global financial architecture and potential reforms following the crisis: promoting (de jure) capital account openness and mobility will not suffice to promote financial integration for poorer countries; it will not automatically lead to economic growth and development; and it will not solve the financial globalisation trap. Poor countries are not only under-represented in terms of voice, but also 'underserviced' on the output side, and this exclusionary nature of the global financial system undermines its legitimacy. To promote economic development, broader financial integration cannot substitute country-specific strategies that focus on the improvement of domestic institutions. As the (private) capital market mechanism will not voluntarily take up this role, there is a case to be made for public intervention to target and support the development of better institutions. An important question is to what extent official financing, and official aid in particular, will serve this purpose (see Chapter 8 in this volume). The global financial system will also have to provide recipient countries with the necessary policy space to develop their own country-specific institutional development paths.

The organisation of this chapter follows the logic of this introduction. Its sections discuss in turn: the recent literature on the relationship between financial development and growth; the relationship between financial integration and growth; and the dynamic relationships between these concepts, which may lead to the possible existence of a financial globalisation trap. A following section introduces a brief empirical test for the trap hypothesis and makes the case for the importance of institutions, while the conclusion discusses policy consequences.

Linking financial and economic development, and the importance of institutions

Banks and other financial intermediaries can perform important functions in the growth process by helping to realise productive investment

Finance, globalisation and economic development 77

opportunities. By screening loan applicants, they address adverse selection in the credit market, helping to channel funds towards productive uses. By monitoring borrowers, they aim to address moral hazard, which helps to ensure that firms stick to their original investment plans. Through long-term bank-borrower relationships, they address both adverse selection and moral hazard, helping to enhance the average productivity of capital.

By and large, the empirical evidence confirms that the development of financial systems and especially banks can have a positive causal effect on economic growth, though there are important exceptions. King and Levine (1993) provide cross-country evidence on the positive effects of finance on growth, which they interpret as causal. However, Demetriades and Hussein (1996) provide time-series evidence from sixteen developing countries which suggests that banking sector development does not always Granger-cause economic growth. If anything, the evidence suggests that the relationship between finance and growth frequently exhibits reverse causality: i.e. it is economic growth that causes financial development and not vice versa.

Follow-up research has advocated further caution in interpreting the relationship between finance and growth in a causal way. Demetriades and Law (2006) provide evidence suggesting financial development has greater effects on growth when the financial system is embedded in a sound institutional framework.[2] They also find effects are most potent for middle-income countries, and rather weak for low-income countries, confirming earlier findings by Rioja and Valev (2004). It thus appears that the finance-growth relationship is sensitive not only to the level of economic and/or financial development, but also to institutional development. Even within similar income groups, the relationship varies substantially according to institutional quality. These studies therefore cast further doubt on the view that financial development, particularly in low-income countries with weak institutions, delivers substantial benefits in terms of economic growth. Financial development may thus not be the quick fix to promote growth in those parts of the world that most need it, such as Sub-Saharan Africa, unless it is accompanied by the strengthening of institutions such as rule of law and property rights. These findings are now increasingly validated in the literature.

Financial development also varies sharply around the world, with some countries experiencing persistently low levels of financial

---

[2] Their sample includes seventy-two countries over the period 1978–2000, using annual data and panel cointegration techniques. Their index of institutional quality is the average of five ICRG measures: corruption, rule of law, bureaucratic quality, government repudiation of contracts and risk of expropriation.

78   *Danny Cassimon* et al.

development. What explains this difference? Four leading hypotheses dominate the literature.

The *legal origins hypothesis* (La Porta *et al.* 1997) argues that common law-based systems, originating in English law, are better suited for the development of capital markets than civil law-based systems, primarily rooted in French law. The main difficulty with this hypothesis is that it is static and can, at best, only explain the relative position of countries at some point in the past.[3] Moreover, the view that common law countries have better shareholder protection than civil law countries has been challenged in an important recent study by academic lawyers at the University of Cambridge.[4] We may therefore conclude that while there is broad consensus that a properly functioning legal system providing effective protection for investors' property rights is important for financial development (and growth), the legal origins view is not widely accepted. Indeed, it has largely been discredited by lawyers.

The *'political view' of state-owned banks hypothesis* suggests that government ownership of banks is widespread because it enables corrupt politicians to direct credit and favours, such as employment and subsidies, to political supporters. Politicians can then garner votes, political contributions and bribes, fuelling a vicious circle of bad economic decisions and the re-election of corrupt politicians. Such a cycle clearly undermines economic growth, not least because credit is channelled to sectors and firms in accordance with political rather than economic priorities. It is further argued that government-owned banks are less innovative and less efficient – plagued by incompetent and unmotivated employees – than private banks, and hence less able to promote financial development. While La Porta *et al.* (2002) provide some supporting evidence for this theory, its significance is often far from convincing. In addition, Andrianova *et al.* (2008) provide a theoretical model as well as empirical evidence which suggest that government ownership of banks may be an effective substitute for weak institutions. Andrianova *et al.* further show that privatising government-owned banks without strengthening institutions that protect depositors from bank failures will likely result in a decline in financial development, challenging the La Porta *et al.* conclusion.[5]

---

[3] There are, however, economic models – of the endogenous growth variety – in which initial conditions can have a permanent effect on the growth rate.

[4] See e.g. Lele and Siems (2007).

[5] Additional evidence warning against the political view of state banks is provided by Demetriades *et al.* (2008) in their analysis of the finance-growth relationship in China, where the banking system is dominated by state banks but has enjoyed very high growth rates over the last twenty years or so.

The *initial endowment hypothesis* (Acemoglu *et al.* 2001) suggests that the disease environment encountered by European colonising powers in past centuries – proxied in empirical studies by settler mortality – was a major obstacle to the establishment of institutions promoting long-term prosperity. When environments were unfavourable, European colonial powers established extractive institutions unsuitable for long-term growth; when environments were more favourable, institutions better suited for growth were put in place. As a corollary, the *economic institutions hypothesis* (Acemoglu *et al.* 2004) addresses the static nature of the endowment hypothesis by proposing a dynamic political economy framework in which differences in economic institutions are the fundamental cause of differences in economic development. While this hypothesis is highly plausible, the jury is still out on the empirical evidence.

The *incumbents and openness hypothesis*, as formulated by Rajan and Zingales (2003), postulates that interest groups, specifically industrial and financial incumbents, frequently stand to lose from financial development because it breeds competition, which erodes rents. They argue that incumbents' opposition will be weaker when an economy is open to both trade and capital flows. This is not only because openness limits the ability of incumbents to block the development of financial markets, but also because the new opportunities created by openness may generate sufficient new profits for them that outweigh the negative effects of increased competition. Hence the opening of both trade and capital accounts is the key to successful financial development.

While this hypothesis has attracted considerable attention in the academic and policy-making community, there is little evidence to suggest that it is relevant to developing countries today. Baltagi *et al.* (2009) address this question utilising panel datasets and dynamic estimation procedures and find that trade and financial openness – alongside economic institutions – are statistically important determinants of the variation we find in financial development across countries and over time since the 1980s. However, there is partial support for the hypothesis that the simultaneous opening of both trade and capital accounts is necessary to promote contemporary financial development. While they find that relatively closed economies stand to benefit most by opening both their trade and capital accounts, opening one without the other can still generate gains for banking sector development.

In sum, all this seems to suggest that political economy explanations of financial development and underdevelopment are the most fruitful ones. Financial and industrial incumbents, income and wealth

80   Danny Cassimon et al.

inequality, and institutions appear to be the players which interact to determine whether financial development in any given country takes off at a particular point in time.

The importance of institutions in linking financial integration and economic development

Through increased efficiency in the global allocation of capital, standard neoclassical growth theory predicts that integration of local financial markets in the global financial system will boost economic development. The scope for improved international risk-sharing and capital deepening should be particularly good news for capital-poor developing economies, which can expect both long-term net flows of capital from industrialised countries and less volatility in income and consumption through newly available insurance instruments. But the reality is different. Observed capital flows from rich to poor countries are far less than what theory predicts (Lucas 1990). In addition, the spate of currency and financial crises in the last two decades are often attributed to unfettered capital account liberalisations – and not only by activists (Bhagwati 1998; Rodrik 1998b; Stiglitz 2000).

As we did above for financial development, we ask here when financial integration is beneficial. Why are some countries able to reap the benefits of financial market integration, while others simply remain unintegrated, and still others experience disaster? Before reviewing the literature, we provide some empirical evidence of the continuing divergence in capital flows between groups of (developing) countries.

Financial integration divergence despite openness convergence

Table 4.1 provides an overview of the evolution of net external capital inflows, as one measure of financial integration, for two groups of developing countries (countries in Sub-Saharan Africa and elsewhere). As the table clearly shows, the two groups continue to experience diverging realities. While middle-income countries are enjoying a growing, albeit volatile, degree of integration in private capital markets, low-income countries remain largely shut out of (private market) integration and remain highly dependent on concessional financing – i.e. official development assistance – to meet their external financing requirements.[6] It

---

[6] This observation is confirmed using stock indicators instead of flow indicators to measure financial integration (see e.g. Lane and Milesi-Ferretti 2006; Rogoff *et al.* 2006).

Finance, globalisation and economic development

Table 4.1. *Evolution of external flows to Sub-Saharan Africa and to other developing countries (US$ billions, 1990–2006)*

	1990	1995	2000	2005	2006 (est.)
Sub-Saharan Africa					
Official flows	**21.3**	**20.9**	**12.4**	**29.4**	**35**
ODA*	17	17.4	11.7	30.1	37.5
Official debt	4.3	3.5	0.7	−0.7	−2.5
Private medium/long term	**0.8**	**3.9**	**5.1**	**12.4**	**14.8**
FDI	1.3	3.3	5.8	10.8	17.2
Portfolio equity	0	0.1	0	0.2	0.1
Bond	0	0.2	−0.2	0	−1.4
Bank lending	−0.5	0.3	−0.5	1.4	−1.1
Private short term	2.3	1.1	−1.4	1	4.6
Other developing countries					
Official flows	**57.1**	**76.4**	**34.9**	**6.2**	**51.9**
ODA*	37.3	41	41.5	76.1	65.7
Official debt	19.8	35.4	−6.6	−69.9	−13.8
Private medium/long term	**30.9**	**158.9**	**183.3**	**465.5**	**639.2**
Private short term	11.5	54.1	−5.3	86.8	84.1

* Official Development Assistance.
Source: Ratha *et al.* (2008: table 1).

is important to note here that this divergence has continued to persist in recent years, despite the significant increase in (de jure) capital account openness among low-income countries in response to pressures from the global financial system. As noted by Chinn and Ito (2006) and Rogoff *et al.* (2006), levels of openness in most low-income countries now approach those of most industrialised countries. For these low-income countries, then, the effectiveness of aid interventions remains highly important (see Claessens, Cassimon and Van Campenhout in this volume).

Threshold effects in linking financial integration and economic development

Rogoff *et al.* (2006) in their review of the voluminous literature on the benefits and costs of financial globalisation note that studies often come to conflicting conclusions. Their explanation for this is that while the literature focuses mostly on the traditional channels through which global financial integration affects growth (i.e. more efficient global capital allocation and international risk-sharing), financial globalisation also serves as a catalyst for certain 'collateral benefits'. These potential collateral benefits include, among others, financial market development, institutional development, improved governance and macroeconomic discipline. Rogoff *et al.* claim that these indirect effects may have a greater role in increasing Total Factor Productivity (TFP) or GDP growth and reducing consumption volatility than financial integration per se.

At the same time, they point to the existence of 'threshold conditions' that interact with financial globalisation – preconditions that need to be in place to reap the benefits of financial globalisation (in terms of better macroeconomic outcomes). They identify financial market development, institutional quality, governance, macro-economic policies and trade integration as these preconditions. If an economy is above a certain threshold regarding these, financial integration will increase TFP and GDP while the risk of crises will diminish. If a country fails to meet these thresholds, financial globalisation will increase the risk of crises while its effect on TFP and GDP remains unclear. They note that:

The framework also points to a fundamental tension between the costs and benefits of financial globalization that may be difficult to avoid. Financial globalization appears to have the potential to play a catalytic role in generating an array of collateral benefits that may help boost long-run growth. At the same time, premature opening of the capital account in the absence of some basic supporting conditions can delay the realization of these benefits, while making a country more vulnerable to sudden stops of capital flows. (Rogoff *et al.* 2006: 4)

This is consistent with the findings of Acemoglu *et al.* (2003) who note that countries that have pursued distortionary macroeconomic policies appear to have grown slower, with higher standard deviations of growth and higher sudden drops in GDP. Acemoglu *et al.* further argue that the main determinants are institutions. For example, institutions that place constraints on the executive, guarantee property rights, a minimum amount of equal opportunity, or relatively broad-based education, lead to higher growth and less volatility. Controlling for the quality of institutions, they find macroeconomic policies do not play a direct role, and thus view distortionary macroeconomic policies not as the cause of low growth or high volatility, but as a symptom of weak institutions. Using the same instruments as Acemoglu *et al.* (2003), Alfaro *et al.* (2005b) also consider endogeneity of institutions and find a causal effect on capital inflows of the quality of institutions. Klein (2005) finds evidence of an inverted U-shaped relationship between the benefits of capital account liberalisation and institutional quality, which is surprisingly similar to the findings of Rioja and Valev (2004) and Demetriades and Law (2006) discussed in the previous section.

Finance, globalisation and economic development

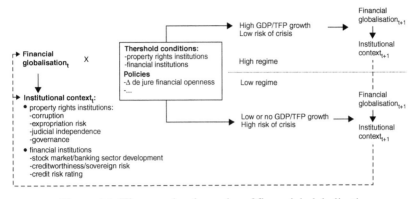

Figure 4.1. The complex dynamics of financial globalisation

From all this, we can conclude that – again – institutions seem to make the difference.

Implications for the dynamics of financial globalisation

In this section, we add a feedback mechanism to the framework of Rogoff et al. (2006), and discuss the implications of the complex relationship between financial globalisation, institutions and economic growth for the dynamics of financial globalisation itself. This can be best explained with the scheme depicted in Figure 4.1, adapted from Rogoff et al. (2006). It shows that de facto financial globalisation at time t affects the institutional context (i.e. collateral benefits). Following Rogoff et al. (2006), we make a distinction between property rights institutions and financial institutions since they may have different effects depending on what is understood by financial integration, e.g. FDI versus other forms of foreign liabilities (Wei 2006). The effect of de facto financial globalisation on GDP and TFP growth and risk of crises depends on some threshold level of institutional quality being present. If financial globalisation occurs in a context of strong property rights and financial institutions, this will lead to high GDP and TFP growth and a lower risk of crises. If financial globalisation occurs in the context of weak institutions, there is no or low GDP and TFP growth, while the probability of crises increases. These outcomes will in turn determine de facto financial integration in the following period, which will again bring collateral benefits.

The link between GDP or TFP growth and future financial globalisation is based on the premise that more productive countries will

84   *Danny Cassimon* et al.

attract more capital, a premise that can be derived from neoclassical growth models when we allow for differences in TFP.

The link between institutions, volatility and financial globalisation is documented by Acemoglu *et al.* (2003). Their main argument is that in institutionally weak societies, there are few constraints on rulers. Following a change in the balance of power, politically ascendant groups may try to use their new power to redistribute assets and income to themselves, in the process creating economic turbulence. The lack of effective constraints on politicians and politically powerful groups implies greater potential gains from coming to power. These higher political stakes may lead to increased infighting, which is again reflected in economic turbulence. Furthermore, in such a context, political leaders may be forced to hold on to power and to pursue unsustainable policies in order to satisfy various groups. They also argue that, with weak institutions, entrepreneurs may choose sectors/activities from which they can withdraw their capital more quickly, again contributing to potential economic instability.

Given the importance of institutions, is there any role left for policies? In theory, the role seems rather limited. Since we define policies as the choices made within a set of institutions, the credibility of these policies will be as good or bad as the institutional context in which they are made. This is indeed what Acemoglu *et al.* (2003) found: once they control for the quality of institutions, policy seems insignificant. However, Alfaro *et al.* (2005a) find that although institutional quality is an important determinant of capital flows, policy is important to explain changes in the level of capital flows (the effects of policies will be investigated later in this chapter).

In analogy to the literature on poverty traps, what we witness can thus be coined a 'financial globalisation trap'. Paraphrasing Matsuyama's (2008) definition of a poverty trap, the 'financial globalisation trap' can be defined as a self-perpetuating condition where an economy, caught in a vicious circle, stays on the edges of the global financial system.

Empirical validation of thresholds and multiple equilibria in the dynamics of financial integration

The above suggests that threshold effects are not only present in the relationship between financial globalisation and economic growth, but in the dynamics of financial globalisation's indicators as well. If an economy is sufficiently integrated within the global financial system, this will strengthen its domestic financial institutions, while a sophisticated and well-regulated financial sector increases the probability

Finance, globalisation and economic development

of participation in the global financial market. We thus see a self-sustaining mechanism, a mechanism that can also work in the opposite direction. An economy characterised by poor property rights institutions will not attract a lot of foreign capital. However, if global financial integration strengthens such institutions as collateral benefits, we again have a self-sustaining effect of a poorly integrated economy trapped at a low-level equilibrium.

The existence of such self-sustaining mechanisms will also be apparent in the evolution of de facto indicators of financial globalisation over time. Economies that meet the necessary preconditions will converge to a high-level equilibrium characterised by a consistently high level of financial integration in the world economy. Economies that do not have the preconditions in place will find it difficult to integrate in the world economy.

In this section, we present the results of piecewise linear autoregressions, which are simple parametric models flexible enough to estimate the threshold and multiple equilibria, to test some of the predictions made above (more detail on the model is presented in the appendix, as well as in Cassimon and Van Campenhout 2008). Specifically, we expect that the interaction of de facto financial globalisation with the institutional context, together with the feedback mechanism, will lead to conditional convergence of financial globalisation. We expect the group of countries with good institutions to converge to an equilibrium characterised by high financial integration in global financial markets. On the other hand, we expect the group of countries with bad institutions to remain on the margins of financial globalisation. The alternative is that there is no such conditional convergence, with all economies converging to the same stable equilibrium. In practice, we will test if a piecewise linear model (that allows for conditional convergence) is statistically significant compared to a simple linear model where all countries converge to the same level of financial integration.

The theoretical framework suggests that threshold effects in the interaction between the institutional context and de facto financial globalisation will cause non-linearities. We thus expect that if we condition on the quality of institutions, this non-linearity will vanish. So, as a second test, we expect that the difference between the linear model and a model that allows for different equilibria will not be significant after controlling for institutional quality in an auxiliary regression. We will also contrast this to the effect of policies. Like Acemoglu *et al.* (2003), we expect the effects of policies (like de jure financial openness) to be of a secondary order. Hence we expect that if we control for such policies, non-linearities in the dynamics of financial integration will persist. The

86   *Danny Cassimon* et al.

difference between a simple linear model and a model that allows for thresholds will remain significant after controlling for policies in the auxiliary regression.

In order to investigate whether there is indeed threshold behaviour in the dynamics of financial integration, we need a suitable measure. In the literature on the relationship between financial openness and economic development, early studies used de jure measures of integration, often based on the IMF's Annual Report on Exchange Arrangements and Exchange Restrictions (AREAER). But over time such measures have come under attack for different reasons. Given the myriad rules and regulations each country applies (e.g. controls on inflows versus controls on outflows, quantity controls versus price controls, restrictions on foreign equity holdings, etc.), it remains unclear how to combine the often qualitative AREAER data with a quantitative measure suitable for multivariate analysis. The main difficulty, however, is that de jure measures do not seem to reflect de facto financial globalisation. Given the framework developed above, this should come as no surprise: the effectiveness of de jure restrictions on financial integration – which can be regarded as policies – hinges on the quality of their institutional context.

Because of the difficulties with de jure measures, we use de facto measures of financial integration. We used Lane and Milesi-Ferretti's (2001, 2006) EWN Mark II database, a data set of consistently defined annual measures for 145 countries' stocks of gross foreign liabilities and assets over the period 1970–2004. Since we want to capture the extent of a country's integration into the global financial system, we sum the stocks of total liabilities and assets, and also use the degree of trade integration as a control. We use the sum of imports and exports as a measure of trade integration. As in Alfaro *et al.* (2005a), we scale by population size rather than by GDP.

Since, arguably, there are other structural determinants of financial globalisation, we tried different controls, all taken from the World Development Indicators On-line.[7] Following the reasoning in Chinn and Ito (2006), we included per capita income in PPP terms, the inflation rate and trade integration (measured as the ratio of the sum of exports and imports to GDP). For low-income countries, concessional loans may be a large part of their total liabilities; since these may be determined differently from other components of financial integration, we decided to use net aid transfers per capita as a control. Data for this variable were taken from the OECD/DAC (Development

---

[7] We also control for country fixed effects.

Assistance Committee of the OECD) on-line CRS system as described in Claessens *et al.* (2007). After including country fixed effects and net aid transfers per capita, we found only trade integration to be significant in the auxiliary regression. As including the other controls did not significantly affect the results, we decided to leave them out for reasons of parsimony.

Our measures of institutional quality are taken from the well-known International Country Risk Guide (ICRG) data collected by the PRS group. We included each of them in turn in the auxiliary regression to see whether this removed the non-linearities in the dynamics of financial globalisation. We also contrast this with relevant policy measures, for which we used the index of financial openness developed by Chinn and Ito (2006), based on principal components extracted from disaggregated capital and current account restriction measures in the AREAER.

The linearity test of our base model (the one based on the residuals of an auxiliary regression without controlling for the quality of institutions) results in a test statistic of 14.84, with a corresponding p-value of 0.015. This means that the dynamics of our measure of financial globalisation is better described by a piecewise linear model featuring two stable equilibria than a simple linear model where every country converges to the same stable equilibrium. The low-level stable equilibrium is estimated at 0.031 US per capita. Countries falling below 0.058 US per capita, i.e. the estimated unstable equilibrium or threshold, will move towards this low-level equilibrium at a speed of about 18 per cent of the deviation from this equilibrium per year. This corresponds to a half-life[8] of about 3.4 years. Countries that have more assets and liabilities than 0.058 US per capita (conditional on the controls included in the auxiliary regression) will move to a high-level stable equilibrium of 0.251 US per capita. However, they will move considerably slower than the group of countries converging to the low-level equilibrium. It will take 7.6 years for a certain deviation from the high-level stable equilibrium to return to half of its initial value. Hence convergence to the low-level equilibrium is more than twice as fast as convergence to the high-level equilibrium.

Now that we have found signs of conditional convergence in the dynamics of financial globalisation, we test if this disappears if we control for the quality of institutions. Although for most indicators of institutional quality the test statistic becomes smaller after controlling for

---

[8] A half-life is the time it takes for a shock away from the stable equilibrium to return to half of its value.

88   *Danny Cassimon* et al.

institutional performance, there are only four measures that make the difference between the linear and the non-linear model insignificant at the 10 per cent level. These measures are: investment profile; corruption; risk for GDP growth; and risk for current account as a percentage of GDP. Controlling for exchange rate stability risk and political risk also reduced the test statistic, but the linear specification still gets rejected at the 10 per cent significance level. We also contrast the effects of institutional quality with the effects of policy by including the index of financial openness developed by Chinn and Ito (2006). As expected, after taking into account the de jure degree of financial integration, the dynamics of international financial integration remain better described by a model that features two stable and one unstable equilibrium.

Conclusion: policy implications

This chapter has brought a number of new perspectives to the finance and growth literature. Taken together, they lead to the following conclusion: while financial openness might stimulate financial development and growth in middle-income countries, it may not do this for the poorest countries. Political economy explanations of financial (under-) development – focusing on the role of incumbents, income and wealth inequality and the evolution of economic institutions – are promising as hypotheses, but need to be further tested.

We have also argued that institutions are important conditioning variables when one examines the effect of financial integration on economic development. We have suggested that the benefits of financial integration in terms of TFP growth and reduced volatility only materialise once a certain threshold of institutional quality has been reached. In a dynamic context, this may lead to conditional convergence in global financial integration, leaving certain countries stuck in a bad equilibrium or 'financial globalisation trap'. Policies, on the other hand, are choices made within particular institutional contexts; their effectiveness depends on the institutional environment in which they are implemented. We thus expect multiple equilibria in the dynamics of financial globalisation to disappear once we control for the quality of institutions, and to persist when we just control for policies.

Using a stock-based indicator of financial integration, we find that there are indeed non-linearities in its dynamics. Adjustment to the low-level stable equilibrium is faster than adjustment to the high-level stable equilibrium. We also find that controlling for the institutional context eliminates the multiple equilibria. Specifically, the preliminary evidence suggests that multiple equilibria are due to contract viability/ expropriation risk, risks related to repatriating profits, payment delays

Finance, globalisation and economic development   89

and corruption. Furthermore, we find that policies – measured by the de jure degree of capital account openness – are not the main determinant of multiple equilibria.

In view of all this, our message should be clear: purely 'economic incentives' to increase financial sector development are unlikely to translate into increased economic development. Similarly, unfettered capital account liberalisation is ineffective at best for countries that have bad institutions. Liberalising financial markets without strengthening institutions will not automatically result in increased financial integration. In the worst case, it will increase volatility and reduce total factor productivity, resulting in even less financial integration in the future.

The evidence presented here makes it clear that a global financial architecture focusing on the promotion of openness as its primary policy output is insufficient to produce economic growth. Going forward, the process of reform should be rather thorough-going, questioning the basic assumptions of the past decades, especially the assumption that financial openness is necessarily positive as a policy stance. The system remains exclusionary, as poor countries are not only under-represented in international policy forums, but also 'underserviced'. This severely damages the legitimacy of the global financial system as well as its effectiveness for poorer countries. It further implies that, in order to promote economic development, financial integration cannot replace country-specific development strategies focusing on the improvement of domestic institutions. As the (private) capital market mechanism will not voluntarily take up this role, there is a case to be made for public intervention directly targeting and supporting the development of better institutions; an important question here is to what extent official financing – and official aid in particular – may serve this purpose. Moreover, the evidence here implies that the global financial system must provide recipient countries with the necessary policy space to develop their own country-specific institutional development paths.

Several subsequent contributions to this volume develop partial answers to the financial globalisation trap. Ocampo and Griffith-Jones (Chapter 15) advocate a 'counter-cyclical' framework to provide greater policy space for countries to escape the trap. Two other chapters address the effectiveness of official aid interventions in targeting institutional thresholds. De Jong and van de Veer (Chapter 7) question the potential catalytic effect of IMF interventions on private financing for low-income countries in debt workout or relief situations. Claessens, Cassimon and Van Campenhout (Chapter 8) discuss the new aid paradigm – highlighting the evolution towards policy dialogue types of conditionality which typically involve negotiating broad institutional reforms – with donors seeking alignment with recipient country priorities and systems.

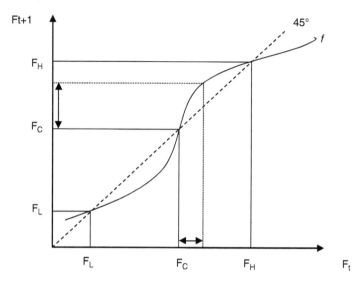

Figure 4.2. Recursion diagram

This, at least in principle, provides real opportunities for targeting aid directly to threshold bottlenecks and increased policy space for recipient countries. But how far this will materialise in practice, and to what extent it will provoke substantial catalytic effects for private sector financing, remains to be seen.

Appendix: brief presentation of the financial globalisation trap model

This appendix provides a brief methodological presentation of the model used to test for the presence of multiple equilibria, and the importance of institutional versus policy variables in explaining these multiple equilibria. Details are available in Cassimon and Van Campenhout (2008).

The resulting dynamics can best be summarised in a recursion diagram as illustrated in Figure 4.2.

In this figure, f is a function that describes how financial integration evolves over time. There are three equilibriums in this figure, two stable (F_L and F_H), and one unstable (F_C). F_C is an unstable equilibrium in the sense that if an economy has an indicator of financial integration equal to F_C in period 1, it is predicted to have F_C in the next period as well. However, if the relationship is stochastic (for instance by adding a mean zero shock ε), then any non-zero shock will drive the economy away from F_C. For instance, if the shock is positive (but smaller than

Finance, globalisation and economic development

F_H), then financial integration will be $f(F_C + \varepsilon)$ in the next period, which is larger than the initial shock. In the second period, without further shocks, the predicted level of financial integration is $f(f(F_C + \varepsilon))$, which is again an increase (again provided that $f(F_C + \varepsilon) < F_H$). This will go on until the economy arrives at F_H, the high stable equilibrium. The reverse happens when an economy starts from the unstable equilibrium and experiences a negative shock. In that case, it will end up at the lower equilibrium F_L. Hence the high and low equilibriums function as local attractors, where the basins of attraction are delineated by the unstable fixed point F_C.

The basic idea behind the econometric model is that the above-mentioned attractors and the threshold can be identified using time series estimation methods. In particular, we can use methods similar to threshold auto-regression to identify the three equilibriums. An added advantage is that we can also get an estimate of the speed at which countries converge to the stable equilibriums. If F_t is an indicator of financial globalisation for a country at time t, a model with two attractors and one threshold can be written as:

$$\Delta F_t = \beta_L.(F_{t-1} - F_L).I_{(F_{t-1} < F_c)} + \beta_H.(F_{t-1} - F_H).I_{(F_{t-1} > F_c)} + \varepsilon_t \tag{1}$$

Here, $I_{(F_{t-1} < F_c)}$ is an indicator function that takes the value of 1 if the condition is satisfied, and is zero otherwise. Defining $\alpha_L = -\beta_L.F_L$ and $\alpha_H = -\beta_H.F_H$, (1) can be rewritten as:

$$\Delta F_t = \beta_L.F_{t-1}.I_{(F_{t-1} < F_c)} + \alpha_L.I_{(F_{t-1} < F_c)} + \beta_H.F_{t-1}.I_{(F_{t-1} > F_c)} + \alpha_H.I_{(F_{t-1} > F_c)} + \varepsilon_t \tag{2}$$

The value of F_C can be found through standard sample splitting and threshold estimation techniques as in Hansen (2000). Furthermore, the low level equilibrium and the high level equilibrium can be calculated from the estimated coefficients as $F_L = -\dfrac{\alpha_L}{\beta_L}$ and $F_H = -\dfrac{\alpha_H}{\beta_H}$ respectively.

In practice, we thus test if the piecewise linear model in equation (2) is statistically significant compared to a simple linear model as in equation (3):

$$\Delta F_t = \beta.(F_{t-1} - F_S) + \varepsilon_t \tag{3}$$

The results and further steps are discussed in the section 'Empirical validation of thresholds and multiple equilibria in the dynamics of financial integration'.

Part II

Assessing the current financial architecture
(how well does it work?)

5 Adopting international financial standards in Asia: convergence or divergence in the global political economy?

Andrew Walter

The last major wave of emerging market crises triggered a global reform project, led by the USA and UK, to bring financial regulation in emerging countries into line with the regulatory standards and practices prevailing in the major countries. As noted in the introductory chapter, emerging market and developing countries had little input into the development of these international standards. Although such standards therefore lacked substantive input legitimacy, the asserted and increasingly widely perceived superiority of the Anglo-Saxon approach to financial regulation and governance gave them a wider degree of output legitimacy. This was certainly the assumption of the G7 countries and the major international financial institutions (IFIs), which put considerable effort into the global dissemination and implementation of international standards and codes on the assumption that this would strengthen the weakest link in the global financial system.[1] This assumption was also shared by many important actors in emerging countries, notably in Asia, who saw the adoption of international standards as a means of importing superior regulatory practices and restraining what they saw as destructive behaviour in their domestic political economies. How successful has this ambitious regulatory reform project been?

In this chapter, I argue that the quality of financial regulation in some emerging market countries has improved considerably since the 1990s, but that there has *not* been systematic convergence upon western

---

I wish to thank participants in the GARNET conference, the editors, and various colleagues who participated in the political economy workshop at the London School of Economics for helpful comments on a first draft of this paper. This chapter draws on a larger research project on East Asian compliance with international financial regulatory standards, published in Walter (2006, 2008).

[1] The Financial Stability Forum (FSF, now Board or FSB), established by the G7 in 1999, referred to twelve 'key standards' listed on its website as 'the various economic and financial standards that are internationally accepted as important for sound, stable and well functioning financial systems' (Financial Stability Forum, 'About the Compendium of Standards', www.fsforum.org/compendium/about.html, accessed 2 May 2008).

96   *Andrew Walter*

regulatory standards. As in the area of exchange rate policy – where researchers have unearthed a large gap between official policies and actual behaviour (Reinhart and Rogoff 2002) – there is often a similarly large gap between words and deeds in financial regulation. Regulatory convergence has in practice been gradual, limited and variable across countries and areas of regulation, and often superficial rather than substantive (what I have elsewhere called 'mock compliance').[2] This is largely because the legitimacy of international standards and associated behavioural practices are often highly contested in the countries that have imported them. The costs of substantive compliance for some actors in developing countries in particular can be high, encouraging these actors to resist compliance. Often, such actors are sufficiently influential that governments have found solutions that fall somewhere between purely formal and substantive compliance but which can be difficult for outside observers to detect.

This argument has three main implications for the broader debates addressed in this volume. First, the relationship between input and output legitimacy in global financial governance is more complex than is sometimes supposed. While developing countries had little input into the standards and codes, there has been less resistance to formal adoption than might have been expected from the low degree of input legitimacy. Formal adoption appeared consistent with best (western) practice, but the considerable scope for de facto domestic adaptation acts as a counterbalance to the undoubted dominance of the major western countries and global financial firms in the process of global financial governance. The assumed mechanisms promoting convergence – specifically market and official incentives – have proven much weaker than the G7 and the IFIs, along with various scholars, initially assumed.[3] If the pressures for convergence were as powerful as some have claimed, we would likely see much more resistance to this form of westernisation at global and regional levels. Second, the formal adoption of international standards has not eviscerated national 'policy space' in financial regulation, either because international standards are flexible in their application or because enforcement by international actors is of limited effectiveness. Regulatory forbearance remains an important option for policy-makers;

---

[2] Walter 2008. In what follows, I use the terms convergence and compliance interchangeably. In a stricter sense, convergence refers to a process by which previously different practices and institutions in national financial systems become more alike, whereas compliance signifies that the behaviour of actors who are the targets of an international rule or standard conforms to its prescriptions.

[3] For official claims about the role of both official and market incentives, see FSF 2000b. For academic claims of this kind, see Simmons 2001; Ho 2002; Soederberg 2003.

Adopting international financial standards in Asia   97

so does window-dressing for many private sector actors. At the same time, fuller convergence remains an option for those actors who perceive gains from substantive compliance. Third, it suggests that national-level private sector actors with little influence in global forums can constrain, modify and sometimes block the implementation of international standards at the domestic level.

None of the aforementioned points constitute grounds for complacency since the approximate political equilibrium produced by national adaptation need not be economically optimal. However, a long historical view casts considerable doubt on the idea that anyone can know what constitutes (or will produce) optimal financial regulation.

The rest of the chapter proceeds in three steps. First, I sketch briefly the unevenness – both across standards and across countries – of convergence upon international regulatory standards.[4] I begin with evidence of convergence at a global level before focusing in more detail on East Asian countries. Second, I discuss some theories that do not adequately explain this outcome, before offering my own. Third, I ask whether this divergence in patterns of financial governance can continue. A final section briefly concludes.

The unevenness of financial regulatory convergence

I focus on four main areas of financial regulation: the Basel Core Principles for Effective Banking Supervision (BCP), the OECD's Principles of Corporate Governance (PCG), the International Financial Reporting Standards (IFRS)[5] and the IMF's Special Data Dissemination Standard (SDDS). Note that these standards range in degree of specificity from the very general to the relatively detailed. At the very general end of the spectrum are the PCG; the BCP include a mixture of general principles and more detailed standards, while IFRS and SDDS are both relatively detailed.

Table 5.1 measures formal compliance with SDDS, IFRS, and with one key aspect of the BCP, the 'Basel I' capital adequacy standard, for different groups of countries just before the recent crisis. It is restricted to these three areas because IMF and World Bank data on compliance with the BCP and the PCG (collected through the Financial Sector

---

[4] For those interested in a more detailed account of financial regulatory reform in East Asian countries after the crisis, see Walter 2006, 2008.
[5] Strictly speaking, since 2001 the International Accounting Standards Board (IASB) issues IFRS, but existing International Accounting Standards (IAS), issued by the IASB's predecessor, the International Accounting Standards Committee (IASC), remain valid until replaced or withdrawn.

98   *Andrew Walter*

Table 5.1. *Formal compliance with SDDS, IFRS and Basel I standards (percentages by country group, end 2007)*

	Percentage of group formally compliant with:		
	SDDS	IFRS	Basel I **
% IMF members *	36%	43%	99%
% OECD members	97%	80%	100%
% Emerging market countries (IMF definition) ***	81%	35%	96%
% Thirteen major crisis-hit countries (since 1990) ****	92%	0%	100%
% Ten major East Asian economies *****	80%	20%	90%

Notes: *The figure for the 'IMF' group for Basel I compliance is for those 143 countries on the Barth *et al.* database, which probably overestimates compliance in this category. **Basel I figures generally are as of end 2007, updated from Barth *et al.* by the IMF's *Global Financial Stability Report, April 2008*. ***The IMF lists twenty-six emerging market countries. ****The thirteen major crisis-hit countries are Argentina, Brazil, Hungary, India, Indonesia, Japan, Korea, Malaysia, Mexico, Russia, Thailand, Turkey and Venezuela (non-compliant). *****The ten major East Asian economies are China (non-compliant), Hong Kong, Indonesia, Malaysia, Japan, Thailand, Singapore, Taiwan Province of China, South Korea and the Philippines.
Source: IMF, *Global Financial Stability Reports*; Deloitte-Touche Tohmatsu; Barth *et al.* (2007).

Assessment Programme, or FSAP) are not publicly available, and because there is no generally agreed measure of compliance in these latter two areas.

Three things stand out about Table 5.1. First, OECD countries exhibit fairly high levels of formal compliance across these three sets of international standards. Second, formal Basel I compliance is almost universal, whereas the pattern for SDDS and IFRS is more variable. Third, among emerging markets (for which the SDDS was primarily intended), formal compliance is high for SDDS and Basel I, but low for IFRS.

Because compliance is a continuous rather than a binary variable, these formal indicators do not fully capture either the reality of legislation or regulatory and private sector practice. For example, although most emerging market countries have not yet adopted IFRS in full, some claim that their domestic accounting standards are 'largely' though not completely based on them (e.g. Korea and Thailand). Even if we could pinpoint where international standards and national regulations diverge, there is the more complex question of whether regulators, banks, companies, and internal and external auditors actually behave in

Figure 5.1. The spectrum of compliance

ways that are consistent with national rules. Mock compliance occurs when actors formally signal their adoption of specific international rules or standards but behave inconsistently with them (see Raustiala and Slaughter 2002: 539; Shelton 2003: 5). In effect, mock compliance can occupy a range of outcomes between the extremes of formal non-compliance and substantive (behavioural) compliance, though it does not exhaust all the possibilities on the compliance spectrum (Figure 5.1); it is analogous to the now widely recognised phenomenon in exchange rate policy where there is often a large divergence between announced and de facto policies (Reinhart and Rogoff 2002). Mock compliance can occur for numerous reasons, including deliberate regulatory forbearance by the government or its agencies, low bureaucratic enforcement capacity or corruption, and behaviour by private sector actors inconsistent with the intent of the rules.

We can be reasonably sure that the level of mock compliance with SDDS is low in most cases. This is because the macroeconomic data that SDDS subscribers are obliged to post on the IMF's bulletin board are based upon publicly available national statistics and must be internally consistent. In addition, the IMF publicly declares whether or not a country posting data meets the requirements of SDDS.[6] The only other financial regulatory standards for which categorical official judgements about (country-level) compliance are made are those for money laundering and terrorist financing.

In other areas, the IMF-World Bank FSAP, which laboriously assesses countries' compliance with all international financial standards, produces reports from which very critical and quantitative judgements about compliance are (at member countries' request) often excised.[7] A quarter of all reports are never published, and many important countries have simply refused to participate in the FSAP (though the recent G20 collective commitment to participation may change this). In areas like corporate governance, bank regulation and accounting, reaching

---

[6] The SDDS is sometimes criticised as insufficient and outdated (e.g. IIF 2006c), though the question of its optimality – or indeed that of the quality of the underlying data – is different to that of compliance.

[7] For the Reports on the Observance of Standards and Codes (ROSCs), see www.imf.org/external/np/rosc/rosc.asp (accessed 3 May 2008).

100   *Andrew Walter*

judgements about degrees of compliance is difficult and often controversial. The FSAP acts as an interlocutor with public sector regulators, but the quality of compliance is at least as much a question of private sector behaviour. For all these reasons, published FSAP reports offer a poor guide to patterns of compliance.

Nevertheless, some FSAP reports are relatively candid and additional anecdotal evidence often does emerge that helps to give a better picture of compliance. Taken together, this can show that formal non-compliance in some areas is considerable and that mock compliance is even more significant. To illustrate, regulatory officials in Korea, among the most avid adherents of the international standards project in Asia, claimed that the country had met or exceeded most international standards by 2002 (FSS 2002: foreword). But the FSAP review team in 2003 argued that the new Korean financial regulator was insufficiently independent from government and industry, as required by the first BCP. Considerable evidence also emerged of regulatory forbearance for banks willing to lend to those large, distressed corporations important to the Korean government's industrial restructuring objectives. For example, foreign-controlled Korean banks complained of government pressure after 2000 to roll over loans to Hyundai, including to its semiconductor affiliate, Hynix. From May 2000 to June 2002, Korean financial institutions, mostly state-controlled, provided new credits to Hyundai group. Half of this financial support went to Hynix, even though it was then uncreditworthy (US ITA 2003: 18). The new financial regulator had allowed banks to classify their Hynix loans through late 2001 as 'normal' or 'precautionary', a relatively lenient treatment that required them to set aside only small provisions (Fitch Ratings 2002: 2–3). Later, in September 2004, once Hynix's prospects had improved, its senior management and auditors were indicted for fraudulent accounts over the whole period 1996–2003.

Evidence of regulatory forbearance can be found in other Asian countries five years or more after the crisis began. One of the main areas of forbearance, as in the Korean case, was loan classification. Singapore's Monetary Authority (MAS) thought so little of Thailand's supposedly improved loan classification regime that it consistently required Singapore-based parent banks with Thai subsidiaries to re-estimate their reported Thai non-performing loans (NPLs) and to make additional provisions against these exposures. MAS' estimates of Thai NPLs were larger than official Thai figures by a factor of five over 2001–3.[8] Lax loan classification means that required provisions are

---

[8] The affected banks were DBS, which controlled Thai Danu Bank, and UOB, which controlled Radhanasin Bank.

Adopting international financial standards in Asia 101

lower than they would otherwise be, artificially inflating net income, retained earnings, shareholder's equity, and hence Basel capital ratios. According to Thai generally accepted accounting principles, Thai Danu Bank had positive net assets but by Singapore's standards it was technically insolvent.[9] Indeed, had most governments in East Asia applied the Singaporean (or US) regulatory regime to their own banks in the period up to 2003–4, additional costly public bail-outs would have been inevitable. This applies as much to Japan as to countries like China, Indonesia, Korea and Thailand (Walter 2006, 2008). Given the political and economic constraints on further bail-outs, it is small wonder that Asian governments turned a blind eye to low NPL recognition and provisioning – a phenomenon being repeated in some advanced countries today. However, it meant that many Asian banks at the time were compliant with the minimum 8 per cent capital to risk-weighted asset ratio (CAR), the core of the Basel regime, in only a very formal sense. It also means that official CARs and NPLs are often not comparable across countries (though such comparisons are often made). Regulatory forbearance in Asia, though arguably justified on various public policy grounds, tended to be hidden rather than admitted because of the perceived need of governments to appear to conform to key international regulatory standards after the crisis. Given the widespread perception that weak or discretionary regulation caused the crisis, forbearance became the sin that dare not speak its name.

Similar outcomes can be found in areas such as corporate governance and accounting standards. In corporate governance, one of the major policy reforms after the crisis was to adopt western-style rules for independent directors on the boards of listed companies and various protections against the exploitation of minority shareholders. Various studies have shown that supposedly independent directors in practice rarely constrain incumbent management or major shareholders – who in Asia are still mostly families and governments – and that minority shareholders can still suffer systematic abuses.[10] As one Asian multicountry survey of public and private sector behaviour concluded in 2005:

A few years ago regulators were praised for tightening up on rules and regulations; today it is apparent that many of these rules have only a limited effect on corporate behaviour. Where implemented, they are often not carried out effectively. (CLSA Emerging Markets 2005: 3)

---

[9] See DBS Group, *Annual Report 2001*, p. 126, and *Annual Report 2002*, p. 80. MAS' relatively strict regulatory treatment probably contributed to DBS' decision to sell its stake in Thai Danu Bank in 2004.

[10] IMF 2003c; Gomez 2004b; Nam and Nam 2004; Nikomborirak 2004; Standard & Poor's 2004a, 2004b, 2004c; CLSA Emerging Markets 2005; World Bank 2005.

Multicountry surveys also show most Asian countries lagging behind the major developed countries in the quality of their financial reporting despite the claimed adoption of IFRS-consistent domestic financial reporting standards.[11] Although it would be wrong to claim that mock compliance does not exist in the USA and UK, particularly after the recent crisis, these surveys suggest that the quality of corporate compliance in countries like China, Indonesia, Korea and Thailand lags well behind that in the USA, UK and regional leaders such as Singapore (Standard & Poor's 2004d; CLSA Emerging Markets 2005).

To summarise, there has been a widespread trend in Asia towards formal convergence upon a variety of international standards that were seen as a solution to the perceived gross failures of financial regulation prior to the crisis of the late 1990s. But beneath this apparent process of convergence lies a more complex pattern. Across standards, the average level of substantive compliance is much higher for SDDS than for those in areas such as banking supervision, financial reporting and corporate governance. In areas like banking supervision, mock compliance with certain core standards such as those on minimum bank capitalisation was extensive in some countries for extended periods. There are also large differences in the level of substantive compliance between countries, with countries like Singapore and Hong Kong at the top and China, Indonesia and Thailand towards the bottom. Beneath these country averages lie even larger variations in the degree of corporate compliance with international and domestic standards.

Explaining uneven convergence

What explains this large variation in the degree of real convergence on international financial regulatory standards? Three related theories claim that external forces promote regulatory convergence, but they overestimate the strength of these forces and do not adequately explain the variation that we see in practice.

One prominent theory is that market forces, facilitated by the globalisation of finance, produce powerful incentives for countries and firms to converge upon western regulatory standards and practices.[12] Incentives for *formal* compliance can be significant, with Basel I and II being the best examples. But in other areas, market incentives for formal compliance are much weaker; for example, national rules on accounting and corporate governance vary greatly. Moreover, market

---

[11] See World Economic Forum (2003: 610); World Bank (2004: 11), and later issues.
[12] See Hansmann and Kraakman 2000; Soederberg 2003; Soederberg *et al.* 2005.

incentives for substantive compliance are often weak even when formal compliance is ubiquitous, as is the case for Basel I. Sometimes market incentives can even be perverse: once foreign capital inflows into Asian stocks revived after 2003, the stocks of companies with *worse* corporate governance practices tended to perform better than average (CLSA Emerging Markets 2005). The one area where market incentives for substantive compliance have been important is macroeconomic data transparency. Here, there is accumulating evidence that compliance with SDDS lowers sovereign borrowing costs marginally, giving both governments and the private sector an incentive to comply.[13] For countries that host large international financial centres, market pressure seems to promote substantive compliance in other areas like banking regulation and accounting standards. Singapore and Hong Kong are important examples, but also rather exceptional ones: for most countries, domestic political pressure appears to trump the desire to appeal to global financial market actors.

Another, related theory is that global convergence on the leader's regulatory standards and practices is produced by financial globalisation and, where necessary, hegemonic coercion (Simmons 2001). There is little doubt that the USA has taken a leading role in the negotiation and promotion of international financial standards in a range of areas and that international standards are often closely related to American national standards (though not always – the PCG and IFRS are cases in point). Simmons' theory, which focuses on the strength of market incentives to follow the leader's regulation and the negative effects of non-followership for the leader, helps to explain why formal compliance is largely voluntary in some cases (e.g. Basel I) and coerced in others (e.g. anti-money laundering rules). But the theory is not well-equipped to explain why the *degree* of compliance in areas where market incentives to emulate the leader are supposedly high (banking regulation, financial reporting) varies considerably across countries. Nor can differential hegemonic pressure explain cross-country variations in compliance: Singapore, Hong Kong and Malaysia have been much less subject to US pressure than have the IMF-intervened countries of Indonesia, Korea and Thailand – but the former have better overall compliance records.

A third common claim is that international institutions promote regulatory convergence. International institutions, both public and private, have been essential to the elaboration and promulgation of international standards. But like market forces and hegemonic states, the

---

[13] See Christofides *et al.* 2003; Glennerster and Shin 2003; Cady 2005.

104   *Andrew Walter*

standard-setters and the IFIs enjoy limited influence over substantive compliance. As noted earlier, even when governments have agreed to participate in an FSAP review of their regulatory practices and have allowed reports to be published, these are often shorn of the most sensitive material. This is not only due to member state reluctance; the IFIs also fear that greater frankness could jeopardise their relationships with member states or trigger capital flight. The reluctance to submit to compliance reviews is apparent in the refusal of many major emerging market countries to participate in an FSAP review (or perhaps to make public its results); as of mid-2008 they included Argentina, Brazil, China, India, Indonesia, Malaysia, South Africa, Thailand and Venezuela. Furthermore, the idea that explicit non-participation has serious negative consequences is implausible as many of these countries have been among the most favoured by international investors in recent years. These nonconformist countries are also in good company: the USA, alone among the G7 countries, refused until very recently to subject its regulatory practices to international review.[14] While IFIs have provided considerable technical assistance in this area in recent years, mock compliance stems more from the deep politicisation of regulation and compliance-avoidance strategies by *private* sector actors.

If a combination of global market forces, hegemonic state power, and international institutional pressure and assistance has been insufficient to promote substantive convergence on many international regulatory standards and practices, it provides a strong hint that domestic political resistance to convergence has often trumped external pressure. But why is domestic political resistance to substantive convergence strong in some areas and countries but not in others? Clearly, we need a theory that explains this variation.

One domestic political economy argument is that variation in regulatory outcomes is primarily a product of administrative capacity (Hamilton-Hart 2002). Without denying this can sometimes be important, particularly in the least developed countries, I prefer to view administrative capacity as endogenous to the political process: governments often underfund regulatory agencies or subvert regulation in other ways if the political incentives favouring mock compliance are strong. Moreover, we sometimes find similar outcomes in cases of relatively low (Indonesia) and high institutional capacity (Korea, Japan).

Another argument focuses on the impact of new ideas on convergence. Hall (2003) argues that the Asian crisis delegitimised the old model of financial regulation in Asian countries and favoured domestic

---

[14] Up until 2008, the US government argued, implausibly, that its need to implement Basel II prevented its participation in the FSAP (IMF 2007: 19).

elites who deployed a new, neo-liberal ideational discourse, which in turn promoted global regulatory convergence. It is true that emerging market financial crises promoted the adoption of western-style regulatory standards and the ideological delegitimation of previous modes of economic governance. This has made it harder for governments to avoid formal adherence to the international standards agenda (even for countries like Malaysia, which have been harshly critical of other aspects of IMF crisis conditionality). But this ideational theory aims to explain convergence rather than divergence and variation. Moreover, Hall ignores the often large gap between policy rhetoric and behavioural reality. Actors, especially those in the private sector, are often much more innovative and less brainwashed than his argument implies, especially when compliance costs are high and when they believe they can hide mock compliance from outsiders. Even committed neoliberal reformers can favour turning a blind eye to private sector mock compliance if substantive compliance would have serious negative consequences for favoured firms, growth or employment (as in Korea and Thailand for some years after the 1997 crisis). It would also be wrong to believe that cross-country variations in compliance can be explained by the degree of commitment to liberal market norms. Singapore, Hong Kong and Malaysia arguably have the best compliance records in Asia, but adhere only superficially to market liberalism: alongside their Anglo-Saxon legal traditions and trade openness, there has been persistent extensive government intervention in the economy, the dominance of state and family ownership in the private sector, limited policy transparency and an unwillingness to accept the norm of politically independent regulators and central banks.

My own explanation is that public and private sector actors are likely to prefer mock compliance when visible non-compliance *and* substantive compliance are both costly to powerful domestic actors. Emerging market crises in the 1990s favoured the formal adoption of international financial standards, by strengthening both the external forces discussed above and those domestic groups that favoured regulatory reform and international convergence. But formal adoption is only part of the battle. Once achieved, much depends on the interaction between the domestic private sector costs of substantive compliance with particular standards and the difficulty that outsiders encounter in monitoring the quality of compliance.[15]

The private sector costs of compliance depend upon the content of standards, including their scope and degree of specificity. Very specific

---

[15] Outsiders include the IFIs as well as most market actors. For elaboration, see Walter 2008, chapter 2.

standards such as the now ubiquitous accounting requirement that listed companies report all significant related party transactions are costly to corporate insiders who have previously used such mechanisms to exploit minority shareholders. Strict compliance with more stringent bank capitalisation standards is very costly for weak banks and their dependent borrowers. More general principles, such as the recommendation in the PCG that '[corporate] boards should consider assigning a sufficient number of non-executive board members capable of exercising independent judgement to tasks where there is a potential for conflict of interest' (OECD 2004: 65) are only potentially onerous: the generality of the recommendation and the difficulty of defining board independence mean that mock compliance with this standard is easy in practice. The costs of substantive compliance are likely to be high and concentrated in financially distressed economies and in those where entrenched insiders will lose from greater transparency and more stringent regulation – even when, as in all of the Asian crisis-hit countries, there are also politicians, reformers, investors and civic activists pushing hard for full convergence. Resistance to substantive compliance is likely to overwhelm the political case for compliance, since the latter derives from its relatively uncertain and more broadly distributed benefits (which possibly include lower systemic financial fragility and gains for minority shareholders). When the costs of compliance are also high for the economy in general, politicians are more likely to listen and put pressure on regulators to exercise regulatory forbearance. By contrast, when private sector compliance costs are low, resistance to substantive compliance will also be low.

The relative difficulty of third-party monitoring will also affect the degree of pressure on the government and on the private sector to comply: when such monitoring is difficult, third-party sanctions are difficult to deploy. Monitoring the quality of compliance with financial regulation, corporate governance and accounting standards is often difficult and costly, requiring not just detailed specific knowledge of particular jurisdictions but also inside information concerning public and private sector behaviour. Monitoring the true level of compliance can be effectively impossible in these areas (Hegarty et al. 2004: 9). This is not only true for private sector monitors. As noted above, the IFIs also have difficulty obtaining inside information about compliance and have no effective means of detecting or sanctioning non-observance within the public or private sectors. In these circumstances, it will often be easier for private sector opponents of substantive compliance to pursue mock compliance strategies than to oppose formal compliance, which is by contrast easily detectable by outsiders (when even the weak can

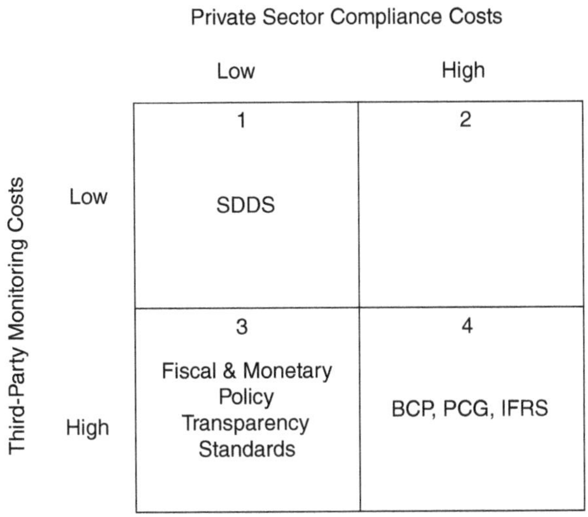

Private Sector Compliance Costs

		Low	High
		1	2
	Low	SDDS	
		3	4
	High	Fiscal & Monetary Policy Transparency Standards	BCP, PCG, IFRS

Third-Party Monitoring Costs

Figure 5.2. Private sector compliance costs and third-party monitoring costs for different international standards

achieve formal compliance, formal non-compliance must signal deep problems!).

Figure 5.2 categorises some of the main international standards into a simple 2x2 matrix. The theory predicts that mock compliance outcomes are likeliest in quadrant 4 and least likely in quadrant 1, which is what we observe in practice (the other quadrants have ambiguous implications).[16] Substantive compliance with SDDS is unusually high because outsider monitoring of the quality of compliance is comparatively easy, because the public sector socialises the costs of compliance, and because compliance produces concrete private benefits (lower sovereign borrowing costs usually also reduce average private sector borrowing costs). By contrast, substantive compliance by the private sector with the stricter components of banking regulation, corporate governance and financial reporting standards is much less likely in countries with high levels of private sector distress and with corporate ownership structures that privilege insiders (as in Indonesia, Korea, Malaysia and Thailand after the crisis). Perceived external pressure for compliance and domestic private sector resistance can put reformist governments in a difficult position, which can only be squared by some form of regulatory forbearance (as in Korea and Thailand). In countries like

[16] Examples of international financial standards in quadrant 2 are difficult to find, but international trade rules on non-tariff barriers may be one illustration (given the

108 *Andrew Walter*

Singapore, where financial distress was relatively low and the government controlled much of the corporate sector, compliance was superior to that elsewhere in Asia. Indeed, Singapore's relatively strong banks share an interest with the government in costly *over*-compliance with international standards, a kind of 'peacock's tail' signalling of their distinctiveness from their mock compliant regional competitors.

Can divergence continue?

The difficulty of third-party monitoring implies that mock compliance can be sustainable over time. But how sustainable can such behavioural divergence be if evidence continues to trickle out into the public arena? In recent years we have witnessed banks that claim to exceed minimum capitalisation rules suddenly collapse after auditors decide their own reputations require that they register an objection to financial accounts (Resona Bank in Japan in 2003); corporate accounting frauds coming to light that reveal past reporting failures (some major banks and companies in Indonesia, Korea and Thailand); and the media publicising egregious cases of controlling shareholders exploiting minority shareholders in some of the region's most important companies (Samsung in Korea and Shin Corp in Thailand). When this happens, regulators may have no choice but to step in and enforce the rules. Markets also typically punish such firms by withdrawing lines of credit or by selling stock. Will market forces, after all, eventually produce convergence even if the process is slower than many first hoped?

There are various reasons to doubt that these long-run forces for convergence will be very strong. One is that governments and regulators often try to isolate firms violating standards as exceptional cases, precisely because of the extensive private and public costs of demanding that all other firms meet regulatory standards in full. In the absence of information about similarly large compliance gaps in other firms, outsiders find it difficult to target them. Moreover, for highly leveraged banks – for which even unsubstantiated market suspicions of undercapitalisation can be disastrous – implicit or explicit government guarantees usually short-circuit market effects, as many advanced countries have more recently discovered. It is public knowledge that the major credit rating agencies believed many Asian banks to be close to insolvent only a few years ago, and that therefore their formal compliance with Basel capital requirements was effectively meaningless. Yet the

relative ease and high incentives for competitors to detect and publicise cheating). I thank Ken Shadlen for this point.

Table 5.2. *Moody's weighted average long-term deposit ratings, bank financial strength ratings and average CARs, Asian and US banks, 2003*

Banks based in:	Moody's weighted average long-term deposit rating, October 2003	Moody's weighted average BFSR, October 2003	Average CARs, mid-2003 (%)
Hong Kong	A2	B-	15.6
Indonesia	B3	E+	21.4
Japan	A3	E+	10.8
South Korea	Baa1	D-	10.4
Malaysia	Baa2	D+	13.4
Singapore	Aa2	B	17.8
Thailand	Baa2	D-	13.6
USA	Aa3	B	12.7

Note: AAA is the highest deposit rating, C is the lowest, with the modifiers 1, 2 and 3 in declining order of quality applied to categories from Aa to Caa. A is the highest and E the lowest BFSR.
Source: Moody's Investor Services and IMF.

same credit agencies rated the liabilities of most of these banks as investment grade rather than 'junk' because they judged the probability of government intervention in the event of a threatened bank failure to be almost certain. Table 5.2 illustrates the distinction between Moody's average credit risk ratings for Asian banks (reflected in the long-term 'deposit rating') and its average 'bank financial strength rating' (BFSR) in 2003. The former is most relevant to creditors because it takes into account the probability of government support, whereas the BFSR does not. The gap between the two ratings, and the lack of relationship between deposit ratings and official capital ratios, are indicators of the variable extent of mock compliance in this sector across Asia. Perhaps most notably, Indonesian banks had the highest average CAR, but their very poor BFSRs suggested Moody's still judged them to be as financially weak as then-tottering Japanese banks (Indonesian deposit ratings were below investment grade because the sovereign rating was so poor).

Does this also mean that the gradual elimination of financial distress in crisis-hit emerging market countries will promote regulatory convergence? There is certainly evidence that after 2004 some governments and regulators stepped up levels of enforcement and reduced regulatory forbearance as economies recovered (Walter 2008). But it would be wrong to expect too much from this process; the financial strength of

110   *Andrew Walter*

emerging market banks remained well below those of advanced countries before the 2008–9 crisis.[17]

The main factor favouring continued divergence is that there are powerful forces of continuity in the political economies of emerging market countries that persist even after financial distress has been largely eliminated. Even if markets did impose costs on all firms in a given category or in a whole economy, key domestic actors may still be willing to pay them because the costs of substantive compliance can be even higher. The families behind most Korean *chaebol* have evidently been willing to pay the additional equity costs entailed by the 'Korea discount' for many years to retain effective control over their corporate empires.[18] Similar points could be made about the very limited concessions to improved corporate governance and full financial disclosure made by many of the ruling business families across Asia (Studwell 2007). Nor are these cases exceptional. Most countries in the world, compared to the USA and UK, have concentrated forms of corporate ownership and control, especially by families and governments (La Porta *et al.* 1998). These insiders do not necessarily share the strong interest of minority shareholders in financial transparency and strict arms-length regulation. As long as corporate ownership and control in Asia and in other parts of the developing world remain so highly concentrated, the domestic political process is unlikely to produce full regulatory convergence.

This points to what could be a more important source of long-term change. The crisis altered ownership structures in the financial sectors of the crisis-hit countries in Asia by substantially reducing family ownership in their banking sectors. Intervened banks were often sold to recoup some of the massive costs of public bail-outs, sometimes to foreign banks or investors. Foreign banks now control about one-third of the banking sector in Indonesia, Korea and Thailand, and 80 per cent of Mexico's. For the twenty-six countries classified as emerging markets by the IMF, the percentage of banking system assets in banks that are at least 50 per cent foreign owned increased from about 20 to 33 per cent between 2000 and 2006, though there are large variations about the mean.[19] This introduced into these countries' financial

---

[17] As of May 2008, Moody's financial strength ratings for Indonesian, Korean and Thai banks still averaged D, C- and D respectively (Moody's Investor Services 2008b).

[18] The Korea discount refers to the lower stock price-earnings ratios of most large Korean firms compared to their global competitors, and is commonly attributed to investor concerns about relatively poor corporate governance practices and weak enforcement in Korea (IIF 2003).

[19] Calculated from the Barth, Caprio and Levine banking regulation and supervision survey, http://go.worldbank.org/SNUSW978P0 (accessed 7 May 2008).

systems relatively strong banks with a correspondingly strong interest in higher sectoral levels of compliance (since this would disadvantage their domestic competitors). Foreign-controlled banks have also sometimes eroded though hardly eliminated the traditional relationship-based links between banks and corporations, and increased the pressure on domestic banks to raise their own standards. Nevertheless, in Asia at least, this is unlikely to produce compliance miracles in the near future since foreign banks often focus on retail rather than corporate lending and because nationalist backlashes before 2008 against foreign banks and investors in Korea and Thailand, heavily supported by elements in the corporate sector, already suggested political limits to their transformative role. The 2008–9 crisis has already produced a degree of de-globalisation of banking, so it might be wrong to expect foreign bank penetration to transform domestic political economies in the near future.

Conclusion

I have argued that although the quality of financial regulation in some emerging market countries has improved considerably since the 1990s, there has been no systematic convergence upon western regulatory standards. For a number of reasons, one of the foundations on which the new international financial architecture was based was less than effectively implemented. This conclusion may be less surprising to students of comparative politics, but it differs from a common view in international political economy that the forces for convergence in financial structures are powerful, particularly for developing countries.[20] Regulatory convergence has been on average limited and variable across countries and areas of regulation. Moreover, there has been a marked tendency for public and private sector actors to engage in mock compliance. In short, this suggests that the external pressures for convergence are much weaker than many expected a decade ago and that considerable policy space remains for both public and private sector actors, though this can easily permit behaviour of a perverse kind. This must be borne in mind as the post-crisis reform process is carried forward.

---

[20] In his contribution to this volume, Zhang argues that financial market structures in Malaysia and Taiwan have moved from being bank-based to securities market-based, a related but somewhat different issue. I believe this claim overstates the degree of structural convergence that has taken place, as the World Bank data set on which it is based does not adjust for the high levels of bank holdings of bonds and the high levels of government and family block equity holdings that characterise Asian financial systems and differentiate them from those in the USA and UK (pre-2008).

I have also argued that the main reason for continued divergence in regulatory outcomes is that powerful private domestic interest coalitions have had too much to lose from the international standards agenda. But interestingly, their preferred strategy has not been to oppose the process of global financial governance for its lack of input and output legitimacy, but instead to engage in less transparent forms of behavioural dissent. Politicians and regulators – even those who have openly embraced international standards as both legitimate and appropriate – have also used the policy space that still exists between formal adoption of international standards and actual behaviour to engage in various forms of regulatory forbearance, because they too have understood that substantive compliance would often entail large political costs. This was the learning experience of even the most committed neoliberal reformers, from the Chuan government in Thailand to the Kim Dae Jung government in Korea. The difficulty that external actors have in assessing the reality of compliance, and sometimes their desire to support domestic reformers, makes it difficult to sanction this behaviour.

The 2008–9 crisis creates considerable uncertainty in this area. Some of its effects arguably favour convergence. Governments and private actors in the major developed countries are now faced with many similar dilemmas previously faced mainly by developing countries. Regulatory forbearance, albeit of a rule-bound kind, appears to be gaining greater legitimacy in the form of a growing consensus in favour of counter-cyclical provisioning and capital requirements for banks. The entry of G20 countries into most of the major international standard-setting bodies puts some emerging country governments in the potential position of being rule-makers rather than rule-takers, which might conceivably raise the political costs of non-compliance. Other effects, such as the potential for a de-globalisation of finance, may promote divergence. The crisis has also dramatically undermined the authority claims of the Anglo-Saxon regulatory model with which many international standards are still associated, which may embolden compliance opponents to be more open in their dissent in the future. In many ways, the politics of regulatory convergence is still in its very early stages.

6 The political economy of Basel II in the international financial architecture

Stijn Claessens and Geoffrey R. D. Underhill

Introduction

The new Basel capital accord (B-II) promulgated by the Basel Committee on Banking Supervision (BC) was intended as a centre-piece of the financial architecture reforms that followed the crises of the 1990s (for the broader context, see Part I of this volume). B-II established a new approach to measuring capital adequacy of internationally active banks in a context of consolidated supervision of increased cross-border banking activities. Its impact will be felt well beyond the BC's G10-member financial institutions.[1] In addition, the BC continues to set a broad range of global standards for financial regulation

---

This chapter is a revised and much abridged version of an article that first appeared in *The World Economy* 31-3, March 2008. The authors would like to thank Erik Feijen and Emile Yesodharan for their excellent research assistance. We are also grateful for funding from the (UK) Economic and Social Research Council's World Economy and Finance research programme (award no. RES-156-25-0009), as well as funding from the EU 6th Framework Programme (Citizens and Governance in a Knowledge-Based Society), part of the GARNET Network of Excellence (work package 5.2.4). The original paper was substantially completed while the first author was at the World Bank. The findings, interpretations and conclusions expressed here are entirely those of the authors; the views expressed do not necessarily reflect those of the World Bank or the IMF.

[1] BC membership was limited to the G10, which was in fact thirteen countries: Belgium, Canada, France, Germany, Italy, Japan, Luxembourg, the Netherlands, Spain, Sweden, Switzerland, the UK and the USA. The Committee itself acknowledged that its standards will be adopted by most countries (see Basel Committee 2006a: 15). The Committee's own website homepage states that 'Over recent years, it has developed increasingly into a standard-setting body on all aspects of banking supervision, including the B-II regulatory capital framework' (web address www.bis.org/bcbs/index.htm). According to the Financial Stability Institute in 2004, some eighty-eight non-Basel Committee supervisors were expected to adopt the framework as of 2006. By 2009, some five thousand banks in seventy-three countries – representing 75 per cent of non-Basel Committee banking assets – would be subject to the standards, the principal motivation being that many of these banks are foreign-controlled by G10 financial institutions (FSI 2004: 5), to which the principles of consolidated supervision (Basel Committee 2006) apply. In 2009, the G20 extended membership of the BC significantly (see below).

and prudential supervision. While B-II is ostensibly, in part at least, about creating a more level playing field among internationally active banks, this chapter provides evidence that the impact of B-II will be far from neutral on competition among different types of banks and, crucially, on the cost and availability of capital for developing countries. Furthermore, we demonstrate how B-II's inherent pro-cyclicality has an especially large impact on developing countries. Combined with B-II's reliance on rating agencies, biases against small and medium enterprises, and high costs of implementation for developing countries (see also chapter by Ocampo and Griffith-Jones in this volume), its potentially distorted impact on competition and pro-cyclicality considerably hampers B-II's effectiveness as a global supervisory standard to provide financial stability. Arguably, B-II and the market-based approach to financial supervision which the BC promoted from the 1996 Market Risk Amendment to B-I were central factors behind the emergence of the global financial crisis.

Despite this central importance of the BC in global financial governance and the application of B-II to banks well beyond the jurisdiction of its current membership, input-side representation during its formulation was highly exclusionary, far more so than for example the International Monetary Fund (IMF) with its broad membership. Powerful private financial interests had more access to the BC decision-making process than developing countries as a whole, and a strong whiff of policy capture is left in the air. Our argument here is that the skewed output is a direct result of the skewed input side of the BC: B-II reflects the preferences of a narrow constituency of interests and confers competitive advantages on the very internationally active banks which originally proposed it. The obvious conclusion is that the BC should be reformed to reflect much better the broader constituencies and interests of those its decisions affect, which would most likely increase the effectiveness of resulting agreements as well. The G20 reform process begun in 2009 goes in that direction, but it is as yet unclear to what extent G10 private sector financial influence will simply be replaced by G20 private sector influence and whether current Basel II reform proposals survive industry counter-attack.

The chapter first examines the process by which B-II was formulated, explaining how the standards were proposed and adopted. In the second section, the chapter employs the BC's own data and related evidence to analyse the likely impacts of B-II on different classes of creditor institutions and borrowers, including some of its effects on developing economies. In the third section, the chapter employs new data to focus on the likely impact of B-II on the cost, availability and

The political economy of Basel II

pro-cyclicality of lending to developing countries. Throughout and in the conclusion, the chapter assesses the likely effectiveness of the agreement in promoting better risk management by individual banks and containment of systemic risk.

Basel II and the new international financial architecture

The development of the B-II accord should be seen in the broad context of the overall international financial architecture reform which began in the wake of the 1994 peso crisis and ended with the post-2001 'period of calm'. In response to the crises, international institutions dealing with financial issues, such as the BC, the OECD, the IMF, World Bank and the newly created Financial Stability Forum (FSF, since 2009 the Financial Stability Board or FSB) promulgated a range of international standards to shape, improve and most of all facilitate market behaviour. In this context, the new B-II market-based approach to banking supervision has a uniquely important place.[2] It is also a representative example of the *process* by which key elements of the new international financial architecture were put in place.

The origins of Basel II

The BC was founded in 1974[3] and consists of the banking supervisor from the central banks[4] of each member country. The BC had in the past earned a reputation for 'Olympian' detachment as guardian of the public interest, with an institutional culture of strict secrecy and relative

---

[2] Although B-II notionally concerns specifically internationally active *banks*, its sectoral and country coverage impact is much broader. The principles embodied in the BC's 'Core Principles' for banking supervision (Basel Committee 2006b) and the 'Basel Concordat' combine with B-II to cover de facto all international banking activities as well as many insurance and capital markets activities of financial conglomerates. This involves in particular the Concordat's principle of home-host supervisory responsibility for cross-border supervision, combined with the principle of consolidated supervision, requiring coverage of financial conglomerates as an integrated whole, i.e. including the securities trading and investment fund activities of commercial banks and their subsidiaries and affiliates. While capital market *regulation* falls under other (international) organisations (such as the International Organisation of Securities Commissions or IOSCO, see Underhill and Zhang 2008), much of banks' activities in capital markets is covered by B-II.

[3] For more on the history of the BC, see Wood 2005.

[4] If this is not the banking supervisor, then there is an additional representative of the national supervisory agency, though this does not add an extra 'vote' and the committee anyway operates on a consensus basis.

insulation from other public and private institutions. The conclusion of the Basel Capital Adequacy Accord (B-I) in 1988[5] was the crowning achievement of the BC and occurred with little formal consultation with 'outside' interests, private or otherwise.

Doubtless up until the negotiation of the 1996 Market Risk Accord amending the 1988 B-I agreement, the Committee did operate in a considerably more detached manner than it does today. However, international-level Olympian detachment and insulation from the traditional politics of government lobbies obscured a more prosaic reality. National financial policy communities, with central banks and autonomous regulatory agencies at their core, were often characterised by 'business corporatism' and the delegation of public authority to private agencies via self-regulation (Moran 1986, 185–201; Coleman 1996). This close relationship between regulatory agencies and their private sector constituencies still characterises the regulatory process today, and is in fact enhanced by the 'Olympian' distance of central banks and other autonomous agencies with supervisory responsibilities from the rough and tumble of traditional policy-making in democratic governments.

While the BC might appear to deliberate in Olympian detachment, the committee's members interact with a small community of private players which share more interests with their 'principals' than with other sectors of the economy and society. Cross-border integration meant regulatory bargains reached at the national level had to be adapted, and B-I achieved this in relation to capital adequacy. Because capital adequacy norms can affect the costs and terms of competition among banks (Oatley and Nabors 1998), calls emerged for the BC to consider more closely the impact of its decisions on the banking sector. The result was the emergence of direct BC consultation with the private sector, particularly with the Institute of International Finance (IIF) based in Washington. The IIF was originally formed as a consultative group of major US and European banks during the debt crisis of the 1980s, but became a more broadly based organisation representing some 350 major banks worldwide. This process expanded with the Committee's 1993 proposals to amend B-I to include bank securities market risks (Basel Committee 1993).

This at first informal (and until then unprecedented) consultation process with IIF began after the latter issued a position paper sharply

---

[5] Capital adequacy refers to the equity and liquidity buffer a bank must have to ensure its ongoing soundness and is measured as a percentage of total bank assets, hence capital adequacy ratio.

criticising the 1993 BC document: the proposals 'fail[ed] to create sufficient regulatory incentives for banks to operate more sophisticated risk measurement systems than those necessary to meet the regulatory minimum' (IIF 1993) meaning it failed to stimulate the use of model-based internal risk control mechanisms. A well-circulated and authoritative paper (Dimson and Marsh 1994) argued that such mechanisms were more effective than the Committee's proposed approach, and this added to the pressure to revamp the proposal. Two consecutive new consultative documents embraced the approach advocated by the IIF (Basel Committee 1995a, 1995b). The pressure had worked, but the Committee's new and soon to become formal interlocutor was hardly representative of the range of parties which would be affected by the amended accord. There was at the time no emerging market representation in the BC and very few emerging market banks were members of the IIF.[6] The process did not extend beyond the traditionally already close relationships between banks and regulators, thus importantly leaving out the consumers of financial services (e.g. corporations, small and medium-sized enterprises (SMEs), households, developing economy sovereigns). Situated at the transnational level, the policy community drawing up international accords was even further removed from traditional domestic lines of democratic accountability than in normal policy-making processes.

Following the successful translation of IIF preferences into Committee policy, the IIF-BC relationship became regular practice in the face of ongoing criticisms of (the still unchanged) B-I treatment of credit risk. The review of B-I began with a study group of the Group of Thirty (G30), a private think-tank-like body of members drawn from public and private institutions in the financial sector alike, many of whom had held prestigious appointments at different times in both. The group issued a report on systemic risk in the changing global financial system (Group of Thirty 1997).[7] In the foreword to the report, Paul Volcker, chairman of the G30 (also former Chairman of the Federal Reserve and now a key advisor leading the US financial reform effort), eulogised the role of global banks in the development of international regulatory frameworks and emphasised collaborative efforts between these institutions and their supervisors as an effective

---

[6] Although the IIF membership did eventually include some emerging market financial institutions, and the BC eventually subsequently began an 'outreach' process involving emerging market economies.
[7] The report includes the names of study group participants and members of the Group itself (pp. 47–8).

118   *Stijn Claessens and Geoffrey R. D. Underhill*

and broadly acceptable contribution towards the process (Group of Thirty 1997: p. ii).

The G30 report also observed that banks' internal risk management controls should play a central role in assuring the stability of financial systems and that 'core' financial institutions should take the initiative to develop a new risk assessment system along with 'international groupings of supervisors'. In essence, financial globalisation had rendered the supervisory process increasingly difficult and beyond the reach of national supervisors. The conclusions of the report argued that regulatory agencies should rely more on the private institutions that they supervised and that the private institutions themselves would accept more of the responsibility to improve the structure of and the discipline imposed by their internal risk management mechanisms (Group of Thirty 1997: 12). In 1998 the IIF issued its own report specifically urging the BC to update B-I on the basis of market-based internal ratings used by banks (IIF 1998).

Here lie the origins of the market-based supervisory approach contained in the three pillars of B-II. Although the BC invited broader consultations on its proposals for B-II, the IIF remained its principal interlocutor, and comments overwhelmingly came from financial institutions in Europe and North America, and to a lesser extent from officials from agencies, a few academics, chambers of commerce and industry producer associations.[8]

While a claim that the BC was a victim of 'policy capture' in the mid and late 1990s may be overstated, there is little doubt that the BC and its member institutions were far more likely to take into account the articulated preferences of private sector interlocutors from developed countries than the interests of developing country supervisors and their corresponding financial sectors. The long-institutionalised relationships between national regulators and the regulated, which had emerged at the transnational level by the mid-1990s, approximate conditions of capture, and B-II clearly has its origins in private sector proposals. It might also be pointed out that there was considerable scepticism about whether this new market-based approach to supervision would indeed prove effective at enhancing financial system stability. Doubts focused in particular on the way in which B-II might increase the pro-cyclicality of lending and risk-taking by banks (see below and Chapter 15 by Ocampo and Griffith-Jones), leading to asset bubbles

---

[8] See Committee website section on comments on proposals at www.bis.org/bcbs/cacomments.htm (comments on second consultative document) and www.bis.org/bcbs/cp3comments.htm (comments on third consultative document), accessed 2 April 2008.

The political economy of Basel II 119

and an increased tendency toward the occurrence of crises. In other words, market forces might make matters worse, not better.

How it works

The three starting points of B-II were better risk exposure measurement, that banks develop better internal controls and risk management, and an increase in the role of market discipline. In B-II this led to the so-called 'three pillars' consisting of (1) minimum capital requirements; (2) supervisory review of capital adequacy; and (3) public disclosure and market discipline (Basel Committee 2003). Under the three-pillar system, bank supervisors would no longer be exclusively responsible for specifying and monitoring levels of capital adequacy; bank risk managers, supervisors and market forces were expected to combine to jointly oversee and to discipline banks.

Pillar One introduced important changes in the way aspects of risks and resulting capital adequacy requirements were to be calculated, also expanding the range of risks to include operational risk. Three different options for measuring required capital became available: (1) the Standard approach for 'less sophisticated' institutions is based on B-I but with enhanced risk sensitivity through differential 'risk weightings' for sovereign and corporate exposures based on external credit assessments, such as by export credit agencies and commercial ratings agencies (Standard & Poor's, Moody's, Fitch, etc.); (2) the 'Foundation' Internal Ratings Based (IRB) approach to risk management allowed for (limited) use by banks of internal Value at Risk (VaR) models; and (3) the 'Advanced' IRB approach for the largest and most sophisticated financial institutions. In the Foundation IRB version, only the probability of default is calculated by the bank, and all other ratios determining capital required were to be specified by the supervisor. In the Advanced IRB version, all aspects of credit risks were estimated by the bank itself. The Committee characterised the Advanced approach as '... a point on the continuum between purely regulatory measures of credit risk and an approach that builds more fully on internal credit risk models', with further movement along the continuum as 'foreseeable' (Basel Committee 2006a: 17).

Essentially, option three was a 'self-supervision' approach, but it was not available to all banks. Under Pillar Two, banks had to qualify for the Advanced option and supervisors must regularly 'stress test' and assess the appropriateness of banks' (use of) risk management models. Pillar Three stressed 'market discipline' in the form of public disclosure of, among others, bank risk profiles and capitalisation and was seen as a *complement* to the first two pillars. This pillar was based on claims, mainly by the industry itself, that market discipline would prove the best guarantor of sound risk management, and that supervisory oversight is essentially redundant in a soundly functioning system of market discipline.[9]

Effectiveness, winners and losers: impact on systemic risk and the terms of competition

The new accord has been subject to criticism on a number of grounds, and these are best revealed by an analysis of how the accord most likely works in practice. The implementation phase officially began toward the end of 2007, though many major banks had begun the transition well before and the 1996 amendment to B-I meant the market-based approach to supervision had indeed been around for some time. This section will argue that while B-II may encourage better internal risk management in the major systemically important banks, it is less clear that the accord reduces the systemic, macro-prudential aspects of risk. Although the outbreak of the financial crisis has somewhat complicated an effective assessment of the results of the accord in 'normal' times, the scale of financial instability certainly weakens arguments that Basel II has either enhanced internal risk management or prevented systemic collapse. Furthermore, the pattern of winners and losers under B-II appears to relate to the pattern of influence observed in the drafting of the accord: large internationally active banks permitted to employ the advanced approach they themselves proposed gained the most. Finally, in part for reasons of lack of representation, B-II has a negative impact on developing countries.

The discussion establishes a number of interrelated points in support of these arguments. First, the systemically most important banks arguably benefited the most from the new regime, in terms of the levels of regulatory capital and the treatment of collateral. Worse still, even on the dubious assumption that the new supervisory approach resulted in better internal risk management within systemically important financial institutions (most of which subsequently collapsed and at time of writing were still on government life-support), this apparently did not aggregate into effective reduction of systemic risk. The accord may

---

[9] While market discipline may assist in sound risk management, it is less clear that it makes supervisory oversight redundant. Even in well-functioning systems with a long history of market discipline, recent corporate (governance) scandals and bank failures in light of the sub-prime crisis, cast some serious doubts on the sufficiency of public disclosure for proper (risk) management.

have helped enhance both the pro-cyclicality and volatility of financial markets. Secondly, under the advanced IRB approach the new accord arguably favours the very sort of financial innovation and risk management practices which led to the current financial crisis. At the same time, the accord discounts the potential benefits of 'relationship banking' as practised by small-scale lenders relative to those of the internal risk management models of the advanced approach. Thirdly, the recent financial crisis has made clear that Pillar Three – market discipline through enhanced disclosure – will not necessarily provide the risk reduction benefits hoped for either at the level of the individual financial institutions or of the overall market. Fourthly, the accord might insufficiently reward the benefits and lower risk correlations of portfolio diversification when bank portfolios include smaller, perhaps individually riskier, but systemically less significant borrowers, including those from developing countries. Fifthly, there remain serious questions about the role of ratings agencies in the new system, particularly regarding the incentives they face and their effects on macro-prudential and systemic risks. And finally, in part because of its complexity, the utility of the accord as a global or even national standard may be questioned; indeed EU and US supervisors have been applying it quite differently within their own jurisdictions while G20 reform discussions emphasise the need for strengthened and harmonised standards and implementation of supervisory practice.

Some of these issues were foreshadowed in the discussion during the run-up to the adoption of B-II. A first distributional cleavage concerned the terms of competition between large, internationally active and smaller banks. This was expressed forcefully by America's Community Bankers (ACB 2003), the German *Bankenfachverband* (small consumer financing banks) and a range of other national and EU-level associations.[10] Their claim was that high development and compliance costs excluded smaller banks from the Foundation and Advanced IRB approaches. A reliance on the Standardised approach leads to either relative or absolute increases in capital charges (relative to B-I) for these banks, and thus to potential competitive disadvantages. This also applies to most banks in developing countries because they cannot use the Foundation and certainly not the Advanced IRB approaches.[11] Arguably, smaller US/EU banks and banks from developing countries

---

[10] These and subsequent references to position papers are available on the BC websites listed in note 10.
[11] Many developing country supervisors were in no position to implement the IRB approaches anyway.

were already at a competitive disadvantage in cross-border markets, and now face higher B-II capital charges. Their weaker internal control systems and developing country context may also render them more risky as institutions, and it was of course the *intention* of B-II to better account for such differences in risk. These banks may, however, have other advantages which offset these risks: smaller banks can take advantage of the 'softer' information on their clients only available in close, relationship-based banking practices, rendering their lending less risky in this regard. As such, both large and small banks have their own comparative advantages in terms of risk management. However, B-II places less value on traditional relationship banking, creating a competitive bias against lending to (unrated) SMEs and giving the large banks an advantage.

The BC's own study reinforces the point of differential impact: the reductions in required capital relative to B-I were much greater under the advanced IRB approach than under the Standard or Foundation IRB approaches (Basel Committee 2006c, especially Table 5).[12] Note that none of the G10 large internationally active (so called 'Group 1') banks were expected to use the Standardised approach anyway, whereas 33 of the 153 smaller G10 banks ('Group 2') were planning to do so. The situation was even starker for the non-G10 countries where 49 of 54 banks in *non*-G10 'Group 2' (smaller) banks were planning to employ the Standardised approach (p. 7, Table 3).[13] For these non-G10 Group 2 banks, the Standardised approach yields a 38.2 per cent *increase* in capital charges relative to B-I, the Foundation IRB approach an increase of 11.4 per cent, and the Advanced IRB approach a modest reduction of 1 per cent (p. 10, Table 5). The impact is clear: substantial competitive and cost advantages to those large banks (mostly in developed countries) who could apply the Advanced approach. In the end, the American small banking lobby bore fruit when the USA decided to apply the new accord to only the 10–20 largest internationally active American banks (a choice the agreement allows national supervisors to make), precisely the group of banks which has collapsed so spectacularly. Meanwhile, and in the face of opposition, the EU stuck to its position that the accord would apply to all banks.

---

[12] The accord stipulates that B-II should not lead to an overall increase in capital requirements compared to B-I; but this is a requirement at the overall banking system level, not at the individual bank level.

[13] 'Non-G10' included Australia, Singapore and seven developing countries. There were only six non-G10 Group 1 banks; the survey was anonymous, but it is highly likely that these were Australian and Singaporean as the criteria for Group 1 banks are: the bank has at least €3 billion in capital, is diversified and internationally active.

The political economy of Basel II   123

Further fears were expressed by banks and clients stuck with the Standardised approach. This approach relies on so-called 'external credit assessment institutions' such as ratings agencies and qualified export credit agencies. Lending to highly rated clients (both financial and non-financial corporations) yields lower capital charges (e.g. AAA to AA-, only 20 per cent; A+ to A-, 50 per cent). While most small credit institutions and their SME clients typically have no ratings (obtaining a rating can be expensive), they are not necessarily more risky, especially when considering their smaller size (given diversification, keeping risk per loan constant, a large pool of SME loans will be less risky in systemic terms than a small number of large corporate loans). However, loans to unrated (SME) corporate clients are subject to a B-II 100 per cent charge (Basel Committee 2006a: 19–23), identical to B-I (when all claims on the private sector were assigned a 100 per cent charge), but certainly higher than lending to highly rated corporate borrowers under B-II.[14] Still, B-II means relatively higher capital costs for the smaller banks and important competitive advantages for those banks that can take advantage of high external ratings of either of the IRB approaches.

The situation for unrated banks or borrowers in developing countries was worse: many sovereigns would attract a 100 per cent (BB+ to B-) or a 150 per cent (below B-) charge, and under the rules no unrated bank or corporate client could have a charge lower than that of the sovereign in which they were incorporated (Basel Committee 2006a: 21–3). For otherwise creditworthy entities within low-rated countries, capital costs would thus rise relative to B-I. Developing country submissions to the BC argued that some banks and corporations in developing countries were sounder than the sovereign and that the ratings of the bank and corporations should be considered in relation to the risks of lending to the entity.[15] Yet their pleas were ignored. By producing relative to B-I an increase in capital requirements for loans to lower-rated sovereigns or banks/firms in such economies, B-II thus affects the cost of capital and the quantity of lending to these borrowers.[16]

---

[14] This final outcome was actually an improvement on earlier proposals which had included a 150 per cent charge for low (BB- and below) and unrated corporations, but strong lobbies in the EU spearheaded by smaller German banks had been effective in obtaining more favourable treatment for SMEs and banks specialising in small-scale lending. See e.g. submissions on www.bis.org/bcbs/cp3comments.htm by the Austrian Banking Industry, the German *Bankenfachverband*, the European Cooperative Banks, the World Council of Credit Unions or the Kredittilsynet-Norges Bank (Norwegian central bank) submission.

[15] See e.g. submission of the central bank of Belize (www.bis.org/bcbs/cp3/belcenban. pdf) and of Burundi (www.bis.org/bcbs/cp3/burcenban.pdf), accessed 2 April 2008.

[16] For additional literature reinforcing these points, see e.g. Griffith-Jones et al. (2002a, 2002b); Persaud (2002).

A related, but more technical aspect of particular relevance for developing countries concerns the risk reduction effects of (international) portfolio diversification. As risks are not perfectly correlated, the sum of capital adequacy requirements applied to *individual* credits is greater than the capital required of the *overall* credit portfolio. B-II acknowledges this diversification effect, but *only* in the IRB approaches. The capital reductions from using (low) correlations are significant and are one of the main reasons why the IRB approach requires less capital than the Standardised approach. Even within the IRB approach, B-II (and earlier B-I) still places insufficient emphasis on the potential risk reduction effects of diversifying portfolios across both developed and developing countries. Developing countries as a group exhibit a lower correlation with developed countries than most other assets with each other. Griffith-Jones *et al.* (2002b) show that the chance of unexpectedly large losses on a portfolio evenly distributed across developed and developing countries is some 25 per cent lower than that of a portfolio distributed only among developed countries. Consequently, the capital adequacy charges should be set lower for a well-balanced portfolio that includes developing countries. But B-II does not allow this, which raises the cost of capital for and lowers the access to external financing for developing countries.

The general underemphasis on the risk reduction effects of portfolio diversification may lead to a higher concentration of lending in less risky, but more correlated segments of the world economy, leading to higher systemic risks. This appears to be precisely what happened in the case of the sub-prime crisis, as banks engaged in creating similar highly rated securitised off-balance sheet assets attracting relatively modest capital charges and which proved quite correlated during financial turmoil. At the least, it does not appear that the B-II process gave proper consideration to this portfolio diversification issue.

Another aspect of relevance for both crisis prevention and workouts in developed as well as developing countries and which came to light in the recent financial crisis is that B-II can increase pro-cyclicality and herd behaviour in lending. Since pro-cyclicality is a key source of systemic risk and the emergence of asset bubbles, B-II would thus actually fail in its key objective to enhance the safety and soundness of the overall financial system (see also chapter by Ocampo and Griffith-Jones in this volume), and there are multiple reasons for this. B-II relies more than B-I on market signals (prices and ratings). This can be beneficial as it avoids relying on the (more) subjective judgements of individual(s) in specific financial institutions, but it is not clear whether good risk management practices in individual institutions leads to stability at the systemic level. If a wide range of banks employing similar

The political economy of Basel II

models respond simultaneously and in similar ways to (perceived) risks and opportunities – as reflected in prices and ratings in the market – downturns and upturns may be reinforced as banks downgrade or upgrade clients and adjust prices on a large scale. This is what happened in the latest, sub-prime crisis and many earlier boom and bust periods in advanced markets. This issue may be of even greater concern to crisis-prone emerging markets whose asset prices and ratings are already very volatile. Of course, if systemic risk is to be reduced and asset bubbles and their consequences avoided, then by nature prudential regulation ought to be counter-cyclical, a principle which B-II appears to violate.

The reliance of B-II on ratings agencies presents other problems. In the first place, the ratings agencies did not foresee many of the 1990s emerging market crises. Figure 6.3 (in the section below) shows that the agencies not only failed to anticipate the Asian crisis, but were also relatively slow to adjust to its outbreak. Nor did they anticipate well the emergence of the sub-prime crisis: while some downgrades began in the summer of 2007 (Morris 2008: 160), many Collateralised Debt Obligations (CDOs) remained AAA-rated well into 2008, even though these and other bundled asset problems were already clear and prices had declined (*Financial Times* 4 January 2008). Questions can thus be raised concerning the capacity of rating agencies to produce information that can help prevent systemic risks.

If rating agencies are successfully to provide the information on credit and other risks which is central to the functioning of the Standard and Foundation approaches, a high degree of objectivity is required. Yet rating agencies face perverse incentives in their relationships with the clients they rate and the financial intermediaries they serve. Ratings agencies are remunerated by the very firms the risks or products of which they are supposed independently to assess. Since lower ratings mean lower capital costs for financial institutions and their clients (Morris 2008: 77), there is at least a notional conflict of interest (*Financial Times* 29 May 2008; 4 June 2008). While consistent mistakes by the agencies would over time reduce their client base and their credibility, the duopolistic dominance of Moody's and S&P in the sector (with Fitch somewhat less influential) mitigates against this.

B-II exacerbated the situation. For one, the conflicts of interest involve not only existing clients. Unrated banks and firms which believe they might enhance their competitive position by obtaining an advantageous rating share an incentive with the rating agencies to seek each other out, vastly increasing the potential client base of the agencies. Furthermore, there are many newly designed financial instruments for which the financial intermediaries which issue them also seek low ratings. Not surprisingly, the agencies did well in recent years (Morris

2008: 77). Furthermore, under B-I, all of this remained more of a private issue: mistakes would be costly for their clients, but not necessarily affect systemic risk. Yet today the agencies have implicitly been assigned new *public* responsibilities and their ratings can affect systemic stability. This indeed happened during the sub-prime crisis when, as ratings were adjusted downwards (having downgraded late in any event), systemic stress rose, a development which questions the B-II practice of giving such a major role to rating agencies in the management of systemic risk.

Other ad hoc criticisms of B-II have been voiced. The hallmark of B-I was its simplicity, at the cost of some lack of subtlety in terms of the range of credit risk. The hallmark of B-II may be its complexity. Satisfying this complexity raises relative compliance costs more for smaller and less sophisticated banks, erecting barriers to entry and hindering competition. Another, more subtle effect of B-II's complexity is that it can generate a false sense of security irrespective of real market conditions and banks and supervisors hide behind technical complexity. Furthermore, it can facilitate regulatory capture as supervisors are overwhelmed by bank-based information. Complexity may also risk widespread 'mock compliance' of the sort referred to by Walter in Chapter 5. And finally, it remains unclear to what extent market pressures will enhance risk management systems since the greater disclosure and transparency required of banks under Pillar Three (for example, of portfolio diversity) have been less forthcoming.[17]

This problem of complexity may especially affect banks in developing countries, whose competitive position may deteriorate relative to B-I since they tend to be smaller, less well-managed and less sophisticated, putting them at a disadvantage relative to the large 'Advanced approach' banks from developed countries. At the same time, supervisors in developing countries have fewer (informational) resources to oversee banks and are thus often more subject to capture in the first place. Even in the USA this small-bank problem was recognised by way of the B-II derogation for smaller banks, casting doubt on the accord as true 'standard' even in the core markets. And market discipline, Pillar Three, is relatively more costly and may be less likely to work well in developing countries.

The analysis in this section has established that the design of B-II is not unrelated to the strength of winners and losers, and that B-II

---

[17] Initial indications were disappointing according to a 2008 still-confidential and interim report by the EU Committee of European Banking Supervisors on Pillar Three disclosure (see site where the data was announced as not yet complete at time of writing, October 2009, www.c-ebs.org/sd/sdtf.htm).

The political economy of Basel II   127

may not reduce systemic risks. In doing so, the analysis has pointed out a number of potential disadvantages of B-II for developing countries. The next section looks specifically at the likely effects of B-II on the costs and availability of capital to poor countries, and in this sense complements the analysis made in Chapter 4 by Cassimon, Demetriades and Van Campenhout.

The impact of Basel II on poor countries

Developing country economies already suffer from limited access to financial services and from pro-cyclical lending patterns, while the level and stability of financial flows to developing countries are closely associated with these countries' development prospects. It is thus important to understand the effects of B-II on the cost and availability of capital to these economies relative to the B-I regime. The previous section has already presented some reasons why B-II might have a negative impact on developing countries (see further the discussion in Claessens *et al.* 2008: 327–8). Several papers have also argued on the basis of external rating agency data that B-II will increase the costs of external financing for many developing countries by increasing risk spreads, albeit modestly (Reisen 2001; Griffith-Jones *et al.* 2002b; Weder and Wedow 2002). These analyses remain incomplete, however, for two reasons: first, the data cover a limited range of countries because many do not have external ratings. Second, B-II puts more emphasis on internal ratings, making analysis based on external ratings potentially less insightful. This section therefore analyses the effects of B-II on the costs and volatility of international capital flows to developing economies, employing the actual internal ratings (IRs) of an internationally active bank and comparing the analysis with data from external rating agencies (ERs). These IRs provide detailed risk assessments for many more countries and cover a longer period than ERs do, so this data analysis significantly enhances our understanding of the impact of IRB models relative to the Standardised approach.[18]

The cost of external financing[19]

We began by mapping IRs from the bank with ERs of S&P and Moody's and creating a scale for the comparison of the forty countries where we

---

[18] Remembering that most developed country lending to developing countries will be carried out by large banks employing the Advanced IRB approach, not the Standardised approach where increases in capital costs are more obvious.

[19] Detailed empirical defence of the points made here, including methodological aspects, is offered in Claessens *et al.* 2008.

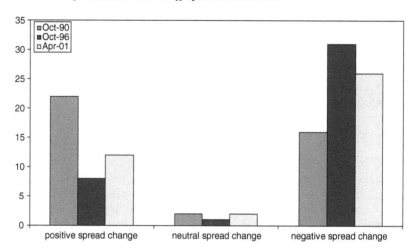

Figure 6.1. Number of countries which have a positive, neutral or negative spread change due to Basel II according to internal ratings in October 1990, October 1996 and April 2001 (total in sample=40)

had both ratings, up to the year 2001. We next recalculated the results for the changes in risk spreads arising from moving to B-II from B-I, substituting the IRs for the usual ERs. The IR results were similar to the ERs: compared to B-I the cost of international bank financing for the worse-rated countries could rise under B-II by up to 1,700–1,900 basis points. The better-rated countries, however, could see their costs decline by up to some 150–180 basis points. The number of countries that would see their cost of external financing increase on the basis of the IRs as of end 2000 was actually less than half (Figure 6.1), and the impact of B-II could be therefore interpreted as on *average* neutral.

The results also showed that the effect in the early 1990s would have been worse on average, but as ratings improved, it became less adverse. Because developing country growth and creditworthiness have improved, both the IRs and ERs have also improved further since 2001, resulting in a more favourable impact on average.

Based on these results, the average impact of B-II appears therefore modest, but some qualifications are in order. The impact remains real for those economies which would face a higher cost of credit (and whose costs were already high in relative terms). For these economies Figure 6.2 shows that, while under both ratings systems the spread change is positive, the average change is higher using IRs compared to using ERs

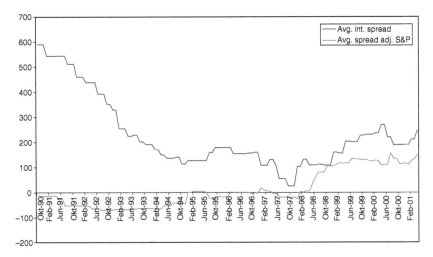

Figure 6.2. Average spread change in basis points under Basel II to produce risk-adjusted return under Basel I based on S&P and internal ratings

because the bank has IRs for more countries, including lower creditworthy countries. The studies based exclusively on ERs thus underestimate the effects on spreads as only the more creditworthy borrowers are rated by S&P and Moody's.

This simple analysis shows that the average cost impact argument is not important for most developing countries, especially *if* ratings improve as they have done in the last decade, but it may well be important for those poor countries with particularly limited access to market-based external financing. At the same time, the analysis has shown that there is little in B-II that specifically addresses the concerns of developing countries or anything that could be attributed to developing countries' specific inputs.

Volatility of external financing

B-II may also adversely affect developing countries by reducing the availability of and increasing the volatility and pro-cyclicality of external financing. Under B-II, banks, relying more on their risk models, may more 'automatically' decrease/expand their lending at times when asset prices are already depressed/elevated, thereby further lowering/raising economic activity and asset prices and producing crises/bubbles.

Furthermore, encouraging banks to develop and use similar sorts of risk models will lead to more herd behaviour, increasing the risks of financial contagion as banks react simultaneously to the same or similar signals. These tendencies may be aggravated as the accord encourages greater use of ERs and IRs, which are arguably somewhat volatile and pro-cyclical (see Lowe 2002). Since developing country assets are already subject to more volatility and pro-cyclicality than other asset classes are, the introduction of B-II might be particularly harmful for them.

If IRs are more volatile than ERs and given that B-II allows greater use of IRs, B-II may actually lead to (even) more volatile lending. Claessens and Embrechts (2003) showed that, while cross-country differences between the two types of ratings are generally small for an individual country, the IRs and ERs are imperfectly correlated over time (see Claessens *et al.* 2008, Figure 5). Importantly, on a simple comparative basis, IRs are much more variable than ERs. Assuming that the behaviour of this bank is representative of the behaviour of others, greater use of IRs could lead to an increase in the volatility and pro-cyclicality of capital flows. If we compare the speed of adjustment in a crisis situation of IRs vs. ERs data (Figure 6.3), we see that IRs adjust faster, show less ratchet and have more one-off effects. More formal tests confirmed these results in many downgrades (Claessens *et al.* 2008: 335–8), although IRs also show more drastic *upgrades* than ERs do. In general, the comparison shows a greater relative willingness of banks compared to rating agencies to change ratings.

These simple comparisons do not imply that either IRs or ERs are worse indicators of the true creditworthiness of countries, since correction needs to be made for the underlying volatility of countries' fundamentals. ERs may not be 'volatile enough' and the higher volatility of IRs may more accurately reflect the higher volatility of the underlying fundamentals. The problem is how to take into account changes in the fundamental creditworthiness of borrowers such that international macro-prudential policies would reduce rather than enhance volatility at the systemic level, particularly in a crisis situation. In any event, this section has provided further evidence of the disadvantages for poor countries of the new Basel regime.

Conclusion

This chapter has argued and offered evidence in support of several points. First, it argued that the input side of the B-II process was dominated by developed country regulators and supervisors involved in close long-term relationships with major developed country private

The political economy of Basel II 131

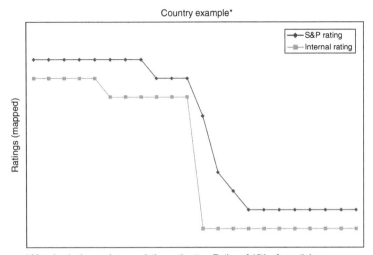

*Mapping is done using correlation estimates. Rating of 15th of month is considered rating of the month

Figure 6.3. Internal and external ratings in the East Asian financial crisis

sector financial institutions, suggesting capture of the policy process underpinning international supervisory cooperation. This may explain why the interests of developing countries might be taken into account so poorly by the BC, despite the fact that the new accord has major implications for banking systems around the globe. The chapter went on to argue that B-II has produced a system of cross-border financial supervision which may enhance internal risk management by individual banks (though the apparently severe undercapitalisation of major financial institutions in the run-up to the crisis militates against such a conclusion), but the new market-based approach to supervision may be less than effective in the reduction of the very systemic risks at which it was initially aimed. The chapter then presented evidence (from the BC itself) that B-II will affect the terms of competition in favour of the very interests which were most influential in the input phase. Finally it also found evidence that B-II will have an adverse impact on the cost and volume of capital flows to some lower-rated developing countries, although the effects on *average* are small. Importantly, it showed that the pro-cyclicality of capital flows to developing countries may increase with the use of internal ratings by internationally active banks. Such an increase would be very unfortunate, given that developing countries already suffer from volatile capital flows.

The effects of the accord thus appear skewed, but where to from here? A core element of the international financial architecture should hardly be abolished during a financial crisis, as was occurring at the time of writing. B-II's greater sensitivity to credit and other risks in complex markets, its emphasis on improved internal risk management and its acknowledgement of the role of market discipline, are also positive developments. First and foremost, the BC input side needs to be reformed to reflect input from the range of countries and constituencies it affects, ensuring a better balance between private interests and the public good.

The accord itself also needs adaptation. There are measures to be taken at the level of individual bank risk management. The most systemically significant financial institutions to which moral hazard so clearly and apparently inevitably applies clearly should have equal or higher, not lower, capital ratios relative to B-I than their smaller brethren Recent BC proposals move in this direction (Financial Times 16 April 2010), but they are also under attack from the financial sector. If it is true that B-II encourages the very risk management practices which led to the current crisis, supervisors need to be far more sceptical about the claims made about the low risks of new product ranges characterised by securitisation, and adopt a 'precautionary principle' whereby the onus is on banks to demonstrate *over time* that new innovations deserve low capital charges because they have limited both bank *and* systemic risks. Until such demonstration, which will require at least one full business cycle, product innovation need not be restrained as such but capital charges on these products should remain high. Supervisors and risk managers also need to be considerably more sceptical of what 'Value at Risk' and other risk management models actually tell us. Models reflect choices made in their design, which are seldom disinterested, reflecting tensions within the individual banks and the incentives structures they face. Furthermore, past price patterns and correlations can tell little about the nature of relationships during periods of financial stress. It has also become blatantly clear that supervisors and markets need to assess financial institutions in their entirety, including all their off-balance sheet activities and hitherto unregulated affiliates (again, BC proposals would establish such measures (Financial Times 4 May 2010)).

An even greater degree of scepticism should be reserved for what these individual bank-based models tell us about systemic risks. This means in particular that supervisors and policy-makers need to 'join the dots' far better: to take into account the dynamic relationships among risk management in individual banks, the pro-cyclicality of credit, the nature of business cycles, and the links between individual risks, the monetary policy stance and global imbalances. Supervisors and market agents still need to develop better tools to assess financial systems as

The political economy of Basel II   133

a whole, given the inherent possibility of market breakdown. Greater emphasis on these macro-economic and prudential aspects could have revealed that individual banks had taken on too much risk relative to capitalisation, and that systemic risks were on the rise prior to the bursting of the sub-prime bubble.

But the most important lesson may be one of overall emphasis. B-II, along with most architectural reforms so far, has emphasised improved facilitation of market processes instead of containment of the systemic risks which these very market processes may represent. Given that the features of the Basel policy process exposed here are common to policy-making in global financial governance generally, it is likely that the outcome observed in the Basel case also applies to a wide range of reform measures. As such, a more fundamental review of input and output aspects of the new international financial architecture may be called for.

Appendix: calculations of required spreads and requirements

The results for Table 6.2 used the following formulas, from B-II modifications as of 5 November 2001 (so as to maintain comparability with the ratings which are also as of end 2001). www.bis.org/bcbs/qis/capo tenmodif.pdf, page 5.

Correlation (R) =	$0.10 \times (1 - \text{EXP}(-50 \times \text{PD})) / (1 - \text{EXP}(-50)) + 0.20 \times [1 - (1 - \text{EXP}(-50 \times \text{PD})) / (1 - \text{EXP}(-50))]$
Maturity factor (M) =	$1 + 0.047 \times ((1 - \text{PD}) / \text{PD}^{0.44})$
Capital requirement (K) =	$\text{LGD} \times M \times N[(1 - R)^{-0.5} \times G(\text{PD}) + (R / (1 - R))^{0.5} \times G(0.999)]$
Risk-weighted assets =	K * 12.50

We assume, like Weder and Wedow (2002), LGD=50 (see their note 6, 'In the consultative document from January 2001, the Basel Committee expressed its belief that a LGD rate of 50 per cent for senior unsecured claims ... represents [a] conservative figure for most banks and countries').

This yields the formula used:

Risk-weighted assets =	$625* N[(1 - R)^{-0.5} \times G(\text{PD}) + (R / (1 - R))^{0.5} \times G(0.999)] (1 + 0.047 \times ((1 - \text{PD}) / \text{PD}^{0.44}))$

For the table, we used the Libor spreads in Table III.1 of Weder and Wedow (2002), and the reported default probabilities of Moody's and S&P in Table II.2 of Weder and Wedow (2002), respectively. The interpretation of the tables is similar to Table III.1 of Weder and Wedow (2002).

7 The catalytic approach to debt workout in practice: coordination failure between the IMF, the Paris Club and official creditors

Eelke de Jong and Koen van der Veer

Introduction

This chapter examines the effectiveness of the 'catalytic approach' to crisis and debt-workout lending in the international financial architecture – the belief that IMF intervention triggers renewed private capital inflows which complement adjustment programmes – in achieving private sector involvement in crisis resolution.[1] A country with external debt problems must find a balance between financing its external deficit and economic adjustment. Financing part of the deficit reduces the burden of adjustment and provides the government with time to implement new policy measures. A gradual adjustment is assumed to lessen the burden on the domestic population. Hence measures that increase private financing in the face of external debt problems should also increase countries' policy space.

Involving private creditors in crisis resolution is crucial for a number of reasons. First, burden-sharing by private creditors is necessary to obtain balance between the pain of adjustment borne by the domestic population and private creditors (see this volume's introduction). Second, private sector involvement is needed to prevent moral hazard and thus reduce the probability of future crises. Third, participation and fresh private capital is necessary since official creditors – the International Monetary Fund (IMF) in particular – generally lack the

Views expressed are those of the authors and do not necessarily reflect official positions of De Nederlandsche Bank. We are grateful to Christine Smolik for data on countries with IMF programmes, and to seminar participants at the University of Amsterdam, Queens University Belfast, Radboud University Nijmegen, the GARNET Conference in Amsterdam (September 2006) and the workshop in Venice (May 2008) for helpful comments on earlier drafts of this paper.

[1] Hence, this chapter focuses on solutions to sovereign debt problems in which the private sector more or less voluntarily takes part. Chapter 10, however, compares a case employing this approach (Brazil) to one in which a solution is enforced on creditors (the case of Argentina).

134

The catalytic approach to debt workout in practice   135

resources to fully meet the financing needs of the crisis-hit country. Last but not least, the extent to which the IMF succeeds in creating a sense of equal burden-sharing between public and private agents is crucial for the implementation of IMF programmes by the authorities of the debtor country, and for the adjustment measures to be accepted by the public. In turn, successful programme implementation increases the chance of private capital inflows. In other words, the legitimacy of IMF policy depends on its output side effectiveness in involving private creditors, and vice versa.

In principle, we can distinguish two forms of private sector involvement in crises. The first concerns the idea of 'bailing in' existing creditors who stand to lose in order to deal with the problem of burden-sharing. Of course 'bailing in' existing creditors is not easy and is unlikely without some form of ad hoc arm-twisting or compulsion or more institutionalised measures which might include debt standstills or an internationally agreed mechanism for dealing with sovereign debt, each attracting uncertain levels of perceived legitimacy in the eyes of the private sector. Second, the catalytic approach involves the voluntary participation of private creditors in the recovery phase triggered by official intervention. The more the first form involves compulsion and a lack of legitimacy, the more it might deter future investors and thus undermine the effectiveness of the second, the catalytic approach. This chapter first addresses the effectiveness of the catalytic approach, and will subsequently address possible alternatives. As noted in this volume's introduction, periods of calm such as between 2002 and 2007 ought to provide the best circumstances for discussing and designing major changes in the international financial architecture, and from this standpoint, the IMF's proposal for a Sovereign Debt Restructuring Mechanism (SDRM) to achieve greater levels of predictability and burden-sharing in post-crisis debt workout situations was well-timed (see Krueger 2002).[2] The proposal, however, was defeated by a combination of intense private sector lobbying, US-based opposition, and the opposition of two key emerging market economies, Mexico and Brazil. With the IMF withdrawing its plan in 2004 (see introduction and Chapter 2),[3]

---

[2] Though now that crisis is once again upon us, we might in consolation take up the widely understood dictum echoed by White House chief of staff Rahm Emanuel, that one should never allow a crisis to go to waste (*The New York Times* 2008).

[3] The SDRM was succeeded by a voluntary private sector initiative developed and led by the powerful representative of the global banking industry, the Institute of International Finance (IIF 2006a). Collective Action Clauses (CACs) for debtors and bondholders, standardised and promoted by the G10, became the market standard.

the international community still relies on the catalytic approach for private sector involvement.

This chapter examines whether and how effectively the catalytic approach has worked since the late 1980s. In some cases, the IMF was successful in attracting private capital: for example to Mexico in 1994 and to South Korea in 1998. In other cases, official rescue loans were not accompanied by an inflow of private capital: for example Thailand and Indonesia in 1997, and Argentina in 2000. An analysis of IMF programmes over this period reveals that IMF intervention generally did not generate new capital by private creditors. In other words, the output legitimacy of this specific element of the global financial architecture is in doubt. We go on to analyse how the concurrently available coercive instrument – the Paris Club's 'comparability of treatment' clause – works in relation to the IMF system. Our findings here lead to our conclusions regarding the reform of the international financial architecture.

Our results indicate that part of the explanation for weakness of the catalytic approach lies in the failure of various multilateral and bilateral creditors to coordinate their crisis lending. In about 25 per cent of all cases, the total amount provided by official creditors exceeded the debtor's financing need. This overlending by official institutions facilitated private sector withdrawal (bail-out) rather than incentives for additional capital inflows. This coordination failure must be surmounted to improve the effectiveness of the catalytic approach in future crises. Yet the essentially voluntary catalytic approach may arguably still require a more or less acceptable coercive instrument to first bail in private creditors. The bilateral creditors assembled in the Paris Club indeed constitute such a coercive instrument; Paris Club debt-restructuring agreements contain a 'comparability of treatment' clause according to which the debtor country must restructure its outstanding *private* debt on comparable terms. Failure to do so supposedly comes at the cost of losing the Paris Club agreement or the refusal of Paris Club members to restructure debt in the future.

We have therefore included the Paris Club's 'comparability of treatment' instrument in our study, for it contributes to our understanding of the effectiveness of coercive instruments. Our findings indicate that only some private creditors are actually bailed in: short-term debts are excluded from the Paris Club's 'comparability of treatment' clause which then does not have the intended effect on total private capital flows because the country's overall balance sheet is not structurally improved. If a coercive instrument is to prove effective, it must encompass all types of private capital flows.

The catalytic approach to debt workout in practice 137

Financing need

Estimated current account deficit	Debt amortisation	Repayment of arrears	Accumulation of net international reserves	IMF repayments

Available financing

Official financing: IMF and other multilateral and bilateral creditors	Total estimated private capital flows	
	Estimated private capital flows	Remaining financing gap: *Catalytic effect*

Figure 7.1. Estimating a country's financing gap

This chapter is organised as follows. We first describe the principles behind the catalytic approach, which essentially assumes official intervention will attract private capital to the crisis-hit country. As the catalytic approach only applies in cases where official financing falls short of the overall financing needs of the country, we proceed to estimate countries' financing needs relative to the official financing offered. Thereafter we turn to the track record of the Paris Club's 'comparability of treatment' clause in attracting private capital. The chapter concludes with a discussion of policy implications – the balance between public and private contributions, and the effectiveness of various options in dealing with the problems of external debt.

The catalytic approach: theory and evidence

The catalytic approach is a strategy of the International Financial Institutions (IFIs) to involve private creditors in solving a country's balance of payments difficulties. These difficulties arise because the country's financing need[4] exceeds the projected inflow of private capital. The gap between a country's financing need and the finance available can be reduced by adjustment measures taken by the country's government to reduce the current account deficit, and by loans provided by official and private creditors. The catalytic effect arises if private sector inflows successfully complement official creditors' contributions to fulfil the gross financing requirement. These private sector loans are represented by the box 'Remaining financing gap: catalytic effect' in Figure 7.1.

---

[4] In IMF documents the financing need is known as 'gross financing requirement'.

But why would private investors provide additional money? Official creditors can trigger private capital inflows (1) by providing liquidity – the *lending* channel – and (2) by their judgement of and influence on a country's policies – the *policy* channel. The mere provision of credit by official creditors can give private creditors an incentive to roll over their existing loans and to supply new loans (Bordo *et al.* 2004: 11). Moreover, the financial assistance of official creditors can tip the balance for the debtor country to embark on an otherwise (politically) unworkable adjustment programme (Morris and Shin 2006), thereby inducing creditors to roll over their loans. By signing an agreement, official creditors signal that a country has sound financial institutions and follows sensible policies. This 'stamp of approval' (Rodrik 1995) or 'good housekeeping seal of approval' (Bordo *et al.* 2004) supposes that official creditors have an informational advantage compared to the private sector. Moreover, after having signed an agreement, the IMF will monitor a country's policies and thus serve as a 'delegated monitor' for private creditors (Tirole 2002).

In the empirical literature, much attention has been given to the catalytic effect of the IMF and to a lesser extent that of the World Bank. The evidence, however, is disappointing, and shows that a catalytic effect is at best present only under specific conditions. When measured as the effect on private capital flows, it is only triggered by bilateral loans (Rodrik 1995) or precautionary IMF programmes (Cassou *et al.* 2006). While Bird and Rowlands (2002) and Cassou *et al.* (2006) present some evidence of a particular type of IMF programme – namely Extended Fund Facilities (EFFs) – having a catalytic effect, Edwards (2006) for these same programmes reports a statistically significant negative effect. When measured as the effect on bond issuances and spreads, the evidence of a catalytic effect seems more convincing (Eichengreen and Mody 2001; Eichengreen *et al.* 2006; Mody and Saravia 2006). But studies present contradictory results. For example, Eichengreen *et al.* (2006) report a significant catalytic effect in countries with a high level of external debt, whereas Mody and Saravia (2006) find evidence of a negative effect for this type of country. Furthermore, it can be questioned whether the catalytic effect should be measured in terms of issuances and spreads. In the end, it is the size of *total* private capital flows that matters in the effort to bridge a country's financing gap. Case studies here underline the poor record of the catalytic approach. Examining seventeen countries under an IMF programme, Killick (1995) found the IMF programme to be associated with larger capital inflows in only two cases, while Ghosh *et al.* (2002), comparing IMF programme projections with outcomes for current and capital account balances, show

The catalytic approach to debt workout in practice 139

that the catalytic effect on which programmes were premised was systematically overestimated.

Estimating the financing gap

A core concept in all IMF programmes is the country's 'financing gap'. This is the difference between what a country needs to raise to pay its maturing debts, arrears, accumulation of net international reserves, IMF repayments and ongoing deficits, and what it is projected to be able to raise from private creditors. In Figure 7.1, the financing gap is the difference between the financing need and estimated private capital inflows. The resolution of any financial crisis entails closing the financing gap through policy adjustments in combination with 'exceptional financing' in the form of official multilateral credit, aid from multilateral and bilateral donor agencies, debt restructurings of bilateral and private debt and *new* sources of private financing (such as direct investment or return of flight capital) (Rieffel 2003: 77–8). For the catalytic approach to work, the total sum of the official financial package must fall short of the financing gap, so that *additional* private capital can fill the remaining gap.

Correctly measuring the financing gap is thus crucial to determine the existence of a catalytic effect. As Figure 7.1 illustrates, all variables other than private capital flows and the current account deficit are ex ante known by the IMF. The question then is: how might one estimate the financing gap? The answer is not straightforward for the following two reasons.

First, *projecting* what can be raised from private creditors is no simple affair. When designing its programmes, the IMF estimates the flow of private capital for the year the programme is approved and for a number of years thereafter. In 60 per cent of cases, the IMF overestimates first-year private capital flows (IMF 2004a: 27). This optimistic bias results from considering constraints on official lending first, and then adjusting estimated private capital flows – which thus do not reflect private investors' willingness to invest in the country (Benelli 2003; IMF 2004a). The maximum amount the IMF can loan to a country is predefined by the country's quota, or in individual cases, limited by political considerations or for reason of the IMF's own financial solidity. Aware of these constraints, IMF staff generate optimistic projections to get large programmes approved by the Executive Board. Benelli (2003) found that the larger the loan relative to the country quota, the greater the projection bias. Optimistic projections were further made to restore confidence, to show that the IMF together with other multilateral and bilateral creditors could fully finance the gap. A striking example of this

140   *Eelke de Jong and Koen van der Veer*

arbitrary adjusting of the financing gap is given in an evaluation report published by the IMF itself:

> In Korea, however, the initial failure of the programme was more directly related to deficiencies on the financing side. The package as announced in the press note included US$20 billion of bilateral assistance as a second line of defence, but there was considerable lack of clarity as to whether this amount was really available. The programme was originally based on the assumption that this amount would be needed to fill the estimated residual financing gap, but it was communicated to the staff at a fairly late stage that it should not count on this amount being available. The estimated financing gap was, therefore, reduced by arbitrarily increasing the assumed rollover rate of short-term debt. (IMF 2003a: 37)

A second difficulty in measuring the financing gap entails defining an acceptable current account balance. When countries are in need of IMF lending, their reserves are by definition insufficient to balance all (private and other) capital outflows. Any change in capital outflows entails a corresponding shift in the current account balance. When designing its programmes, the IMF estimates the size of private capital flows and uses this estimate to project changes in the current account balance. But as outlined above, the IMF often overestimates available private capital, thereby underestimating both the actual adjustment of the current account balance and the financing gap.

IMF projections are thus unreliable measures for estimating financing gaps. To standardise the measurement of official lending, we thus employ the easier to measure concept of 'financing need'. The question then becomes: what proportion of a country's financing need is taken up by multilateral and bilateral creditors? This is also the measure used by private creditors, who face the same difficulties as the Fund in estimating the financing gap. Its use allows us to more easily construct a reliable measure for the future current account balance.

In one study, the IMF itself uses a country's debt-stabilising current account balance as a benchmark to calculate its current account adjustment when evaluating its programmes (IMF 2004a). The 'debt-stabilising current account balance' is that which stabilises the external debt ratio given the historical performance of the economy. The intuition behind this measure is that a country's external debt-to-GDP ratio remains constant if external debt increases by the same rate as GDP. Since an increase in external debt is equal to the current account deficit, the 'debt-stabilising current account' equals the growth rate of GDP times the external debt level.[5]

---

[5] See IMF (2004: 30) for the exact formula of the debt-stabilising current account balance.

Table 7.1. *Official lending in countries with an IMF programme*

Number of observations	External debt / GDP < 40	External debt / GDP 40 – 60	External debt / GDP > 60	Total
< 100% of financing need	30 (65%)	56 (82%)	103 (75%)	189 (75%)
> 100% of financing need	16 (35%)	12 (18%)	34 (25%)	62 (25%)
Total	46	68	137	251

Using the debt-stabilising current account balance to calculate financing need thus surpasses the problem of biased current account balances within IMF programme documents. We thus measure a country's financing need by calculating the debt-stabilising current account balance (using data from the World Development Indicators) and adding this value to the values for debt amortisation, repayment of arrears, accumulation of gross international reserves, and IMF repurchases and repayments as provided by the IMF from its MONA database. Thereafter, total official financing is measured as the total of the net use of Fund credit, official borrowing from multilateral and bilateral lenders and net official transfers as a percentage of the financing need.

Official financing and the effect on private capital

This section's analysis is based on annual data covering the years 1988–2004 for sixty-five developing and emerging market economies (see van der Veer and de Jong 2007). For all years, both countries with and without an IMF programme were included. Due to missing observations, the entire set is an unbalanced panel with a maximum of 722 observations. Out of these 722 observations, 251 refer to country-year combinations in which an IMF programme was in effect, and for which we have data from the IMF's MONA database. We estimated the total financing need of these countries using the procedure set out in the previous section, and found that in 25 per cent of the observations, official financing exceeded the country's financing need (Table 7.1). In such cases public financing, rather than catalysing private capital, is likely to facilitate its exit. Note also that overlending is not limited to countries with a high level of external debt.

To determine whether IMF programmes lead to additional private capital inflows, we estimate an equation of private capital inflows in

142 *Eelke de Jong and Koen van der Veer*

Table 7.2. *Official financing and the catalytic effect of IMF programmes*

Sample	Full sample	< 100% of financing need	> 100% of financing need
Stand-By Arrangement	−1.375 (−2.00)**	−1.061 (−0.82)	−1.444 (−2.07)**
Extended Fund Facility	−1.288 (−1.25)	−1.900 (−1.04)	−1.038 (−1.33)
Poverty Reduction and Growth Facility	0.096 (0.12)	2.558 (1.64)*	−1.519 (−1.76)*
Observations	722	248	474
F-test	0.00	0.00	0.00

Significance level: *** = 1%, ** = 5%, * = 10%.
Regressors not reported: export growth, external debt as per cent of gross domestic product (GDP), GDP per capita, inflation rate, interest rate, investment rate, reserves in months of imports, real GDP growth, short-term debt to reserves, short-term debt to total external debt, total debt service as per cent of exports, lagged dummy for IMF programme.

which the explanatory variables are a set of control variables explaining capital inflows under normal conditions, and a dummy variable which is 1 if the country has signed an IMF programme. The control variables include three groups of indicators representing: (1) long-term potential growth and market size; (2) the country's capacity to pay or reimburse investments; and (3) macroeconomic performance and stability.[6] A two-step Heckman selection procedure is used to control for sample selection (see the appendix). The equation is estimated for each of three types of IMF programmes: Stand-By Arrangements (SBAs), Extended Fund Facilities (EFFs) and Poverty Reduction and Growth Facilities (PRGFs). SBAs aim to solve short-term balance of payments problems; EFFs are geared to alleviate protracted balance of payments problems; and PRGFs are concessional loans to low-income countries. SBAs and EFFs are mostly used by middle-income countries.

The results for the full sample suggest that SBAs facilitate the exit of private investors, whereas no effect on private capital flows is found for the other two programmes (Table 7.2, first column).

As stated above, a catalytic effect can only materialise if official finance falls short of the amount needed. Distinguishing between observations where official finance is larger or smaller than the country's financing need indeed reveals that overlending negatively affects private capital flows in countries with an SBA (Table 7.2, last two

---

[6] See table A-3 in van der Veer and de Jong (2007) for the list of variables used.

The catalytic approach to debt workout in practice 143

columns). In these cases the private sector is effectively bailed out. For PRGFs a marginally significant positive (negative) effect was found for cases where total official financing was smaller (larger) than the financing need. These results suggest that if we can expect any catalytic effect, it is for PRGFs.

The overall conclusion is that the catalytic effect remains elusive: official creditors thus cannot rely on private investors to voluntarily provide finance to crisis-hit countries. These disappointing results underpin the case for employing more coercive instruments to achieve private sector involvement in crisis resolution.

The Paris Club and coercive 'comparability of treatment'

The difficulty of predicting the reaction of private capital markets is an important and often-heard argument against the introduction of coercive instruments to achieve private sector involvement. Fear of increased borrowing costs indeed informed Mexico and Brazil's opposition to the SDRM. The international financial architecture nevertheless contains, and has been using since the mid-1950s, the coercive 'comparability of treatment' instrument in Paris Club debt-restructuring agreements. According to the 'comparability of treatment' clause, debtor countries must arrange agreements on comparable terms with private creditors. Paris Club agreements are thus ideal cases to study how private capital markets react to coercive instruments to achieve private burden-sharing. This section examines these Paris Club agreements, and thereby contributes to understanding the (in-)effectiveness of coercive instruments more generally.

The Paris Club is an informal group of creditor governments that meets regularly in Paris to restructure official bilateral debt. It has nineteen permanent members (mainly OECD countries), though other creditors can participate on a case-by-case basis.[7] Since 1956 the Paris Club has reached 406 agreements concerning 84 debtor countries; the total debt covered in agreements since 1983 has been $509 billion. In spite of this activity, the Paris Club is strictly informal and is usually described as a 'non-institution'.[8]

In order to reach agreements – which are individually implemented by creditor countries – a number of rules and principles were codified in

---

[7] The permanent Paris Club members are: Austria, Australia, Belgium, Canada, Denmark, Finland, France, Germany, Ireland, Italy, Japan, the Netherlands, Norway, Russian Federation, Spain, Sweden, Switzerland, the UK and the USA.

[8] See the Paris Club website, www.clubdeparis.org.

a United Nations resolution at the end of the 1970s. The following rules and principles are operated today: (1) decisions are made on a case-by-case basis; (2) decisions require consensus; (3) only countries with an IMF programme can apply; (4) creditors agree to implement the agreed terms; and (5) 'comparability of treatment' obliges the debtor country to seek debt restructuring with other bilateral and private creditors on comparable terms. This final principle of 'comparability of treatment' creates a direct link between a Paris Club agreement and the debtor country's decision to service its outstanding private debt. In order to support the case-by-case norm, the Paris Club has developed a series of 'terms' that allow for more flexible and generous treatment of debt.[9]

The Paris Club introduced the possibility of debt reduction in 1988. In debt rescheduling, the entire stock of debt on which the debtor defaults is never rescheduled (Brown and Bulman 2006: 18); only a part of the arrears on debt-service payments, as well as those obligations due over a specified period of time, are consolidated into a new loan. This effectively adds a second layer of debt to what already exists, increasing the country's total outstanding external debt. Debt rescheduling by the Paris Club thus failed to adequately address the chronic debt problems of many low-income countries. Subsequently, for roughly forty heavily indebted poor countries (HIPCs), the Paris Club departed from its normal rules to grant progressively more generous debt reduction, with a view to reducing the burden of foreign debt below an agreed threshold (Rieffel 2003: 57). The Paris Club maintained its policy of no debt reduction for middle-income countries until 2003. In that year the Paris Club agreed on the Evian Approach for non-HIPC countries, which gave creditors the option of debt reduction for these countries as well.

The principle of 'comparability of treatment' requires countries benefiting from Paris Club debt restructuring to seek similar (comparable) relief from their private creditors. As the principle has no legal basis, its effectiveness depends on the Paris Club's threat of cancelling the agreement, and being less cooperative in future negotiations. For its part, the debtor country can use the threat of default to push other creditors to agree to a comparable restructuring. But as a former insider in the Paris Club notes: 'the basic flaw in the comparable treatment principle is the absence of a consideration of how the application of the principle in a

---

[9] Ordered from no debt reduction to more than 90 per cent debt reduction, these terms are: classic (no debt reduction); Houston (some debt reduction); Toronto (33 per cent); London (50 per cent); Naples (>50 per cent); Lyon (80 per cent); and Cologne (>90 per cent). In addition, ad hoc terms are sometimes applied as well. See www.clubdeparis.org.

The catalytic approach to debt workout in practice 145

particular case will affect future flows of private capital to the debtor country' (Rieffel 2003: 284).[10]

The 'comparability of treatment' clause is essentially a coercive mechanism to achieve private sector involvement in crisis resolution. Its effectiveness in safeguarding net total private capital inflows, however, is questionable. Apart from its non-legal basis, the 'comparability of treatment' clause only applies to debt with a maturity of more than one year; it thus excludes short-term debt.[11] In addition, even if the Paris Club through the clause is successful in involving private creditors with outstanding accounts, private capital markets may more generally shy away from investing in countries where they perceive they may be forced to agree to less advantageous interest and repayment conditions in the future.[12] In this respect, it also matters whether the Paris Club agrees to rescheduling or to bilateral debt relief. Under 'comparability of treatment', debt rescheduling implies fewer concessions by private investors than debt reduction, and thus less incentive to disinvest. On the other hand, rescheduling debt neither reduces future debt services nor improves the (long-run) financial position of the country. Private agents could thus interpret a rescheduling agreement as lowering the possibility of repayment of their own claims, inducing them to withdraw their money.

In sum, whether the 'comparability of treatment' clause in Paris Club agreements helps or hampers the IMF to catalyse private capital is an empirical matter, which we settled in van der Veer and de Jong (2007). In that paper we distinguished between countries that had signed an IMF agreement only and those that had signed a Paris Club agreement in addition to an IMF agreement. As in the previous section, we distinguish between three types of IMF agreements: SBAs, EFFs and PRGFs. It appeared that a Paris Club agreement reduces net private capital inflows when a country has signed an SBA or an EFF, and increases private capital inflows when a country has signed a PRGF. Hence a Paris Club agreement may have variable effects, depending on whether the country has signed an SBA, EFF or a PRGF.

Van der Veer and de Jong (2007) offer two, partly complementary, explanations for these differing effects: (1) the nature – debt

---

[10] Lex Rieffel participated in numerous Paris Club negotiations since the 1970s during his eighteen years with the US Treasury Department.

[11] The Paris Club does not deal with short-term debt as its restructuring can significantly disrupt the capacity of the debtor country to participate in international trade. See www.clubdeparis.org.

[12] This was observed in the 1999 agreement between Pakistan and the Paris Club creditors when the private financial community opposed inclusion of bond restructuring under the 'comparability of treatment' clause (see IMF 2001a: 5).

rescheduling or debt reduction – of the Paris Club agreement; and (2) the term structure of the country's external debt.

First, the contradictory effects of Paris Club agreements could be explained by the different incentives that result from debt rescheduling and debt reduction. A deal involving debt reduction improves both a country's short- and long-term financial position; debt rescheduling only improves a country's short-term position while its long-term position deteriorates. If 'comparability of treatment' is applied, the private sector has to agree to larger write-offs under debt reduction. Private investors then have to weigh their own share in debt reduction against the positive effects of the country's enhanced ability to pay its arrears. Regression analysis reveals that a Paris Club rescheduling will most likely lead to an outflow of private capital, whereas a debt reduction enhances the inflow of private capital (van der Veer and de Jong 2007: table 6). Most debt relief is granted to countries with a PRGF, and thus to low-income countries. Here Paris Club debt reductions can result in debt cancellations of up to, and even over, 90 per cent under the 'Cologne terms'. As such, the resulting positive effect on total private capital inflows is more likely to be evidence of a catalytic-type effect – in accordance with debt overhang theory – than evidence of effective enforcement of private debt reductions following the 'comparability of treatment' clause.

A second and complementary explanation for the varying effects of Paris Club agreements lies in the term structure of a country's external debt. Private investors can easily withdraw their money if short-term debt constitutes a relatively high proportion of a country's external debt. The ratio of short-term debt to total external debt is 13, 11 and 7 per cent for countries with an SBA, EFF and PRGF, respectively. The negative effect of a Paris Club agreement on countries with an SBA or EFF may thus reflect the greater mobility of private capital in these countries, combined with the negative assessment of the country's financial position due to the rescheduling of debt (the dominant type of Paris Club restructuring in countries with an SBA or EFF).

From these results, van der Veer and de Jong (2007) conclude that how private capital markets assess the overall financial position of the country after debt restructuring is more important than the losses incurred by private creditors in the process. Stated otherwise, bailing in private creditors will not have the intended effect on total private capital flows if the country's balance sheet is not structurally improved. Essentially, private investments are based on considerations regarding the probability of future repayment. Debt reduction by bilateral donors implies a reduction in the amount a country must eventually pay its official creditors, while debt rescheduling effectively increases a country's future payment obligations. Private investors are thus more willing to provide fresh capital in cases of Paris Club reductions.

Conclusion

Private sector involvement is a crucial element of crisis resolution. It contributes to equal burden-sharing, prevents moral hazard, and supplements necessarily limited official funding. The extent to which the IMF succeeds in creating a sense of equal burden-sharing between public and private agents is crucial for the implementation of IMF programmes by debtor country authorities, and for public acceptance of the adjustment measures as legitimate. In turn, successful implementation of adjustment measures increases the chance of private capital inflows. This highlights the importance of involving private sector creditors as part of an effective debt workout if IMF policy is to be perceived as legitimate on the output side.

This chapter investigated the effectiveness of the catalytic approach in achieving this private sector involvement in crisis resolution, as well as the effectiveness of the Paris Club's more coercive 'comparability of treatment' clause. In the period examined, coordination failures among official creditors worked against catalysing private sector involvement. Addressing this problem of coordination within the current international financial architecture may improve output side effectiveness of external debt workout processes and increase policy space for countries experiencing difficulties.

Our evidence revealed the failure of various multilateral and bilateral creditors to coordinate their crisis lending. A prerequisite for private sector involvement is that the public sector does not bail out private creditors; the total amount provided by official agents should fall short of the debtor's financing need. But in about 25 per cent of cases, official institutions provide more than is needed. Regression analysis shows that in these cases IMF programmes lead to an outflow of private capital. In other words, when official creditors overlend, official money is likely to facilitate a rush to the exit by private investors. In cases where the amount of official finance is less than the financing need, regression analysis shows only weak evidence of an inflow of private funds, and only to low-income countries that have signed a PRGF. Even if official finance falls short of a country's financing need, the catalytic approach appears unreliable as a policy to achieve private sector involvement.

A second coordination failure emerged from our study of the Paris Club's coercive 'comparability of treatment' instrument, whereby debtors are obliged to strike a deal with the private sector comparable to that made with the Club. Attempts by the IMF to catalyse private capital in countries with an SBA or EFF were counteracted by Paris Club involvement in these cases. Paris Club debt rescheduling in these countries – which effectively increases a country's external debt – in combination with the Paris Club's coercive bail-in of private creditors, conflicts with the IMF's aim of voluntary private sector involvement via its catalytic approach. Estimations, therefore, showed that the Paris Club clause generally did not have the intended effect on net total private capital flows. The Paris Club agreements gave rise to additional inflows of private capital only in low-income countries that had signed a PRGF *and* where the Paris Club had decided to reduce bilateral debt. Given the high level of Paris Club debt reductions in these cases, we interpret this result as evidence of a voluntary catalytic type of effect, in line with debt overhang theory. In all other cases these deals led to an outflow of private capital.

In sum, coordination failures among official creditors in general and the IMF and the Paris Club in particular have worked against effective catalysis in particular cases. While overcoming these coordination failures is warranted, the catalytic approach – even with improvements in the current international financial architecture – may still prove insufficiently reliable as a core policy to achieve private sector involvement. Creating a more coercive instrument to bail in private creditors might in the end prove necessary. Yet our results also show that the coercive bailing-in of only some private creditors – with short-term debts excluded from the Paris Club's 'comparability of treatment' clause – will not have the intended effect on total private capital flows if the country's balance sheet is not structurally improved. Private capital markets will generally react negatively to a worsening balance sheet, overriding any positive effect on net total private capital flows as a result of an effective but partial bail-in. Hence any potential coercive instrument must encompass all types of private capital flows. From this perspective, debt standstills are a likely candidate for future policy development.

Appendix: the estimation procedure

As in other empirical studies on the effects of IMF programmes, a two-step Heckman selection model was used to obtain the estimations presented in the text. The first step involved estimating a probit model for the chance a country has signed an IMF programme. The results of this estimation were used to construct a selection bias control factor – lambda – equivalent to the Inverse Mill's Ratio. This factor is a

The catalytic approach to debt workout in practice

summary measure, reflecting the effects of all unmeasured characteristics related to whether a country has signed an IMF programme or not. This lambda was added to the list of explanatory variables of the 'equation of interest'. Both equations in the Heckman selection model were estimated simultaneously by using a maximum likelihood procedure:

$$B = \gamma Z + u_2 \quad \text{(selection equation)} \tag{1}$$
$$y = \beta X + u_1 \quad \text{(equation of interest)} \tag{2}$$
$$u_2 \sim N(0, 1), u_1 \sim N \quad (0, \text{sigma}) \text{ and corr}(u_1, u_2) = \rho$$

where 'B' is a binary variable indicating whether the country signed an IMF programme; 'Z' is a vector of variables indicating a country's economic conditions which determines a country's probability of having signed an IMF programme; 'y' is one of the four types of private capital flows; and 'X' is a vector of variables determining private capital flows, including the lambda mentioned above.

8 Empirical evidence on the new international aid architecture

Stijn Claessens, Danny Cassimon and Björn Van Campenhout

Introduction

As highlighted in Chapter 4 of this volume, lower-income developing countries are not fully integrated in the global financial system. They are not only under-represented in major decision-making forums; they also remain largely excluded from the flow of substantial private external financing. To correct this architectural weakness, the international community has stepped in to provide substantial amounts of bilateral and multilateral official financing, either through grants or concessional lending. This concessional official financing – generally described as 'development aid' – makes up the lion's share of external capital flows to low-income countries (see Chapter 4, Table 4.1). The aid architecture thus remains an important subset of the global financial architecture. It can be defined as the set of rules and institutions affecting aid flows, including the way aid is allocated, the modalities through which it is delivered and its accompanying conditionality requirements.

Although only loosely linked to changes in the overall global financial architecture, the aid system over the last few years has been witnessing a transformation, with policy changes at both the bilateral and multilateral donor levels and actions at the level of individual recipient countries. Overall, these changes aim to considerably improve the effectiveness of aid, to the extent that aid scholars refer to a 'paradigm shift' (Renard 2006). We thus aim to document how changes in this subset of the overall international financial architecture have affected actual behaviour.

The findings, interpretations and conclusions expressed in this paper are entirely those of the authors. They do not necessarily represent the views of the IMF, its executive directors or the countries they represent. The work has been supported by the UK Economic and Social Research Council's World Economy and Finance research programme (award no. RES-156-25-0009) . For more detail on the empirics reported in this paper, we refer to Claessens *et al.* 2007.

Table 8.1 provides an overview of the rationale, key elements and some strengths and weaknesses of this new aid 'paradigm' relative to two earlier approaches: project aid (the 'default' mode at least until the beginning of the 1980s) and the structural adjustment programme. The new approach was largely born out of the perceived failure of these earlier approaches and has been accompanied by a number of major architectural changes. These have included: specific international actions such as coordinated debt relief for a large number of poor countries; 'institutional' changes such as the move away from project lending towards programmatic lending; greater emphasis on coordination among donors (the so-called 'harmonisation' effort) as well as between the donor community and recipient countries (so-called 'alignment', whereby donors align with recipient country priorities, institutions and systems); and greater ownership by the recipient country (and not only its government). These shifts have been accompanied by changes in the development approach more generally, including the greater use of Poverty Reduction Strategy Papers (PRSPs), the explicit introduction of Millennium Development Goals (MDGs) and the enumeration of the objective of scaling up aid. Importantly, the new approach has put greater weight on some elements of the Washington Consensus approach, including good governance and a sound institutional environment as preconditions for development and receiving aid. These new principles have also been translated into the 2005 Paris Declaration on Aid Effectiveness, a framework of concrete indicators and targets to be fulfilled by all signing (bilateral and multilateral) donors.

As aid-dependent countries are largely decoupled from the global financial system, aid architecture changes are not driven by major financial crises; rather, they are prompted by the observed failures of former aid approaches. Changes in the aid architecture are thus only loosely linked to changes in the overall global financial architecture. One element linking both is the recognition of the failure of the Washington Consensus-driven structural adjustment programme, which led to a round of changes in both the global financial and aid architecture at the end of the 1990s. The change in the aid architecture was made possible by a remarkable coalition of NGO and public opinion pressure, policy-based academic research (most of it funded by donors such as the World Bank) and recipient country pressure for more policy space and ownership.

As aid traditionally substitutes public intervention to correct the failures of the market-based approach, studying the aid sub-architecture provides insight into the question of the balance between the public and private spheres in the global financial system. The new approach

Table 8.1. *Overview of the paradigm changes in the international aid architecture*

Aid approaches	Description of logical framework	Type of conditionality	Typical aid modalities	Supportive international consensus	Strengths	Weaknesses or problems
Project aid	- Aid allocation level: aid as a foreign policy instrument - Lack of trust of the recipient country public sector calls for donor-driven aid projects, executed in non-aligned and non-harmonised ways	- Buy political and commercial (through aid tying) support - Poverty focus through micro earmarking	Project aid, minimally harmonised and aligned (e.g. parallel Project Implementation Units (PIUs))		- Development impact closely controlled, monitored and attributed (donor constituency accountability) - High donor ownership	- Political and commercial tying - Fungibility - Lack of sustainability
Structural Adjustment Programmes (SAPs)	- (Good) projects do not 'work' in a distorted sectoral and macro-environment - Aid must be used to buy reforms that promote economic growth and also increase the development impact of project aid	- Ex-ante conditionality: aid to those that promise to promote macro-stabilisation and political and economic reform through SAPs - Bilaterals delegate SAP contents and monitoring to IFIs	- Policy-based aid, such as BoP and sectoral support - Sometimes explicitly supported by similar bilateral aid - Largely coexistent with bilateral project aid modality	Washington Consensus	Focus in principle on key bottlenecks to growth and development	- Lack of recipient country ownership - Unable to prevent nor cure debt problems - Growth-focused, not poverty-focused - Difficult to address political reforms - Aid cannot *buy* reform
New aid paradigm	- Long-term aid effectiveness requires aid channelling through the recipient country public sector	- Selectivity: give aid only to needy and deserving - Ex-post conditionality:	- Harmonised sectoral support (pooled funds, SWAPs, Sector Budget support	- MDGs - PRSP and HIPC Initiative/MDRI - Paris Declaration on Harmonization and Alignment	Increased aid effectiveness through: - Increased ownership, in principle also solving fungibility	- Only few countries meet preconditions - Involvement of civil society not fully validated, problem of representativeness

- Increased ownership requires donor-recipient country government partnership with policy dialogue and results based-monitoring under mutual accountability - Harmonisation needed among donors, and alignment with recipient country priorities and systems - Disengagement by donors from local (project) level requires civil society to check local development impact - Civil society for checks and balances	rewarding recipient countries that have shown to deliver - Policy dialogue - Broad poverty earmarking through recipient country-owned PRSPs - Bilateral donors should put politics on the table	- General Budget support - Debt relief - Projects 'new style' (H&A)	- Poverty, rather than growth-oriented - Increased H&A - Results-based - Strengthening central recipient country institutions (Public Finance Management (PFM), etc.) and reducing its transaction costs	- Loss of attribution to donor constituencies - New (bilateral, multilateral and private) donors don't always abide by the new logic - Greater fragmentation and proliferation

Source: Based on authors' interpretation and compilation of e.g. Molenaers and Renard 2008.

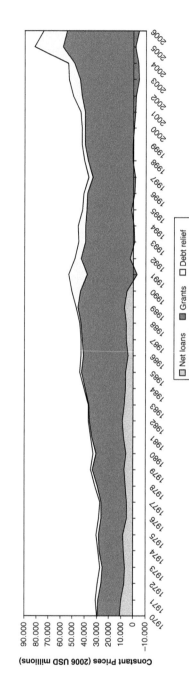

Figure 8.1. Bilateral net ODA transfers, 1970–2006
Source: DAC online ODA statistics.

Empirical evidence on international aid architecture 155

to public intervention aims to link improved input (better consultation procedures and institutions) to improvements in output (aid effectiveness). By stimulating both donors and recipient countries to abide by mutually accepted rules and institutions, it should in principle increase the legitimacy of the decision-making process. By fostering recipient country 'ownership' and therefore increased alignment of aid to recipient country preferences, such as in the PRSP approach (that challenges some elements of the Washington Consensus), output legitimacy and 'policy space' should likewise be enhanced. In this way increased inclusion on the input side should enhance the effectiveness of policy.

These changes in the aid architecture should increase its effectiveness through at least two channels. First, the revised approach can be expected to affect the *allocation of aid* among countries in several ways, the so-called *selectivity* issue. Recipient countries that abide by the new paradigm should see themselves rewarded with more aid on more concessional terms, while debt reduction should reduce the pattern of 'defensive' lending where more indebted countries were receiving more aid flows to keep up with payments to (multilateral) creditors (Birdsall *et al.* 2003). Institutional and policy changes should lead to fewer coordination problems, resulting in better aid allocation. And there should be less influence of historical, (geo-)political and other non-economic or developmental factors in aid allocation. Thus the first empirical question this paper addresses is whether there have been any significant recent changes in the *actual behaviour* of donors.

Under the new aid architecture, aid allocation will be less 'tied' and delivered on a more predictable basis. It will employ more harmonised and aligned procedures among donors, in principle resulting in increased efficiency and effectiveness. This study therefore also investigates how far the donor community has moved from rhetoric to reality by drawing on survey results from the monitoring of the Paris Declaration indicators.

The profound changes in the aid architecture are obviously not limited to the bilateral donor community. One of the key developments in the new aid architecture is the entry of new players which may or may not abide by the new paradigm rules, but in any case has led to increased proliferation and fragmentation at the global level: bilateral donors (the new EU countries as well as richer developing countries including China and India); multilateral donors (including so-called vertical funds); and private actors (large international NGOs and private foundations such as the Bill & Melinda Gates Foundation).[1] As

---

[1] See e.g. Kharas 2008 for an insightful analysis of this new 'global aid reality'.

156   *Stijn Claessens* et al.

reliable data are unfortunately only available for bilateral donors which are members of the OECD's Development Assistance Committee (DAC), we limit our analysis to them.

Figure 8.1 presents the evolution of DAC member bilateral Official Development Assistance (ODA, in constant dollars) over the period 1970–2006, expressed as net transfers, i.e. including interest payments. It disaggregates these transfers in its grant, loan and debt relief components. Overall, the figures reveal an increase in the absolute volume of aid until the beginning of the 1990s, with the following downward trend arrested at the beginning of the new millennium – hinting at some scaling up, albeit only at levels comparable to that of the 1990s. The recent spike is mainly due to a (temporary) increase in debt relief, accounted for as aid.

But what do these aggregate figures conceal about changing patterns in aid allocation (selectivity) and its modalities? While we observe overall increases in aid selectivity and the use of appropriate modalities, we also observe significant differences between donors. What explains these differences? We hypothesise that the quality of donors' own institutional environments matters, suggesting that the problem lies at home where low transparency and limited voice and accountability, possibly combined with a perverse political economy, make donors deliver aid poorly.

The remainder of the paper is structured as follows. The next section describes the issue of selectivity and examines changes in the actual aid allocation behaviour of bilateral donors over time. The following sections then summarise preliminary evidence on changes in aid delivery mechanisms induced by the new architecture, as proxied by the Paris Declaration indicators, and discuss the link between aid selectivity and donors' institutional environments. The concluding section outlines implications for a further reform agenda.

Increased aid effectiveness through selectivity

The allocation of aid is a much analysed topic (Easterly 2003 and Radelet 2006 provide general reviews that also cover the aid allocation literature), with empirical studies dating at least as far back as the 1960s.[2] The general finding of this literature is that, at least until the early 1990s, political and strategic interests overshadowed concerns of growth, poverty reduction and other economic objectives. In other

---

[2] Seminal early studies include Little and Clifford 1965; OECD 1969; Bhagwati 1972; Dudley and Montmarquette 1976. McKinlay and Little 1977 introduced econometrics; Trumbull and Wall 1994 and Wall 1995 introduced panel data econometric techniques.

Empirical evidence on international aid architecture 157

words, donors allocated their own money with little concern for its impact on development. There was little impetus for change until the end of communism, the growth of globalisation and the revitalisation of the academic literature on the topic.

The end of the Cold War had great consequences for international aid. First, it reduced many of its political motivations. Second, the ensuing progress in reforms, improved growth and success in reducing overall poverty reduced many countries' need for concessional aid. For some countries, globalisation and increased private capital flows came to meet their financing needs. Many of these changes were driven by changes in the overall development model triggered in part by the breakdown of communism.

Academic research also contributed to change. Aid allocation has received renewed attention in recent years, starting with the work of Alesina and Dollar (2000) which presented solid evidence of the importance of non-economic factors in determining aid (a finding which has since been confirmed by several papers).[3] In part due to changes in geopolitical and global economic circumstances, and perhaps due to these new insights from research, donors have since the mid-1990s been adapting their programmes and altering their policies. Recent empirical studies reveal (indirectly) how (some) donor countries have changed their practices: e.g. Berthélemy and Tichit (2004); Roodman (2005); Dollar and Levin (2006); and Sundberg and Gelb (2006) all find that donors' selectivity has improved.

While many studies find improvements, a contrarian view comes from Easterly (2007) who does not find consistent evidence of increased selectivity with respect to economic policies, such as trade openness, and only temporarily increased selectivity in the late 1990s regarding corruption. The issue is thus not fully settled; nor do we know which specific institutional changes may (or may not) have been driving these changes in actual behaviour.

One recent feature of the new aid architecture is the growing importance of debt relief. (Almost) all donors have engaged in bilateral (official) debt reduction, most recently through the (enhanced) Heavily Indebted Poor Countries (HIPC) initiative with 100 per cent write-offs. Multilateral debt reduction is also underway through the Multilateral

---

[3] France, Great Britain and Japan, for example, were found by Alesina and Dollar (2000) to favour their former colonies in the allocation of aid, and they, together with the USA and Germany, were found to allocate more aid to recipients that vote in unison with them in the UN. The political regime in recipient countries did not seem to matter much; Alesina and Weder (2002) for example find no evidence that less corrupt governments receive more aid. Others confirm similar patterns regarding specific donors. Kuziemko and Werker (2006) find that US aid increases by 59 per cent and its UN aid by 8 per cent when a country rotates onto the UN Security Council, suggesting bribery.

158　*Stijn Claessens* et al.

Debt Reduction Initiative (MDRI). Earlier work has shown aid flows to be a function of the level and structure of a country's debt obligations, including its outstanding debt to bilateral and multilateral financial institutions (Birdsall *et al.* 2003). This suggests HIPCs kept receiving resources due to their high indebtedness or large size, supporting the hypotheses of defensive lending and defensive granting – that is, situations in which donors continue to give loans and/or grants to prevent default on past loans and to avoid admitting 'mistakes'. These perverse effects of high debt stocks and certain debt compositions are an argument in favour of debt relief, which can help 'restore policy selectivity'. Conversely, as debt relief has now been implemented in a number of countries, we need to ask how it has affected the amount and destination of bilateral aid flows, and if indeed it has been successful in eliminating defensive lending.[4]

A companion paper to this chapter, Claessens *et al.* (2007), provides some additional recent evidence on changes in bilateral aid selectivity for the twenty-two DAC reporting bilateral donors over the period 1970–2004, focusing explicitly on changes induced in recent years by the new aid architecture.[5] Here we summarise the general results, focusing on the evidence that relates to the institutional environment of donors.

Using panel regressions that explore variations across time, donors and recipients, Claessens *et al.* (2007) have investigated how bilateral aid flows respond to a variety of factors including: recipient country level of income, a proxy for poverty; its size (as proxied by its population); its debt burden; and bilateral factors such as trade relationships as well as colonial and political linkages between donor and recipient. Generally, and as documented in the literature, we find that poorer countries receive more aid; larger countries receive less aid; and countries with closer trade and other ties with the donor receive more aid. Significantly, we found those countries with higher-quality policy and institutional environments, as measured by the World Bank's CPIA (Country Policy and Institutional Assessment) index, to have received more aid, suggesting selectivity. Neither the total debt burden nor the share of bilateral and multilateral debt within it significantly affected aid transfers over the whole period. This suggests that while there may have been defensive lending in sub-periods, as earlier findings suggest, defensive lending practices did not drive aid flows over the whole period.

---

[4] With the increase in official debt reduction in the 1990s, some have investigated the motivations for debt relief (Chauvin and Kraay 2007).

[5] See the appendix of this chapter and Claessens *et al.* 2007 for a detailed description of the data sources, data and the methodology we used to investigate these questions.

Empirical evidence on international aid architecture 159

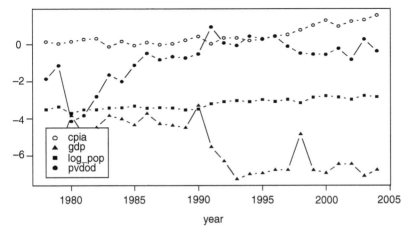

Figure 8.2. Responsiveness of aid to countries' income, policy, population and debt
Note: The figure presents time-varying sensitivities of aid to policy (cpia), poverty (gdp per capita), population (log_pop) and debt burden (pv of debt over exports, pvdod) respectively. Higher aid selectivity refers to more positive scores on cpia, more negative scores on gdp, zero or positive scores on population and zero or negative scores on pvdod respectively.
Source: Claessens *et al.* 2007.

The results over the whole period, however, hide important changes over time and improvements in donor aid practices. One way to document these changes is to allow the coefficients to vary over time, specifically year by year.[6] Figure 8.2 plots these coefficients for the most important sensitivities. It shows bilateral net aid transfers became increasingly sensitive to poverty level (measured by GDP per capita), to policy (measured by the World Bank's CPIA), to country size (measured by population) and to the country's debt burden (measured by present value of debt over exports). The figure shows that while some improvements began a decade ago, others have begun more recently. It strongly suggests that donors are taking needs (poverty) and policy

---

[6] Another way is to split the data into three sub-samples: 1970–89, 1990–8 and 1999–2004 (see Claessens *et al.* 2007). The first period is similar to earlier studies and coincides with the period before the fall of the Berlin Wall; splitting the ensuing period in two lets us see whether a new aid architecture has emerged. The cut-off point, 1998, roughly coincides with the start of the new literature on aid effectiveness and major changes in the international aid architecture (e.g. the World Bank Aid Effectiveness study in 1998 and the launch of the HIPC/PRSP framework). Viewing results by these sub-periods confirms the picture derived from the year-by-year changes.

160 *Stijn Claessens* et al.

selectivity more seriously, have less of a small country bias, and engage less in defensive lending.

Econometric analysis provides further evidence of reduced defensive lending, with the importance of debt composition (high bilateral or multilateral debt shares) in aid flows declining after 1990, and even further after 1999. This suggests that the various debt-reduction initiatives have paid off in weaning creditors from ever-greening loans through new loans (and grants) to the point that heavily indebted countries actually received more net transfers than other comparable countries. Analysis also suggests beneficial effects from the Poverty Reduction Strategy Papers (PRSP) and the HIPC initiative at the individual country level, where their adoption has increased net aid flows, enhanced policy selectivity, and reduced the perverse role of debt composition in driving aid flows.

Overall, these empirical findings are reassuring in that the new international aid architecture appears to be leading to improvements in the actual behaviour of donors. But there is evidence of continuing bad behaviour as well. Increasing aid flows in the early 2000s may have been a temporary surge. Preliminary ODA data for 2007 show a fall, mainly due to the reduction of debt relief.[7] Overall, in terms of scaling up, donors seem to have a hard time meeting their promises, such as the fifty billion dollar increase of aid to Sub-Saharan Africa by 2010.

In this chapter we complement our analysis in Claessens *et al.* (2007) with evidence on individual bilateral donors, using the same data and methodology. Figures 8.3–8.6 provide evidence of change in selectivity among the twenty-two traditional DAC-reporting donors, expressed as changes in responsiveness to our four main variables (income, policy, debt and small country bias) over three periods: 1970–89, 1990–8 and 1999–2004 – the pre-and post-Cold War periods, and the new aid architecture period.

Overall, these results confirm the general hypothesis of increased selectivity over time, especially in the most recent period. They also reveal marked differences in selectivity between donors. Take for instance the evolution of donor-specific sensitivities to the quality of recipient country policy and institutions (proxied by the CPIA) in Figure 8.3. Here, a more positive figure refers to improved effectiveness, higher aid per capita then responds to a higher CPIA score. The results show an overall improvement in effectiveness after the Cold

---

[7] Debt relief may be a poor substitute for other aid flows since many of the debts were not being repaid anyhow. In some countries, this means the donor development ministry essentially repays the finance ministry. The recipient country, however, would not necessarily receive real extra net transfers.

Empirical evidence on international aid architecture 161

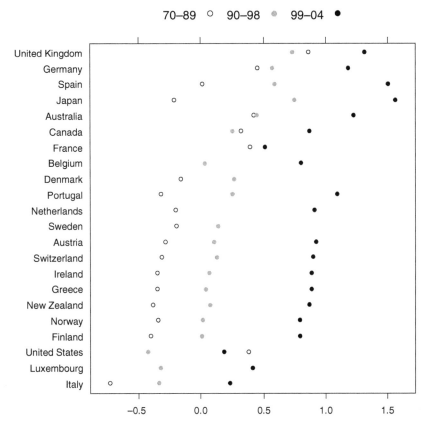

Figure 8.3. Time-varying, donor-specific sensitivities for CPIA

War, with improvements being most pronounced in Japan. One of the notable exceptions here is the USA, where the end of the Cold War did not lead to higher aid selectivity. Overall, the more pronounced improvements in CPIA selectivity have been recorded in the most recent period as a result of the new aid paradigm, with all countries, including the USA, becoming somewhat policy-sensitive. As for poverty selectivity (Figure 8.4, with aid effectiveness presented as a more negative sensitivity), improvements have been less pronounced, except for countries such as the UK and the USA that were already relatively poverty-selective. Here many bilateral donors remain largely poverty-insensitive, even in the most recent period. The next section examines a second dimension of aid effectiveness: the quality of aid delivery mechanisms.

162 *Stijn Claessens* et al.

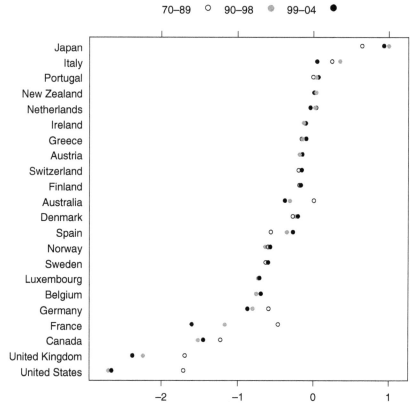

Figure 8.4. Time-varying, donor-specific sensitivities for GDP

Increased aid effectiveness through improved delivery

Alongside desired improvements in selectivity, the aid business also suffers from longstanding weaknesses linked mainly to lack of coordination (between donors and with the recipient country) and high transaction costs, showing a continued fragmentation among donors, projects and purposes. The average donor still disburses to too many countries and runs too many small projects. Countries are thus overburdened by multiple reporting, numerous missions, volatility in flows, lack in continuity of donor staff, etc. While the problems are well-known and longstanding (Easterly 2007 has quotes going back several decades on the same issue), limited progress has led to aid fatigue. The new aid architecture has thus embarked on an ambitious quest to tackle these thorny issues, not only by making it the centrepiece of the new paradigm, but also by establishing a concrete framework to induce, measure and monitor

Empirical evidence on international aid architecture 163

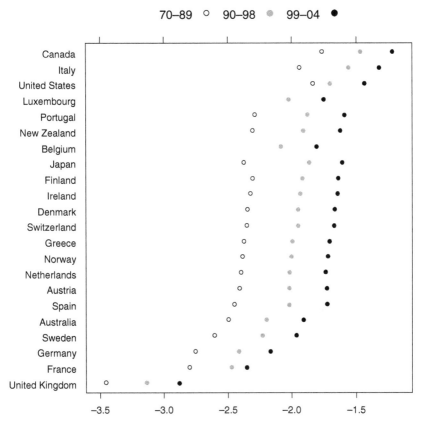

Figure 8.5. Time-varying, donor-specific sensitivities for population size

progress through the Paris Declaration on Aid Effectiveness (hereafter PD) process agreed in March 2005. Table 8.2 provides a brief overview of the elements, indicators and targets that make up the PD consensus; it also includes the baseline situation as of 2005 (from survey results), as well as the 2010 targets.

The 2005 baseline results reveal an interesting picture of the current state of aid delivery, especially regarding harmonisation and alignment efforts. It shows that although some indicators show relatively high performance (such as aid untying, recipient country budget reporting, in-year predictability), performance in other areas remains weak. The baseline results again show marked differences among individual bilateral donors (OECD 2007). These observations largely confirm our aid selectivity results – namely that there are substantial differences

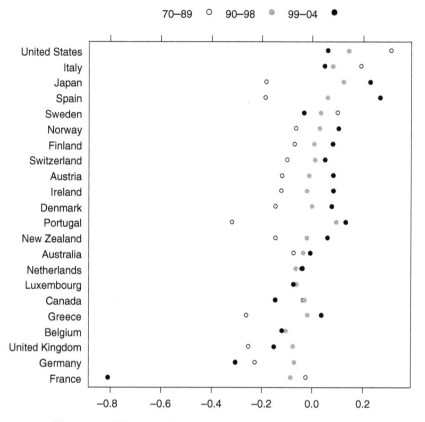

Figure 8.6. Time-varying, donor-specific sensitivities for debt outstanding disbursed

between donors – in the area of aid delivery practices as proxied by PD harmonisation and alignment indicators.

An alternative and broader framework to measure the quality of aid, and that of broader 'development friendliness', has been pioneered by the Commitment to Development Index (CDI) of the Center for Global Development. The CDI assesses donors in terms of aid, trade, investment, migration, environment, security and technology (see Roodman 2005), and reports significant differences among the twenty-one donors it covers: the overall CDI score (from 0 to 10) varies from 3.1 to 6.6, while the aid allocation-specific score varies from 1.1 to 10. The two before last columns in Table 8.3 indicate the average CDI Aid Quality Index and overall CDI scores for our sample of bilateral donors. Again we observe major differences between them.

Empirical evidence on international aid architecture 165

Table 8.2. *Monitoring the Paris Declaration commitments: 2005 baseline and 2010 targets*

	Indicator	2005 Baseline	2010 Target
Alignment	2a Quality of Public Finance Management (PFM) system	31% of countries meet criteria	Half of partner countries increase their scores
	2b Quality of procurement system	Not yet available	One-third of partner countries increase their scores
	3 Aid reported on budget	88% (average: 42%)	94%
	4 Coordinated capacity development	48% (average: 42%)	50%
	5a Use of country PFM systems	40% (average: 33%)	80%
	5b Use of country procurement systems	39% (average: 38%)	80%
	6 Parallel Project Implementation Units (PIUs)	1,832 (average: 61 per country)	611
	7 In-year predictability	70% (average: 41%)	87%
	8 Untied aid	75% (average: 82%)	Progress over time
Harmonisation	9 Use of programme-based approaches	43% (average: 35%)	66%
	10a Coordinated missions	18% (average: 29%)	40%
	10b Coordinated country analytical work	42% (average: 52%)	66%

Notes: The baseline is the weighted average of the survey results, except for the average of indicator 3. Larger donors (World Bank, EC, UK) thus have more weight.
Source: OECD 2007.

Implications for changes needed at the donor level

Our review of the literature, our empirical findings, and review of the latest patterns in aid allocation and delivery suggest that although aid architectural reforms have led to real improvements on the input side, the output (i.e. aid effectiveness) is still far from perfect, especially when we look beyond overall improvements and focus on individual (bilateral) donors. What explains the observed differences among donors in aid allocation and delivery behaviour and development friendliness?

Table 8.3. *Measures of aid quality and governance of bilateral donors*

Country	Voice and account-ability	Political stability	Government effectiveness	Regulatory quality	Rule of law	Control of corruption	CDI AID	CDI overall	PD average
Australia	1.45	0.85	1.94	1.67	1.81	1.99	2.50	5.50	24%
Austria	1.55	1.04	1.62	1.53	1.87	1.99	2.70	5.40	36%
Belgium	1.46	0.74	1.64	1.32	1.45	1.40	5.10	4.90	39%
Canada	1.46	0.94	2.03	1.53	1.85	1.90	3.30	5.20	51%
Denmark	1.72	0.82	2.29	1.81	2.03	2.39	10.00	6.40	53%
Finland	1.63	1.47	2.08	1.70	1.95	2.57	3.90	5.40	53%
France	1.40	0.46	1.20	1.06	1.31	1.44	4.10	4.60	42%
Germany	1.48	0.83	1.52	1.39	1.77	1.78	3.30	5.30	48%
Greece							2.70	4.00	
Ireland	1.42	1.16	1.53	1.75	1.62	1.60	5.90	5.00	69%
Italy	1.14	0.28	0.38	0.84	0.37	0.31	1.60	4.30	34%
Japan	0.91	1.11	1.29	1.27	1.40	1.31	1.10	3.10	49%
Luxembourg	1.63	1.51	1.73	1.79	1.83	2.01			40%
Netherlands	1.67	0.77	1.86	1.65	1.75	2.05	8.50	6.60	67%
New Zealand	1.62	1.27	1.94	1.68	1.93	2.38	2.20	5.60	32%
Norway	1.64	1.21	2.10	1.34	2.02	2.13	9.30	6.20	65%
Portugal	1.27	0.85	0.95	1.00	0.97	1.11	2.30	4.80	40%
Spain	1.05	0.33	1.05	1.06	1.10	1.18	2.50	4.80	30%
Sweden	1.55	1.13	2.00	1.44	1.86	2.24	9.80	6.30	53%
Switzerland	1.72	1.40	2.13	1.45	1.96	2.19	4.80	5.20	49%
United Kingdom	1.42	0.46	1.83	1.76	1.73	1.86	4.60	5.10	73%
United States	1.08	0.31	1.64	1.47	1.57	1.30	2.20	5.00	34%

Source: Kaufmann *et al.* 2007; Roodman 2005; authors' calculations based on OECD 2007.

Empirical evidence on international aid architecture   167

One possible explanation is that we are observing a progression in learning among donors who are still internalising the lessons. Further improvements may thus come, as implied by the PD framework's 2010 targets. Furthermore, our state of knowledge remains imperfect, with many outstanding questions on the general process of development and the effectiveness of aid. The current bilateral aid allocation and delivery system, and possibly by implication the whole current international aid architecture, may thus be optimal as it combines focusing on the knowns and experimenting on the unknowns.

But it is doubtful that lack of knowledge and ongoing learning are the main reasons behind the still disappointing manner in which aid is allocated. As many others have argued (e.g. Easterly 2007), much more is known than is currently applied by the development community, and more specifically by bilateral donors. The reason why this knowledge is not being more effectively used, we argue, lies in donors' own institutional environments. Similar to the role of the institutional environment in recipient countries affecting the impact of aid, it is likely that variations in the quality of aid arise in part from different institutional environments in donor countries. Donor countries' institutional environments determine how the aid allocation budget is decided in government, parliament or otherwise; what targets and policies are set; how aid is accounted and reported for; and whether the (specialised) agencies involved are independent, accountable, transparent and operate with integrity. These and other institutional differences influence outcomes: whether the donor's aid is selective and development-friendly, or whether it largely ends up supporting narrow local, geopolitical or other interests.

We can get some insight into this relationship when we relate data on aid quality with data on donors' institutional environments. Specifically, we can correlate donor scores on the two CDI proxies and the average PD with Kaufmann, Kraay and Mastruzzi's (KKM) various governance indexes.[8] We do this for the year 2006 for the twenty-one countries for which we have data for both sets of indexes (the CDI is not available for Luxembourg). Table 8.3 presents the data. Surprisingly, we find strong positive correlations: donor countries with better governance tend to be more committed to development and provide aid in a more development-friendly manner. The strongest correlations are between the overall CDI index and the KKM indicators. Here, the strongest correlation is with the Voice and Accountability KKM index (0.81), followed by the Government Effectiveness and Control of Corruption indexes (both 0.75). The lowest correlation is with the Political Stability index (0.26).

---

[8] The KKM indexes have been widely used in assessments of countries' governance. They cover six dimensions: voice and accountability, political stability, government

168 *Stijn Claessens* et al.

The correlations are somewhat less strong for the specific CDI Aid Quality index. The correlation with the KKM Voice and Accountability index, for example, is now 0.67. This somewhat lower correlation suggests that aid allocation is not just related to donors' overall institutional environments but also to the institutional set-up, and consequent behaviour, of the specialised agencies involved in aid budgets. Finally, the KKM governance indicators also correlate with the unweighted average PD indicator measure, with correlations ranging around 0.40.

These high correlations and their ordering suggest that how citizen preferences in the donor country are taken into account impacts the quality of aid (including how aid gets allocated) and that less corruption in the donor country makes selectivity more likely. This suggests that the limited selectivity of some donors in part reflects weaknesses in the specialised processes by which aid priorities, modalities, commitments, etc. are set. Better quality development ministries and other relevant agencies would presumably help. But, and probably more important in the long run, weaknesses reflect the quality of dialogue in individual countries, the population's involvement in discussions about aid and the general voice of the public in decision-making.

Concluding policy recommendations

Our finding that the international aid architecture must take into account not just the policy and institutional environment in recipient countries, but also in donor countries, suggests a number of possible reforms in the international aid architecture that may, over time, improve the quality and impact of aid. Very broadly, these include: increased disclosure and transparency, better governance, reduced conflicts of interest, more accountability, more harmonisation, greater benchmarking and better analyses. Changes in policy can further help improve outcomes.

Greater disclosure and transparency can help put pressure on aid agencies and other actors to justify their actions, thereby reducing the risk of non-development factors driving aid flows. A greater use of benchmarking and (ex-post) evaluation of donors could pressure agencies to reform (further). Further tools to evaluate donors such as the CDI could also be developed and disseminated more widely. The OECD-DAC assessment of aid agencies could be conducted more intensively, in the form of an annual score card. As the Paris Declaration process is so far the most

effectiveness, regulatory quality, rule of law and control of corruption, www.govindicators.org.

Empirical evidence on international aid architecture

tangible framework for assessing and monitoring aid delivery performance (on Harmonisation and Alignment), many observers are calling for it to cover more players in the aid business, including private donors.

There is also a need for more, better-focused research on donor and recipient country policy and institutional environments' impact on aid. Further precision in the institutional factors driving changes in behaviour would require good measures of changes in, say, financial policies, transparency, coordination, etc. at the donor country or international level. Current available data, however, still limit the possibility to do so. Further work on documenting institutional changes over time in a rigorous and quantitative way would help to identify which changes are the most influential. More generally, making more and better data available to researchers would allow for better analysis. One particularly useful source of data to be made public is the World Bank CPIA. More microanalysis on the impact of aid would help to clarify the impact of aid flows, while the bundling of policy analysis and research efforts, especially in Europe (a European Centre for Global Development?), would help to create greater clarity and more unity of purpose.

While there has been much talk of harmonisation, alignment and increased knowledge-sharing, results have been limited. Standards for aid projects, loan terms, uniform reporting, mutual recognition of reporting among donors, etc. could be enforced more rigorously to minimise costs and coordination problems, while more multilateral rather than bilateral approaches to aid would overcome some of the coordination issues that still plague the industry. To create accountability requires well-informed stakeholders. Often the right questions are not being asked by those responsible for overseeing budgets. More knowledge dissemination to and learning by parliamentarians and executive directors on the intricacies of aid and development would help, as would general public outreach.

Whether all this will occur is uncertain, and there are risks to consider with donor institutional reforms as well. Ocampo and Griffith-Jones in this volume have noted that using more formal aid selectivity tools can increase sensitivity to short-run measures of performance, and thereby possibly increase aid volatility, including possible pro-cyclical effects. More transparency may lead to pressure on aid agencies to improve policies, but may also require them to listen to constituencies with volatile preferences. For these and other questions it would be desirable if future research takes into account not just the policy and institutional environment in recipient countries, but in donor countries as well, and how they may (or may not) translate into improved selectivity.

Appendix: aid allocation model structure

This appendix provides some detailed information on the empirical model used in the second section of this chapter to test changes in aid allocation by bilateral donors over time (as in Claessens *et al.* 2007). The model uses annual data for the 1970–2004 period (subscript t), and measures how 21 bilateral donors (subscript i) allocate their aid towards 147 recipient countries (subscript j).

$$a_{ijt} = \alpha + \beta x_{ijt} + \mu_{ij} + \theta_t + \varepsilon_{ijt}$$

The dependent variable studied (a) is the annual aid from donor i to recipient j. Aid is defined in net transfer terms as the total resources provided by a specific donor in the form of grants, loans and debt relief, net of any loan principal repayments and interest payments on the loans the country makes to the donor, and scaled by recipient country population. Aid data are derived from OECD/DAC ODA official statistics.

We are interested in what drives aid allocation, and to what extent it has become more 'selective'. To measure selectivity, we use four main indicators: policy selectivity (as measured by CPIA); poverty selectivity (GDP per capita); population (to account for the so-called small country bias); and defensive lending bias (as measured by debt over exports). The model also includes a (time-invariant) bilateral dummy for colonial ties. Most other control variables we use are common in the literature: bilateral trade flows (to control for the role of non-aid economic relations between the two countries); net aid provided by other donors (to control for aid coordination and complementarity or substitution among aid flows); and total aid provided by the specific donor to all countries (to control for the overall level of aid generosity of the donor country).

To check whether structural changes in the 1990s affected aid allocations and their relationships to our need and selectivity measures, we split the sample into three sub-samples, 1970–89, 1990–8 and 1999–2004, and use dummies for each period. Additionally, we interact dummies for every year with these four variables to provide a picture of the year-by-year evolution of these sensitivities, to provide the results as presented in Figure 8.2. Furthermore, we run the same regressions for each individual donor, using the same sub-periods, to present time-varying donor-specific sensitivities for our four main factors, as shown in Figures 8.3–8.6.

For specific estimation methodology, rather than using fixed or random effects models, we use the Hausman-Taylor (HT) methodology, similar to what is often used in gravity models. The HT model allows

Empirical evidence on international aid architecture

Table 8.4. *Fixed effects, random effects and Hausman-Taylor estimations*

	(1)	(2)	(3)
	Fixed effects	Random effects	Hausman-Taylor
Lagged GDP/capita	−0.651**	−0.323**	−0.598**
	(0.046)	(0.035)	(0.043)
Log (population)	−2.055**	−0.808**	−1.013**
	(0.45)	(0.063)	(0.097)
CPIA	0.0795+	0.109*	0.0898*
	(0.045)	(0.044)	(0.044)
PV debt	−0.00331	0.00123	−0.00366
	(0.011)	(0.010)	(0.010)
Net aid others	6.080**	9.262**	6.602**
	(1.12)	(1.06)	(1.10)
Donor net aid sum	−0.297**	−0.205**	−0.252**
	(0.044)	(0.043)	(0.043)
Lagged bilateral trade	12.22**	19.83**	13.22**
	(1.11)	(1.02)	(1.09)
Multilateral debt share	−0.114	0.285	−0.161
	(0.35)	(0.31)	(0.33)
Bilateral debt share	0.231	0.347	0.171
	(0.27)	(0.26)	(0.27)
Colony	−	7.379**	7.543**
	(−)	(0.56)	(0.90)
Constant	34.86**	13.76**	18.13**
	(7.09)	(1.08)	(1.58)
Observations	47,883	47,883	47,883
Number of bilateral effects	2,349	2,349	2,349

Note: Robust standard errors in parentheses; ** $p<0.01$, * $p<0.05$, + $p<0.1$. Hausman specification test comparing fixed effects and random effects: Chi(36)=496.89 (p=0.000); Hausman specification test comparing fixed effects with Hausman-Taylor: Chi2(36)=46.55, p=0.112. The variables Lagged GDP/capita, Bilateral debt share, Multilateral debt share, Net aid others, Lagged bilateral trade, PV debt and CPIA are endogenous in Hausman-Taylor.

the estimation of time-invariant effects (here the colony dummy), without imposing the strong assumption that all variables should be uncorrelated with the individual specific effects. Table 8.4 provides the basic results.

9 Who governs and why? The making of a global anti-money laundering regime

Eleni Tsingou

Anti-money laundering (AML), while clearly a financial architecture issue in principle and in practice, stems from policy preoccupations external to the domain of financial and monetary governance. Impetus for the AML regime, in contrast to other policy areas covered in this volume, came from outside the financial policy community and the emerging rules are generated from a more heterogeneous set of actors. Yet it is important to look at the AML regime when discussing cross-border financial integration as, to fulfil its purpose, it is likely to constrain rather than facilitate the mobility of capital in a global era.

This chapter analyses the institutional and regulatory evolution of the regime developed over the past thirty years to fight money laundering. It identifies its characteristics as deriving mostly from the perception of policy-makers that they must be seen to be taking robust action to address a diverse set of public policy goals. These are often in tension with each other: related to criminal justice and security issues (corruption, drug trafficking and most recently terrorism) on the one hand, but also addressing global competitiveness issues between member countries of the Organisation for Economic Cooperation and Development (OECD) and offshore finance. As a side effect, the regime also shapes private sector practices in a way which can consolidate and strengthen the position of the largest global financial players. Despite the regime's ambitions, its achievements remain modest at best while many of its effects raise serious concerns about its substantive functioning, efficiency and legitimacy.

The regime's ineffectiveness in particular raises a paradox. The input side of the policy process lies outside the traditional financial policy community, and is centred on a series of powerful agencies involved in security and criminal justice issues at the core of the state. At first glance, the regime appears to challenge the private sector and the market-friendly financial architecture by imposing substantial compliance

---

I wish to thank the editors and participants in this project, and in particular Eric Helleiner and Elliot Posner for their comments on earlier drafts.

The global anti-money laundering regime   173

costs on banks and nominal impediments to global financial integration. But its ineffectiveness belies this initial conclusion and may enhance the legitimacy of the regime with the financial policy community whose position it appears to challenge yet undermine the legitimacy of the regime in general. At the same time, input-output considerations are also relevant in light of the core OECD nature of the regime: policy-making is excluding input from developing economies, and the emerging AML regime may well have detrimental consequences for the financial development of low-income countries.

The chapter is organised in four parts. It first explores the institutional structure of the AML regime and its key actors, and shows how this area of financial governance is more 'state-centric' than others, with costs of implementation borne primarily by the private sector. The chapter then proceeds with an analysis of the regime's effectiveness. While the secretive and illegal nature of money laundering makes assessments of both the problem and the regime's effectiveness problematic, evidence suggests that tensions within the AML regime are such that clear benefits are hard to detect. The chapter thus examines alternative explanations for the regime's momentum, in particular its symbolic nature and the extent to which AML rules and regulations affect the workings of the financial system, in fact protecting OECD financial centres from the competitive pressures of offshore finance and shaping private sector practices in ways that consolidate the position of the largest global financial players. Finally, the chapter focuses on the regime's side effects: the marginalisation of certain financial activities within OECD countries, as well as consequences for developing economies. Overall, the chapter confirms that in the AML regime, there is no trade-off between effectiveness and legitimacy; rather, the legitimacy of the regime, which is being questioned on both the input and output sides, is further damaged by its effectiveness shortcomings.

Presenting the global anti-money laundering regime

Money laundering is the process of disguising the illegal origin of the financial proceeds of crime. Following intense policy attention on the illegal narcotics trade, money laundering became a financial governance issue in the 1980s, culminating in the 1989 establishment of the Financial Action Task Force (FATF). Based in Paris, FATF has thirty-five members.[1] Its role is to issue regularly updated recommendations

---

[1] FATF member countries are: Argentina, Australia, Austria, Belgium, Brazil, Canada, China, Denmark, Finland, France, Germany, Greece, Hong Kong-China, Iceland,

174   *Eleni Tsingou*

which aim to set legislative and regulatory AML standards. The recommendations deal with an extensive range of themes, from the general (adoption of background AML policies, adjustment of banking secrecy laws, participation in multilateral initiatives and solutions, criminalisation of money laundering, legal frameworks for seizure and confiscation) to the institution-specific (customer identification and record-keeping rules, increased diligence of financial institutions, exchange of information and legal facilitation of mutual assistance).[2] Following the terrorist attacks of 11 September 2001, FATF issued a further nine recommendations focusing on the combating of terrorist financing. Though earlier recommendations were flexible in their guidance, FATF has evolved and is now able to draw on a pool of expertise. Recommendations have become more precise and prescriptive while the organisation issues Special Interpretative Notes in support of its work.

The monitoring of implementation takes two forms. First, all member countries carry out self-assessments. Second, FATF has a mutual evaluation procedure that allows on-site visits by legal, financial and law enforcement experts from other member governments. In 1999 FATF took a further step, a 'naming and shaming' campaign to identify countries and territories (beyond its membership) guilty of non-cooperation. The first 'Non-Cooperative Countries and Territories' (NCCT) report was made public in 2000. The report has been regularly reviewed, though the programme currently lies dormant.[3]

FATF does not work in isolation. Its efforts are aided by the work of regional task forces which follow the FATF format at the regional level; the Egmont Group of Financial Intelligence Units, which annually brings together representatives of the relevant national agencies; and the United Nations Global Programme against Money Laundering. The International Monetary Fund (IMF), as part of its work on financial

---

Ireland, Italy, Japan, Luxembourg, Mexico, Netherlands, New Zealand, Norway, Portugal, Russia, Singapore, South Africa, South Korea, Spain, Sweden, Switzerland, Turkey, the United Kingdom and the United States. The European Commission and the Gulf Cooperation Council are counted as members. The FATF also counts one observer country, India.

[2] The recommendations were most recently revised in 2003 to create a 'comprehensive, consistent and substantially strengthened international framework for combating money laundering and terrorist financing'. Changes include tougher provisions for high-risk customers, the extension of anti-money laundering measures to several non-financial businesses, the extension of existing requirements to cover terrorist financing, and the prohibition of shell banks. For comprehensive information on the forty + nine recommendations, see the FATF website www.fatf-gafi.org.

[3] Instead, the International Cooperation Review Group has, since 2007, been analysing high risk and non-cooperative jurisdictions and has become more pro-active in the aftermath of the crisis.

integrity, is now examining AML standards in its financial sector reviews and, where appropriate, offers technical assistance (Johnston and Abbott 2005). FATF, the IMF and the World Bank use similar assessment procedures and documentation in their AML evaluations.

The main initiator of much of the activity at the global level is the United States, which led the way in the criminalisation of money laundering in the 1980s.[4] There were apparently good reasons for this early and sustained interest: according to a 2001 report by the Federal Bureau of Investigation, approximately half of the money laundered worldwide goes through the US financial system while the US Treasury estimates that 99.9 per cent of such funds are laundered successfully (Mitchell 2003). But while a series of high-profile scandals involving financial institutions including the Bank of Credit and Commerce International, Citibank and Bank of New York brought attention to the issue throughout the 1990s, there was little interest in pursuing matters beyond the FATF framework or in ways that would lead to additional legislation or reinforced AML functions for regulators. In fact, there was no impetus for additional regulation or legislation prior to the terrorist attacks of 2001: while the US Senate Permanent Subcommittee on Investigation of the Committee on Governmental Affairs repeatedly pushed for legislation (US Senate 1999 and 2001), its efforts were mostly ignored or derided. Hearings showed consistent and adamant opposition from the private sector but also from public regulators and supervisors. After September 2001, these discarded bills provided the bulk of an AML package ready for speedy inclusion in the US Patriot Act, Title III.

Seen against this ambitious global regime of standard-setting and prevention, international coordination in law enforcement is a slow and underdeveloped process. Limited inter-state cooperation takes place in the context of Interpol (and Europol), where FATF is at times involved. It remains unclear, however, whether the AML regime has led to actual changes in the practices of law enforcement agencies and the establishment of effective communication channels.

As this brief overview shows, the regime is at first glance state-driven and state-focused. Yet while most of the public AML discourse refers to countries and criminals, the actors at the forefront of AML activities

---

[4] For an analysis of the role of the United States in the development of global prohibition regimes, including in money laundering, see Andreas and Nadelmann (2006). The literature on global prohibition regimes is particularly useful in explaining the role of powerful states in the development, adoption and implementation of particular prohibition norms and in the global acceptance and compliance processes that make them into a regime. The literature, however, does not explicitly distinguish between regimes' legal and regulatory components, nor does it address the impact of such regimes in terms of effectiveness and costs.

176   *Eleni Tsingou*

in a practical sense are primarily private. Financial institutions have clear incentives to take AML measures seriously, mainly to do with reputational and legal issues (Basel Committee 2001a). Indeed, they have long complied with its regulatory requirements. These include special identification measures – the 'know your customer' mantra applied to all financial services; monitoring based on internal systems and a comprehensive system of dealing with suspicious activity; up-to-date training programmes; the implementation of auditing procedures and accountability measures such as signed attestations of knowledge of AML measures and evaluations thereof; the setting-up of specialised AML units; and the full participation of senior management (Vitale 2001).

However, the dominant view in the private sector is that 'when the total costs to the banking system of the myriad anti-money laundering reporting requirements are correctly measured, few anti-money laundering efforts are cost effective' (Rahn 2003). This was confirmed in a comprehensive post-September 11 survey by the American Bankers Association, which placed bank secrecy and AML requirements first in the ranking of compliance costs faced by banks (ABA Banking Journal 2003: 35, 38). A more recent international survey of 224 banks in 55 countries provides further evidence of the mounting (and unexpected) costs of AML compliance, mostly due to transaction monitoring and staff training (KPMG 2007). Industry participants also appear to be engaged in pre-emptive moves, thus inadvertently contributing to regulatory creep and its associated costs. At the same time, the ability of public agencies to effectively monitor private sector compliance is in doubt, raising questions about the effectiveness of the current system of private sector incentives.[5]

Private sector concerns emphasise the 'private costs of a public policy' (Serrano and Kenny 2003) and to some extent exemplify how some regulatory measures are technical and difficult to implement, as well as highlighting the growing trend towards passing compliance responsibility to the private sector. They also highlight the less tangible costs associated with being assigned the legal role of 'capable guardian' (Levi and Maguire 2004: 417). This development appears to be at odds with trends observed in other areas of financial governance: public-private sector dynamics seem to be working to the financial detriment of the latter, with limited private access to policy debates and decision-making.

---

[5] Observations based on comments of public and private sector AML practitioners in Washington DC and New York (March 2008).

The global anti-money laundering regime 177

Goals and tensions: what is the regime for?

This section addresses the developing AML regime in terms of its effectiveness and, in turn, its legitimacy. Key challenges include the tracing of illicit financial flows, inconsistencies within the institutional set-up, the differing priorities of prevention and enforcement, and the introduction of terrorist financing into the regime. The continuing difficulties in establishing an effective regime eventually highlight its legitimacy problems and call it further into question.

What makes money dirty and how much of it is out there?

The nature of money laundering lies at the heart of the challenges to the AML regime. While there is a widely accepted general definition of money laundering, international harmonisation on which crimes are relevant is much more recent. Traditionally, rules and laws evolved from the domain of narcotics, but a wide range of crimes have since been added in different jurisdictions (in some jurisdictions such as the UK, all crimes are considered relevant).[6]

Attempts to measure money laundering pose further difficulties. Its secretive and illegal nature means that data are scarce, while the practice encompasses activities in both the formal and informal sectors of the economy. Nevertheless, there have been several attempts to calculate it, the most often quoted figure coming from the IMF which estimates total money laundered to be between 2 and 5 per cent of world GDP. Another set of figures puts laundered drug money at 2 per cent of total financial flows (*The Banker* 2003). The methodology used for these estimates, however, is widely challenged, leading one commentator to remark that 'given the credibility of the methodology, the only thing that can be stated with certainty is that the actual figure is not likely to be less than 0% or more than 100%' (Naylor 1999: 30). Indeed, while attempts at measurement often lead to claims of 'sizeable' sums (see Unger 2007), no background is provided on the criteria employed in making these judgements. It is significant that FATF's own project to calculate the extent of money laundering between 1996 and 2000 failed (Reuter and Truman 2004). These limitations clearly matter: without an accurate understanding of the extent of the problem, we cannot make objective assessments of the emerging regime's

---

[6] A comprehensive discussion of the problems arising from the diverging crimes included in AML legislation (including within the European Union) can be found in Unger 2007.

178   *Eleni Tsingou*

effectiveness. Furthermore, there is no clear benchmark of what would constitute success or what an 'acceptable' figure for global laundered funds might be.

In search of legitimacy and efficiency

Examining the main actors within the AML regime offers insights into why the regime has developed the way it has. At its core, FATF promotes global standards. Yet FATF is essentially a political organisation in its practices and membership. While its scope is de facto global, to qualify for membership a country must be 'strategically important' (as is boldly stated on the organisation's website). Indicatively, Russia joined FATF soon after being de-listed from the NCCT list; this can be seen as symptomatic of the organisation's political character, as well as its emphasis on form over practice. This charge is not unjustified; recent work on the 'scale and impacts of money laundering' confirms that 'giants wash more' (Unger 2007). Yet the AML regime affects many more countries for which applying the recommendations may be a less than necessary 'investment'.

The broadening of participation in the AML regime has been restricted to opening new regional agencies. FATF's narrow membership, its peer review procedure and its (to date) limited reprimands have cast doubt on the organisation's legitimacy yet no doubt reduce the costs to the private financial sector. The NCCT process has also been criticised for being wound down despite its effect on regulatory and legislative frameworks and, more importantly, for its arbitrariness. The list of countries that never made it onto the NCCT list (the United Arab Emirates for example) seems to reinforce the political character of FATF and the influence of core G7 countries within it. Other countries were removed from the NCCT list following reviews of their regulatory and legislative frameworks. That this was generally not accompanied by improvements in reputation or market access casts further doubt on the credibility of the process.

Nor has the role of the IMF been without controversy. Succumbing to US and G7 campaigning, the IMF began as a reluctant participant, 'piggy-backing' money laundering issues on top of its financial integrity work.[7] Its endorsement of FATF recommendations was based on a compromise that included winding down the NCCT list, to be replaced by working through consensus, cooperation and a transparent

---

[7] This point was supported by IMF staff, as expressed in confidential interviews in June 2004.

The global anti-money laundering regime   179

methodology. While inclusion of the IMF addressed some of the membership shortcomings of FATF, it also raised questions on whether financial assessments can efficiently and legitimately deal with standards closely linked to criminal justice.

The often haphazard implementation of AML provisions at the national level adds another level of difficulty. In the United States, a wide range of agencies including the Financial Crimes Enforcement Network (FinCEN), the dedicated Treasury Department authority and the new Department of Homeland Security have all been trying to determine 'who does what' and 'who should be doing what', while financial regulators and supervisors remain unenthusiastic participants. The approach is thus far from uniform.

Reconciling the goals of the regime: prevention and enforcement

The AML regime is developing on two fronts: prevention and enforcement. Prevention is a regulatory tool and focuses mostly on sanctions, regulatory and supervisory rules and standards, reporting and customer due diligence. Enforcement is a legal tool, concentrating on investigation, confiscation, prosecution and punishment. Despite the criminalisation of money laundering and the now prominent role of enforcement agencies, the AML regime is primarily a regulatory process. Its participants' roles, however, are blurred: are regulators and banks becoming law enforcement officials? How can law enforcement best be integrated in the institutional framework, and at which level does policing work best? While guidance, feedback and cooperation are welcome, the different objectives of regulators and law enforcement officials need to be reconciled, or at least acknowledged.

At both national and regional-global levels, cooperation between regulators and supervisors (and the financial institutions they oversee) and law enforcement agencies remains uneven. Their relationship is patchy, often adversarial or inconsequential. Tension can arise from the lack of established procedures but also from their different interpretations of results: the financial sector measures success by lack of problematic instances, while law enforcement bodies focus on confiscated sums and convictions. Regulators and law enforcement agents indeed have different strategies: the first group focuses on the process, including persuasion, cooperation, self-regulation, risk-based discretion and 'private remedies'; the second group stresses prosecution, external regulation, and public justice and punishment (Croall 2003: 46). In essence, the AML regime is trying to reconcile two rather different goals: compliance and results. This creates contradictions and further hampers the

180   *Eleni Tsingou*

effectiveness of the regime. It also affects the legitimacy of the regime as two possible legitimation avenues, through regulation or through law enforcement and compliance contradict rather than complement each other.

Introducing terrorism

Another, at first surprising dimension of the AML regime is the inclusion of provisions, post-9/11, to combat the financing of terrorism (CFT). Fighting terrorist financing was an 'uncontroversial' early measure and had immediate effect through the freezing of assets (Navias 2002: 58–9). FATF responded by designing additional specialised recommendations; its efforts were mirrored in the adoption of related regional standards and were further consolidated through national regulation and legislation, most notably the US Patriot Act.

In practice, however, CFT measures can only have limited effects. When the US Federal Bureau of Investigation tried to profile terrorists' use of banks, it highlighted the practice of making a large deposit and then withdrawing small amounts of cash at frequent intervals, a profile that matches one in four customers according to practitioners (*The Economist* 14 December 2002). Forensic work by FinCEN on the 9/11 terrorists showed that money laundering tools cannot spot the financing of terrorism. An additional problem is one of methodology: terrorism is often funded by clean money. 'Success' here would require banks to make value judgements about the future use of money as well as about customers' potential to act unlawfully in the future. This is subjective, time-consuming and can lead to discrimination on the basis of ethnicity; it also requires consistent, forthcoming and up-to-date intelligence. Finally, the sums involved in financing terrorism are small. The 9/11 attacks may have cost less than $500,000; raising such an amount would have met limited challenges as transactions below $10,000 do not require the same level of scrutiny.

Indications are that most of the measures taken since the terrorist attacks of 2001 will have little impact on the financing of terrorism. FitzGerald (2004: 398) argues that they have failed to 'create positive economic incentives for compliance in order to counteract the existing disincentives for disclosure experienced by financial intermediaries and regulation jurisdictions'. Others have argued that control functions have been 'outsourced' to the private sector without adequate direction (Passas 2006) or, indeed, customer protection. It also remains unclear whether the AML regime is the appropriate setting for dealing with terrorist financing though this debate at the policy level appears closed.

The global anti-money laundering regime 181

While many acknowledge the inconsistencies of dealing with the two issues together from a regulatory point of view, the regulatory and legal channels in place in the USA – establishing a link between addressing money laundering, terrorist financing and national security – are unlikely to be challenged. Elsewhere, this link has often been grudgingly accepted as a political decision.

Explaining the anti-money laundering regime

Is money laundering a genuine threat to the financial system? Is inclusion of some 'dirty money' in the system an acceptable price to pay for efficient financial markets as promoted by regulators and the private sector over the past thirty years? This goes to the heart of long-established principles of what is appropriate in global financial governance. While 'money laundering, financial crime and terrorist financing have shattered the myth of capital neutrality' (Unger 2007: 184), the elimination of money laundering would require a reworking of the system, one which would change our understanding of the concept of free movement of money.

From the outset, the official rationale for addressing money laundering has focused on criminal behaviour and seldom on explicit questions of financial governance as such. Public officials have consistently presented the AML regime as a way of: (1) tackling the drugs trade, the arms trade, human trafficking and other organised criminal activity; (2) supporting the integrity of the financial system, including supporting good governance and transparency, especially in the developing world; (3) combating corruption and its economic and political consequences; (4) promoting economic development and ensuring that funds are channelled to appropriate economic endeavours that contribute to tax revenues; and most recently, (5) targeting the financing of terrorist activities (McDowell and Novis 2001). AML measures furthermore have a foreign policy component with their focus on problem countries and politically exposed persons, as in the case of the sanctions programme of the US Treasury Office of Foreign Assets Control (OFAC).

It nevertheless remains difficult to separate the above concerns from less touted yet significant reasons why money laundering matters to policy-makers, especially within OECD countries. The lines between money laundering and tax havens or banking secrecy are blurred; formally they are distinct concerns as money laundering is unequivocally illegal. As the FATF focus on NCCTs has shown, however, an important part of the global strategy against money laundering has revolved

182   *Eleni Tsingou*

around improving practices and promoting transparency in offshore centres. Offshore centres, which represent 1.2 per cent of the world's population and account for 3.1 per cent of its GDP, handle a quarter of the world's financial assets (Levin 2002). The drive towards building an AML regime is thus inevitably connected to questions of competitive pressure and establishing a regulatory level playing field (Sharman 2006a).

The downside of the regime is also felt in OECD countries, most notably in those that have strong private banking traditions (e.g. Switzerland and Luxembourg). The European Union (EU), through three European Commission Money Laundering Directives (1991, 2001 and 2005), has to some extent harmonised practices and standards in the EU, though this has fuelled tension between member states. The EU AML drive has revealed that there are strong linkages to FATF discussions and the (often binding) standards, that the G7 members such as the UK and France are at the forefront of proposals for comprehensive regional standards, and that countries with long-established offshore status, most notably Luxembourg, are under intense pressure (at the political and regulatory levels, but also in the media) to address weaknesses. This pressure has only increased since the movement towards reform advocated in the wake of the financial crisis.

While the private sector – which bears the costs of compliance – may be the overall 'loser' in the emerging environment, compliance affects small and large institutions differently despite the adoption of 'risk-based' principles in the AML regime.[8] Major industry players, through the establishment of the Wolfsberg Group of Banks, have attempted to position themselves so as to seize the initiative on creating appropriate standards.[9] Created in 2000, the Wolfsberg Group issues global AML and CFT guidelines for international private banks, focusing primarily on correspondent banking relationships; the harmonisation of principles and the strengthening of the private sector's reputation and credibility are the reasons given for the voluntary code of conduct (Pieth and Aiolfi 2003). While membership of the group remains restricted, the initiative now includes an annual 'Wolfsberg Forum' which brings together a wider spectrum of financial institutions (fifty of the world's largest banks), as well as representatives from regulatory and supervisory

---

[8] Interviews with public and private sector officials in the USA, UK, Switzerland and Luxembourg over a four-year period confirm this point.

[9] The group consists of: ABN Amro, Banco Santander Central Hispano, Bank of Tokyo-Mitsubishi UFJ, Barclays, Citigroup, Credit Suisse, Deutsche Bank, Goldman Sachs, HSBC, JP Morgan Chase, Société Générale and UBS. For more information see www.wolfsberg-principles.com.

The global anti-money laundering regime

agencies at the national and global level (e.g. the Basel Committee on Banking Supervision) and FATF (Pieth 2006).

Another by-product of the AML/CFT regime has been the development of global compliance programmes that also serve as sophisticated databases and marketing tools for the major financial institutions. At the 'high end' of the market, banks and securities firms use complex compliance programmes that enable client identification, the monitoring of their transactions, the reporting of suspicious activities, and the regular updating of global regulatory and legal requirements. These programmes are developed using a risk-based approach where customers are categorised as high, medium or low risk in their dealings with the financial institution, in which the most important factor seems to be the customer's nationality. While the initial cost of such programmes is high, financial institutions admit they have valuable uses, including getting to know more about clients' individual needs, offering consistency to clients who have global financial relationships, and creating sophisticated 'valuable customer' profiles.[10] Big institutions are also more likely to have confidentiality arrangements in place that facilitate business-wide programmes and overcome restrictions imposed by banking secrecy and data protection provisions. These methods have been endorsed by the Wolfsberg Group, which promotes a risk-based approach focusing on country, customer and services variables.

The burden of compliance is greater for smaller, local institutions, where 'know your customer' and reporting requirements are less automated. While a risk-based approach is also applied to small private institutions and their regulators alike, it is unclear how this would impact on fines or criminal investigations in the case of irregularities. The reactive role of the private sector in the AML/CFT regime thus disproportionately affects small institutions, highlighting their justified concern for policies that are proportionate to the effectiveness of the regime.

The considerations above show that the regime is state-centric and reflects rich-nation and, in particular, US interests (its domestic criminal agenda, foreign policy and financial competitiveness). It does not, however, aim to control money laundering in an unequivocally effective manner, as this would affect the very nature of the global financial system. Instead, the regime meets the more modest standard of visible public action while strengthening the position of the largest players. Under the current regime, 'traditional' financial centres can reassert

---

[10] Proprietary information on these programmes was discussed in interviews with private sector compliance officers in Zurich and New York (June 2004) and again in Washington DC and New York (March 2008).

184   *Eleni Tsingou*

their position vis-à-vis offshore centres while the largest financial institutions can further consolidate their positions, not only by turning requirements into marketing advantages, but by creating market entry barriers for smaller institutions.

Establishing costs and side effects

There are quieter but widespread concerns regarding the costs of the regime, especially to non-OECD countries. While a credible cost-benefit analysis of the AML regime may elude us, some analysts have reached conclusions using qualitative methods. Geiger and Wuensch (2007) found limited benefits in developed financial environments such as Germany, Singapore and Switzerland. On the other hand, Sharman (2006b) found AML/CFT measures to have had a markedly negative impact on Barbados, Mauritius and Vanuatu, suggesting similar effects may be found elsewhere in the developing world. Developing nations may find strict AML rules damaging to their development strategies. In principle, they have few incentives to join the fight against money laundering; only strong leadership from other countries and the embarrassment of being blacklisted may persuade them (Simmons 2001: 605–7).

Studies have shown that money laundering and corruption, especially in the developing world, are often linked to detrimental results (Duffy 2000). But can the AML regime be part of a development strategy? Developing countries have limited financial and human resources,[11] which are now being diverted to comply with global AML requirements. Yet there seems to be little political space to discuss the potentially complementary (and arguably useful) issues of capital controls and tax evasion. The focus of AML requirements is thus often at odds with the real needs of developing nations. At the UN crime conference in Bangkok in 2005, core countries blocked a drive by developing countries for a new UN AML treaty. The focus remained on existing FATF standards mostly relevant for banking issues despite many developing countries' concerns that they do not address issues associated with real estate financing, a more pressing concern for many participants.

The side effects of this focus on banking issues go further. Significant parts of the population in some countries lack the necessary documentation to participate in the formal banking system (de Koker 2006). The marginalisation and financial exclusion of students, migrants and informal economy workers through 'know your customer' banking

---

[11] For an analysis of the allocation of resources and its effects in developing countries, see Rodrik (1998a).

The global anti-money laundering regime 185

practices, and the increasing criminalisation of cash, though addressed in academic circles (de Goede 2003; Amoore and de Goede 2005), remain outside the scope of official concern. This affects the weakest and poorest members of society in the developing and developed world alike. Regular remittance systems are being marginalised, with money service businesses (MSBs) finding it difficult to maintain relationships with the formal banking sector. A growing number of banking institutions in the USA are finding that compliance costs outstrip the narrow profit margins that business with MSBs offers; remittance accounts are thus being closed.[12] Alternative remittance systems have also been targeted, most notably *hawala*, which avoids wire transfers, paper trails and formal banking (Biersteker 2002; de Goede 2003). Finally, charities are put under the spotlight and though many have been targeted for their knowing or unknowing support of al-Qaeda terrorists, standards lack concrete measures (other than encouraging charity verification field trips) and have not produced a comprehensive approach.

Conclusion

This chapter has provided an overview of a specialist regime, both central (in terms of its actors) and peripheral (in terms of its content) in global financial governance. It has shown how political considerations are integrated in broader financial governance arrangements and how distinctions between domestic and global security issues and the political economy can become blurred. At first glance, the AML regime seems determined to place controls on the financial system in order to serve specific (financial and non-financial) policy goals, imposing costs in terms of compliance. At the same time, the technical nature of the recommendations and evaluations and the evolving role of international organisations such as the IMF within the regime indicate AML's normalisation in the financial governance framework. The relatively successful targeting of countries with irregular banking sectors also points to the achievement of a 'level playing field' and the harmonisation of practices. The financial policy community in the major financial centres does not lose much after all.

The chapter, however, has certainly cast doubt on the regime's effectiveness. The absence of data on money laundering and terrorist

---

[12] Interviews with private sector officials in the United States (March 2008) suggest that maintaining links with MSBs poses unacceptable reputational risks (with the exception of California, such links are relatively inconsequential in profit terms). While public sector agencies appear aware of the issues and the particular problems facing the underbanked, solutions are not forthcoming at this stage.

financing, as well as on prevention and convictions, severely limits any assessment of the efficiency of a 'proceeds of crime' and 'proceeds for crime' approach. The lack of evidence, especially on the regime's benefits, undermines the validity of cost-benefit analyses, whether at the national or global level. But despite the difficulty of providing concrete justification for the regime, its development and purpose are seldom questioned. In turn, this lack of effectiveness further weakens the already fragile legitimacy of the regime.

Parallel, unofficial concerns served by AML and CFT measures contribute to the continued existence of the regime as it is. There is a clear need to address complex public issues such as drug trafficking, corruption and terrorism; the resulting policies, however, amount to little more than rhetoric and offer regulatory and bureaucratic solutions to ill-defined problems.[13] Similarly, despite the emphasis on financial integrity, there is a strong perception of competitive pressures from specialised and offshore financial centres; the globalisation of AML/CFT standards appeases only some of those worries. The private sector – or more accurately, certain segments of it – is not always the loser. The major players have been able to use the opportunity to develop sophisticated marketing techniques and to consolidate their expertise, while their smaller competitors have been more exposed to the costs.

The regime falls short in effectiveness while imposing detrimental effects on the weaker and least influential economies in the system. Given the inherent contradiction between an 'effective' AML regime and global financial integration as witnessed over the past thirty years, one questions whether stamping out money laundering is (or ever was) a serious goal. Truly effective AML/CFT controls are inherently incompatible with the free cross-border flow of money; the regime is thus most likely destined to remain largely symbolic.

---

[13] In interviews with public regulators and enforcement officials in the United States, the point that the recent wave of AML/CFT activity does not take into account any of the lessons learned from the war on drugs of the 1980s was often reiterated (March 2008).

10 Brazil and Argentina in the global financial system: contrasting approaches to development and foreign debt

Victor Klagsbrunn

Introduction

Over the past decade, Brazil and Argentina have found very different answers to a very similar problem: an excruciating debt burden denominated in a foreign currency, a phenomenon that has haunted a range of emerging market economies over the past decades. While Brazil toed the line prescribed by Washington-based institutions – the IMF in particular – Argentina defaulted on its foreign debt in 2002 instead of giving in to creditor pressure. And while Argentina reacted against the 'rules' of the system to carve out its own 'policy space' to ease the domestic costs of adjustment and debt workout, Brazil followed the recipe and appeared to suffer (somewhat) greater costs. Two questions follow: how can the highly divergent policy responses of these two countries be explained? And how are the two policy routes to be evaluated with the benefit of hindsight? These are the two central issues addressed in this chapter.

The divergent stories contain possible lessons: first and foremost, they show that the 'policy space' available to national economies during financial crises may be greater than is often assumed in the literature or by those who designed the financial architecture. The case of Argentina contradicts common assertions that globalised finance leaves no alternative to 'orthodox' policies (see Chapter 11 by Zhang). Second, it shows that following heterodox policies was not only possible, but at least in Argentina's case, probably beneficial: in spite of hardships, Argentina in the end fared slightly better than Brazil. Third, one central reason for the 'unorthodox' route chosen by Argentina was the IMF's continued insensitivity to the legitimate interests of developing countries (and domestic political pressures within them). In both cases, this insensitivity led to less than optimal results. Argentina defaulted, dealing a blow to cooperative solutions to financial turmoil; Brazil largely stuck to the orthodox policy mix but paid a heavy economic cost, particularly in the form of excessively high interest rates to attract foreign capital, which through an overvalued exchange rate impaired international competitiveness. In sum, more openness on the policy input side of global financial governance may have opened space for a middle way leading to more desirable outcomes than was achieved by either country.

Historical background

Both Brazil and Argentina are no strangers to financial turmoil. The foreign currency-denominated external debts of emerging economies led to a series of moratoria known as the Developing Country (largely Latin American) Debt Crisis of the 1980s. Debtor countries had little option but to turn to the IMF. Exposed US banks faced bankruptcy, leading to considerable US as well as Fund intervention during the workout. While debtors agreed to service their debts, banks were pressed to lend into arrears; eventually debt was swapped for bonds underpinned by international guarantees, or discounted altogether. During the second half of the 1990s, the spectre of emerging market debt returned to haunt international financial markets following a near decade-long wave of enormous capital inflows. Contributing to this gigantic flow were policies that kept interest rates high and which aimed to attract foreign capital, all within the framework of high international liquidity and financial market growth.

The currencies of these countries generally suffered significant over-valuations that corroded their capacity to maintain healthy trade balances and to guarantee returns on invested capital from the industrialised world. Dependence on growing inflows of capital to equalise the balance of payments made it essential to maintain and to accelerate the overvaluation of currencies by means of increased domestic interest rates. This, of course, is the variable over which local monetary authorities have the greatest control. While deficits in the current accounts and in the balance of trade can be offset by the inflow of foreign capital, this depends on the outlook for returns.

The moment of truth came with the Asian crisis in 1997, though it was foreshadowed by the attack on the Mexican currency three years earlier. Readjustments of exchange rates spread through practically all emerging markets as authorities realised the need to abandon their policies of overvaluing their currencies. Without a doubt, the most painful and longest period of readjustment took place in Argentina, culminating in 2002 in the moratorium and forced restructuring of its foreign debt.

Following the debt crisis of the 1980s, the majority of emerging countries were heavily influenced by what is commonly referred to as the Washington Consensus, a new form of liberal market reform supposedly tailor-made to solve these countries' ongoing external problems. The Washington Consensus, even after the serious world economic recession of 1991–2, no longer had to be imposed by IMF fiat; monetary authorities in emerging economies were already sufficiently 'convinced' that liberal principles were the only ones that would allow them to take part in the paradise promised by globalisation, especially the financial globalisation that was then making a beachhead in emerging markets.

As a result, the multilateral institutions that controlled the international financial system were taken out of the spotlight in international economic relations. Nonetheless, national policies differed from one another to a certain extent regarding the acceptance and application of IMF prescriptions. This allows us to conclude that there was always a certain margin for manoeuvre, even during the Washington Consensus' period of dominance over the economic policies of emerging countries – either by imposition (as during the external debt crisis of the 1980s) or through persuasion (by the so-called consensus of the 1990s).

Focusing on Brazil and Argentina's foreign debt workouts since the mid-1990s therefore allows us to evaluate the tensions between internal and external imperatives and to analyse the extent to which the external adjustment pressures of the market and IMF conditionality, as well as internal commitments to market reform, permitted divergent policies. The pressure to pursue divergent policies had of course never been absent, given the internal dynamics of each country.

What is certain is that post-2002 and the acute crisis in Argentina, many developing countries entered a benign trajectory in their external (particularly current account) balances and debt. Fuelled by rising commodities prices and exports – wherein a long run of unfavourable terms of trade for developing countries was apparently reversed – emerging markets now enjoyed buoyant and balanced growth. Brazil and Argentina have been among the main winners of this trend, accumulating huge trade surpluses while simultaneously liquidating external debt (see Figures 10.1–10.3). While the onset of crisis in the USA and recent developments in the external balances of developing countries indicate that this period may have come to an end, the crisis has yet to strike emerging markets directly.

Policies to reduce foreign debt since 1999

Both Argentina and Brazil eventually overcame their foreign debts, but through very different means. Which international and internal factors

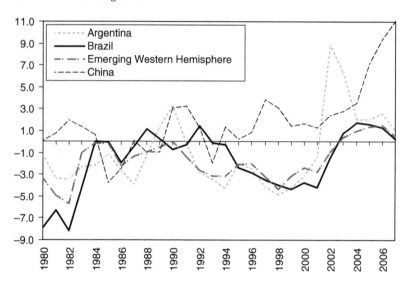

Figure 10.1. Current account balance as % of GDP
Source: IMF.

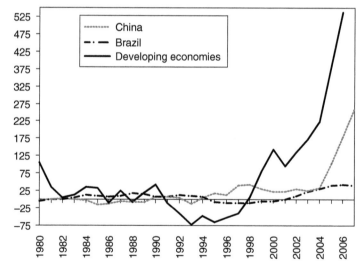

Figure 10.2. Trade balance selected developing countries in US$ billions – I
Source: UNCTAD database and Central banks.

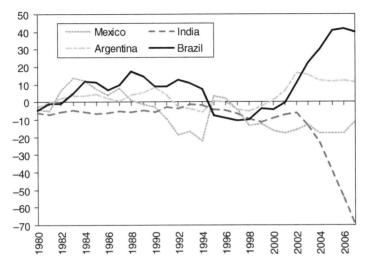

Figure 10.3. Trade balance selected developing countries in US$ billions – II
Source: UNCTAD database.

led them on their respective paths? Argentina, attending to internal social and political pressures, broke out of its extremely unfavourable 2001–2 situation by defaulting on external obligations altogether. In addition, it benefited from Washington's changed stance towards a potential default. For strategic as well as ideological reasons, the Bush administration found a default that would punish international investors much more acceptable than had been the case for the Clinton government (Helleiner 2005). Brazil benefited from a highly favourable and unusual external situation (which also favoured Argentina) in the first seven years of the new century and carefully reduced its foreign debt, particularly the indebtedness of private enterprises. The Brazilian monetary authorities preferred a more 'orthodox' approach, using their current account surpluses to accumulate international reserves, and not to reduce public foreign debt. The favourable external situation attracted foreign capital: to production and the financial sphere in Brazil and to production in Argentina. This further contributed to the accumulation of international reserves.

Little can be said about the advantages of one set of economic policies over another during periods of prosperity; it is times of crises that allow us to see which are more risky. For this reason, it is necessary to evaluate countries' foreign debt, exchange rate and interest rate policies in light of what we may expect to happen under emergency conditions.

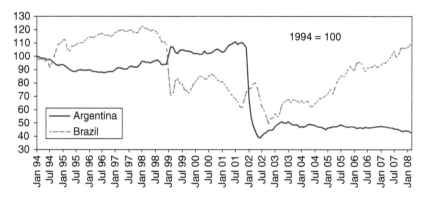

Figure 10.4. Effective real exchange rates
Source: www.bis.org.

Even though Argentina and Brazil were both members of MERCOSUR, after 1999 they adopted contrasting and even competing emergency measures. The key variable in evaluating their policies is exchange rates, which in the short run are largely determined by interest rates. Because the domestic interest rate is the easiest variable for monetary authorities to control, it is the basic differentiating element in the analysis of the two countries' respective economic policies.

Effective exchange rates in the 1990s: different routes to similar results

Argentina and Brazil both adopted policies to anchor their currency to the US dollar in the early 1990s. Despite the seemingly radical nature of Argentina's 1991 law on convertibility, the scope for appreciation of the Brazilian currency was even higher. During the second half of the 1990s, both currencies appreciated significantly in real terms. In both cases this was caused by higher domestic interest rates and increased capital inflows.

In Brazil the index for the effective exchange rate (taking into account the difference between the domestic inflation rate and that of foreign countries weighted by their bilateral trade)[1] increased by 35 per cent between July 1994 (the onset of the Real Plan) and January 1998; Argentina's increased by 26 per cent between August 1996 and October 2002. As a result, the trade balance of both countries deteriorated in the second half of the 1990s.

---

[1] See BIS on effective exchange rates, www.bis.org.

Brazil

At the beginning of the Real Plan in July 1994, the Brazilian government abruptly reduced the amount of money in circulation, especially the banking system's access to new credit. This resulted in a sharp increase in domestic interest rates which attracted large amounts of foreign capital. Both trends were responsible for the appreciation of the currency, which was welcomed by monetary authorities as a means to strengthen their ability to control inflation by reducing the cost of imported products.

Contrary to Argentina, Brazilian monetary authorities did not formally peg the real to the US dollar. This allowed the Brazilian currency to fluctuate and devalue during the Mexican crisis, going from 0.82 to the dollar to 1.20 in just a few months, providing a breathing spell for the country's trade balance. But even with lower, albeit persistent, inflation, the government once again insisted on permitting and even encouraging another currency appreciation, caused by high domestic interest rates.

It only took a new financial crisis in the emerging countries of Asia in 1997 for the government to again raise domestic interest rates in an attempt to maintain the capital inflows necessary to stabilise the balance of payments. The same happened when the crisis in Russia broke out in 1998. As in Mexico in 1994–5, the policy of high interest rates and currency overvaluation received a breather with the massive loan and shield coordinated by the IMF at the end of President Fernando Henrique Cardoso's first term in 1998. Even so, growing trade and financial deficits due to the mass outflow of dollars mandated, less than two months later, the sudden abandoning of the policy of currency overvaluation.

The policy of maintaining excessively high interest rates and the subsequent appreciation of the Brazilian currency continued into the new century, even after President Luis Inácio Lula da Silva took office in 2003. All recent Brazilian administrations have continued to be cooperative with the international banking system and to insist upon, or at least not oppose, the overvaluation of the real. Between October 2002 and March 2008, the real gained 73 per cent in effective value against the US dollar. This of course presents a threat to Brazilian (particularly industrial) exports. But as Brazil's export commodities maintained their high prices, and as the export of industrialised goods continued to grow especially to other countries in Latin America, this overvaluation was not reflected in Brazil's current accounts until the first half of 2008.

Using high interest rates as the privileged instrument to control inflation has a monetarist hue, and leads to the appreciation of currencies.

194   *Victor Klagsbrunn*

This measure is supported by the IMF, not as an ongoing policy, but to stop the bleeding of foreign exchange in times of crisis. In contrast, the basic principles long outlined by the IMF, and included in the guidelines of the so-called Washington Consensus (see e.g. Williamson 2002), are to impose *competitive* interest rates. Nevertheless, the IMF and international financial markets accepted and sustained the policies of most emerging countries during the second half of the 1990s.

Argentina

Argentina employed similar if far more radical policies by adopting a currency board system of official parity to the dollar, established by law in 1991. This type of currency board – which behaves in a way similar to a fixed standard, previously tied to gold and now to the US dollar – prevents monetary authorities from adopting defensive devaluations in light of current account deficits. This causes external adversities to be reflected immediately and with great intensity in the reduction of economic activity.

One does not need to be clairvoyant to see that the legal adoption of parity with a key world currency makes it very difficult and painful to later abandon such a rigid scheme. Argentina maintained the parity of its currency with the dollar for an excessively long period and the adverse effects of this delay were far more pernicious than in other countries. The country as a result went through a period of economic and political turmoil. In the end, through a democratic election, a political line was victorious which once again embraced a radical line, this time a doctrine of confrontation with the international banking system under the stewardship of the IMF.

Argentina has since sought to avoid the appreciation of its currency. Since its current account balance returned to black in 2003, it has intervened energetically in the currency markets with the declared objective of increasing exports, discouraging imports, and promoting the growth and vitality of its domestic economy. We once again see a much more resolute policy than Brazil's, in the interests of domestic growth and avoiding the mortal consequences of overvaluing its currency and excessive dependency on capital inflows.

IMF policies, the Washington Consensus and currency appreciation

The maintenance of a competitive exchange rate, included in Williamson's fifth 'commandment' of the so-called Washington

Consensus, does not constitute anything novel.[2] In light of unforeseen events in the balance of payments, the IMF has for decades proposed or imposed the devaluation of currencies under attack *as the first step* in putting a country's house in order. This is simply because the entry of risk capital or capital invested at high interest rates cannot for long resist persistent trade deficits, especially in emerging economies dependent on world financial markets.

As is widely known, the IMF sanctions or even imposes policies of fiscal austerity, cutting expenditures and increasing taxation in order to put governments' accounts in order. The Fund is opposed to interference in the mechanisms of the marketplace (that is, with regard to prices) and proposes or imposes, in exchange for its support in emergency operations, avoidance of any type of subsidy or price support. On the other hand, the Fund very clearly demands changes in policies regarding remuneration of the work force and the correlation of forces in the labour market. These generally result in a reduction in real wages to ensure the greatest mobility of labour and to cut the aggregate demand, seen as the principal cause of inflation.

In order to eliminate the causes of inflation, seen as resulting from excess demand, the package is completed with the adoption of high interest rates. The establishing of the interest rate for government bonds depends on the willingness of the public to purchase government paper at a given rate (the minimum level of the market of interest rates) and the willingness of the government to pay out higher rates for its debts. Since it is lower-risk debt, all the other interest rates tend to accompany the government's own policy of paying high rates.

It should again be pointed out that for the IMF, interest rates should not remain high for long periods, only the length of time necessary to put the brakes on pent-up demand to avoid fuelling domestic price increases and to check the exit of foreign currency. This is the meaning of the fourth Williamson 'commandment', the only one he formulated in vague terms[3] – liberalising interest rates – and which the author preferred to rewrite later in even vaguer terms as 'liberalisation of financial markets'. To a certain extent Williamson is right in his correction of

---

[2] Williamson (2004): '5. A Competitive Exchange Rate. Note 2: I have seen it asserted that a competitive exchange rate is the same as an undervalued rate. Not so; a competitive rate is a rate that is not overvalued, i.e. that is *either* undervalued *or* correctly valued. My fifth point reflects a conviction that overvalued exchange rates are worse than undervalued rates, but a rate that is neither overvalued nor undervalued is better still.'

[3] Williamson (2002: 1): 'Liberalizing Interest Rates. In retrospect I wish I had formulated this in a broader way as financial liberalization, and stressed that views differed on how fast it should be achieved.'

196   *Victor Klagsbrunn*

the text since liberalisation of interest rates is something that no central bank does or wishes to do, precisely because this constitutes its most important instrument of short-term monetary policy, especially in light of the danger of an assault on the currency.

The 1990s was a decade of exuberant accumulation of financial surpluses coming from industrialised countries. This was the result of high interest rates in all financial markets, owing to the restrictive monetary policies in force in the principal industrial economies and the modest productive accumulation of the period. This was the case not only in the industrialised world but also in emerging countries. This situation continued during most of the 1990s, fuelled by the financial speculation – especially in emerging countries – that exploded in the various financial crises in Latin America, Asia and Russia at the end of the decade.

In the emerging countries, the inflow of funds and the high interest rates in place prevented their currencies from devaluating in order to accompany the rise of domestic prices, higher than in industrialised countries. Consequently, the problems of foreign trade merely worsened. In terms of the balance of payments, this bleeding of money in foreign trade was offset, to the extent possible, by the inflow of capital in pursuit of high interest rates.

Without an acceptable trade balance, at some point the inflow of capital is no longer sufficient and the ability to honour obligations comes into doubt. Any attempt to maintain the high quotations for local currencies merely acts to postpone the solution and to increase the effects of any unforeseen withdrawals of currency. This occurred in Brazil before its disorganised devaluation in 1999, and in Argentina – the last country to abandon its overvalued currency – as late as 2001.

The IMF – against what it had itself prescribed – now mobilised considerable resources to support attempts to maintain high quotations for the real one month before the devaluation of 1999, and for the Argentine peso in 2000 and 2001. How can this be explained? The intense political pressure exercised by the Fund's principal 'stakeholder' – the USA – both inside the Fund and in the international financial system is a large part of the story.[4] In the final analysis, the purpose of these

---

[4] It is worth comparing the press releases on the shielding of the Mexican peso and those pertaining to the emergency measures adopted by the Fund for the Brazilian and Argentine currencies. The 1 February 1995 press release on the shielding package for Mexico explicitly mentions the previous appreciation of the peso: 'At the same time, there was a substantial real appreciation of the new peso and a sharp increase in the external current account deficit' (p. 1) as well as the devaluation of the peso after the exchange crises: 'The substantial devaluation of the exchange rate that has taken place is expected to contribute to a significant improvement in the current account of the balance of payments' (p. 3). But the 2 December 1998 communication on the

Brazil and Argentina: contrasting approaches 197

emergency packages was to back administrations in both countries that applied policies very sympathetic to international banking institutions by privatising state-owned enterprises, liberalising financial markets and stimulating direct foreign investment.

They were thus programmes dictated by political considerations, which did not anticipate any way out, not even in the short run. In Brazil the central bank was obliged to abandon the overvaluation of the real less than two months after a gigantic loan package coordinated by the IMF. In Argentina the agony continued for years afterwards, provoking an even deeper and longer crisis which to a large extent dismantled the productive and financial systems of the country. They were politically determined rescues by an institution – the IMF – whose decisions are mainly taken by governments, which act politically.

Rising capital inflows and compliance with the demands of international creditors, 2003–2007

Brazil

As trade surpluses returned in 2003, Brazil enjoyed rapidly increasing capital inflows, both as direct investment and into its stock market. Emerging economies generally did well in these years and Brazil and Argentina were no exceptions. The period of surpluses – in trade, current accounts and capital inflows – reached its end in mid-2007. Current account deficits reappeared in 2008 due to the drastic but predictable decline in the trade surplus and increased remittances of profits and dividends by the subsidiaries of foreign companies, needed to cover falling profits in their headquarters. Figure 10.5 shows that Brazil's foreign debt has declined drastically since its high point in 2000, and very rapidly since 2003. Brazil's reserves also grew over these years, exceeding its total external debt in 2008. Already in 2000 the Brazilian monetary authority had exchanged Brady bonds for others (Globals) with lower interest rates and with longer periods of amortisation, which resulted in the nominal reduction of the foreign debt by two billion dollars.

In 2002, companies in the Brazilian private sector had difficulty turning over their foreign debt. For this reason Brazil's foreign accounts could only be balanced with resources from the IMF's Financial Assistance Program. The year 2003 witnessed increased international reserves, but only due to a further US\$7.3 billion owed to the IMF; this

shielding package for Brazil (Press Release 98/59), and those for the Argentine peso in 2000 (00/17) and 2001 (01/03 and 01/37), have no reference whatsoever to the overvalued exchange rate.

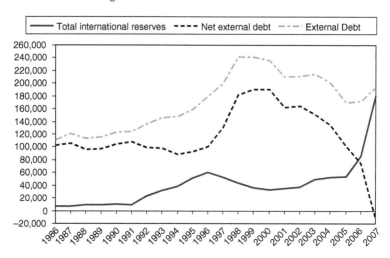

Figure 10.5. Brazil: international total reserves, total external debt and net external debt
Source: Banco Central do Brasil <www.bcb.gov.br>.

was the first year of the Lula government, which was initially distrusted by international financial markets. In 2004, total debt was particularly reduced by private debt, only 65 per cent of which was turned over (Banco Central do Brasil 2004: 147–8). In contrast, the foreign debt of the federal government remained stagnant, as can be seen below:

Beginning in September 2004, following several months of devaluation, the real began to appreciate against the US dollar. The trend accelerated over the following years with the central bank continuing its policy of rebuilding its international reserves, made possible by the high level of liquidity in international markets (Banco Central do Brasil 2005: 105–7). The central bank intensified its interventions in local exchange markets (either directly or by swap operations), buying foreign currency to slow the appreciation of the real. These interventions were insufficient as the Brazilian currency has continued to appreciate. Capital inflow continued at a swift pace due to Brazil's high interest rates, justified by rumblings of a new spike of inflation (though inflation was clearly losing ground).

The current account surpluses were used to liquidate Brazil's debts to the IMF (totalling some US$21 billion) and to the Paris Club. The authorities substituted the Brady bonds with others of a longer maturity, with the objective of prolonging the public foreign debt and reducing servicing costs. With this move, the gross foreign debt once again began to climb in 2006, though this was more than offset by the fantastic increase in the country's international reserves. The policy of

Brazil and Argentina: contrasting approaches   199

Table 10.1. *Brazil, external debt of central government*

Year	2000	2001	2002	2003	2004	2005	2006
External debt of central government (directly contracted) in US$ millions	72,592	71,191	75,323	76,729	75,345	75,161	63,942

Source: Banco Central do Brasil.

increasing reserves while maintaining the level of public foreign debt is costly; US government bonds yield much less than what is paid to service the debt. The current account surplus and the dollars acquired in the domestic market could be better used to liquidate a portion of the foreign debt. The Brazilian Central Bank, however, justifies the policy by arguing that huge international reserves increase global confidence in the Brazilian economy. The central bank maintains its public foreign debt at an unnecessarily high level; reasons for this policy have not been explained and could only be the subject of speculation.

Argentina

As is well known, beginning in 1998 Argentina suffered a long process of deteriorating foreign accounts and a dire domestic economic situation. Over the course of 2001 the Minister of the Economy recognised there was no way for Argentina to repay its foreign debt. In December of that year he announced a default, only months after the IMF had conceded an enormous stand-by credit package of US$20 billion. It was not until January 2002 that Argentina finally abandoned the parity of its peso with the dollar. Negotiations with creditors were concluded during the government of Néstor Kirchner, who managed to exchange government bonds (total value: US$104.4 billion) for new paper worth 35 per cent of their face value. In addition, the government in 2005 imposed a longer repayment period for its remaining debt (a record forty-two years) and slashed the interest rate from 5 to 2 per cent per year for the first ten years. Such results were previously unheard of in restructuring sovereign debt, and led to a sharp reduction of Argentina's external debt (see Figure 10.6).

This debt restructuring was achieved after three years of growth in the Argentine economy and its international reserves. As the country no longer seemed to be in such dire straits, many wondered if the Argentine government could not have agreed to a somewhat higher payment. The government's position, however, enjoyed tremendous popular support,

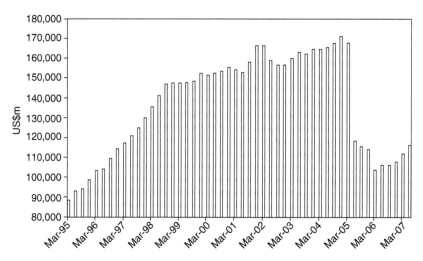

Figure 10.6. Argentina: total external debt, 1995–2007
Source: Banco Central de la República Argentina.

forcing the majority of creditors to either accept the proposal or to remain in doubt as to whether they would some day receive something for their paper.

The reaction of the financial markets and the international ratings agencies in the wake of the unilateral restructuring is telling. As the indicators measuring the sustainability of Argentina's foreign debt improved, the rating agencies in quick succession improved the standing of its sovereign bonds. Highly liquid international financial markets in 2005 and 2006 began accepting the new papers with a spread comparable to that of countries with a very different recent history of payments, such as Brazil (see Figures 10.7 and 10.8).

Conclusion: contrasting policies and attitudes to international market pressure

Brazil, the prodigy of the IMF and the international banking community, takes pride in its record in the serial emerging market crises (see Banco Central do Brasil 2005: 107). On the basis of its adherence to Washington's teachings, it tries to extricate itself from the image of an emerging country beset with problems, particularly in comparison to Argentina. Ever since the crises in Mexico in 1995, in Asia in 1997, in Russia in 1998, and in Argentina beginning in 1998, the Central Bank of Brazil has attempted to convince international financial markets,

Brazil and Argentina: contrasting approaches 201

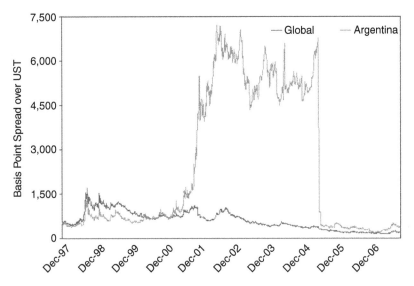

Figure 10.7. EMBI spread Argentina vs. global, 1998–2007
Source: JP Morgan. Cited by LatinFocus.

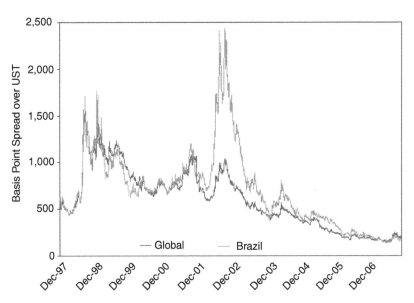

Figure 10.8. EMBI spread Brazil vs. global, 1998–2007
Source: JP Morgan Securities Inc., Emerging Markets Research.

202   Victor Klagsbrunn

with limited success, that its case is different. More recently, Brazil has benefited from favourable economic circumstances to ease the pain of adjustment, enjoying growth, a sound external balance and debt load.

But Argentina's situation following its financial earthquake has also been quite enviable. Argentina's international reserves grew tremendously between 2004 and 2007; the weight of servicing its external debt, at least for the first ten years after the mega-swap, is significantly lighter than Brazil's. While it is true that the Argentine government's confrontational stance towards the IMF and creditor banks has frightened creditors, this is something all involved must learn to live with. Recent experience shows that Fund directors are quite capable of accepting political *faits accomplis* in the countries where they operate (IMF 2004b).

The argument is not that default is the best policy. Yet when confrontation with creditor banks brings the IMF on stage, the situation becomes economically and politically dominated by governments of wealthier countries – whose decisions are also political, given their close ties to their own private sector financial institutions. Nonetheless, the actions of the Argentine government demonstrate that debtor economies, responding to democratic social and political pressures and acting on the basis of their sovereignty, can achieve results under adverse conditions. Like developed countries, they too have an obligation to negotiate considering their own domestic political and economic imperatives, which are not necessarily those of (private) creditors. The performance of the Argentine government demonstrates that there may be a far wider margin of manoeuvre than is generally thought to exist. It is unrealistic to try to impound the assets of the debtor country; private creditors, the IMF and creditor governments alike will find it difficult to force indebted countries with a current account surplus to adopt policies that challenge the government's domestic and democratic imperatives.

In other words, when confronted with adverse conditions, both creditors and debtors are forced to the negotiating table. The attitude the Argentine government assumed in the negotiations was key. Precisely because the country had already passed the worst of the crisis, creditors had an interest in seeing Argentina restructure its debt in the hope that at least limited debt servicing would be restored. The comparison with Brazil shows that the *via crucis* of the neighbour to the south was initially more painful, but that in the end Argentina found its future development less compromised by past debt. Assuming that the impact of the sub-prime crisis does not compromise the situation unduly and/or enduringly, Argentina may continue to take a path to economic growth that does not entail currency appreciation, a path that creates incentives to export and, by inhibiting imports, to produce locally.

In light of the government's policy to protect the peso from overvaluation, large multinational companies were in the 'period of calm' beginning to invest in Argentina to take advantage of its conditions of production and its exchange rate that favours exports within MERCOSUR. Foreign capital is attracted to Argentina, as to all countries, when there is growth in the market, either internal or external. This is also true of large Brazilian companies more and more inclined to invest in their neighbour country.

The ability of countries to pursue more autonomous policies depends on the international situation, their foreign accounts and the political priorities of government officials. Pressure from international markets to accept the 'generally applicable' rules of 'rational' economic policy will of course try to ensure that external debt servicing remains the priority. But depending on the degree of domestic public support, creditor banks appear realistic enough to accept *faits accomplis* when national governments do not accept what the IFIs attempt to impose – at least for a period.

This applies not only to the emerging economies: the IMF is also a critic of the behaviour of core economies, though neither the Fund nor creditor banks so far have the power to enforce changes. While emerging economies have had their share of financial turmoil from 1980 to 2002, (so far) it seems that the United States and other central economies will be the principal victims of the crisis that began in 2008. The developed country sub-prime financial crisis represents another serious twist in the story, the full effects of which are not yet clear. The G20, Bank for International Settlements and other international governance bodies will assist as central banks in the core economies come in by supporting their banks. It is a fair bet that it will then be clear to all that the central economies always decide their own economic policies (including those that affect international finance) on the basis of their national interests – a right rarely claimed by emerging markets.

11 Global markets, national alliances and financial transformations in East Asia

Xiaoke Zhang

In East Asia – as in many other developing regions – the liberalisation and globalisation of financial markets over the past two decades has led to the exponential growth of stock markets in traditionally bank-based systems. The increased importance of equity finance has fuelled incentives for industrial firms to rely on stock markets instead of banks for external financing. The collective outcome of these individual choices has been the rapid securities market orientation of national financial systems. East Asian financial capitalisms, however, have not converged on the liberal market model epitomised by Britain and the United States. As we will see below, regulatory regimes, market operations and corporate governance models continue to diverge from those of financial liberalism.

The central proposition advanced here complements the major themes of this volume by viewing successful financial market reform and governance as a function of interacting systemic and domestic factors. It contains the normative implication that while global market integration has reshaped national institutions, the international architecture developed to manage the process needs to be sensitive to policy imperatives associated with national configurations of power and interest: effectiveness requires the articulation of national preferences on the input side, and policy space on the output side. Otherwise national systems will likely react against the architecture, impairing the necessary political cooperation underpinning regional and global governance.

Since the late 1990s, structural reforms promulgated in the context of the new international financial architecture have reinforced pressures for the marketisation of financial systems in emerging markets. Regardless of national differences in the political underpinnings of financial development, these reforms were seen to have essentially universal application (Rodrik 1999). However, as shown in this and several other chapters in this volume, there are real and potential tensions between harmonising liberal market structures and national institutional legacies and political

Markets, alliances and transformations in East Asia 205

imperatives. Large-scale convergence of national systems on a particular model of financial governance is thus unlikely in the near future, as the evidence on the adoption of global standards (Chapter 5) and Basel II (Chapter 6) illustrate. If this realisation is to be better reflected in the output side of global financial governance, it is paramount that we better understand the interplay of global and national forces that generate the actual trajectories of national financial development. This chapter therefore exposes the complex interplay of external and internal factors that characterises financial reform, heightening the need for global governance standards to consider input legitimacy in order to make them fit better with national political conditions.

In more concrete terms, this chapter aims to explain a process of institutional change in national financial systems that has produced apparently converging but non-liberal outcomes. It does so by focusing on two prominent East Asian emerging markets, Malaysia and Taiwan. The cases were selected chiefly because national reforms in both countries have led to exponential stock market growth. From 1988 to 2005, the ratio of stock market capitalisation to GDP jumped from 59 to 143 per cent in Malaysia and from 67 to 134 per cent in Taiwan (Beck 2007). Direct financing by private firms from stock and bond issues in Malaysia rose from a mere 10 per cent of total external funds in 1980–5 to 43 per cent in 1999–2003 (BNM 1996: Chart IX.2; BNM 2006: Chart 1.1). In Taiwan, such financing jumped from 14 per cent in 1982–6 to 38 per cent in 1998–2002 (Shi and Chen 2003: 26). Financial structures and corporate finance became so capital market based that in the importance of equity finance, Malaysia and Taiwan began to rival Britain and the United States. Their financial systems are among the most capital market oriented in the world (Demirgüç-Kunt and Levine 2001; Levine 2002).

But crucial differences remained. While financial structures became increasingly capital market based, the outsider model of corporate governance through the enforcement of shareholder rights and the market for corporate control did not materialise in either Malaysia or Taiwan. Second, and in contrast to the traditional market-based model where banks stay clear of stock markets, Malaysian and Taiwanese bankers have acted as market makers. And finally, while the Anglo-American model is based on securities regulation by independent agencies, Malaysian and Taiwanese regulatory agencies have operated under the direct influence of state and societal actors aiming to harness stock markets to pursue their policy interests.

Clearly, then, Malaysia and Taiwan share striking similarities in terms of the growth of their securities markets, while at the same time

206   *Xiaoke Zhang*

offering a contrasting model to the Anglo-American model of financial governance.[1] This chapter aims to account for the political process through which financial transformations have followed apparently converging patterns but have diverged significantly from typical cases of financial liberalism. It locates the sources of institutional change and continuity in Malaysian and Taiwanese finance in the interaction between international market forces and domestic interest alliances. This interactive process has not only oriented the national financial architecture towards stock markets but also made market-oriented transformations different from the neoliberal paradigm. The argument both contrasts with and complements the central proposition of Chapter 5 (by Walter) that emphasises external pressures as the primary driving force behind policy and market reforms but wherein national pressures often yield mock compliance with global standards.

The chapter first specifies the analytical framework and then provides empirical support for the argument. It concludes by discussing policy implications for the good governance of the international financial system.

Global markets, national alliances and market changes

The shift towards market-oriented financial systems in Malaysia and Taiwan was the result of actors reconstructing the political underpinnings of national financial governance in line with their changing preferences. Private market agents, public financiers and politicians pursued capital market-oriented reforms and crafted new institutions to enhance market performance, to improve policy-making efficiency and to achieve policy objectives. By altering the constraints and opportunities they faced within domestic settings, global forces enhanced their preference for marketised finance. Structural pressures and domestic interests thus combined to facilitate the emergence and consolidation of de facto alliances for pro-market reforms, policies and institutions.

Private bankers in Malaysia and Taiwan became champions of the stock market largely due to changes in bank-industry relations. Against the backdrop of liberalisation and globalisation in the 1980s and 1990s, such relations became increasingly distant as banks gained greater freedom to manage their assets. This was manifest in the steady decline of banks' asset portfolio exposure to industry. In Malaysia the ratio of

---

[1] It should be clear that there are important historical differences between the American and British financial systems, particularly with regard to the development of corporate bond markets and regulatory frameworks.

loans to manufacturing industries to total bank loans dwindled from 25 per cent in 1989 to 16 per cent in 2002 (BNM various issues); in Taiwan it declined from 27 per cent in 1986 to 15 per cent in 2000 (CBC various issues). While big business groups began to diversify into the banking sector in the 1990s, many had their core businesses in property, construction, finance and other industries with short-term horizons (Amsden and Chu 2003: 119–60; Gomez 2004a).

The increasingly arms-length relationship led banks to define their interests in isolation from those of industrial firms and to shun corporate investments with long payout periods. Global market integration not only expanded the possibilities for banks to engage in short-term transactions but forced them to do so as mobile international capital dwarfed their capacity to provide cheap funds for investment. As their lending operations became short-termist, banks sought to maintain liquid asset positions and found stock markets excellent outlets for lending. Private bankers increasingly came to see stock markets as vehicles to enhance their profitability; they have thus had strong incentives to push for stock market growth through pro-market regulatory change.

In their efforts to push for such change, private bankers sometimes found allies in the large corporate sector. Large firms, due to their strong capital base and cash flow, often enjoyed access to relatively cheap funds in the stock market. Stock market growth decreased their dependency on bank loans and, more importantly, shielded them from intervention by state-owned institutions. On the other hand, the growing disintegration of the bank-industry nexus reduced traditional sources of industrial financing and forced large firms to raise funds in domestic and even international capital markets. New entrepreneurs seeking to expand venture capital activities, especially in high-tech and capital-intensive sectors, found bank credit inadequate and were willing to go public. They resorted to direct financing and thus supported the growth of stock markets (Felker 2001; Chow 2005).

While corporate finance became increasingly market oriented, shares of listed and non-listed firms often remained in the hands of relatively small groups of block shareholders in both Malaysia and Taiwan. The private benefits of concentrated ownership – the ability to expropriate minority shareholders and invest in high-risk projects – are great; blockholders have thus been at the forefront of resistance to corporate governance changes towards the Anglo-American shareholder model. As blockholders typically controlled more than 50 per cent of listed firms and dominated corporate decision-making, market-based contests for control have been rare in Malaysia and Taiwan, as has been the case in many other East Asian economies (Chang 2006).

208   *Xiaoke Zhang*

Private market agents, particularly bankers, were well-positioned to translate their preferences into policy outcomes, partly because they maintained close ties with financial and regulatory authorities. More importantly, financial globalisation rendered state financial agencies and their long-standing policy instruments ill-suited for market regulation. In contrast, private financial firms led the way in product development and were heavily involved in shaping market rules. Crucial know-how is today the proprietary domain of market actors, which state regulators find difficult to match. Increasingly they have had to draw upon the expertise of the private sector and rely upon public-private cooperation for governing rapidly changing financial markets. Such relationships provided private financiers with enhanced entry into financial policy-making.

Private sector preferences did not produce pro-market reforms on their own; central bankers and finance ministry officials formulated reform strategies in line with their desire to diversify the financial sector and improve its efficiency in the face of growing competitive pressure. The continued process of financial liberalisation in the 1980s and 1990s rendered interest rate and credit controls (on which financial authorities had traditionally relied for achieving policy objectives) increasingly ineffective. They were thus keen to supplement these instruments with open market operations, particularly in the money market. The money market in Malaysia and Taiwan, however, remained shallow and inactive, mainly because there were few active participants. The growth of stock markets – which encouraged investors and market institutions to obtain funds from the money market to finance stock purchases and market operations – would thus lead to a deeper and more active money market and facilitate official efforts to control money supply through open market operations.[2]

Alongside their own policy preferences, public financiers took into account the desire of their private counterparts to maintain liquid asset structures and expand income bases through stock transactions. As the fortunes of private banks were increasingly tied to such transactions, financial authorities grew more inclined to promote stock markets in order to bolster the profitability of the banking sector. Given their symbiotic relationship, public financiers have been sensitive to the preferences and concerns of the private financial community (Wang 1996: 93–133; Gomez and Jomo 1997; Guo *et al.* 2000; Gomez 2002).

---

[2] Author interviews with former deputy governors of the CBC/finance ministers, Taipei, 3 and 13 November 2002, and with a former assistant governor of the BNM, Kuala Lumpur, 3 July 2005.

Markets, alliances and transformations in East Asia 209

Private and public financiers contended for control over financial policy within a broader structure of political interests and power that supported their pro-market preferences. The political incentive to facilitate market-oriented changes derived in part from politicians' desire to use the stock market to privatise state-owned enterprises (SOEs). In Malaysia and Taiwan, privatisation programmes began to gather momentum in the late 1980s and 1990s as political leaders sought to improve national economic competitiveness in the face of systemic market pressure. These programmes stimulated politicians to promote stock markets so privatised companies could get listed and their shares adequately subscribed (Semkow 1994: 173–7; Jomo 2003: 110–32).

In Malaysia, market changes were also associated with the ostensible agenda of inter-ethnic redistribution. As government controls over banks were progressively weakened in the 1980s, leaders of the United Malay National Organisation (UMNO), the dominant party in the ruling National Front coalition, increasingly turned to the stock market to widen corporate shareholding among *bumiputera* or Malay investors. In the 1990s, many *bumiputera* individuals and institutions acquired controlling interests in the securities industry (Chin and Jomo 2001), prompting UMNO politicians to more vigorously develop the stock market to ensure 'indigenous' dominance in the commanding heights of the national economy.

Government efforts to foster the growth of capital markets were also part of larger strategic objectives. Throughout the 1990s, Malaysian and Taiwanese political leaders in their jockeying for foreign capital, economic status and regional influence promoted their respective capital cities as important financial centres in the Asia-Pacific region. Promoting stock markets and financial market economies – the primary institutions of regional financial centres – became the linchpin of this strategy.

In Taiwan, efforts to promote a financial market economy have geopolitical significance as well. With its international recognition diminishing, Taiwan was a diplomatic pariah in the 1980s and 1990s. To bolster its precarious security position, governments since the early 1990s – under both the Nationalist Party or Kuomintang (KMT) and the Democratic Progressive Party (DPP) – have been bidding for membership in international economic organisations. Political elites supported a more market-oriented financial system as a sign of their commitment to market-led development and conformity to the neoliberal credos espoused by international financial institutions and leading industrial countries. They hoped pro-market policies would promote the overseas profile of the island and render it more admissible to multilateral institutions and processes (Noble 1997; Chao 2002: 188–90).

While political leaders decided on the overall direction of market reforms, they depended on private agents for their formulation and implementation. Private banks and firms possessed the detailed and up-to-date information on financial markets and changing economic and business conditions needed to effectively implement policies. While state elites relied on private market agents to achieve their political objectives, the latter used the favourable policy environment to advance their own agendas. They thus formed a de facto policy alliance to create a new market order in line with their interests and goals.

This chapter argues that fundamental shifts in the financial architecture of Malaysia and Taiwan have been predicated on the emergence and consolidation of a powerful pro-capital market alliance – a political construction initiated and promoted by private market agents, public financiers and political elites with a shared interest in market-oriented change as a response to economic and political imperatives both at home and abroad. It has transformed the political structure of finance in which the norms that underpinned bank-based systems have been reinvented and market-friendly values embraced. In Malaysia and Taiwan, market-oriented change reflected the agency and ability of political actors to break through institutional heritages to build new market orders.

External pressures were certainly at play in the orientation towards stock markets in Malaysia and Taiwan and accounted for the simultaneity of their efforts to enact market-oriented reforms in 1980s. But these pressures were transmuted by and through the interest alliances of private and public actors. Such alliances facilitated the absorption of market-oriented practices into domestic policy and the national institutions of financial governance. State and societal actors manipulated systemic pressures and pursued their reform strategies to align financial market changes to their own policy goals. This interactive process where international structural trends were embedded within domestic processes while being reconfigured by the interests of political actors explains the institutional divergences from the liberal-market paradigm.

Financial transformations in Malaysia and Taiwan

This section examines the political processes through which Malaysian and Taiwanese financial market structures changed, particularly after the Asian crisis of 1997–8. The purpose here is not to provide a full account of financial transformations over the past decades (which is far beyond the scope of this chapter) but to illustrate the causal links between global forces, domestic alliances and market changes.

Malaysia

In the late 1980s and early 1990s, financial policy-makers in Malaysia intensified their efforts to promote stock markets by allowing banks to increase lending for share purchases, by removing barriers to portfolio investments by foreigners, and by privatising SOEs. These were accompanied by longer-term policy changes that liberalised the institutional framework for the trading of shares, modernised the trading system of the Kuala Lumpur Stock Exchange (KLSE), and fostered the growth of institutional investors such as unit trusts and investment funds. The reform efforts squared closely with UMNO leaders' desire to increase wealth in *bumiputera* hands. They were supported by private financiers who, reluctant to commit to long-term industrial investments, found the grass greener in the asset management and stock-broking niches (*MB* (*Malaysian Business*) 1–15 May 1990: 47–8; Scott and Wellons 1996: 24). Pro-market regulatory changes set the stage for the rapid growth of stock markets in the early and mid-1990s.

In the wake of the Asian crisis in late 1997 and early 1998, the stock market tumbled amid a massive unloading of shares, particularly by foreign investors. Financial authorities moved swiftly to rescue the stock market by rehabilitating stock-broking firms and directing institutional investors to bolster share prices. These efforts, however, failed to stem the market's downward spiral as underlying economic conditions continued to worsen. Looming conflicts between Prime Minister Mahathir Mohamad and his deputy Anwar Ibrahim over a range of economic and political issues further unnerved investors and depressed market sentiment (MacIntyre 2003: 79–90). The political uncertainty was short-circuited in September 1998 when Anwar was ousted and Mahathir centralised policy-making power in his own hands. The government quickly introduced capital controls which eliminated the offshore ringgit market and prohibited the repatriation of portfolio funds for twelve months.

While the economic effects of capital controls were at best mixed (Kaplan and Rodrik 2001; Jomo 2004), there is little doubt that there was an explicit economic as well as political agenda to revive the stock market. Mahathir himself made it abundantly clear that he intended to rescue the stock market through capital controls and was obviously elated when the market rose by an astonishing 38 per cent following their announcement (Mahathir 2003). The controls were successfully installed in part because they had a political constituency in the financial community: technocrats in the central bank and the finance ministry eager to restore financial market stability (*ID* (*Investor Digest*)

September 1998: 6–8). Private financiers, whose assets were wrecked and profits reduced by the battered stock market, applauded the controls which enlivened transactions (*ID* September 1998: 6–8; Johnson and Mitton 2003).

With the capital controls in place, financial authorities turned to recapitalising the banks and creating an institution to manage non-performing loans. Given the inextricable ties between banking institutions, stockbrokers and securities industries, these efforts aimed to revive not only the banking sector but the stock market as well. To further strengthen the pivotal role of banks in the revitalisation of the financial market, authorities pushed for a merger plan to consolidate seventy-odd commercial banks, merchant banks and finance companies into thirty institutions under ten anchor groups. Big banks, which successfully lobbied to be designated anchor institutions by dint of their government ownership or connections to UMNO politicians, saw the consolidation as an opportunity to expand their business and enhance their control of the financial sector (Gomez 2002: 109; Jomo 2003: 224).

The stock market steadily gained ground in early and mid-1999 against a backdrop of ample liquidity in the financial system as well as encouraging progress in bank recapitalisation. The stock market recovery, however, was short-lived: it began to dip again in late 1999 and remained bearish in 2000, despite 8.3 per cent growth that year. Alongside contagion effects from the major regional and US markets, the slow pace of corporate reforms and the selective bail-outs of business elites dampened the confidence of investors, particularly foreign investors. Despite the easing of capital controls in 2000, foreign investors who had bolstered the earlier vigour of the Malaysian bourse now shied away from it (*FEER* (*Far East Economic Review*) 29 June 2000: 51; Rodan 2004: 128–31).

The political costs of the dismal stock market were looming large in the minds of top UMNO politicians. Millions of *bumiputera* investors in unit trusts, many of them poor villagers, saw their investments and life savings eroded. The bail-out of business elites, in contrast to the anxieties and hardships endured by unit investors, fuelled widespread discontent. This could not have come at a worse moment as the government was confronted by a growing reform movement galvanised by popular outrage over Anwar's purge. The opposition rode on this social and political ferment to make surprisingly large gains in the general elections of late 1999 (Khoo 2000). For Mahathir and his associates, a key to placating disgruntled *bumiputera* investors, stemming the opposition's electoral gains and maintaining the hegemonic position of the UMNO rested in getting the stock market back on the high-growth track. This in turn required the resurrection of investor confidence. Despite ranting about the iniquities of the global financial system, Mahathir worked to lure back foreign portfolio investors by accelerating corporate and market reforms.

Early 2001 witnessed a flurry of policies pertaining to the speedy reform of corporate governance. The government introduced stronger, regularised procedures in the corporate sector emphasising transparency and good governance.[3] To implement the regulatory reforms, Mahathir appointed young technocrats to the major regulatory and corporate restructuring agencies while edging out the finance minister who had been closely associated with the unpopular bail-out deals (*Asiamoney* December 2001: 25–9; *FEER* 14 June 2001: 24–8). This paved the way for the government to strip business elites who had benefited from the bail-outs of their positions and assets, force major shareholders of conglomerates to bear their own losses, and direct state-owned enterprises to reform the management structures that spawned corruption. In acknowledgement of these initiatives, leading US credit rating agencies upgraded their evaluation of sovereign risk in Malaysia while foreign portfolio investors flocked back during the second half of 2001, sparking an 18 per cent rally on the stock market by early 2002 (*FEER* 14 March 2002: 42).

Technocrats followed up with more liberalising measures to place the stock market on a sustained growth trajectory. Alongside corporate restructuring, they prepared the Financial Sector Masterplan (FSM) during 2000 in close consultation with private financiers (*ID* March 2001: 16–7; *NST* (*New Strait Times*) 29 December 2000: 26, 29 March 2001: 23). The document outlined a ten-year strategy for financial markets which began its staged implementation in March 2001. Several key regulatory changes, implemented in the first stage of the FSM during 2001–3, allowed banks, financial companies and stockbroking firms within banking groups to fully engage in investment banking and fund management under an integrated legal entity; the new rules also allowed well-capitalised banking institutions to lend, virtually without limits, for share purchases (BNM 2002: 115–22; 2003: 116–9; 2004: 207–8). These changes not only facilitated the efforts of banking groups to attain higher levels of efficiency and economies of scale but also enabled them to provide a wide range of banking and securities-related products and services.

---

[3] For more detailed discussion on these regulatory changes, see *Asiamoney* April 2001: 55–6; *ID* May 2001: 4–14; Rodan 2004: 131–6.

214   *Xiaoke Zhang*

The market-oriented reforms reflected the long-running interests of bankers to control the securities industry as well as the desire of public financiers to improve banking efficiency and stock market performance. As the ownership structure of financial markets became ever more concentrated, private financiers gained enhanced political leverage. Policy favours were provided to them as quid pro quos for their cooperation in the design and implementation of the FSM. They now had full access to all market segments of the securities industry and committed more loanable funds to share purchases, unit trusts and other securities investments. Combined with steady foreign portfolio inflows, this greatly enhanced the liquidity and trading activity of the stock market. The merger of the Malaysian Exchange of Securities Dealing and Automated Quotation, the exchange established in 1997 for high-tech and high-growth companies, with the KLSE in early 2002 and the further streamlining of listing procedures encouraged an unprecedented number of firms to go public. Over the next three years, the Malaysian bourse remained buoyant, with market capitalisation steadily increasing. Even Mahathir's shock announcement in mid-2002 that he was resigning as prime minister did not disrupt the upswing in the stock market.

While post-crisis policy and institutional reforms appear to have put capital market growth on a sustained footing, they did not signify unreserved convergence towards the liberal market model. Nowhere was this more manifest than in the continuation of concentrated corporate structures in which controlling shareholders remained dominant and minority and institutional investors subordinate (Cheah 2005; Gourevitch and Shinn 2005: 232–7). This prevented the development of an active market for corporate control and an outside model of corporate governance. Market-oriented reforms were initiated in response to external pressures and development imperatives, but the enactment of these reforms reflected the political dynamics of interest alliances in which UMNO leaders were beholden to influential *bumiputera* bankers and business tycoons who were eager to keep outsiders at bay. Efforts made by Abdullah Badawi, Mahathir's reform-minded successor, to change the oligarchical corporate structure often hit snags when they conflicted with business interests (Ooi 2008; Walter 2008: 120–5). While the financial system has become more market oriented, the mode of corporate governance is likely to remain divergent from the essence of financial liberalism.

Taiwan

In the late 1980s, financial officials embarked on reforms to promote the growth of the Taipei Stock Exchange (TSE) in order to channel

Taiwan's swelling trade surpluses into industrial investment and to more effectively control money supply (Woo and Liu 1994; Shea 1995). Over the next few years, the government passed numerous amendments to the Securities and Exchange Law and implemented a wide range of reforms that allowed banks to engage in the full spectrum of securities businesses, promoted institutional investment and provided more favourable policies for share trading. These reforms resulted in a sustained boom for the Taiwanese bourse over the first half of the 1990s.

The weaknesses of bank-based financing exposed by the Asian crisis of 1997–8 as well as the looming domestic banking crisis in 1999–2000 underlined the importance of avoiding excessive reliance on bank credit and developing a more market-based corporate capital structure. There was renewed consensus among key policy-makers that a well-developed capital market would help Taiwan cope with pressures created by globalisation (Shen 2005). The economic rationale for further market-oriented change was reinforced by the desire of political leaders to promote the TSE as a tool to boost the international visibility and status of Taiwan. The plan to turn Taiwan into a regional financial centre made a forceful comeback in 2001 when the government crafted a more practical strategy – with pro-market reforms at its centre – to achieve this goal (Ye 2005). These considerations generated bipartisan interest in the further development of the stock market and rendered the ruling and opposition parties willing to cooperate on major reform policies designed to strengthen market institutions.

Enhanced official interest in market-oriented reforms was tied to the efforts of banks and securities firms to advance their own policy agendas. Following the financial crisis, private banks scaled down their lending to the manufacturing sector (Chen and Wang 2005) and pushed for official intervention to bolster declining share prices; as a large proportion of their assets was tied up in stock market transactions, they actively contributed to a stock market stabilisation fund (*FEER* 10 December 1998: 72; *TianXia* 1 February 2001: 154). Private bankers also sided with financial technocrats against industrial and planning officials who, wishing to direct more funds to small firms, opposed such a fund (*EIUCR-Taiwan* 1st quarter 1999: 21). As securities-related businesses became an increasingly important source of income and profit, private financiers pressed for full access to the securities industry. In June 2001 the government pushed through the bills that cleared the way for the establishment of financial holding companies structured around leading banks; the new legislation allowed these companies to operate right across the financial services spectrum.

216   *Xiaoke Zhang*

Despite efforts to boost share prices, the TSE remained depressed for over a year following the Asian crisis amid growing financial sector weaknesses, political uncertainties created by the electoral alternation of power and the global economic downturn. As a large proportion of Taiwan's population owned listed shares,[4] the continued underperformance of the stock market had grave political consequences, with economic woes undermining the credibility of the new DPP government (Wu 2002). With market-rescuing efforts proving ineffective and domestic investors unnerved by unsettled political and market conditions, the government had no choice but to turn to foreign investors.

Until the late 1990s Taiwan had operated a tightly controlled capital account and had maintained extensive restrictions on foreign portfolio inflows, primarily due to concerns over the impact of foreign capital inflows on macroeconomic stability (Zhang 2003a). But with domestic investors shying away from the TSE and politicians under pressure to revitalise the stock market, the government had little choice but to turn to foreign investors and further liberalise the capital account.

While domestic pressures were sufficient to produce policy change, this does not preclude a role for external forces. Following the financial crisis, many Asian states in order to revive their stock markets engaged in a competitive deregulation of restrictions on foreign portfolio inflows. This intercountry rivalry forced the Taiwanese government to eventually abolish the system of only allowing qualified foreign institutional investors to buy shares, and to scrap the investment cap for foreign institutional investors in 2003. The policy shift prompted Morgan Stanley, a leading international investment bank, to increase the weighting of Taiwanese stocks in its regional stock indices, which many global investors used as a guide. Foreign portfolio investment began to flow back and kept the TSE buoyant for the next few years.

In parallel with their efforts to stabilise the demand side of the stock market, financial authorities moved to broaden its supply side. Trading in TSE-listed securities had traditionally concentrated on a small set of big companies, mainly due to the reluctance of major shareholders to trade their control shares. In the early and mid-1990s the government enforced stricter shareholding dispersal requirements which achieved a modicum of success. Frustrated in their attempts to open up closely held companies,

---

[4] More than 30 per cent of Taiwan's population owned stocks in the late 1990s (*Forbes*, 1 June 1998: 122), compared with 8 per cent in Korea and 26 per cent in the UK in the period 1997–2000 (ASX 2003: 2).

policy-makers in the post-crisis period turned to fiscal incentives as an alternative way to promote listings and increase tradable shares. In 1998 the finance ministry eliminated the taxation of company dividends paid to shareholders; this was followed by the integration of business taxes which, as part of the overall official effort to boost investment activity, removed the double taxation of shareholders and investors.

There were, however, limits to how far the government could cut taxes in order to promote listings, mainly due to Taiwan's rising budget deficits in the aftermath of the financial crisis and the ensuing recession (Chen 2005). Securities market regulators thus explored the possibility of easing listing requirements and streamlining cumbersome application procedures. This policy change also reflected growing demand for the reform of listing rules from high-profile Taiwanese companies that increasingly resorted to the capital market for long-term financing as well as from private financiers who stood to benefit from a broader market (Economist Intelligence Unit, November 2000: 28; Shi and Chen 2003). The relaxation of listing rules, combined with fiscal incentives, saw the number of listed companies on the TSE more than double from 338 in 1996 to 697 in 2004.

The impact of fiscal incentives and listing deregulation on the breadth of stock trading was further magnified by the renewed efforts of the government to privatise SOEs. In late 1996 the bipartisan National Development Conference decided to accelerate privatisation in its aim to broaden the capital market, boost state offers and improve the declining competitiveness of the Taiwanese economy. Despite its pro-labour stance, the DPP government stuck with the reform programme and saw through the privatisation of many major SOEs, in defiance of strong protests from trade unions (Wu 2003). Between 1998 and 2004 the government transferred six large manufacturing and transportation companies to private hands and sold its shares in nine financial institutions to the public, significantly increasing the market capitalisation of the TSE (CEPD 2005).

Conclusion: implications for global financial governance

While this chapter demonstrated how structural pressures and interest alliances have interacted in the financial transformation of Malaysia and Taiwan, the argument developed here has broader implications for current debates about the political and normative underpinnings of global financial governance. Although the case selection is not broad enough to allow fully generalisable conclusions, these two examples of national reform in a global context provide a number of important points for further discussion.

First of all, while liberal market pressures have generated similar patterns of financial market change in Malaysia and Taiwan, they have not confirmed any linear or uncompromising shift towards financial liberalism. As noted earlier, increasingly marketised financial systems in Malaysia and Taiwan have displayed important divergences from the Anglo-American model of finance in modes of corporate governance, stock market operations and securities regulatory regimes. There is thus much greater indeterminacy in the transformation of national financial systems than the 'new' international financial architecture implied. In Malaysia and Taiwan, as in many other emerging market economies, market-oriented change did not preclude nationally distinctive policy paradigms and regulatory regimes unamenable to homogenising forces.

This means that international policy-makers must adequately recognise the ways in which common external stimuli for national market change unleashed by global market integration are mediated by the incentives, preferences and strategies of domestic political actors. When such mediations are factored into the analysis of national capitalisms, it seems far from inevitable that market changes would converge towards a universal model of financial development and governance. Institutional changes, even in response to systemic factors, are likely to involve complicated and differentiated political processes shaped by domestic power structures. This also suggests that divergent political processes may sustain convergent changes across national political economies. Finding the right balance between legitimate national political processes and systemic pressures for institutional change is a crucial normative underpinning for global financial governance.

Finally, the empirical findings of this chapter strongly support one of the major arguments of this volume: that the market-oriented model of financial governance does not transfer easily from one national context to another, while domestic dynamics will almost certainly mediate the impact of systemic pressures on patterns of market reform. This underlines the need for greater attention to the diversity of national political structures that underpin financial markets, and for more policy space than is currently allowed in the international financial architecture erected and consolidated during the period of calm. If reform is once more on the cards due to the outbreak of crisis, a legitimate and effective approach to global financial governance needs to take into account national configurations of political power and interest. Equally important, if national financial systems in East Asia are not expected to converge towards the liberal-market model and if the political underpinnings of financial markets remain different, mutual respect for national differences and policy spaces should be a guiding principle in intergovernmental efforts to enhance regional financial cooperation.

Part III

Does the future hold? Reactions to the current regime and prospects for progress (where is it going?)

12 Changing transatlantic financial regulatory relations at the turn of the millennium

Elliot Posner

US and European banks, insurance companies, asset managers and other financial services firms have long competed in multiple jurisdictions with distinct and sometimes incompatible regulatory systems. As transatlantic market integration proceeded throughout the 1990s, problems sparked by these regulatory differences were the focus of a host of often intense conflicts. This chapter explains an unexpected shift in the way American and European authorities managed these conflicts: from cooperation skewed heavily towards the preferences of US officials, and accepted grudgingly by European counterparts, to a Euro-American regulatory condominium characterised by close interaction among decision-makers and mutual accommodation. Why did US officials become more accommodating and European authorities more influential, and why did more balanced cooperation begin in 2002–3 in some sub-sectors but only more recently in others?

This chapter thus examines change in a core G7 relationship during the 2002–7 'period of calm'. My findings highlight the role of political authority, institutions and power in reconfiguring transatlantic regulatory cooperation. Lobbying by financial services companies, in part driven by market forces, also played an important role, ensuring that conflicts were resolved through deeper cooperation. But the preferences and actions of private actors were ultimately contingent on political developments tied to the fifty-year-old European integration project. In emphasising official sector decision-making and political power over private influence in public policy, this chapter parallels the contributions by Helleiner and Pagliari, Walter, and Baker in this volume.

But in contrast to classic state-centric accounts, my argument points to the enhanced structural power of a regional polity, the European Union (EU). Institutional change inside the EU recast the North

---

This is a considerably abridged and modified version of 'Making rules for global finance: transatlantic regulatory cooperation at the turn of the millennium', *International Organization* 63(4) (October 2009), 665–99.

Atlantic distribution of regulatory leverage and reshaped transatlantic relations. The degree to which regulatory authority was 'centralised' to the EU level was a primary causal factor behind the timing of change and pattern of cooperation.[1] In each of this study's six cases, the turn to more regionally centralised authority bolstered Europeans' ability to affect the behaviour of American regulators. Efforts to establish EU-wide rules and rule-making set off a sweeping process, first by altering the expectations of US financial services companies (with lucrative operations in Europe) and later those of European firms and officials as well as those of American authorities. Despite widespread scepticism over EU regulatory capacities (Véron 2007; Pauly 2008), perceptions of a new European ability to retaliate against US unilateral rule-making, to increase regulatory costs and to narrow opportunities for regulatory arbitrage in Europe ultimately generated new American incentives for accommodation and closer transatlantic coordination.

The governance of transatlantic financial services still frequently sets best practice in multilateral arenas, and regional cooperation increased EU influence. In this sense, input into global standard-setting has been broadened, thereby levelling the playing field for companies from Europe and other non-US countries with similar regulatory approaches and capacities – and thus enhancing input legitimacy, at least in the eyes of non-US developed-country firms and officials. As the concluding section discusses, the critical question concerns what greater EU influence will mean in the post-crisis era. Before 2008, EU representatives were satisfied with levelling the playing field within a normative framework developed under decades of American dominance. Will political responses to crisis ultimately take either the EU or the USA away from the orthodox model for organising global financial governance? Will the two regulatory powers adopt common positions at the multilateral level or offer competing models?

Explaining financial regulatory cooperation

In assuming continued US dominance in global financial regulatory developments, few analysts contemplated the possibility of change; explanatory models thus do not account for it or its possible implications (Oatley and Nabors 1998; Sobel 1994; Simmons 2001; Singer 2007).[2] For example, in a frequently cited explanation for cross-border

---

[1] In the extended article version of this chapter, I compare and weigh the importance of EU 'centralisation' to other possible causal variables.

[2] Exceptions include Cerny 1993; Coleman and Underhill 1995.

financial regulatory interaction, Simmons (2001) sees 'financial power' as the source of US dominance. She maintains that as a financial hegemon, the USA (sometimes in tandem with the UK) does not need to adjust its own policies in response to external pressures. This model employs variation in incentives tied to different issue areas to explain whether the USA will expend resources to achieve its goals or wait for market forces to pressure others to adjust (Simmons 2001: 592–601). While it accounts fairly well for regulatory relations across sub-sectors in the 1980s and 1990s, it does not predict the development of regulatory cooperation in subsequent years.

Asymmetric interdependence and power

Political economy approaches that treat economic interdependence as a potential source of external influence see market power and ultimately bargaining strength as stemming from 'foreign reliance' (Hirschman 1980/1945; Aggarwal 1985; Krasner 1991; Vogel 1995). Influence over global rules, by this logic, derives from the relative concentration of foreigners willing to accept a regulator's decisions in order to gain access to customers or suppliers. As Simmons and others maintain and substantiate, the international influence of US securities regulators in the post-Bretton Woods era emerged largely from the number of foreign firms that depended on US financial markets and therefore complied with SEC rules.

A corollary of this reasoning – that bargaining dynamics should vary with shifts in relative dependencies – can be used to generate causal propositions to explain *change* in regulatory relations. A relative increase (or decrease) in the concentration of foreign firms operating in a given jurisdiction should enhance (or reduce) the bargaining strength of officials representing it. The logic here suggests at least two routes by which the numbers of foreign companies under an authority's jurisdiction might change. One is an increase in the size of markets within the same political boundaries. This tends to be the default hypothesis, with scholars assuming that markets and by extension foreign firm concentrations grow because of exogenous economic and technological forces. At least in the transatlantic arena, such an argument leads to predictions of continued US dominance in the securities market sector. If this were the case, we would expect American officials to have made fewer, not more, adjustments in recent years, gaining bargaining strength relative to their European counterparts. While Europe extended traditional strengths in a few niches (such as in the management of high net worth individuals) or narrowed the US lead in others (such as in the

226   *Elliot Posner*

turnover of exchange-traded derivatives), in most areas of the securities industry the USA maintained or expanded its global position.[3] The US-to-European ratios for equity market capitalisation and total value of share trading, for example, increased from approximately 2:1 in 1994 to 2.5:1 in 2003.[4]

The regionalisation of rule-making and enforcement is a second reason why the number of foreign firms operating in a jurisdiction might change as the expanding territorial boundaries of regulatory authority capture a greater number of foreign firms. In contexts characterised by fluid jurisdictional boundaries, explanations of bargaining strength built on standard statist assumptions of congruence between regulatory authority and national borders run the risk of missing shifts in the distribution of power and their effects.

Financial regulatory cooperation in the North Atlantic

In the EU, political and institutional centralisation occurs when informal and formal decision-making processes, authority and rules move from the many national capitals to the EU. Since the mid-1990s, this has occurred in the domains of financial and monetary governance. The introduction of the euro rapidly accelerated and qualitatively changed what had until then been a gradual and uncertain shifting of authority towards the centre of the region (Coleman and Underhill 1995; Underhill 1997a; Posner 2005, 2007, 2009; Jabko 2006; Mügge 2006; Quaglia 2007). The transfer is far from complete and the new rule-making apparatus – comprised of multiple committees and a delicate balance of power between member governments, the European Parliament and the European Commission – hardly fits classic notions of hierarchical administration. However, at least from the viewpoint of market participants and foreign authorities, single sets of rules increasingly govern firm behaviour across the entire continent (including the City of London) and are produced and implemented by an EU process – even when enforcement remains in the hands of national authorities.

In particular, the EU effort to harmonise rules and centralise rule-making led directly to two interlinked internal projects. The Financial Services Action Plan (FSAP) of March 2000 tabled the legislation deemed necessary to integrate European national financial services

---

[3] International Financial Services, London, 'Financial Market Trends: Europe vs. US', October 2004; 'Rising Financial Activity in London Points to Increasing Global Influence of London', Press Release, 18 October 2004, www.ifsl.org.uk.

[4] World Federation of Exchanges, www.world-exchanges.org. For the USA, I combined figures from the NYSE, Nasdaq and Amex. For Europe, I added the figures from the LSE, Euronext and Deutsche Boerse.

Changing transatlantic financial regulatory relations 227

industries (European Commission 1999, 2006a). The new laws central-ised regulatory authority by harmonising national rules to a much greater extent than in the past, often requiring a single set of EU standards and regulations with equivalency clauses for foreign firms overseen by home regulators. The second EU project, the Lamfalussy Process, alters rule-making procedures for financial services legislation and supervi-sion (Lamfalussy 2001)[5] by delegating the creation of detailed rules to the Brussels bureaucracy and using new bodies, comprised of national regulatory authorities, to advise and to coordinate transposition, imple-mentation and enforcement. The Lamfalussy Process marks a historic shift away from an arrangement that was primarily the sum of multiple and idiosyncratic national decision-making regimes to Brussels-based procedures. Most rules now originate through these channels and while national agencies are responsible for on-the-ground implementation, interpretation and supervision, EU mechanisms increasingly constrain their actions. To a much greater extent, the application of centralised legislation in EU member countries no longer results in differing rules on the ground.

To evaluate the effects on transatlantic regulatory relations of this massive, two-pronged project, I focus on the timing of new pieces of legislation and the degree to which they centralise regulatory authority. When Europeans rely heavily on principles such as complete standard-isation, mandating a single set of rules with which local and American firms must comply, we would expect an increase in EU relative bar-gaining strength and (eventually) more accommodative behaviour on the part of US regulators because EU policy-makers would be setting the terms of competition for a greater number of US firms or their affiliates operating in Europe. EU officials could credibly threaten to use their authority in ways that might damage the businesses of a larger number of US firms or affiliates. In such a scenario, European author-ities would gain the same potential to harm foreign businesses and retaliate against foreign government measures that US authorities have long possessed. Unlike in the past, EU authorities could take unilateral actions that would change the 'payoff matrix'. The EU would become a rule-maker rather than a rule-taker. Such 'highly centralised regula-tion' characterises several sub-sectors covered by the FSAP.

In contrast, looser forms of regulatory integration, such as the prin-ciple of mutual recognition when accompanied by only minimal levels of harmonisation and standardisation, do not create a single set of rules for companies operating in the EU. We would not therefore expect a

---

[5] Originally, the Lamfalussy Process only included the securities industry but was expanded to banking and insurance in 2003.

228 Elliot Posner

Table 12.1. *Empirical expectations of regulatory centralisation explanation*

		(t_2) Expectations for management of EU-US conflicts
(t_1) EU chooses regulatory principles	**Highly centralised**	*US inclined to make adjustments. Terms of cooperation reflect mutual accommodation.*
	Minimally centralised	*No change in US behaviour. US reluctant to make adjustments. Terms of cooperation reflect US preferences.*

change in Europe's bargaining power with the USA or more accommodative behaviour on the part of American officials. Such 'minimally centralised regulation' typified efforts before the FSAP and the Lamfalussy Process. These empirical expectations are summarised in Table 12.1.

A pattern of change in transatlantic regulatory cooperation

This section briefly documents the pattern of change in the way US and European authorities have managed regulatory disputes. Throughout the 1980s and 1990s, national central bankers, treasury and finance ministry officials, and securities supervisors interacted in a web of bilateral relations and multilateral forums. Between 2002 and 2007, in contrast, transatlantic cooperation was institutionalised; led and coordinated by the US Treasury and the European Commission, a mesh of ongoing and formalised dialogues not only added a layer to and changed the tenor of the old country-to-country bilateral and multilateral interactions but also shifted attention to EU-US bilateralism. The 'EU-US Regulatory Dialogue on Financial Services' introduced in May 2002 produced negotiations in accordance with the September 2002 Norwalk Agreement, the March 2003 initiated SEC-CESR (Committee of European Securities Regulators)[6] cooperative framework, and the June 2005 CESR-CFTC (Commodity Futures Trading Commission) 'Common Work Program to Facilitate Transatlantic Derivatives Business'. Whereas in the past US regulators interacted primarily with their *national* European counterparts, today EU member states are also represented by several European-level bodies and, indirectly, by the International Accounting Standards Board

---

[6] CESR, created in June 2001, is comprises of the EU national securities regulators and a representative from the European Commission.

Table 12.2. *Transatlantic dispute management over time – the turning points*

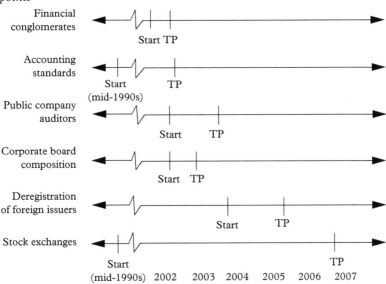

Start = Start of dispute; TP = Turning point from cooperation based on US preferences to cooperation based on mutual accommodation.

(IASB).[7] The European Commission initially played the most important European role, engaging directly in discussions with the US Treasury, Federal Reserve Bank, the SEC and the Public Company Accounting Oversight Board (PCAOB). Between 2002 and 2007, exchanges between high-level financial authorities gave the new cooperative relationship stature and publicity. In April 2007, US President George Bush, German Chancellor Angela Merkel (acting in her capacity as European Council President) and European Commission President José Manuel Barroso signed the 'Framework for Advancing Transatlantic Economic Integration' which featured financial markets as a target area.[8]

In addition to new faces and forums, the pattern of change in transatlantic regulatory relations, as sketched in Table 12.2, includes a shift in the terms of cooperation. Low-intensity disputes festered during the 1990s as the SEC jealously guarded US sovereignty, refused to agree to European demands for mutual recognition, and set the agenda which in 1989 began to include regulatory in addition to enforcement issues.

[7] See below for details.
[8] 'Framework for Advancing Transatlantic Economic Integration between the United States of America and the European Union', 30 April 2007, www.ec.europa.eu.

230 *Elliot Posner*

During a brief two-year span in 2002–3 several conflicts became acrimonious. Then Euro-American dispute management entered a period based on mutual accommodation rather than US preferences, with American authorities making significant concessions in several high-profile transatlantic conflicts. European regulators did not achieve all of their goals but did much better than in the past.

Dispute management reflecting US preferences

Of the six major disputes, the two that began in the mid-1990s exemplify the lopsided nature of transatlantic relations. The conflict over accounting standards started when Europeans proposed a mutual recognition regime whereby EU companies with listings in the USA would use their own national accounting standards and vice versa (European Commission 1995). American regulators, however, showed little interest in mutual recognition regimes or convergence initiatives. The SEC's view was that the rest of the world would eventually adopt US standards (Simmons 2001: 611 fn 93). US Generally Accepted Accounting Principles (US GAAP) were already accepted by all EU national regulators and the SEC did not consider European standards and International Accounting Standards (IAS) to be as rigorous.[9]

The conflict over the rules governing stock exchange competition also emerged in the mid-1990s. It began with European demands for a change away from transatlantic competition based on national treatment to a mutual recognition regime, whereby European stock exchanges would place their screen monitors on traders' desks in the USA and vice versa without having to comply with additional host regulatory requirements (Franke and Potthoff 1997).[10] The European entreaties met steadfast US resistance. Emphasising the dangers to investors of sharing regulatory sovereignty, the SEC argued that mutual recognition could threaten the ability to carry out their primary domestic mandate – protecting shareholders.

Dispute management by mutual accommodation

The year 2002 marks a discernable turning point, after which making mutual adjustments became a routine part of managing conflicts. The

---

[9] See Arthur Levitt, 'The World According to GAAP', *Financial Times*, 2 May 2001, p. 21; telephone interview with former SEC chief accountant, 8 July 2007.

[10] Author's interview with Federation of European Securities Exchanges (FESE) official, Brussels, 9 June 2004.

Changing transatlantic financial regulatory relations   231

shift is observable in all six cases though the turning points occurred at different moments over a five-year period.

The conflict over the 2002 EC Financial Conglomerates Directive (FCD)[11] was only resolved after months of acrimony and suspicion. The FCD requires that the holding company of non-EU financial companies be subject to consolidated supervision. This means that a single regulator must oversee all parts of large financial conglomerates, including their domestic and foreign banking, insurance and securities operations. A home-regulator can be the supervisor under the new directive only so long as its regulatory system meets EU equivalency standards (Tafara 2004). US financial services firms, especially investment banks operating in Europe, complained loudly. At the time of the directive's adoption, US supervision was based on a different operating principle and would not have met the new EU standards. An EU finding of non-equivalency could have hit US-based investment banks with costly and unwanted changes that included accepting an EU authority as their global consolidated regulator. The conflict crested in early 2002 with American suspicions that EU officials wanted, in the words of one Washington official, to 'push back on the US apparent hegemony of financial market regulation ... and impose EU supervisory rules on banks'.[12] Some US supervisors expressed surprise and consternation that the EU and its member state supervisors would presume to pass judgement on US rules and supervision.[13] Others suspected the Europeans were reneging on a 1989 agreement that allowed US banks to continue to operate in the EU under the national treatment principle, rather than comply with new requirements (Underhill 1997a: 117).[14]

By mid-2002, American and EU officials had arrived at a common understanding. Instead of ignoring the conflict, retaliating, or pressuring the EU to make adjustments, US regulators made a major adjustment by making their own rules more compatible with the new EU law.[15]

Three transatlantic disputes arising from the passage of the US Sarbanes-Oxley Act of 2002 were also eventually managed through a process of mutual accommodation. The first involved provisions that required foreign auditors of US-listed firms and of foreign affiliates of

---

[11] Directive 2002/87/EC of the European Parliament and of the Council of the European Union.

[12] Former US Treasury official's correspondence with author, 31 May 2006.

[13] Former US Treasury official's correspondence with author, 31 May 2006.

[14] Author's interview with senior staff official, US House of Representatives, Washington, 6 May 2004.

[15] The SEC created the supervised investment bank holding company (SIBHC) and then the consolidated supervised entity (CSE), but the large US investment banks

232   *Elliot Posner*

American companies to register with a new body, the Public Company Accounting Oversight Board (PCAOB), and be subject to inspections, investigations and disciplinary proceedings (Ross 2004). The acrimony did not subside until late 2003.[16] At the time, 333 European companies were publicly listed in the USA and were audited by 58 EU-based auditors (Ross 2004). The initial US position of making modest accommodations gave way to greater flexibility in implementing the act.[17]

The second Sarbanes-Oxley spillover concerned new requirements for corporate board and audit committee independence, putting some European companies with US listings, especially German firms, in an untenable bind (Tafara 2004; Vitols and Kenyon 2004: 31–4). This issue was resolved more quickly than the first, with the SEC making concessions to affected European firms in April 2003 (Campos 2003; Tafara 2004).[18] Finally, the increasing costs of maintaining a listing on US stock exchanges under the Sarbanes-Oxley regime triggered a third transatlantic dispute in February 2004 over reporting and registration obligations. Taking a conciliatory tone, the SEC adopted new rules (Campos 2006; European Commission 2006b; GAO 2006).[19]

In the accounting standards dispute, simmering since the 1990s, the SEC began to make concessions to the EU in 2002. The Norwalk Agreement of that September committed IASB, the new EU standard setter,[20] and the Financial Accounting Standards Board (FASB), the US standard setter, to making existing IFRS and US GAAP fully compatible.[21] The SEC also worked closely with the European Commission to prepare for an eventual mutual recognition regime, with the SEC

---

chose the latter. See Alix 2004, p. 3 fn 8. See GAO 2004, p. 88 for the effect of the new rules on Basel II and US bureaucratic politics.

[16] *Financial Times*, 'US Refuses to Exempt EU Auditors From Registration With Financial Regulator', 12 June 2003, p. 8; 'Sarbanes-Oxley and Europe: US Legislation Finds a Friend Across the Water', 23 April 2004, p. 9; European Council 2003, 2,513rd Council Meeting, Economic and Financial Affairs, Luxembourg, 3 June, 9822/03 (Presse 149), p. 16.

[17] *Wall Street Journal*, 'US and EU Reconcile Audit Issues', 26 March 2004, p. B2; PCAOB Rule 2105; PCAOB Release 2004–005 (9 June 2004, PCAOB Rulemaking Docket Matter No. 013); 'PCAOB to Consider Proposal to Enhance International Cooperation in Inspections', 26 November 2007, www.pcaobus.org.

[18] SEC Releases 33–8220; 34–47654; IC-26001; File No. S7-02-03, 25 April 2003, www.sec.gov.

[19] *New York Times*, 'S.E.C. Changes Its Tune on Letting Foreign Securities Leave', 7 December 2006, p. C6; SEC Final Rule, Release 34–55540, 27 March 2007.

[20] EU legislation mandates that IASB standards used by European companies be endorsed by the European Commission.

[21] The Norwalk Agreement, www.sec.gov. International Financial Reporting Standards or IFRS is the new label for IAS.

Changing transatlantic financial regulatory relations   233

and CESR launching a joint work plan.[22] By November 2007, the US regulator's turnabout had produced a new rule eliminating the requirement of US GAAP reconciliation for foreign issuers using IFRS as published by IASB (Nicolaisen 2004; SEC 2004, 2005; Cox 2007a).[23]

The position of US officials on the rules governing stock exchange competition began to change in early 2007. Until then, the SEC had avoided making accommodations despite the greater frequency and intensity of EU complaints in 2003. In early 2007, however, the SEC Director of the Office of International Affairs published a plan for a mutual recognition regime (Cox 2007b; Tafara and Peterson 2007).[24] In August 2007, moreover, the SEC solicited comments from the Federation of European Securities Exchanges (FESE) on the transatlantic extension of mutual recognition to the sector.[25] On 1 February 2008 the SEC signed a joint statement with the European Commission endorsing mutual recognition as a governing principle for transatlantic securities markets.[26] And in June the US agency proposed a rule change that would expand exemptions from registration for certain types of foreign securities firms – a rule change that would meet some, though not all, EU demands.[27]

The management of these six conflicts thus follows a common pattern: change in the terms of transatlantic regulatory cooperation with American regulators becoming as likely to make adjustments as their European counterparts. This change occurred in the various disputes at different moments between 2002 and 2007.

An empirical investigation into the pattern of change

The evidence summarised in Table 12.3 suggests a fairly close correspondence between the centralisation of EU regulatory authority and transatlantic cooperation in four of the six cases. The other two raise new questions that call for different investigative techniques.

In the financial conglomerates conflict, EU member states agreed to apply the principle of highly centralised regulation in May 2002 by replacing national approaches with a single set of rules. Soon afterwards, in response to the equivalency provisions of EU law, the SEC

---

[22] SEC Press Release, 'SEC and CESR Launch Work Plan Focused on Financial Reporting', 2006–130, 2 August 2006.

[23] SEC Press Release 2007–235.

[24] *New York Times*, 'Should US Markets Be Wide Open?', 9 February 2007, p. C1.

[25] Jukka Ruuska, Letter to Christopher Cox, 17 August 2007, www.fese.be.

[26] 'Statement of the European Commission and the U.S. Securities and Exchange Commission on Mutual Recognition in Securities Markets', SEC Press Release 2008–9, 1 February 2008, www.sec.gov.

[27] SEC Proposed Rule, Release No. 34–58047, 27 June 2008.

Table 12.3. *Transatlantic dispute management over time – EU centralisation*

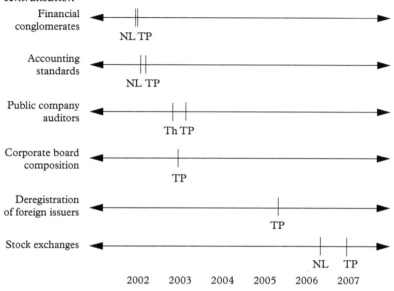

NL = New legislation that centralises regulation; Th = Threat to create new legislation that centralises regulation; TP = Turning point from cooperation based on US preferences to cooperation based on mutual accommodation.

began a two-year process of making adjustments to US rules. The accounting standards conflict followed a similar pattern. Three months after European policy-makers passed a July 2002 regulation mandating companies listed on EU stock exchanges to apply the same set of accounting standards by 2005,[28] US officials began what became a series of conciliatory policies.[29] The public company auditors' dispute veers slightly from the pattern, in that American authorities made conciliatory changes following European threats to adopt legislation (rather than actual passage of a law based on the principle of highly centralised regulation). In July 2003, US officials began to back down from a narrow interpretation of the Sarbanes-Oxley Act after EU officials threatened to retaliate by creating future EU auditing legislation that would have the same extraterritorial effects as the US law.[30] There was basic

---

[28] Regulation (EC) 1606/2002.
[29] Herdman, Robert K., 'Moving Towards the Globalization of Accounting Standards', speech by SEC staff, Cologne, 18 April 2002.
[30] *Financial Times*, 'SEC May Limit Regulator's Global Reach', 9 July 2003, p. 29; 'Sarbanes-Oxley and Europe: US Legislation Finds a Friend Across the Water', 23 April 2004, p. 9. Author's interview with European Commission official, Brussels, 9 June 2004.

Changing transatlantic financial regulatory relations 235

congruence between my expected causal factor (a change in the level of regulatory centralisation) and outcomes in the stock exchange dispute as well. Here EU policy-makers did not agree to higher degrees of centralisation until September 2006; a minimally centralised regime[31] based on the principles of mutual recognition and minimal harmonisation thus characterised the sub-sector in Europe. While US officials had previously refused to bend to demands for a transatlantic mutual recognition regime, SEC officials signalled a new willingness to make adjustments in early 2007, in advance of the 1 November implementation of a new EU law. The EU legislation, Markets in Financial Instruments Directive or MiFID, centralises the rules governing stock exchanges, albeit by increasing the degree of harmonisation and coordination rather than imposing a single set of rules.[32]

The corporate board composition and deregistration of foreign issuers conflicts, which I discuss in detail below, also ended with the US making adjustments. However, these outcomes occurred in the absence of centralising EU regulation in the respective sub-sectors.

Further investigations

Careful inspection of event sequence shows that the first disputes to be resolved through mutual accommodation affected the outcomes of later cases. This conclusion goes a long way to explain several cases, especially the two that were not consistent with my original expectations. In the corporate board and the deregistration cases, where no new EU legislation preceded US concessions, EU authorities made linkages to the existing conglomerates legislation which contained an equivalency clause, their strongest ammunition for punishing US financial services companies.[33] By dragging out the process for accepting US holding company regulation in Europe, EU officials were able to influence the other disputes (Lackritz 2005).

Given these dependencies among the cases, the causes behind the new terms of cooperation in the first dispute – the financial conglomerates conflict – are important for explaining later outcomes as well. What then accounts for the management of the conglomerates dispute? The answer turns on the SEC's new holding company rules for

---

[31] The regime was based on the 1993 Investment Services Directive (Council Directive 93/22/EEC). See Coleman and Underhill 1995; Steil 1998.

[32] MiFID (Directive 2004/39/EC of the European Parliament and Council of the European Union) repealed the ISD. While passing the law in April 2004, EU policy-makers did not clarify the degree of harmonisation until September 2006. Compare Article 42 of the MiFID with Article 15 of the ISD.

[33] *Financial Times*, 'Brussels Turns Up Pressure Against US Audit Rules', 16 June 2003, p. 8; *Financial Times*, 'SEC May Limit Regulator's Global Reach', 9 July 2003, p. 29.

broker-dealers. Is there an observable mechanism connecting EU regulatory centralisation to the SEC decision, as my hypothesis contends? Careful examination strongly suggests the answer is yes. The SEC was responding largely to the lobbying of American investment banks, concerned about the possible negative implications of the new EU financial conglomerates directive to their European businesses.

Beginning even before Brussels formally opened the directive's consultation period in December 2000, US financial services companies ceaselessly pressured US lawmakers and regulators until their interests were protected (SEC 2003: 62911; Alix 2004: 3). Represented primarily by the Securities Industry Association (SIA), the US investment banks successfully persuaded politicians in Congress as well as officials at the SEC and the Treasury to find a solution to the dispute and develop more cooperative relations with their European counterparts.[34] In addition to a paper trail that includes press reports, transcriptions (and my own observations) of testimony before the US Congress, and SIA documents, my interviews on both sides of the Atlantic without exception confirm the significant role of this lobby group in convincing US authorities to make adjustments, end the conglomerates dispute and institutionalise transatlantic regulatory dialogue.[35]

It is hard to imagine US regulators joining the new dialogue, creating new holding company rules (embodied in Consolidated Supervised Entities), and doing so when they had other options acceptable to American investment banks. The FCD thus deeply constrained the choices available to American officials. Making no adjustments was unacceptable to US firms, which successfully lobbied Congress and found support for their cause in an SEC eager to expand its powers. Despite scant evidence of actual EU regulatory capacity or intentions, the US made concessions because Wall Street firms argued that making no adjustments would place them in a precarious position and would jeopardise the role of the SEC as their primary regulator.

The hardest case

The accounting standards case was the most challenging of the six because multiple factors, including market pressures (Simmons 2001), contributed to the changed transatlantic regime. Yet the historical record strongly suggests that EU regulatory centralisation ranks

---

[34] The SIA changed its name to Securities Industry and Financial Markets Association or SIFMA, www.SIFMA.org.

[35] Interview with staff official, US House of Representatives, Washington, 6 May 2004; former US Treasury official's correspondence with author, 31 May 2006.

Changing transatlantic financial regulatory relations 237

among the more salient of these causes. European officials believed that their new accounting standards laws gave them capacities, which they deliberately used to pressure US authorities to make adjustments. Side legislation related to the EU accounting standards regulation contains equivalency clauses (European Commission 2007).[36] For foreign firms raising capital or listing securities through regulated markets, the legislation requires either adoption of the new accounting standards or approval that home accounts meet EU requirements. The EU thus placed itself in a position to decide whether over 200 US companies had to reconcile US GAAP with IFRS.[37] European policy-makers used the equivalency clauses first to pressure the SEC to make concessions, and then for the SEC to live up to its commitment to implement a mutual recognition regime (Dam and Scott 2004: 4).[38] In fact, the European Commission delayed clarifying the meaning of equivalency until the SEC agreed to recognise IFRS without the reconciliation requirement.[39]

Transmission mechanisms

Among the six disputes, the stock exchange conflict stands out for its longevity. Why did the SEC's more conciliatory stance emerge five years after the resolution of the financial conglomerates dispute? Despite persistent EU demands and threats, as well as successful management of regulatory conflicts overall, the SEC avoided making accommodations through 2006. Even then, US authorities only gradually moved towards cross-Atlantic liberalisation of the sector. The timing of the shift, as shown above, corresponds well with regulatory centralisation. But there are interesting differences between the mechanisms at work in this case and the others. In the conglomerates dispute, US financial services firms responded to the new EU law and acted as the main conveyers of European developments to US authorities. Other transmitters, in addition to pressure from US firms, contributed in the subsequent cases. A new confidence in the ability to retaliate against US

[36] See Commission Regulation (EC) 809/2004 of 29 April 2004 (Prospectus Regulation) and Directive 2004/109/EC of the EP and the Council of 15 December 2004 (The Transparency Directive).

[37] See CESR, Ref: CESR/07–138, 6 March 2007, www.cesr-eu.org.

[38] *Financial Times*, 'Europe Urged to Be Cautious on US Change', 8 November 2005, p. 28. Interview with European Commission official, Washington, 5 May 2004; CESR, 'CESR's Advice on the Equivalence of Chinese, Japanese and US GAAPs', CESR/08–179, March 2008, www.cesr-eu.org.

[39] Charles McCreevy, 'EU-US Cooperation on Reporting Standards, Audit Oversight and Regulation', Brussels, 27 November 2007, SPEECH/07/757; and Proposal for a Commission Regulation (EC), 2 June 2008, www.europa.eu.

238 *Elliot Posner*

policies emboldened European officials and companies, often working in tandem, to press for US concessions to old and new grievances; the institutionalised dialogue gave them a forum. Unlike earlier cases, by 2007 SEC officials were all too aware of EU developments and needed neither US-based financial companies nor Europeans to prompt reconsideration of the decades-old insistence that foreign stock exchanges register with the SEC and be subject to its oversight before gaining access to American investors.

More centralised EU legislation was certainly a factor behind the SEC's new interest in mutual recognition; MiFID's implementation promised to capture a large number of US securities trading firms, including parts of the merged NYSE-Euronext, under a comprehensive set of rules. As changes within the EU unfolded, US authorities felt the impact of Europe's massive regulatory project via an increasing number of channels, indicating deep and pervasive structural change. The turn towards mutual recognition, relabelled 'substituted compliance', was the SEC's bid to ensure that the onslaught of new European rules would meet US standards, to prevent regulatory arbitrage and, more broadly, to win back the initiative in setting international regulatory trends (Tafara and Peterson 2007).

Conclusion

These conclusions engage the volume's theme on the relationship between private financial interests and public authority. Although the influence of private interests on US and EU authorities was tangible, the cases demonstrate a phenomenon distinct from regulatory capture. Private influence was a necessary but not a sufficient condition for the observed changes. Internal EU regulatory centralisation changed the market opportunities and expectations of US-based multinational firms operating on European markets, and their lobbying in turn sparked a complex sequence of events. Over time, coordinated private lobbies on both sides of the Atlantic increasingly constrained political authorities' room to manoeuvre. Because a breakdown in longstanding (and lucrative) cooperation was deemed unacceptable, US officials found ways to accommodate EU positions.

Between 2002 and the onset of the financial crisis, rule-making in the governance of transatlantic securities markets became considerably more inclusive. Although well short of legitimate in the sense used by Underhill, Blom and Mügge in the introduction to this volume, US authorities could no longer set rules without considering EU positions. European negotiators represent not only the democratically

Changing transatlantic financial regulatory relations 239

elected governments of twenty-seven countries, but also the European Parliament and the European Commission, both of which sought to broaden participation in financial rule-making.[40]

This broader participation on the input side had already altered transatlantic financial governance before the crisis. Regarding rules of access to foreign markets, the new power balance had furthered liberalisation, with both sides embracing the sovereignty-sharing principle of mutual recognition as of 2007. For EU-based companies, this shift removed asymmetrical access rules which imposed additional regulatory costs to operate in the United States. However, firms domiciled elsewhere but operating within the Atlantic zone faced the possibility of competitive disadvantages (as mutual recognition regimes by definition exclude others, even those with similar rules and enforcement apparatuses). Foreign authorities had two, not necessarily mutually exclusive, options: bring home regulation in line with the transatlantic consensus, or promote their own financial centres as functionally equivalent alternatives.

There is some evidence that the EU's role as a global rule-maker improved regulatory effectiveness. SEC chairman Christopher Cox, for example, apparently believes the 2004 introduction of the Consolidated Supervised Entities programme, created to be equivalent to the new EU financial conglomerates regime, prevented an even worse crisis than what he faced in 2008. 'It is extremely fortunate that the [Consolidated Supervised Entities] programme existed', he stated in an 8 May 2008 speech, 'so that when the Federal Reserve Bank of New York came into Bear Stearns on short notice in March, they could see Basel ratio calculations they were familiar with, and they could immediately review both capital and liquidity assessments on a consolidated basis'.[41] Nevertheless, the principles underlying pre-crisis EU regulatory measures largely mirrored those developed in the decades of US dominance. Transatlantic regulatory cooperation had in fact accelerated and intensified cross-border harmonisation, convergence and sovereignty-sharing along the 'orthodox' model, giving hope to multinational financial firms of a united transatlantic front dictating outcomes at the multilateral level.

EU-US dominance in setting the terms of securities market governance is likely to continue into the near future. Helleiner and Pagliari

---

[40] On the EP's efforts, see Pervenche Berès, 'La construction d'un marché financier intégré: le rôle du Parlement Européen', 10:50, 16 January 2007, www.pervenche-beres.fr. The European Commission created the Financial Services Consumer Group (FSCG), www.ec.europa.eu.

[41] Christopher Cox, Address to the Security Traders 12th Annual Washington Conference, Washington, 7 May 2008, www.sec.gov.

and other contributors to this volume remind us that Europe's financial arrival coincides with macro-processes of equal magnitude in other world regions. Yet institutional and other domestic factors have thus far delayed the translation of growing capital markets into regulatory heft for their respective authorities. It will likely take many more foreign financial firms falling under China's ambit before officials there would have the international leverage (though not necessarily the desire to influence) of their European counterparts. Increasing foreign access to its financial services industry might quicken the process, but so might a regulatory combination with Hong Kong. For the time being, only the EU – apart from the USA – is in a position to forward alternatives should the current crisis undermine the basic governance principles developed under American hegemony.

How durable is the pre-crisis normative framework? Might Europe actually produce an alternative and extend it to the international level? EU legislation, passed in 2008 and 2009, certainly lessens firm discretion, and the initiative to use the G20 as a mechanism for revamping international financial regulation and extending to the global context EU governance mechanisms, such as colleges of supervisors, appear early indications of European determination. Yet Europe's international role in the area of financial governance and the future of the existing regulatory framework and the EU-US condominium depend on ongoing internal EU and domestic US developments as well as their interdependencies. Inside the EU, unlike at the turn-of-the-millennium when Alexandre Lamfalussy's committee deliberated, the central debate in the post-crisis era turns on cross-border prudential supervisory arrangements. Will they provide the contours of a novel approach to financial governance? Will they be compatible with American ones?

13 Monetary and financial cooperation in Asia: improving legitimacy and effectiveness?

Heribert Dieter

Introduction

Since the turn of the century, countries in Southeast and East Asia have been embracing regional cooperation and integration in monetary and financial affairs.[1] The 1997–8 Asian crisis, the successful introduction of the euro and, more recently, the collapse of the hitherto praised Anglo-Saxon model have been important catalysts for this emerging process. The Asian crisis demonstrated the lack of options for emerging economies in financial crisis. The policies of the International Monetary Fund (IMF) were suboptimal to say the least, and revealed a clear lack of output legitimacy. The creation of a single currency in Europe then showed that such integration was possible in practice, and not just in theory. Asian observers see that the euro is providing enhanced economic stability and strengthening Europe's position in global affairs. This, of course, is important in a region where more and more citizens wish to break free from the dominance of the United States in both economic and security affairs. More recently, the sub-prime crisis has reminded Asian policy-makers of the lectures they endured in 1997 and 1998: personal ties between lenders and borrowers were then termed 'crony capitalism'. Today we see that the American financial system has generated the largest financial crisis since the Great Depression, while we even hear calls for a return to 'good old fashioned banking'.[2] The contrast between the IMF's approach to Asian countries in the late 1990s and to the United States a decade later serves as a stark reminder of the disproportionate influence western OECD countries exercise over global

---

[1] Asia below refers to East and Southeast Asia, i.e. the countries that constitute ASEAN+3 (China, Japan and South Korea).

[2] British Chancellor of the Exchequer Alistair Darling suggested in September 2007 that 'there are times when going back to good old-fashioned banking may not be a bad idea', *Daily Telegraph*, 13 September 2007.

242   *Heribert Dieter*

financial governance, thus bringing the lack of input legitimacy of such governance into sharp relief.[3]

Against this background, Asian policy-makers continue to question both the effectiveness of the current regime as well as its legitimacy. While there was little, if any, cooperation between central bankers before the Asian crisis, monetary regionalism – alongside bilateral trade agreements – is now receiving significant attention in Asia. However, the two processes – integration in trade and in finance – are not occurring in the same forums. While trade agreements in Asia are currently bilateral, monetary cooperation is a regional endeavour.

Monetary regionalism characterises a process of supranational regional integration that deals primarily, though not exclusively, with monetary and financial issues. In contrast to conventional regional integration, which emphasises the early integration of trade and production, monetary regionalism stresses the integration of financial markets, the stabilisation of exchange rates and the development of cooperative mechanisms in finance.[4] In Asia today, regional cooperation in monetary affairs can be observed on four levels: the networking of currency swaps under the Chiang Mai Initiative (CMI); the monitoring of short-term capital flows and other surveillance measures; initiatives to strengthen regional bond markets; and the emergence of cooperation on exchange rates.

This chapter analyses the emergence of monetary regionalism in East and Southeast Asia since 2000. The first sections give an overview of the rationale for monetary and financial cooperation; issues of sequencing within regional integration; the Chiang Mai process as one of the more tangible results of Asian monetary cooperation; and the rivalry between China and Japan for regional leadership. Subsequent sections then analyse potential exchange rate regimes for the region and the evolution of regional bond markets. The conclusion addresses the institutional dimension of monetary regionalism and its future.

The rationale for monetary regionalism

There is virtual unanimity among academic and political observers that the legacy of the Asian crisis of 1997 is the single most important reason for pursuing monetary and financial cooperation in Asia today.[5]

---

[3] For a discussion of the influence of transatlantic powers on economic governance see Dieter 2009.
[4] For details see Dieter 2000; Dieter and Higgott 2003.
[5] See for example Dieter 2000; de Brouwer 2002; Ryou and Wang 2003; Milner 2003; Kohsaka 2004; Stevenson 2004; Wang 2004; Dayaratna-Banda and Whalley 2007.

Regardless of their individual merits or problems, countries in Southeast and East Asia then received identical treatment by international financial institutions, and this shared experience has fuelled a sense of shared destiny. The IMF's provision of liquidity – a key element in any crisis management – was much too slow in 1997. Particularly South Korea had to endure weeks of negotiations while its currency lost much of its value and credit was not rolled over in foreign financial markets.[6] In addition, those countries affected by the IMF's decisions had very little say in the formulation of its policies.

The unprecedented build-up of foreign reserves by Asian governments reflects the political will to avoid a repetition of the events of 1997–8. Dayaratna-Banda and Whalley (2007) argue that emerging monetary regionalism in Asia aims to achieve region-wide financial stability even in the midst of global instability. It further aims to increase the ability of countries to pursue domestic objectives while encouraging intraregional capital flows. As exchange rate volatility increases uncertainty, hampers trade and complicates investment decisions, the new arrangements seek to allow individual countries a degree of choice in exchange rate policies – which also need to remain sustainable under crises and contagion. The new arrangements further aim to prevent speculative attacks on currencies by supporting exchange rate systems that do not allow one-way bets on their external value.

Nevertheless, the Asian crisis alone would not have generated sufficient momentum for the current drive towards monetary regionalism. The frustration of Asian policy-makers with the slow reform of the international financial architecture and the dominance of Washington in regional and global affairs is equally important (Sakakibara 2003: 232f; Wang 2004: 940). Insuring against future crises, then, is not the only motive; the enhancement of regional power is another:

Countries realize that the only way for the ascending region to exert power comparable to that projected by the United States and Europe is for its members to act collectively. They understand that regional problems like the underdevelopment of local financial markets will be easier to solve if they act collectively rather than individually. This new commitment to regional cooperation is evident in the Chiang Mai Initiative and the Asian Bond Fund. The readiness of

---

[6] The rapid provision of liquidity by both the American Federal Reserve and the European Central Bank in 2007 and 2008 underlined the utility of immediate liquidity provision. However, it is not clear that it constituted prudent lending. Walter Bagehot's nineteenth-century rules for last resort lending – lend freely, at penalty rates, against good collateral – were implemented in a number of cases, most notably in the bail-out of the investment bank and brokerage house Bear Stearns in March 2008. The Fed accepted mortgage-backed assets, for which there was no market at the time, as collateral.

244 *Heribert Dieter*

East Asian governments and central banks to commit meaningful financial resources to these regional initiatives signals a departure from the status quo ante. (Chung and Eichengreen 2007: 14f)

As the problems of effective global financial governance will not be solved overnight, and as national regulation is no longer sufficient, the region – at least in theory – might better be able to provide these structures (Sakakibara 2003: 234). The question is whether East and Southeast Asia are ready to embark on a process of integration that will eventually lead to an integrated monetary and financial sphere. Here we need to consider two factors: whether the region is sufficiently integrated economically and whether countries in the region are able to cooperate politically.

Sequencing

While I will not analyse the region's economic interdependence in detail, it is necessary to address the issue at least briefly. With the rapid rise of intraregional production networks, economic interdependence in Asia has been growing rapidly. Bayoumi, Eichengreen and Mauro suggested in 2000 that ASEAN economies, in terms of interdependence, were as plausible candidates for monetary integration as European economies (Bayoumi *et al.* 2000: 122). While Bayoumi *et al.* were primarily looking at ASEAN, Masahiro Kawai has argued that Southeast and East Asia together are as interdependent as Europe was in the early 1990s when the decision for a single currency was made (Kawai 2007: 109).

The issue of sequencing is central to any analysis of regional integration. The conventional sequence starts with trade and is followed by monetary integration at a much later stage. While Europe successfully followed such a path, the reverse strategy might be more sensible today. Since tariffs are much lower than they used to be in the 1960s and 1970s, the benefits of regional free trade are now more limited. Financial instability on the other hand can cause severe damage to economies – an incentive to concentrate on finance first, followed by the integration of markets for goods and services (Dieter 2000; Shin and Wang 2002; Pomfret 2005).[7]

A sequencing pattern which is different from the traditional trade-based model of integration has been suggested by Dieter (2000) and

---

[7] We observed a very different process in the EU. The debate on monetary integration in the European Economic Community only became significant after the customs union was completed in 1968. The Werner plan of 1970, the so-called snake in the tunnel of 1972, and the creation of the European Monetary System took place only after the integration process was well-established. In contrast, monetary regionalism in Asia is a process that is not embedded in a broader integration project.

Monetary and financial cooperation in Asia 245

developed further by Dieter and Higgott (2003). Rather than starting with a free-trade area, followed by a customs union, a common market, an economic and monetary union, and finally a political union, it has been proposed to start with the pooling of foreign reserves, followed by the creation of a regional exchange-rate regime, an economic and monetary union and a political union. Instead of postponing the benefits of monetary integration, this four-stage approach would begin with a monetary measure.

What are the advantages of pursuing monetary integration first? Shin and Wang suggest that a monetary union would accelerate intraregional trade without requiring free-trade agreements or other measures (Shin and Wang 2002: 11). Reducing the costs of hedging against currency volatility is an advantage that can be quantified by individual companies as well as countries. The cost of insuring against volatility can reach 5 per cent of the value of an export item, which is substantial by any standard. A common currency would also increase bilateral trade; numerous empirical studies have shown that trade is facilitated by monetary stability in space, i.e. a single currency between countries (Pomfret 2005: 117). Kazuko Shirono, who confirms these findings, suggests that a common currency in Asia would lead to a doubling of trade in the region. Excluding Japan, the expected welfare gains for participating economies would be around 3.7 per cent of GDP, while the largest welfare gains would accrue for an extended currency union comprising the ASEAN+3 countries, Australia and New Zealand. The expected welfare gain would then be 6.2 per cent (Shirono 2007: 14).

Cooperation in monetary and financial affairs would thus benefit participating economies. Nowhere is this more evident than in the provision of liquidity. The unilateral accumulation of reserves, which we have observed over the past decade, is a costly form of insurance against exchange rate and credit market volatility. Asian policy-makers have responded to this challenge by initiating the so-called Chiang Mai process.

The Chiang Mai Initiative and the pooling of reserves

The Asian crisis was a traumatic experience for policy-makers in Asia. Since then, foreign reserves have risen to unprecedented levels. Between 1999 and 2007, foreign reserve holdings by Asian economies quadrupled, from 900 to 3,640 billion dollars (see Table 13.1).

Table 13.1 reveals a clear pattern. The bulk of the region's foreign reserves in 2008 (84 per cent) were held in East Asia, primarily by

246   *Heribert Dieter*

Table 13.1. *Total reserves minus gold of selected Asian economies (US$ billions, end of year)*

Country	2004	2005	2006	2007	2008
Japan	834	834	880	953	1,009
Hong Kong	124	124	133	153	182
South Korea	199	210	239	262	201
Singapore	113	116	136	163	174
Taiwan	242	253	266	275	280
China	615	823	1,068	1,530	2,110*
India	127	160	171	267	247
Indonesia	35	33	41	55	50
Malaysia	66	70	82	101	91
Philippines	13	16	20	30	33
Thailand	47	51	65	85	1,086
Vietnam	6	9	11	23	24
Total	2,422	2,670	3,115	3,898	4,511

Source: IMF, International Financial Statistics, July 2009. *EIU estimate.

China and Japan.[8] Those of Southeast Asian countries, with the exception of Singapore, were modest in comparison; the reserves of those ASEAN countries not listed in the table were insignificant.

In response to the crisis, the leaders of ASEAN invited China, Japan and South Korea to join efforts to deepen economic and monetary cooperation. The ASEAN+3 Summit in November 1999 released a joint statement covering a wide range of potential areas for cooperation (Wang 2004: 941); the first major result was presented by ASEAN+3 finance ministers less than one year later. The ASEAN swap agreement, originally from August 1977, was now widened to cover all ASEAN members, while the amount available was raised from $200 million to $1 billion in May 2001. The second development, also under the umbrella of the Chiang Mai Initiative (CMI), was the development of a full series of bilateral swap and repurchase agreements between the ASEAN+3 countries. Countries could swap their local currency for major international currencies for up to six months, for up to twice their committed amount (Pomfret 2005: 114).

The CMI began as a cautious endeavour. Observers were surprised by the decision to limit the amount available under the swap at the discretion of the two countries involved to 10 per cent of the total, and to

---

[8] Accumulating reserves is fiscally expensive as countries effectively swap high-yielding domestic assets for lower-yielding foreign ones (Rajan and Siregar 2004: 293). For a detailed discussion see Green and Torgerson 2007.

Monetary and financial cooperation in Asia 247

require IMF consent for the remaining 90 per cent (e.g. Dieter 2001). Diplomatic considerations informed this initial caution; the ASEAN+3 countries had no desire to give Washington and the IMF an opportunity for renewed criticism. Since then there have been notable developments: the 2007 ASEAN+3 Finance Ministers Meeting in Kyoto agreed on the multilateralisation of the fund.[9]

Notably, efforts to deepen financial cooperation in Asia did not suffer a setback in the 2008/9 financial crisis. Instead, ASEAN+3 ministers agreed to enlarge the multilateralised CMI to 120 billion dollars, of which 80 per cent would be provided by China, Japan and South Korea (Arner *et al.* 2009: 29). While European cooperation did suffer a setback in the crisis – Hungary needed the IMF for a bail-out – Asian policy-makers have continued and expanded their cooperation, which is a remarkable achievement.

Nevertheless, the CMI continues to have significant shortcomings and its ultimate purpose remains ambiguous. Is it the nucleus of an emerging process of monetary regionalism in Asia? Or is the goal much more limited, i.e. a joint liquidity programme? The main reason for the deadlock can be found in the political divisions that overshadow the CMI. Tension between Japan and China is hampering the further deepening of the CMI.

China-Japan rivalry for regional leadership

In 1997 Asia was hit by a financial shock that was, until the sub-prime crisis, probably the most severe financial crisis in the postwar period. While Japan was the only country that could have beaten the panic, it failed and missed what Walden Bello called its 'golden opportunity'. Japan's failure occurred on two levels. First, instead of increasing its imports from the countries in crisis, it reduced them – in some cases by over a third (Dieter 2005: 129). Rather than becoming the regional consumer of last resort, Japan left this role to the USA. Second, and more

---

[9] Ministers agreed in principle, but not on all the details: 'Proceeding with a step-by-step approach, we unanimously agreed in principle that a self-managed reserve pooling arrangement governed by a single contractual agreement is an appropriate form of multilateralisation. We recognised the consensus reached as a significant achievement towards an advanced framework of regional liquidity support mechanism. We instructed the Deputies to carry out further in-depth studies on the key elements of the multilateralisation of the CMI including surveillance, reserve eligibility, size of commitment, borrowing quota and activation mechanism.' The Joint Ministerial Statement, 10th ASEAN+3 Finance Ministers' Meeting, May 2007, Kyoto, Japan, www.mof.go.jp/english/if/as3_070505.htm.

248   *Heribert Dieter*

importantly, Japan failed to pursue its own 1997 proposal for an Asian Monetary Fund out of deference to Washington. This failure to utilise the opportunity provided by the Asian crisis has crucially harmed Japan's leadership aspirations (Dieter and Higgott 1998). China, of course, snapped up the opportunity.

The rivalry between China and Japan overshadows monetary cooperation in the region. Although one could argue that both countries have pursued a constructive relationship in recent years – and both the CMI and the bond market initiatives (see below) confirm this – the unresolved nature of the two countries' relationship is the decisive issue for all types of integration in Asia. But this judgement requires qualification. As Keohane suggested back in 1984, there can be 'power without hegemony' (Keohane 1984).

China's position in Asia was much weaker in the beginning of the 1990s than it is today. At that time it did not enjoy full diplomatic relations with Indonesia, South Korea or even Singapore, while relations with Russia, India and Vietnam were hostile (Shambaugh 2004: 66). But the situation has since changed dramatically. David Shambaugh has emphasised that China is the fundamental cause of change in Asia, altering the traditional underpinnings of international relations in the region. China, moreover, is seen less and less as a threat:

most nations in the region now see China as a good neighbour, a constructive partner, a careful listener, and a nonthreatening regional power. This regional perspective is striking, given that just a few years ago, many of China's neighbours voiced growing concerns about the possibility of China becoming a domineering regional hegemon and powerful regional threat. (Shambaugh 2004: 64)

Over the past two decades, China has become an economic hub in Asia. Both in trade and production, countries in the region are increasingly benefiting from intense links with the country. Today nearly 50 per cent of China's trade is intra-regional, and it has no large trade surplus or deficit with any country in the region (Shambaugh 2004: 83). By opening itself to foreign investment and trade, China has not only become an indispensable trading partner, but also of strategic interest to many foreign companies (Zakaria 2005). Chinese diplomacy has encouraged this company-level development by portraying the country as the benign emerging giant of East Asia.[10]

With hindsight, the Asian crisis has been an opportunity for China, and an opportunity it has exploited. The decision not to devalue its

---

[10] For example, China offered an asymmetrical opening of its markets five years ahead of the opening required by its ASEAN trading partners (Cai 2003: 396).

Monetary and financial cooperation in Asia 249

currency in 1998 was wise and probably stemmed further panic (Dieter and Higgott 1998). While the USA initially refused to participate in the bail-out of Thailand, China in contrast offered aid packages to several Southeast Asian states. The Chinese approach was appreciated in the region, and stood in stark contrast to the authoritarian way the IMF and other international creditors imposed their programmes (Shambaugh 2004: 68). The rise of China's influence has been most significant where America's influence has declined: in South Korea and in Southeast Asia (Shambaugh 2004: 90). This is no coincidence. America's position deteriorated most in those countries that were affected by the Asian crisis and had to deal with IMF programmes. In these countries, China appears a more benign partner.

China's rise has been particularly damaging to Japan's leadership aspirations. In the monetary sphere China and Japan have reached a situation akin to the one described by David Rapkin in 2001, in which neither Japan nor the United States could advance a specific project because the other had the power to block it (Rapkin 2001). Today, the lack of progress in monetary regionalism can partly be explained by the willingness of both China and Japan to block any initiative that would improve the other's position in the region.

In trade, the rivalry between the two countries has led to a complex network of bilateral agreements that is making both regional trade and the deepening of regional production networks more difficult.[11] China took the lead by suggesting the establishment of an ASEAN-China free trade agreement in 2001; a similar agreement was then proposed by Japan. Competition between China and Japan has since then contributed to an ever more complex trade regime in the Asia-Pacific. Rather than developing a regional integration project that would eventually create an Asian common market, China and Japan are engaged in a struggle for superiority.

Stabilising exchange rates and surveillance

Exchange rates have a prominent place on Asian policy agendas. In Asia, as elsewhere, periods of high growth have usually been accompanied by stable exchange rates. This was the case in Japan's era of high growth in the 1950s and 1960s when the yen's peg to the dollar enabled Japan to transform itself into a manufacturing powerhouse (Chung and Eichengreen 2007: 1). Other Asian countries, including

---

[11] On the drawbacks of bilateral trade agreements see Dieter 2006; on the effects for production networks see Dieter 2007.

250   *Heribert Dieter*

Thailand, Indonesia and South Korea, have witnessed a similar correlation between high growth and stable exchange rates.[12]

Exchange rate regimes in the region today differ substantially. Japan in recent years has an arrangement resembling a free float although its central bank has been intervening heavily in foreign exchange markets over the last decades. A range of countries have intermediate regimes. Indonesia, Laos and Cambodia use managed floats with high flexibility while many other countries manage their exchange rates and permit relatively little fluctuation. The ASEAN members Singapore, Thailand, the Philippines and Vietnam operate such a regime, as do South Korea and Taiwan. China and Malaysia have a managed float vis-à-vis a basket of currencies. Hong Kong and Brunei use a currency board arrangement, that is, a hard peg (Kawai 2007: 103). Although exchange rate stabilisation has been much debated, in reality there has been very little formal cooperation; exchange rate policies in the region are set unilaterally, and the trend is towards managed or independently floating rates rather than a cooperative exchange rate arrangement (Dayaratna-Banda and Whalley 2007: 27).

Successful monetary integration in Asia requires steps beyond the CMI. A number of options are available. First, East Asian countries could develop a single currency, which would of course be very ambitious. Second, the ASEAN+3 countries could agree on a regional exchange rate mechanism similar to the European Exchange Rate Mechanism (ERM). In essence, participating countries would have stable but adjustable exchange rates in the region, but float vis-à-vis the rest of the world. Third, countries could abandon their dollar pegs (formal or informal) and jointly agree to peg their currencies to a single currency from the region, either the yen or the yuan. Fourth, countries could decide to peg their individual currencies to a basket of currencies, which could for example comprise the dollar, the euro and the yen (Dayaratna-Banda and Whalley 2007: 35). While the options continue to be discussed, the adoption of a single currency appears for the time being a distant prospect. And while an Asian Exchange Rate Mechanism remains possible, it would require substantial policy coordination and the subordination of national monetary policies to the goal of regional stability.

The third and fourth alternatives, however, are more realistic options. In pegging the region's currencies to a single currency other than the dollar, the question arises whether it should be the yen or the yuan.

---

[12] Stable does not mean fixed exchange rates. For example, Indonesia prior to 1997 implemented a crawling peg to the dollar that took into account diverging inflation rates.

Monetary and financial cooperation in Asia 251

Japan continues to be the leading supplier of foreign direct investment to the region while China has already become Asia's leading trader, in both imports and exports (Chung and Eichengreen 2007: 4). The fourth option – pegging to a basket of currencies – is much less problematic and has economic and political advantages. Kawai suggests the use of a basket comprising the dollar, the euro and the yen. This would provide greater stability for the real exchange rate and would make Asian countries less susceptible to fluctuations between the three currencies (Kawai 2007: 114).

Barry Eichengreen has suggested that a parallel currency could be introduced in Asia, not to replace national currencies but to exist alongside them. This Asian Currency Unit would be a weighted average of Asian currencies and could be used for invoicing in regional trade and to denominate bonds (Eichengreen 2007: 138). A parallel currency was used in Europe, where the European Currency Unit (ECU) was adopted in 1975 as a unit of account for the European Development Fund (Eichengreen 2007: 140). The European experience, however, shows that one should not expect too much. Despite the fact that European integration was firmly established by the mid-1970s, the ECU was never widely used. Transactions continued to be denominated in national currencies or the dollar; only the European Community used the ECU for budgetary purposes (Eichengreen 2007: 142). The parallel currency played a very limited role in fostering European monetary integration, and it is hard to see why its role in Asia would be significantly larger. Additionally, China-Japan rivalry may yet interfere with the necessary degree of cooperation required to realise any such project: it is not clear to what extent proposals such as the Kawai basket-based currency unit might fit with the recent suggestion by the Governor of the central bank of China that the IMF's Special Drawing Rights (SDRs) might be considered for its potential role as a reserve asset in international exchange rate and adjustment of payments imbalances.[13]

Enhanced regional surveillance is another ingredient for deeper cooperation in monetary affairs, not only to further regional integration but to combat the risk of contagion. The Asian crisis powerfully illustrated the need for regional monitoring (Giradin 2004: 345). But again, the benefits of surveillance should not be over-estimated. While some institutions such as the IMF believe it can be a powerful tool in the prevention of future financial crises, on closer inspection this is doubtful. There was no lack of data for both the Asian boom prior to 1997 and for the dotcom bubble before 2000. There simply is no

---

[13] See Zhou Xiaochuan, 'Reform the International Monetary System', speech 23 March 2009, text available at www.pbc.gov.cn/english/detail.asp?col=6500&id=178.

252 Heribert Dieter

working formula that does not predict too many crises while alerting us to the crucial ones. No forecasting model exists that would have predicted the Asian crisis (Frenkel and Menkhoff 2000: 29).[14] And where data were available – as in the USA in the years before the sub-prime crisis – 'financial innovation' made it difficult for supervisors to maintain a clear picture of developments. Consensus in Asia on which micro- or macroeconomic indicators should be monitored furthermore remains elusive (Dayaratna-Banda and Whalley 2007: 27).

The deepening of regional bond markets

Before the Asian crisis, many companies in the region borrowed funds from western financial institutions, usually denominated in foreign currency; the absence of an Asian bond market left enterprises in Asia little choice. Being able to use the region's savings without facing exchange rate risk or having to hedge against such risk would represent a major improvement in the region's financial architecture. It should be remembered that the combination of declining exchange rates and the unwillingness of international lenders to roll over existing debt were two main factors in the financial meltdown of 1997. Initiatives to create regional bond markets as well as to strengthen national bond markets have taken various forms: the Asian Bond Market Initiative (ABMI) proposed by the Japanese Ministry of Finance in 2002, the Asian Bond Fund (ABF) and the initiatives of the Executives' Meeting of East Asia and Pacific Central Banks (EMEAP). These will be discussed in turn.

The ABMI aims to create a suitable environment for the emission of bonds in regional financial markets (Arner *et al.* 2009: 31ff; Tourk 2004: 862). The development of bond market in Asia is currently hampered by weak financial institutions, the lack of financial intermediaries such as insurance companies and pension funds, and the unwillingness of international ratings agencies to provide credit ratings for Asian companies – many of which are family-owned and unable to provide the data required for analysis by independent evaluators. Without improvements in the above areas, companies in Asia will remain reluctant to use these instruments as unsecured corporate bonds will be significantly more expensive than bank loans.[15] The Asian Development

---

[14] The crisis which erupted in summer 2007 underlines the weakness of surveillance systems. While it was obvious that the USA was borrowing and spending beyond its means, financial markets preferred to ignore the fundamentals for years. On the (un)-sustainability of American economic development see, for example, Dieter and Silva-Garbade 2004.

[15] Tourk suggests unsecured bonds would require interest coupons of more than 18 per cent per annum (Tourk 2004: 862).

Monetary and financial cooperation in Asia 253

Bank supports ABMI by issuing bonds denominated in Thai baht and Philippine pesos (*Financial Times* 15 April 2005: 9).

The ABF was established in 2003. China, Japan, Hong Kong, Malaysia, Indonesia, the Philippines, Singapore, South Korea and Thailand have all agreed to contribute 1 per cent of their foreign reserves to the fund, which will invest in Asian debt securities (Tourk 2004: 865). The ABF initiative underlines the willingness of Asian governments to actively promote the deepening of their financial markets. Rather than waiting for the private sector to develop these structures, governments are seeking to speed up the process by creating the necessary market environment.

In contrast to the other projects, EMEAP is not a purely Asian venture. Membership is similar to the ABF, with the significant addition of Australia and New Zealand, two economies with well-developed financial markets and central banks possessing useful expertise. EMEAP is one of the older dialogue institutions in the region, having been set up in 1991 at the behest of the Bank of Japan (Castellano 2000: 1f). Few concrete steps were taken in its first years of existence, but since the turn of the century it has become an important – if underrated – venue for central bank cooperation in the region. While the USA remains excluded from EMEAP, its importance has not escaped Washington's attention.[16]

The first EMEAP Asian bond fund was launched in June 2003. Its $1 billion capital was invested in a basket of *dollar-denominated* bonds, issued by governments in all EMEAP countries except Japan, Australia and New Zealand (which already had well-developed bond markets). The fund was managed by the BIS in Basel (Battellino 2004: 13; Tourk 2004: 860; de Brouwer 2005: 8). The next phase, Asian Bond Fund 2, comprises a Pan-Asia Bond Index Fund (PAIF) and a Fund of Bond Funds (FoBF) consisting of eight separate country sub-funds (Battellino 2004: 13). PAIF is a single bond fund investing in sovereign and quasi-sovereign *local-currency-denominated* bonds issued in the eight EMEAP markets, again excluding Australia, Japan and New Zealand (EMEAP Press Statement 12 May 2005).

The importance of the EMEAP initiatives is considerable.[17] Central bankers from the region's larger economies have taken active steps to broaden and deepen the region's financial markets. If successful, these

[16] According to well-informed circles in Canberra, the Federal Reserve Bank in recent years expressed its interest in participating in EMEAP, only to be turned down by Asian central bankers.
[17] EMEAP itself claims the launch of the Asian Bond Fund 2 represents a milestone in central banking cooperation in the region, a rather unusual expression of excitement from central bankers (EMEAP press statement, 16 December 2004).

254   *Heribert Dieter*

efforts will in the long run result in reduced risk and better management in Asian financial markets. At the same time, the willingness to exclude the American Federal Reserve underlines central bankers' willingness to emancipate themselves from US authority; this dimension is as important as the bond market initiative itself. Nevertheless, a note of caution is appropriate. Regional bond markets are not a substitute for the reform of national financial markets. Furthermore, it is illusionary to think that regional bond markets can thrive while exchange rate volatility persists (Chung and Eichengreen 2007: 8). Stable exchange rates in the region would make cross-border investment – including portfolio investment – significantly more attractive. The development of regional bond markets and cooperation on exchange rate stability thus are inevitably linked.

Conclusion

The countries of East and Southeast Asia have been responding to obvious shortcomings in the effectiveness and legitimacy of the current regime of global financial governance. Thus far, regional cooperation has delivered clear improvements in legitimacy. Though governments are now working together within several regional initiatives, including the Chiang Mai Initiative and those for the creation of bond markets, they are not yet particularly effective as the ASEAN+3 economies continue to pile up costly reserves. While Asia has started to emancipate itself from western dominance in financial governance, the price of this liberation is considerable.

The financial crises of the 1990s were a traumatic learning experience. Especially some of the weaker states now appreciate the need to shed a little sovereignty in order to preserve wider state-building capacities and regional stability. Vulnerability to financial market volatility is now the major challenge to policy autonomy. This sense of vulnerability may well be the key to the further development of regional collective action in the monetary sphere. The current financial crisis is serving as a reminder for Asian economies that their efforts for deepening regional monetary cooperation continue to be of high importance. At the time of writing (autumn 2009), we can observe a fading willingness of western economies, in particular the USA and the United Kingdom, to change the regulation of their own financial markets. If the interests of Wall Street will once again prevail, this will probably fuel efforts in Asia for developing their own regimes of crisis prevention and crisis management. Asian countries may enhance input-side legitimacy by strengthening cooperation and participation of Asian countries in determining their destiny in the global monetary order, and simultaneously enhance output-side legitimacy and policy effectiveness by better aligning policy output and results to their interests and normative preferences.

In conclusion, this analysis confirms that monetary regionalism in Asia will be a complex endeavour and will only be achieved in the long run, if at all. Progress in monetary and financial integration in Asia must still overcome substantial technical problems. Currently, it also appears unlikely that Asian governments will be willing to give up a substantial degree of sovereignty over macroeconomic affairs – let alone push for the creation of an Asian supranational fiscal and monetary authority – unless China and Japan develop some form of joint leadership. Nevertheless, the discussion has shown that substantial economic benefits can be expected from monetary regionalism, and to assume that Asian countries will permit this opportunity to pass is probably a delusion.

14 From microcredit to microfinance to inclusive finance: a response to global financial openness

Brigitte Young

This chapter concerns the place of poor developing countries in the financial architecture and 'microlending' as a potential means for alleviating poverty. It critically examines the exponential rise of microfinance institutions (MFIs) and asks why they have become so central within strategies to combat poverty around the globe. Poverty alleviation has so far played a subordinate role in the design and functioning of the global financial system, at least in part because developing countries' concerns have been largely absent from the input side of global financial governance. Microlending is thus first and foremost a response to the exclusion of the poor from global and national financial systems. In important ways, the growth of microfinance is also a reaction to the dilemmas of financial openness and debt traps (Cassimon *et al.*, Chapter 4 in this volume) and the tendency of capital to flow 'uphill' from poor to developed economies (Prasad *et al.* 2006). Thus the crisis-prone process of global financial integration over the last thirty years is arguably the key to understanding this paradigmatic shift in international aid delivery. Global financial crises have increased economic instability for many among the poorest of the poor, who often bear the brunt in developing (and increasingly also developed) countries.

As the majority of the world's poor are women, women are also the most affected as the aid and financial architecture restricts the policy space available to national authorities. Aid and adjustment packages have often involved restrictive macroeconomic policies such as balanced budget requirements and specific limits on the debt to GDP ratio. Poor women (as well as men) have very little 'voice' in the national or global financial system; nor do they have the option to 'exit' macroeconomic instabilities since poor women in particular are often bound to specific places by virtue of their role in social reproduction (Elson 2006; Bakker 2007).[1]

---

[1] Social reproduction refers to biological reproduction, reproduction of labour power, and social practices connected to caring, socialisation and the fulfilment of human needs (Bakker and Gill 2003: 4).

From microcredit to microfinance to inclusive finance 257

The combination of financial turmoil and input-side exclusion is a striking illustration of the growing tension between the extended power of capital and the viability of human and economic development for people caught in cycles of poverty. Indeed, debates on the reform of financial architecture have largely ignored access to financial services for people from the lowest social strata – though they remain the most affected by the instabilities of financial openness (Young 2003; Ocampo *et al.* 2007).

The first section of the chapter provides a short overview of the normative shift in international aid allocation where inclusion of the poor in decision-making has followed the delegitimisation of earlier top-down approaches (Qudrat-I Elahi and Rahmann 2006). The second section begins with a description and clarification of the functional and conceptual differences between 'microcredit' programmes and 'microfinance' institutions (MFIs); it introduces data and examples of microfinance that show that since the 1990s loans have mainly gone to women. The third section focuses on the increasing role played by large private financial actors and global capital markets in the emerging microfinance system. An additional question has arisen in the past year of crisis: is microfinance a cushion for the poor in the current financial meltdown (since at the very bottom there is not much wealth to be destroyed)? Or will the current disinvestment and de-leveraging of many institutions have an impact on the growth plans of MFIs? The shift to 'inclusive finance' – which aims to provide access to credit for all 'bankable people and firms, to insurance for all insurable people and firms and to savings and payments services for everyone' (UNCDF 2006: 5) – raises normative and moral dilemmas that are discussed in the final section.

Changing norms: microlending, international aid and the financial architecture

In recent years a dramatic shift has taken place to integrate the poor into the financial system via microfinance, part of a larger trend in the governance of the 'international aid architecture' (Claessens *et al.*, Chapter 8 in this volume). The change in strategy was due to the failure of top-down aid allocation approaches to include the poor in the policy process and to effectively reduce poverty (Nourse 2001; Qudrat-I Elahi and Rahmann 2006).

The 1970s witnessed growing scepticism over the benefits of large development projects; state involvement and top-down approaches, previously seen as the cure, were increasingly cast as the problem (Kaul 2000). North-South public transfers through national and

258   *Brigitte Young*

international agencies in the 1960s and 1970s had fallen short of their aims largely because they excluded intended beneficiaries from decision-making (Benería 2003; Qudrat-I Elahi and Rahmann 2006). The 'Washington Consensus' of the 1980s and 1990s fared little better; IMF and World Bank conditionality excluded developing countries from ownership of top-down rules. Strictly enforced structural adjustment programmes further restricted the policy space of governments in developing countries to address poverty (Stiglitz 2005; Rodrik 2007). Cuts in public spending to achieve fiscal balance and the erosion of public revenues were particularly devastating for many among the poor, who in times of crisis only had the state to turn to. While macroeconomic policies to defeat inflation stabilised monetary regimes, high interest rates further undermined poor people's access to credit (Bakker 2007). As pointed out in this volume's introduction, pressures exerted by the norms of global financial integration not only limited the policy space available to developing countries; it put into question the political legitimacy of governments as well as the legitimacy of the entire financial system and aid architecture. Capital did not necessarily flow to where it was scarce and to where development needs were greatest, while the market did not replace the old system of aid transfers.

The delegitimising of previous approaches opened a 'policy window' for new ideas (Goldstein 1993). The recognition that financing for development affected not only capital flows and financial markets but all segments of society (Stiglitz 2005; Bakker 2007) informed a new strategy focused on the 'social dimension' of development policy. The World Bank, which since the early 1980s had focused on economic growth – the trickle-down effects of which would reduce poverty – changed course in the early 1990s to become a leading advocate of the new participatory approach. Social development together with economic growth now became the building blocks for the alleviation of poverty. The pillars shifted once again towards the end of the last decade. The emerging development agenda now suggested that social investment and investment in human capital were not enough to reduce poverty, which required focusing on a combination of political, economic, institutional, cultural and social factors – the prerequisites for long-term economic growth (Vetterlein 2007; Young 2008).

With this latest shift, the World Bank has fundamentally revised its traditional ideas and premises, recognising that there can be 'no economic growth without a social foundation' (World Bank 2001). 'Opportunities, empowerment, and security' for the poorest members of society are now central in its fight against poverty. The poor are

From microcredit to microfinance to inclusive finance 259

no longer seen as beneficiaries of top-down aid; instead, their individual powerlessness, voicelessness, vulnerability and fear are part of the matrix to facilitate economic growth (World Bank 2001: v). Normative concepts such as ownership, self-initiative, self-reliance and good governance are the pillars of this bottom-up approach and challenge our current understanding of poverty reduction and financial governance alike. In particular, past financial service provision to the poor was treated exclusively as part of social policy – distinct from the rest of the financial system. As a result, the initial microcredit revolution was dominated by non-profit organisations emphasising social over financial returns.

The new more market-oriented principles can be seen in many multilateral and bilateral frameworks and conventions including the Poverty Reduction Strategy Papers (PRSPs), the Millennium Development Goals (MDGs) and the 2003 proposal by the United Kingdom to create the International Finance Facility (IFF). The Monterrey Consensus adopted by heads of state and governments at the International Conference on Financing for Development in 2002 declared that 'microfinance and credit for micro-, small and medium enterprises ... as well as national savings schemes are important for enhancing the social and economic impact of the financial sector' (United Nations 2002) which requires adequate attention to 'financial inclusion today, tomorrow, and the next day' (UNCDF 2006: iv). The United Nations General Assembly, in declaring 2005 the International Year of Microcredit, focused on those factors that exclude people from full participation in the financial sector, while concrete indicators and targets for financial inclusiveness were part of the Paris Declaration on Aid Effectiveness in 2005 (Bakker 2007). These changes signal for the first time recognition by the international donor community that the poor need reliable access to banking systems, which can also be an important institutional building block for economic growth.

The ascendancy of microfinance can thus be seen as both a reaction against the contemporary global financial order, but also as an integral part of global finance. This seemingly contradictory stance suggests that while microfinance initially developed as a counter-reaction and as an avenue out of poverty for those sidelined by the global financial reform agenda, it later was coopted by finance once the traditional view changed to the idea that 'the poor are bankable'. This shift in emphasis from providing 'the passive poor' with top-down aid to providing them with the means to harness their own initiative in ways of their own choosing is the 'driving force' behind the microfinance ascendancy. Historically, lending to the poor was considered a socially worthy cause

260   *Brigitte Young*

but did not attract institutional and individual investors. Typically, donor-driven, NGO-dominated microcredit institutions provided small loans to the poor who, since they possessed neither land nor collateral, were viewed as excessive security risks by commercial banks. But now the microfinance sector is in a transition from a largely NGO-dominated governance structure towards the increasing involvement of large private investors; the traditional view of the poor has given way to the idea that 'the poor are bankable' and that the banks extending the loans are 'bankable as well' (UNCDF 2006: 47; Commonwealth Secretariat 2007). Professional investors – pension funds, insurance companies, universities and religious institutions, philanthropic foundations and large investment banks such as Deutsche Bank, Citigroup, Commerzbank, HSBC and ABN Amro – now see microfinance as an important investment opportunity (*The Economist* 3 November 2005).

The shift towards new forms of financial service delivery to the poor has important normative implications. The 'bottom-up' approach of microfinance suggests that the inclusion and integration of large segments of the poor into the stream of global finance not only has the potential to improve the effectiveness of aid, but in the process may also strengthen the legitimacy of governance. Instead of starting from the assumption that there is a trade-off between economic effectiveness and input legitimacy, the new 'socially responsible investments' strategy suggests that economic efficiency can, at least in theory, be combined with social efficiency.[2]

The move towards inclusion and the effects of financial volatility mean that we now face a new reality. Large private financial investors are eager to enter the microfinance business and to link poverty alleviation to capital markets via microfinance. Even Muhammed Yunus advocates the idea of a 'social-consciousness-driven capitalism'; it certainly fits Bill Gates' call for a new form of 'creative capitalism' to utilise those aspects of capitalism that have served the wealthy so well to equally serve the poor (*Financial Times* 25 January 2008). In this process, commercial profits are seen as compatible with socially responsible investment (Deutsche Bank Research 2007).

It is this market-driven focus of microfinance that is being questioned by many (feminist) development experts. They agree that gaining access to credit is vital for the poor (particularly poor women) to counter the cycle of poverty. But they argue that such access is insufficient to

---

[2] Social efficiency is a broader concept and includes input and allocative efficiency in comparison to the more narrow concept of economic efficiency which stresses competition and private market discipline (Bakker 2007: 19).

From microcredit to microfinance to inclusive finance 261

guarantee financial sustainability and transform traditional asymmetric gender relations (Goetz and Sen Gupta 1996; Scully 1997; Hanak 2000; Mayoux 2000, 2002; Lucarelli 2005). Feminists criticise further that the discourse on female empowerment present in many microfinance programmes veils the hierarchical power relations of the global economy to the detriment of poor developing countries and their citizens (Rankin 2002; Weber 2002, 2004, 2006; Brigg 2006; Fernando 2006). The jury is still out on whether the integration of poverty alleviation with financial returns is a viable strategy. In the worst-case scenario, it may be little more than 'old wine in new bottles' – that is, furthering the process of financial integration with questionable benefits for the poor.

The next section provides an overview of the functional and conceptual differences between microcredit and microfinance and presents some data on the number of MFIs, average loan size, borrowers per region and the number of poor women served.

From microcredit programmes to microfinance institutions

The literature invariably uses the terms 'microcredit' and 'microfinance' interchangeably. There are, however, important differences in the types of financial services they offer and their conceptual dimensions (Qudrat-I Elahi and Rahmann 2006). Microcredit programmes are associated with small-sum credits for poor self-employed individuals. The term 'microcredit' – while still in use, witness the 'Microcredit Summit'[3] – is associated with the first phase of giving credits to the poor in the 1950s. The focus then was on small-scale male farmers (Matin *et al.* 2002). Yet the strategy to provide the poor with small amounts of credit was not new. According to Seibel (2005), India's indigenous microcredit predates the German *Raiffeisen* system by around 300 years. Postal systems have also been major providers of savings and payment services, not just in Europe since the nineteenth century, but in Japan and elsewhere. Government-run credit programmes and government-owned banks were another source of small loans to the poor in Asia, Africa and Latin America.

The *Raiffeisen* system of the 1860s was an important Austro-German initiative with some interesting parallels to the modern microcredit/

---

[3] The 'Microcredit Summit' consists of banks, educational institutions, international development organisations, international financial institutions, NGOs and governmental organisations, www.microcreditsummit.org.

262   *Brigitte Young*

microfinance movement. Consisting of savings and credit cooperatives based on the self-help principle, the system was a response to high
interest rates in the poorer areas of Germany which could reach up to
700 per cent per annum. *Raiffeisen's* credit unions were member-owned
banks, initially based on group-based lending techniques; they were
bottom-up institutions that combined poverty outreach with financial
sustainability (Seibel 2005; UNCDF 2006: 8).

Despite their early successes in the 1960s, microcredit programmes
reached their functional and organisational limits in the mid-1970s.
As 'credit only' facilities, their function was limited to providing small
sums of money and overseeing the repayment of loans through com-
pulsory saving. This ignored the development of other important cus-
tomer-oriented financial services. First, reliance on donor institutions
meant microcredit programmes did not focus on their members' savings deposits. Public subsidies thus produced negative effects. Subsidies
were not used to pay for the daily operational costs of microcredit programmes, but for the provision of 'cheap credit'. As a result, microcredit
institutions became more and more reliant on public grants. In addition, few regulatory mechanisms and supervisory authorities existed to
control the distribution of credit. Hence a lot of money ended up in the
pockets of local elites.

On top of this, restricting loans to individual borrowers led to attri-
tion of the more successful and affluent recipients who shifted to formal banking institutions. Not only did this reduce the total number
of credit applicants, it also interfered with the sustainability of microcredit institutions and in the long run limited the allocation of credits to the poorest of the poor (Hollis and Sweetman 1998; Robinson
2001).[4]

While the micro*credit* movement was geared to lend to the poor and
is generally referred to as the first revolution, micro*finance* institutions
(MFIs) ushered in the second revolution and are the forerunners of
the movement today. Although the allocation of credit still plays an
important role, today's MFIs differ from their predecessors by offering more services (i.e. the administration of small savings accounts,
insurance policies to protect against natural crises and death, money
transfers and remittances from and to foreign countries). Most importantly, MFIs differ from microcredit programmes in two ways. First,
MFIs are 'for profit ventures' (Qudrat-I Elahi and Rahmann 2006).
In contrast, non-governmental and non-profit organisations focus on
the reduction of poverty and not on financial return. Second, MFIs

---

[4] Also Jouben, Lindsay 2008. 'The Illusively Sustainable Development: Microfinance,
Gender, and the New World Order', unpublished thesis, Rutgers University-Newark.

From microcredit to microfinance to inclusive finance 263

are less dependent on public subsidies and other donor organisations. Many have grown independent of government and political influence and place great emphasis on economic efficiency.

The promoters of microfinance differ in another vital aspect. Microcredit was product-centred; business was essentially organised around small loans but did not develop additional products to match evolving demand (Qudrat-I Elahi and Rahmann 2006). Viewing the poor as customers with specific needs for financial services led to a shift in perception: the poor became clients rather than beneficiaries (Nourse 2001). This led to the realisation that the poor do indeed have the ability to save and that sustainable microfinance strategies must include insurance coverage to protect against unexpected catastrophes. The new approach centred on the idea that 'what households need is access to credit, not cheap credit' (Morduch 1999, 2000; Matin *et al.* 2002: 285).

Microfinance services are currently provided through NGOs, private banking institutions, state-based banks, postal savings banks, financial institutions (i.e. insurance companies), credit institutions and a variety of other lending institutions. Many of these are large institutions offering diverse products and services. MFIs thus represent a special type of financial organisation; as they can be registered as NGOs, cooperative societies, or banks with special charters like the Grameen Bank, they can be classified as 'semi-informal'.

The microfinance revolution began with the experiment of the Grameen Bank in Bangladesh in 1976. The concept of its founder, Muhammad Yunus, recipient of the 2006 Nobel Peace Prize, was to extend small loans to poor people without collateral. In fact, inspiration for the Grameen Bank is rooted in the German credit cooperative movement. The government of Madras in southern India, part of the British Empire in 1880, adopted the principle of credit cooperatives to reduce widespread rural poverty. The cooperatives spread from there to Bengal, where the group loan idea stayed alive and eventually inspired the Grameen model (Morduch 1999).

According to the Grameen Bank website of February 2010, the Bank operates 2,563 branches providing services to 81,343 villages with a total staff of 23,275. The banks serve over 8 million members, of whom 97 per cent are women. They generally charge a nominal interest rate of 20 per cent (the real rate is approximately 15–16 per cent) which can vary between institutions. Loans are typically granted for one year and average US$134 (Morduch 1999: 1574; Brigg 2006). While the Grameen Bank website states the official repayment rate is 98 per cent, this is rather questionable. *The Economist* (2005) assumes not all repayments are accurately reported in rural areas.

264 *Brigitte Young*

An interesting aspect of microfinance, for which the Grameen Bank is a good example, is the shift towards women as its business base. Between 1980 and 1983, women accounted for 39 per cent of clients. But this changed drastically in subsequent years. Already in 1991–2 women accounted for 93 per cent of all creditors (Goetz and Sen Gupta 1996). This rose to 97 per cent for the Grameen case in 2009. Clients of MFIs in Asia are virtually all women, while women make up 67 per cent of clients in Africa, 66 per cent of clients in the Middle East and North Africa, and 59 per cent of clients in Latin America and the Caribbean (Commonwealth Secretariat 2007: 9). This gender-specific shift reflects the new 'social dimension' in the fight against poverty. The current focus on gender, combined with higher repayment rates among women, has made women the explicit target of microfinance (*Financial Times* 28 September 2006; World Bank 2006b). Not only 'reaching' but 'empowering' women became the second official goal of the Microcredit Summit Campaign to reach the Millennium Development Goals (Commonwealth Secretariat 2007).

It is estimated that there are over 10,000 MFIs around the world: credit unions, NGOs, cooperatives, government agencies, and private and commercial banks. Average loans in 2006 ranged from US$149 in Asia and US$235 in Africa to US$678 in Latin America and the Caribbean and US$1,597 in Eastern Europe and Central Asia. Borrowers make up 2 per cent of the population in Eastern Europe, 20 per cent in East Asia and 51 per cent in South Asia (Deutsche Bank Research 2007: 3–4).

The 'Microcredit Summit' wants 175 million families to have access to small cash loans by 2015. The 3,552 MFIs reporting to the Microcredit Summit currently reach 154.8 million clients; about 106.6 million were very poor when they started the programme. Of the more than 106 million poorest clients with a loan at the end of 2007, 83.2 per cent or 88.7 million are women. The number of very poor women reached has thus risen from 10.3 million at the end of 1999 to 88.7 million at the end of 2007 – an additional 78.4 million women, or a 764 per cent increase between 1999 and 2007. Approximately 90.6 per cent of the poorest clients live in Asia, home to approximately 63.5 per cent of the world's population living on less than one dollar a day (Daley-Harris 2009, 23, 25, 29).

Linking microfinance to global capital markets: inclusive finance

Microfinance in recent years has become a highly attractive investment strategy for private institutional and individual investors. High

From microcredit to microfinance to inclusive finance 265

repayment rates among micro-borrowers minimise the risk. As the *Financial Times* (13 February 2006) noted, financial investors have recognised that 'banking on women' can be a highly profitable investment strategy as well as a form of foreign aid. Within the growing movement championing socially responsible investment, large private investors such as Deutsche Bank suggest the much discussed trade-off between social returns and financial profitability can be minimised, and that new patterns of governance in global finance can be developed that are both effective and include a wide range of stakeholders (Goodmann 2006; Matthäus-Maier and von Pischke 2006; UNCDF 2006; Deutsche Bank Research 2007; MiX (Microfinance Information eXchange) 2007).

But this is not the whole story. Central to understanding why private investors are keen to enter emerging microfinance markets is the expected steep rise in demand for financial services. Estimates forecast a large gap between supply and demand while pundits in the field argue that only by integrating MFIs into capital markets can this shortfall be met. Subsidised loans alone are no longer sufficient to cover the expected funding needs of MFIs. Deutsche Bank estimates that MFIs currently serve an estimated 100 million micro-borrowers,[5] but that potential demand is closer to one billion borrowers. With current loans totalling an estimated US$25 billion, this translates into an estimated funding gap of US$250 billion. The estimated untapped growth factor of ten represents enormous potential for institutional investors.

Since 2004, international public and private sector investors have more than doubled their investments to US$4.4 billion. It is expected that large investors will further increase their investments to around US$20 billion by 2015. It should come as no surprise that large private actors are much less interested in the 90 per cent of MFIs (mostly NGOs) that are either unprofitable or barely approaching profitability. Their interest is in the top 10 per cent of mature, regulated and financially sustainable MFIs (around three hundred of them) as well as smaller MFIs approaching profitability (Deutsche Bank Research 2007: 6).

While many unregulated NGOs and microfinance institutions rely on grants and concessional funding as well as bank lines of credit, experts predict that the future sustainability of MFIs depends on tapping a broader range of funding sources, both domestically and internationally. As can be seen in Figure 14.1, the largely unregulated MFIs

---

[5] The estimate of 100 million cited by Deutsche Bank differs from the 133 million cited in the Microcredit Summit Report. There are no reliable data on the number of clients served by MFIs.

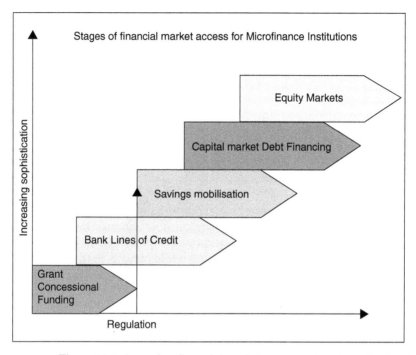

Figure 14.1. Accessing financial markets: progressive stages for MFIs
Source: UNCDF 2006: 76.

at the bottom of the pyramid rely mostly on concessional grants and subsidised loans. Access to diverse funding sources and longer maturities is possible only at the upper stages of financial markets – through bond issues, securitisation and equity finance (UNCDF 2006: 76).

However, international intermediaries who invested in MFIs before the global financial crisis are now in the process of reconsidering their investment policies. The increasing liquidity constraints are forcing many institutions (such as endowment or pension funds, foundations, governmental agencies for development, etc.) to de-leverage and sell their assets. Roberto Moro Visconti, a financial consultant, suggests that the main casualties in the microfinance funding situation during this economic crisis are the structured products that were being used to raise capital, such as Collateralised Debt or Loan Obligations (Visconti 2009). It is estimated that more than 25 per cent of non-deposit-taking MFIs decreased their lending in the past twelve months globally. However, others argue that the present slowdown is an opportunity to take stock, bolster governance and improve services such as financial literacy for customers.

Nancy Berry, the former president of Women's World Banking, sees a silver lining in the present slowdown of growth in the MFI sector. 'I hope we do have a slowdown. The industry was in a race to grow with little depth. That creates serious credit risks' (Financial Times 23 March 2009). Agreement seems to exist among microfinance experts that in spite of uncertain conditions, the long-term outlook for microfinance is largely positive though the sector's astronomical growth will slow.

There is another reason why corporations, investment banks, pension funds and telecom companies (e.g. Vodafone) are entering and will continue to enter the microfinance market. Quite apart from the humanitarian promise of 'inclusive finance', these investors are interested in minimising risk and see new opportunities. The UNCDF report *Building Inclusive Financial Sectors for Development* (2006) states that weak institutional banking structures in most developing countries discourage inclusion of the poor in the financial circuit. Under current conditions, banks are unlikely to provide the needed regulatory framework for sustainable MFIs, which in turn limits bank involvement (Schmidt and Winkler 2000).

The answer lies not in simply linking microfinance institutions to capital markets. We need new governance structures to reform the legal and regulatory financial environments of domestic markets. Small banking structures are seen as impediments to achieving economies of scale. Thus 'financial sectors with a limited range of institutions, limited total assets in the banking system in relation to GDP, and underdeveloped financial markets are far less likely to offer access to financial markets by MFIs' (UNCDF 2006: 77).

According to this story, the bottom line is that institutional factors limit the ability of MFIs to access financial markets in many developing countries. Surely institutional reforms make sense, especially if existing institutions block poor people from participating in the financial system. The promotion of 'inclusive finance', however, does not provide a detailed blueprint for institutional reform. If it is a market-driven model primarily focused on competition, stricter regulations and 'effective' supervision, we need to ask if such a system can serve the poorest of the poor at all. It is not altogether surprising that the Microfinance Information eXchange calls for a reorientation of MFI operations to 'develop new products and services that will help them [MFIs] move traditional clients up the income ladder and also meet the demands of the existing middle class' (MiX 2007: 4).

While data are unavailable to judge whether 'inclusive finance' can be squared with effective development strategy, it seems plausible that

268   *Brigitte Young*

the upper strata of the poor and the lower middle class poor in many developing countries would benefit from such a system. What seems less likely is that the poorest of the poor, living on a dollar a day, would benefit. As Matin *et al*. and many others have noted, 'microfinance is not a magic sky-hook that reaches down to pluck the poor out of poverty. It can, however, be a strategically vital platform that the poor can use to raise their own prospects for an escape from poverty' (Matin *et al* 2002: 273).

Conclusion

This chapter has critically examined why microfinance institutions grew to prominence within global poverty alleviation strategies in the 1990s. A closely related question was why large private investors have entered the largely donor-driven, NGO-dominated governance structure of microfinance. The two most plausible driving forces behind the microfinance revolution are the 'aid architecture' debate and its attendant reforms; and the problems of financial openness with its macroeconomic instabilities and constraints on 'policy space'. The alleged failure of subsidised and public transfer payments alongside debt and financial crisis provided the underlying rationale for the microfinance revolution.

Global financial openness with its periodic volatility reduced the 'policy space' for many governments in developing countries to respond to financial upheavals. At the same time, the effects of macroeconomic adjustment opened 'policy space' for bottom-up aid approaches as both the exclusion of the poor from the global financial system (input legitimacy) and the effectiveness of top-down approaches (output legitimacy) were challenged outright. The resulting normative shift to integrate the poor via microfinance and the *subsequent* realisation that the 'poor *are* bankable' and that the banks extending loans are 'bankable *as well*' attracted large private investors; the latter now advocate that economic efficiency and the integration of a large segment of the poor into the stream of finance are mutually compatible goals. The new 'private initiative capitalism' with its emphasis on self-initiative and self-reliance has become the road map to 'financial empowerment' for individuals caught in the vicious circle of poverty. At the same time, due to some of the sector's intrinsic characteristics, such as closeness to clients and limited risk and exposure, microfinance tends to behave in an anti-cyclical manner, thus providing a shelter in the present economic recession (Visconti 2009).

From microcredit to microfinance to inclusive finance 269

The integration of the poor into global capital markets raises important normative issues. Nobody would dispute that the poor need convenient, safe, reliable and affordable access to financial services. But we should also keep in mind that 'inclusive finance' may yet again expose the poor to the very problems of volatility in capital flows and exchange rates that come with financial openness. It is thus not surprising that many critics of market-oriented microfinance view the 'win-win' approach of large financial corporations with growing scepticism.

Ultimately, it may be more honest to recognise that there are different strata of the poor with very different needs. Privately funded MFIs linked to capital markets may work well for particular social strata, but may not be appropriate for the most vulnerable people whose circumstances require much more than access to financial services. The recognition that there is no 'one-size-fits-all' strategy to mitigate poverty and that there are different strata of the poor with unique needs may open policy spaces to provide custom-made access to financial services. Such a strategy may in the end help to reach the Millennium Development Goals more effectively and with more legitimacy.

15 Combating pro-cyclicality in the international financial architecture: towards development-friendly financial governance

José Ocampo and Stephany Griffith-Jones

Introduction

As noted in several earlier chapters (e.g. the Introduction by Underhill, Blom and Mügge; Chapters 3 by Baker and 9 by Tsingou), developing countries have had relatively little influence on the development of the existing international financial architecture. Whether the term is actively used or not, there is an odour of policy capture by private interests circulating around public decision-making processes in financial governance (e.g. Chapter 6 by Claessens and Underhill; Chapter 2 by Helleiner and Pagliari), indicating a lack of input-side legitimacy within the current international financial architecture. This limited input legitimacy has contributed to building a system which is far from development-friendly, particularly for the poorest countries. This in turn limits the output-side legitimacy (i.e. the effectiveness) of global financial governance from the standpoint of a wide range of developing economies (see Chapter 4 by Cassimon, Demetriades and Van Campenhout). This limited output legitimacy is particularly visible in the highly pro-cyclical, market-based nature of the system, limiting policy space for developing countries and enhancing the possibility of costly bubbles and crises. This chapter argues that one of the major functions of an effective international financial architecture should be to mitigate the pro-cyclical effects of financial markets and to open 'policy space' for counter-cyclical macroeconomic policies in the developing world. The chapter goes on to provide recommendations to enhance the development-friendliness of the international financial architecture in this respect.

Professor and Co-president of the Institute for Policy Dialogue, Columbia University; and Professor and Director of the Financial Markets Programme at the Institute for Policy Dialogue, Columbia University, respectively. This chapter builds on our paper 'A Countercyclical Framework for a Development-Friendly International Financial Architecture', published in J. M. Fanelli (ed.) *Macro-Economic Volatility, Institutions and Financial Architectures* (Palgrave, 2008).

Combating pro-cyclicality in financial architecture 271

The boom-bust patterns of financial markets and their highly negative effects have been evident in numerous developing country crises since the 1980s, especially in the East Asian and Russian crises of 1997–8 and the Argentine/Turkish crises of the turn of the century. But the resulting reform of the international financial architecture has been disappointing.[1] Reform of governance in the International Monetary Fund (IMF) has been unsatisfactory, while reform in other bodies (e.g. the Basel Committee) has until recently not happened at all. This is particularly worrying at a time when a major financial crisis has broken out centred in the USA and the developed world. Indeed, the current crisis provides further evidence that unless properly regulated, financial markets anywhere, at any time, are prone to harmful boom-bust patterns (Kindleberger 1982; Soros 2008). The new crisis has been accompanied by serious and large-scale macroeconomic global disequilibria and has now given birth to renewed debate and new initiatives on financial regulation, including the need to introduce counter-cyclical elements into the architecture.

This negative picture contrasts with (at least so far) more positive trends across a range of developing countries that have improved their macroeconomic management and domestic financial regulation as well as developed local bond markets, especially in domestic currencies. Furthermore, they have 'self-insured' themselves against financial crises by accumulating extremely high foreign exchange reserve buffers. These reached the unprecedented amount of five trillion US dollars in late 2007, to which should be added three trillion US dollars in foreign sovereign wealth funds (Griffith-Jones and Ocampo 2008). The reserves in particular reflect, at least in part, a lack of confidence in existing collective mechanisms for official liquidity provision during crises.

While this chapter focuses principally on the design of a counter-cyclical framework for global financial governance, this needs to be seen in the broader context of a reformed international financial architecture as analysed throughout this book, both in terms of decision-making processes and outcomes (see in particular the Introduction and the chapter by Underhill and Zhang).[2] The input-side governance of the system should give developing countries sufficient representation to reflect their growing role in the world economy, while more attention should be paid to avoiding policy capture by private interests.

---

[1] There is a very large literature on this subject. See for example Underhill and Zhang 2003 for a comprehensive analysis. For our own work, see Griffith-Jones and Ocampo (2003).

[2] There are also important issues relating to regional financial architecture, which we have not included.

272   *José Ocampo and Stephany Griffith-Jones*

The chapter proceeds as follows. In the next section we set out the current pro-cyclical tendencies of the international financial architecture and analyse the negative effects of the financial instability it tends to generate. In the following section we discuss the implications of this general context for promoting development-friendly international financial governance. The following four sections then discuss several concrete proposals aimed at reducing the pro-cyclical bias of private financial markets, thus opening 'policy space' for counter-cyclical macroeconomic polices especially in emerging markets and developing countries. As we will show, these measures can be both market-based and regulatory, national and multilateral. The final section concludes by summarising our proposals.

The current international financial architecture: capital account volatility in the developing world

From a development perspective, the international financial architecture has four main aims: (1) to promote the consistency of national macroeconomic policies with stability at the global level, thereby avoiding negative macroeconomic policy spill-overs from some (especially large) countries to others; (2) to provide transparency and ensure appropriate and comprehensive regulation of banking and capital markets both nationally (especially in the main financial centres) and internationally; (3) to supply sufficient international liquidity during crises, providing a complement to national lenders of last resort; and (4) to provide adequate international mechanisms for orderly debt and financial crisis workouts. These aims imply that developing country interests must be comprehensively addressed before any form of international financial governance may be understood as effective.

The current global financial architecture is deficient on all these counts. A central problem is the essential pro-cyclicality of the contemporary market-based order. During the last three decades, those developing countries that became more integrated into world financial markets experienced highly pro-cyclical volatility in their external financing. This financial volatility directly affected both their balance of payments and domestic financial markets, and through them damaged domestic economic activity and other macroeconomic variables. Given this volatility, developing countries lost 'policy space' to adopt autonomous counter-cyclical macroeconomic policies and faced great difficulties creating the deep financial markets which many associate with successful economic development. A vicious circle emerged involving pro-cyclical financing, underdeveloped financial markets and institutions, and external constraints on macroeconomic policy autonomy. The unfortunate outcome was that 'twin' external and domestic financial crises became far more frequent after the breakdown of the Bretton Woods exchange rate arrangements (Bordo *et al.* 2001).

Trade volume and terms of trade fluctuations typically play a major role in the determination of business cycles in developing countries, particularly in commodity-dependent economies. Nonetheless, since the 1970s business cycles in developing countries have been characterised by the leading role played by *capital* account fluctuations. This has been particularly true for economies more integrated into world financial markets, the 'emerging market economies'. Boom-bust cycles in capital flows reflect investor herding and associated contagion – of both optimism and pessimism. Volatility is associated with significant changes in risk evaluation, involving alternating periods of 'appetite for risk' (more precisely, underestimation of risks) and 'flight to quality' (risk aversion). Market-sensitive risk management practices as well as the evaluation of managers against competitor performance serve to increase herding (Persaud 2000). Furthermore, due to information asymmetries, different assets tend to be pooled together in risk categories viewed by market agents as strongly correlated. This practice turns such correlations into self-fulfilling prophecies. These problems have been dramatically evident in 2007–8, particularly in the United States.

Boom-bust cycles have renewed the relevance of the endogeneity of financial market instability as analysed by Minsky (1982), who demonstrated how financial booms generate excessive risk-taking by market agents, which eventually leads economies into crises. From a different theoretical perspective, a similar explanation has been suggested by White (2006) who argues that the 'search for yield' characteristics of low interest rate environments generate incentives for credit creation, carry trade and leverage that easily build up asset bubbles. 'The main risks to the financial sector could stem from financial excesses linked to a generalised complacency towards risk reinforced by a benign short-term outlook' (BIS 2005: 120). These analyses appear particularly prescient in the light of recent events.

In developing countries, fluctuations in capital markets have been reflected in the pro-cyclical pattern of spreads, variations in the availability of financing (absence or presence of credit rationing) and in maturities. This involves short-term volatility, such as intense upward movement of spreads and periods of interruption (rationing) of financing during crises. More importantly, they also involve *medium-term* cycles as witnessed over the past three decades (see Figure 15.1 in

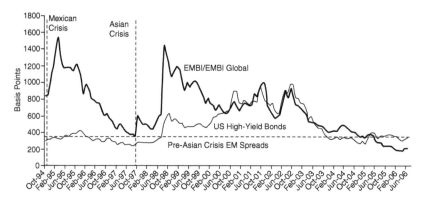

Figure 15.1. Emerging market spreads on JP Morgan EMBI global and US high-yield bonds, October 1994 to June 2006
Source: ECLAC, on the basis of data from Merrill Lynch's US High-Yield Master II Index (H0A0); JP Morgan Chase's EMBI and EMBI Global.

relation to spreads since 1994). This period saw two full medium-term cycles: a boom of external financing in the 1970s followed by a major debt crisis in the 1980s; a new boom in the 1990s followed by a sharp reduction in net flows after the Asian and Russian crises of 1997–8. Since 2002–3, a new cycle has been in place which has most likely deteriorated into a downward phase as a result of the current crisis.

Different types of capital flows show different volatility patterns. The higher volatility of short-term capital indicates reliance on such financing is highly risky (Rodrik and Velasco 2000) whereas the lower volatility of FDI is considered a source of strength. However, 'financial engineering' may be making these erstwhile different flows increasingly convergent in their behaviour. Particularly the use of securitised risk management techniques by multinationals, via derivatives, may mean that in critical moments FDI flows contribute to volatility. For example, foreign subsidiaries in emerging markets (which are likely to have a net foreign exchange risk exposure vis-à-vis strong currencies) may not hedge this exposure permanently but only once pressure on the local currency starts emerging. By engaging in such a 'dynamic hedging strategy' their hedging transactions which will increase pressure on the currency will materialise exactly when that pressure is already there (Dodd and Griffith-Jones 2007).

During booms, developing countries viewed by markets as 'success' stories are almost inevitably drawn into the capital account boom, inducing private sector deficits and risky balance sheets (French-Davis 2001;

Marfán 2005). But even countries with weak 'fundamentals' may be drawn into the boom (see for example Calvo *et al.* 1993) while all countries, again with some independence from their 'fundamentals', will be drawn into 'sudden stops' (Calvo and Talvi 2004). Conditions become particularly difficult in developing countries during crises because rising risk premiums and the reduced availability of external financing may eliminate room for counter-cyclical monetary and fiscal policies and may rather force them to adopt pro-cyclical ones – i.e. high interest rates and tight fiscal policies. While industrial countries can smooth pro-cyclical effects of credit and asset prices through counter-cyclical macroeconomic policies (as is occurring in the current crisis), developing countries may be forced to adopt pro-cyclical macroeconomic policies that reinforce the movements of financial markets.

There is also widespread evidence that ample private sector financing encourages pro-cyclical macroeconomic policies during booms. Unstable external financing distorts incentives that both private agents and authorities face *throughout* the business cycle, inducing the pro-cyclical behaviour of economic agents *and* macroeconomic policies (Kaminsky *et al.* 2004). In the words of Stiglitz (2003), increased exposure to financial market risks has replaced Keynesian automatic stabilisers with automatic *de*-stabilisers. Contrary to the view that liberalised financial markets would play a disciplining role, dependence on financial swings has encouraged the adoption of pro-cyclical monetary and fiscal policies.

Although pro-cyclicality is inherent in financial markets, domestic financial and capital account liberalisation in the developing world have accentuated its effects. A lag in developing adequate prudential regulation and supervision frameworks further increases the risks of financial liberalisation, and the costs of such financial volatility in terms of economic growth are high. There is now overwhelming evidence that pro-cyclical financial markets and macroeconomic policies have increased growth volatility and have not encouraged growth in the developing world (Prasad *et al.* 2003), while efficiency gains from financial market integration are swamped by the negative effects of growth volatility. Eichengreen (2004) estimated that over the past twenty-five years, currency and banking crises have lowered the income of developing countries by 25 per cent. Others have estimated even higher average annual costs of crises. Indonesia experienced larger falls in output and income during the Asian crisis than the United States did during the Great Depression.

Each medium-term financial cycle may have specific features. The cycle leading up to the current crisis was characterised by an unprecedented accumulation of international reserves and reduced debt ratios – 'self-insurance' by developing countries against the financial instability experienced in previous crises. While such 'self-insurance' together with booming exports and the development of local-currency bond markets may have changed the conditions surrounding developing country financing in recent years, new risks have emerged or become more prominent. First, new sources of potential pro-cyclicality have emerged, particularly related to the explosive growth of derivatives worldwide. In developing economies, derivative contracts are used both to hedge risk and for international hedge funds and investment banks to speculate, for example via the 'carry trade'. Large segments of these derivative markets are unregulated (as they operate in the over-the-counter market and offshore). Nor have existing regulations fully incorporated the risks derivatives pose in situations of stress, when they can add to systemic risk.

Second, uncertainties associated with the disorderly unravelling of accumulated global imbalances and the effects of the current financial turmoil may undermine the prospects of developing economies. Paradoxically, developing country 'self-insurance' measures (large current account surpluses, increased international reserves and reduced indebtedness) are *part* of global imbalances. Developing countries' new sources of strength when viewed on a country-by-country basis are one of the elements of vulnerability for developing countries as a whole. A global cooperative approach to the provision of 'collective insurance' and the management of global imbalances would thus be a more desirable solution (Griffith-Jones and Ocampo 2008).

Implications of financial volatility for financial governance

Developing countries are plagued by myriad financial market imperfections, particularly currency and maturity mismatches. Risks associated with financial instability can be corrected in part through domestic policy involving variable mixes of accumulating foreign exchange reserves during booms, counter-cyclical fiscal policies, strengthened prudential regulation and supervision, exchange rate intervention, management of the capital account (including through incentives to reduce debt or improve its term structure during booms), and use of the margins that these policies generate for counter-cyclical monetary policy (Ocampo 2005). These actions, however, are not without costs. The accumulation of international reserves to cover risks associated with short-term capital is usually expensive. While the risks faced by the domestic financial

Combating pro-cyclicality in financial architecture 277

sector can be counterbalanced by stricter prudential regulations, this raises the cost of financial intermediation.

The wave of crises in the developing world has underscored the need for a broad framework for macroeconomic stability. In the recent debate, this has been reflected in the focus on *sustainability*, including external, fiscal and financial sector sustainability (IMF 2004c). But given the pro-cyclical bias of financial markets and the incentives to adopt pro-cyclical macroeconomic policies, equal emphasis should be given to the *counter-cyclical* dimensions of macroeconomic and financial policies and to the policy space thus required.

Counter-cyclical dimensions have received much less attention until recently. This is reflected in the absence of the concept in the IMF Medium-Term Strategy which was proposed in 2005 (IMF 2005a). This contrasts with the explicitly counter-cyclical focus of macroeconomic policies in some industrial economies, particularly the United States (indeed, even the IMF has urged the USA to pursue counter-cyclical policies in the current slowdown). The IMF's lack of explicitly counter-cyclical objectives also contrasts with the call of the major grouping of developing countries for financial issues, the Group of 24 (2005), to make them part of its support to developing countries. There is now increasing consensus on the need to use expansionary periods to strengthen fiscal positions, as well as more limited recognition of the need to avoid contractionary fiscal policies during crises.

Preventive (prudential) macroeconomic and financial policies, which aim to avoid the accumulation of unsustainable public and private sector debts during periods of financial euphoria, have become part of the standard recipe. However, even well-established counter-cyclical prudential practices, such as the Spanish system of forward-looking provisions, have until the credit crunch received limited attention. Nor was the need to reduce pro-cyclicality given adequate attention in the revision of the Basel standards. The original Basel II may indeed increase the pro-cyclicality of both international and domestic bank lending (see below and Chapter 6 by Claessens and Underhill in this volume). As a result of the current crisis, the Basel Committee has agreed to develop a new framework for counter-cyclical capital buffers. It is unclear, however, how this new counter-cyclical framework will affect bank lending to developing countries, i.e. whether it will also work counter-cyclical for developing country capital flows.

Managing counter-cyclical policies in the current globalised financial world is no easy task as financial markets generate strong incentives to adopt pro-cyclical policies. It is thus essential for international cooperation to address these incentives and constraints. This means that the first function of international financial governance, from the point of view of developing countries, should be to *mitigate the pro-cyclical effects of financial markets and open 'policy space' for counter-cyclical macroeconomic policies*. This can be achieved by smoothing out boom-bust cycles at the source through regulation; helping to partially cover or diversify the risks (especially of a cyclical nature) developing countries face in international capital markets; and increasing the ability of developing countries to adopt counter-cyclical policies.

A number of measures can be suggested: (1) explicit introduction of counter-cyclical criteria in the design of prudential regulatory and supervisory frameworks, in capital source and developing countries; (2) designing market mechanisms that better distribute the risk faced by developing countries throughout the business cycle (GDP-indexed and local-currency bonds); (3) instruments that encourage more stable private flows, such as counter-cyclical guarantees; and (4) counter-cyclical official liquidity to deal with external shocks.

Counter-cyclical prudential regulation and supervision

The origins of problems that erupt during financial crises are associated with excessive risk-taking during booms. Weak prudential regulation of domestic financial systems exacerbates this. One of the major problems seems to be the focus of prudential regulation on microeconomic risks, and the tendency to underestimate risks that have a clear *macroeconomic* origin. The basic problem is the inability of individual financial intermediaries to internalise collective risks assumed during boom periods.

Moreover, traditional prudential supervision, including both Basel I and Basel II standards, has a pro-cyclical bias. As loan-loss provisions are tied to loan delinquency or to short-term expectations of future loan losses, the system is ineffective in reducing excessive risk-taking during booms, when expectations of losses are low. The sharp increase in loan delinquency during crises reduces financial institutions' lending capacity, triggering 'credit squeezes' and reinforcing the downswing in economic activity and asset prices. Since credit ratings are also pro-cyclical, basing risk assessments and charges on such ratings is also pro-cyclical (see also Goodhart and Persaud 2008).

Given the influence of banking regulation on credit availability, a crucial step is to introduce a counter-cyclical element into prudential regulation and supervision. A major innovation is the Spanish system of forward-looking provisions, introduced in 2000. Here provisions are made for expected losses ('latent risks') when loans are disbursed,

Combating pro-cyclicality in financial architecture 279

estimated on the basis of a full business cycle (Fernández de Lis *et al.* 2001). Under this system, provisions are built up during economic expansions and are drawn upon during downturns. It can be complemented by strictly counter-cyclical prudential provisions which can be decreed by the regulatory authority for the financial system as a whole, or for some financial agents on the basis of excessive growth of credit (relative to some benchmark).

The introduction of counter-cyclical elements within prudential regulation and supervision should thus become a central concern of the Basel Committee. The benefits to developing countries would accrue through both a less pro-cyclical supply of credit and more resilient domestic financial systems. In developing countries these provisions should be supplemented by more specific regulations aimed at controlling currency and maturity mismatches (including those associated with derivative operations) and at avoiding the overvaluation of collateral generated by asset price bubbles. Regulations can be used to establish higher provisions and/or risk weightings for these operations, or a strict prohibition on lending in foreign currencies to non-financial firms without revenues in those currencies.

The best option may be capital account regulations to avoid inadequate maturity structures of borrowing in external markets by all domestic agents and currency mismatches in the portfolios of those agents operating in non-tradable sectors. So long as there is no international lender of last resort, international rules should continue to provide room for the use of capital account regulation by developing countries. Public good considerations need to override private financial interests to allow such controls. Furthermore, evaluating the vulnerability of domestic financial systems and developing regulatory and supervisory frameworks are essential elements of financial sector assessments undertaken by the IMF and World Bank. It is essential that counter-cyclical dimensions of prudential regulation and supervision be incorporated into such assessments and advice.

More broadly, Basel II has a number of problems that require attention: it is complex where it should be simple; it is implicitly pro-cyclical when it should be explicitly counter-cyclical; and although it is supposed to more accurately align regulatory capital to the risks banks face, in the case of lending to developing countries it ignores the proven benefits of diversification. In particular, by failing to consider the benefits of international portfolio diversification, capital requirements for loans to developing countries will be significantly higher than is justified on the basis of actual risk. There are thus fears that Basel II may sharply reduce bank lending to developing countries, particularly during crises (thus enhancing the pro-cyclicality of such lending), and increase the cost of much of the remaining lending, particularly for low-rated borrowing countries (Griffith-Jones and Persaud 2008). To a great extent, the pro-cyclicality problems of Basel II on the output side can be explained by the input-side functioning of the Basel Committee, with until recently no representation from developing countries and heavy influence from the large banks. Both these issues may yet be adequately addressed as a result of the reforms stemming from the current crisis, with the afore-mentioned counter-cyclical capital buffers framework and an extension of the Basel Committee membership to all G20 countries.

One clear way to improve Basel II would be to introduce the bene-fits of diversification into the internal-ratings-based approach. One of the major benefits of investing in developing and emerging econ-omies is their relatively low correlation with mature markets. This has been tested empirically using a wide variety of financial, market and macro variables. Simulations comparing the estimated losses of port-folios diversified across both developed and developing countries with the losses of portfolios in developed countries only indicate losses for the former were 19–23 per cent lower (Griffith-Jones *et al.* 2002b). If risks are measured precisely, this should be reflected in lower capital requirements. Taking into account the benefits of diversification will also make capital requirements less pro-cyclical – significant as Basel II currently increases the pro-cyclicality of capital requirements by rely-ing on banks' own models (which are inherently pro-cyclical) for cal-culating capital.

Market instruments

GDP-indexed bonds

GDP-indexed bonds could be particularly beneficial to smooth debt service payments by linking annual debt servicing to growth in the debtor country's GDP (Griffith-Jones and Sharma 2006). The inter-est coupon would be totally or partially tied to the issuing country's growth rate. Given the requirement of many institutional investors to hold assets that pay a positive interest rate, a floor can be determined beneath which the rate cannot fall.

GDP-indexed bonds could be beneficial for all countries, but espe-cially for developing countries. They would provide two major benefits. First, they would stabilise government spending and limit the pro-cyclicality of fiscal pressures by requiring smaller interest payments at times of slower growth – thus providing space for higher spending or

Combating pro-cyclicality in financial architecture   281

lower taxes during crises. They would also curb excessively expansionary policy in times of rapid growth. The issuance of such bonds would make it easier for governments to follow counter-cyclical fiscal policies. Second, by allowing debt service ratios to fall in times of slow or negative growth, they reduce the likelihood of defaults and debt crisis.

Simulations indicate that gains for emerging-economy borrowers would be substantial. Borensztein and Mauro (2004) show that had half of Mexico's government debt consisted of GDP-indexed bonds, it would have saved about 1.6 per cent of GDP in interest payments during the Tequila crisis of 1994–5. To help create a market for such instruments, it may be better if countries with greater credibility issued them first. Two such groups of countries can be identified: developed countries and developing countries like Mexico or Chile that remain attractive to markets. The precedent of introducing collective action clauses into bonds, done first by developed countries and later followed by developing ones, shows that demonstration effects can be effective when introducing financial innovations.

GDP-indexed bonds may also provide benefits for issuer industrialised countries, especially in Europe. They may be particularly attractive to EMU countries, given that the 'Stability and Growth Pact' tends to render their fiscal policies pro-cyclical if they near the maximum allowed deficit of 3 per cent of GDP. They are also attractive to countries such as Italy where pensions are indexed against GDP growth.

Investors will likely have two main benefits from the introduction of GDP-indexed bonds. First, they allow taking a position on countries' future growth prospects. Though this is possible to a degree through stock markets, they are often not representative of the economy as a whole. Since growth rates across emerging markets tend to be fairly uncorrelated, a portfolio including GDP-indexed bonds of several economies would have the benefits of diversification, thus increasing the return/risk ratio. Second, investors would benefit from a lower frequency of defaults and financial crises, which often result in costly litigations/renegotiation and sometimes in outright losses.

On a broader level, GDP-indexed bonds can be viewed as desirable vehicles for international risk-sharing, as a way of avoiding disruptions from formal defaults and as a mechanism to help smooth growth. They have the characteristics of a public good as they generate systemic benefits above those going to individual investors and issuing countries. The positive externalities provide justification for public action; the World Bank and regional development banks could play the role of 'market makers' for GDP-indexed bonds (Ocampo et al. 2007: chapter 2). These institutions could begin by developing a portfolio of loans with repayments indexed to debtor countries' growth rates; a portfolio of such loans to different developing countries could then be securitised and sold in the international capital markets. Such a portfolio would be particularly attractive to private investors as it allows them to take a position on the growth prospects of a number of emerging economies simultaneously. As correlations among developing countries' growth rates tend to be lower at the global level, the World Bank may be best placed to do such securitisation.

Local-currency bonds

Local-currency-denominated bonds are another alternative for better managing the risks faced by developing countries throughout the business cycle. These bonds can counter the currency mismatches that often characterise the debt structure of developing countries. The development of domestic capital markets, especially bond markets, creates a more stable source of local funding, mitigating difficulties created by sudden stops in cross-border capital flows. Domestic bond markets in developing countries have been booming since the Asian crisis while international markets increasingly issue local-currency-denominated bonds.

Nevertheless, domestic markets for these instruments tend to be less liquid than similar markets in industrial countries while the reduction of currency mismatches comes at the cost of additional maturity mismatches (Jeanneau and Tovar 2006). For international investors, the attractiveness of these instruments depends on expectations of exchange rate appreciation; demand may thus be subject to strong pro-cyclical swings. Thus the advantages of reduced currency mismatches might not be accompanied by less volatile external capital flows. While minimum holding periods or exit taxes could be useful, they may reduce the liquidity of these instruments.

Innovative proposals have been advanced to make local-currency investments more consistently attractive to international investors. Dodd and Spiegel (2005) have suggested raising capital in international markets by forming diversified portfolios of emerging market local-currency debt issued by sovereign governments. These portfolios would – by using risk management techniques of diversification – generate return-to-risk ratios that competed favourably with other major capital market security indices. A similar effect can be achieved by multilateral development banks raising funds in local developing country markets. The World Bank already has a pilot project of diversified bond issues; the second Asian Bond Fund launched in December 2004 is also a pilot project of this type.

Counter-cyclical guarantee facilities

International financial markets overestimate risk in difficult times and underestimate it in good times; private lenders' resulting boom-bust patterns are often more determined by changing global risk appetite and/or contagion than by country fundamentals. This provides a strong case for public institutions to play an explicitly counter-cyclical role to help counter the inherently pro-cyclical tendencies of private flows. While this is widely recognised in IMF lending, it applies equally to multilateral development banks (MDBs) and export credit agencies (ECAs). Guarantees on long-term trade credit for investment in infrastructure is a case in point: private investment in infrastructure grew significantly in the early and mid-1990s but fell sharply in the wake of the numerous crises (Griffith-Jones and Fuzzo de Lima 2006).

There are two paths for increasing the counter-cyclical role of international financial institutions in this area. One would be for MDBs to increase counter-cyclical lending (e.g. for infrastructure). Another path, which will give the public resources they manage greater leverage, would be for MDBs and ECAs to issue guarantees to private sector lenders with an explicitly counter-cyclical element in their associated risk evaluations. This would require MDBs and ECAs to assess risk using a longer-term perspective than is typically done by commercial banks. When banks or other lenders lower their exposure to a country, MDBs or ECAs would increase guarantees if they considered the country's long-term fundamentals sound. When market risk evaluations improve and willingness to lend increases, MDBs or ECAs could then decrease their exposure.

To the extent that MDBs and ECAs use models to assess risks, taking a longer-term view requires using models with longer-term perspectives than those used by private lenders. These models would presumably be better at 'seeing through the cycle'. It is also important that guarantees be tailor-made to correct market imperfections and to avoid moral hazard. They must maintain private investors' incentives to choose only good projects and to run them efficiently. Guarantees can also impose excessive costs on taxpayers or consumers and expose them to too much risk; to overcome this, it is crucial that contingent liabilities be carefully monitored and risks assessed. In the case of infrastructure projects, the risks to be guaranteed must be defined in such a way that private agents assume normal market risks, whereas non-market risks (such as regulatory risk or force majeure) should more readily be guaranteed by public authorities.

The international provision of counter-cyclical official liquidity

For capital account-led crises

At the country level, central banks have acted for many decades as lenders of last resort to prevent financial crises and their deepening. Equivalent international mechanisms, however, are still at an embryonic stage. As there is no automaticity in the availability of financing during crises, current IMF arrangements operate more under the principle of the 'emergency financier'. Enhanced international provision of emergency financing in response to external shocks is essential to lower unnecessary burdens of adjustment and to avoid the spread of crises. Appropriate facilities should include a liquidity provision to cover large capital flow reversals and volatility in real export earnings.

In recent decades, capital account liberalisation and volatility has greatly increased the need for official liquidity to deal with large reversals in capital flows. There is a growing consensus that many of the recent crises in emerging markets have been triggered by self-fulfilling liquidity runs. The enhanced provision of emergency financing in the face of capital account crises is thus important not only to manage crises when they occur, but to prevent such crises and to avert contagion (Griffith-Jones and Ocampo 2003; Cordella and Yeyati 2005).

To address this obvious need, the IMF has made efforts to improve its lending policy during capital account crises. The Supplemental Reserve Facility was established in 1997. Evidence that even countries with good macroeconomic fundamentals might be subject to sudden stops of external financing gave broad support to the idea that a precautionary financial arrangement, closer to the lender-of-last-resort function of central banks, had to be added to existing IMF facilities. In 1999 the IMF introduced the Contingent Credit Line (CCL). The facility, however, was never used and was discontinued in November 2003. Among the factors that contributed to countries not using the CCL, observers have emphasised 'entry' and 'exit' problems (Buira 2005b). Using the CCL could be seen as an announcement of vulnerability that would harm confidence.

Since the expiration of the CCL, the IMF has been exploring other ways to achieve its basic objectives. As it has recognised, instant liquidity provided by a well-designed contingency line 'would place a ceiling on rollover costs – thus avoiding debt crises triggered by unsustainable refinancing rates, much in the same way as central banks operate in their role of lenders of last resort' (IMF 2005b). The IMF's Medium-Term

Strategy (2005a) thus includes a provision for continued dialogue on a mechanism for contingency financing. This has resulted in the so-called Flexible Credit Line (FCL), which has already been adopted by several emerging markets including Mexico and Poland. This facility uses prequalification made at the country's request. However, there is no automacity in access to the FCL, which would be essential for pre-empting liquidity runs.

For compensating terms of trade shocks

The provision of official liquidity to avoid costly and unnecessary adjustment to temporary terms of trade shocks is essential, particularly for low-income countries that suffer larger negative effects on growth and poverty (Collier and Dehn 2001). While the IMF has facilities to compensate for terms of trade shocks, they are much too limited. The major IMF facility designed in the 1960s to deal with these shocks, the Compensatory Financial Facility (CFF), has been used less and less, especially as its conditionality has been tightened. Indeed, since upper tranche conditionality was introduced in 2000, the CFF has not been used at all. It was now abolished.

For low-income countries with access to the Poverty Reduction and Growth Facility (PRGF), the preferred route to dealing with terms of trade shocks has been augmentation of this programme. While this has the advantage of concessionality, it is linked to a highly conditional Fund arrangement, inappropriate for shocks caused by external events. As the IMF recognises, PRGF augmentation has been small compared to the impact of shocks, and has been granted to only half the PRGF countries experiencing them (IMF 2005c). In 2005 the IMF established a second concessional PRGF 'window', the Exogenous Shocks Facility (ESF), for countries without a PRGF programme. The ESF, which also covers natural disasters, is a high conditionality arrangement and its scale is limited. The IMF doubled access for all facilities for low income countries in 2009.

IMF facilities should be modified following two criteria. First, far lower conditionality should be attached to lending for externally caused shocks, whether to middle or low-income countries. The original CFF and the Oil Facilities of the 1970s had low conditionality and were amply and efficiently used; they recognised the principle that countries should not adjust policies (if they are reasonable) when faced with purely exogenous and temporary shocks. Second, the scale of existing facilities, including the concessional component in the case of low-income countries, should be significantly expanded to compensate for the much larger proportion of losses caused by temporary shocks. This would reduce the unnecessary negative effects on growth and poverty reduction (for a recent discussion, see Griffith-Jones and Ocampo 2008).

The IMF's lack of concessional resources is often cited to explain the small scale of ESF and PRGF augmentation. In the context of scaling up aid flows, more resources should be allocated to the IMF for financing the subsidy element within compensatory lending to low-income countries.

Conclusion

The tendency towards pro-cyclicality and contagion in international financial markets has increased the incidence of financial crises and growth volatility in the developing world and reduced the national 'policy space' to adopt counter-cyclical macroeconomic policies. This chapter has therefore argued that a principal task of a development-friendly international financial architecture is to mitigate the inherent pro-cyclical effects of financial markets and to reopen 'policy space' for counter-cyclical macroeconomic policies in the developing world. Given the role of global imbalances in the credit crunch and current crisis, such measures would have beneficial effects for developed countries as well.

To achieve these objectives, the chapter has explored a series of useful policy instruments: the explicit introduction of counter-cyclical criteria in the design of prudential regulatory and supervisory frameworks; designing market mechanisms that better distribute the risk faced by developing countries throughout the business cycle (GDP-indexed and local-currency bonds); multilateral instruments that encourage more stable private flows, such as counter-cyclical guarantees; and better provision of counter-cyclical official liquidity to deal with external shocks. A reform of the input side of international financial and regulatory institutions, rendering them more inclusive, would increase their legitimacy and make them more likely to introduce these desirable output-side proposals. The importance of achieving this should not be underestimated, given the dynamics of major changes in the world economy and the implications of the current crisis.

16 Public interest, national diversity and global financial governance

Geoffrey R. D. Underhill and Xiaoke Zhang

Radical reforms of the international financial architecture were urgently discussed following the outbreak of currency and financial crises in East Asia and other emerging market economies in the late 1990s. By the time the Argentine and Turkish crises erupted in 2000–1, the broad contours of the post-Asian crisis global financial architecture were set. The reforms had been limited to a focus on technical deficiencies in the functioning of markets. The Introduction and several chapters in this volume argued that this pattern of governance reflected the preferences of an alliance of powerful transnational market players and the official national and multilateral agencies of financial and monetary governance based in advanced industrial countries, economies which had hitherto avoided most of the consequences of financial instability experienced by developing economies. A range of chapters also argued and presented evidence that the current financial architecture lacks effectiveness and suffers legitimacy problems on both the input and output sides of the equation, and that limited participation on the input side was related to ineffectual and illegitimate policy output.

The post-2001 period of relative calm ended with the outbreak of the sub-prime crisis in 2007. This serious crisis at the heart of the global financial system, occurring despite the reform of the financial architecture and beginning in the most robust financial systems, should stimulate urgent reflection on the nature of contemporary financial governance. The long-run political sustainability of the liberal financial order is still poorly understood, while current problems demand

---

We wish to thank the anonymous reviewers and many commentators in workshops and conferences where earlier versions of this work were first presented, all of whom contributed to its development and improvement over time. The flaws remain ours alone. The authors also wish to acknowledge the generous funding from the (UK) Economic and Social Research Council's World Economy and Finance research programme (award no. RES-156-25-0009), funding from the EU 6th Framework Programme (Citizens and Governance in a Knowledge-Based Society) as part of the GARNET Network of Excellence, and funding from the EU Framework 7 programme PEGGED (award no. SSH7-CT-2008-217559).

much more than further improvements to the technical functioning and implementation of the current architecture. There has been a general failure to reflect broadly upon the requisite normative and political underpinnings of cross-border financial governance in an integrated market system. Until the latest crisis, complacency had become a palliative for the genuine loss of direction in the further reform of the global financial regime, and this complacency and the patent weaknesses of the 'new' financial architecture as revealed throughout this volume had much to do with the eruption of this new and far more serious crisis, the effects of which will be with us for some time. The considerable input-side influence on the design of the international financial architecture of the very private financial interests which stood most to benefit from the facilitation of cross-border market integration and activity must be directly associated with the causes of the crisis. The outbreak of crisis was in no small way a policy process problem as much as a financial market failure. How the liberal order and market-based approach to governance came about had much to do with its failure.

This analysis has important implications for the reform measures which lie ahead. As set out in the Introduction, four issues addressed in this volume relate closely to the legitimacy and effectiveness of global financial governance: (1) the proper balance between private interests and public policy processes; (2) inclusion of low-income countries in the policy-making process; (3) policy space for national governments in a global financial system; and (4) the relations between different 'levels' (national, regional and global) in the contemporary global financial architecture. This chapter argues that a more effective and legitimate governance of global finance lies in explicit consideration and incorporation of essential political and normative prerequisites. It focuses on two such prerequisites that are an integral but seldom-discussed aspect of the global financial architecture. The first is that the international financial order be predicated upon an appropriate and politically sustainable balance between private and public forms of authority, which should include the interests of emerging market and low-income countries. The second prerequisite is that the global financial architecture be rendered more compatible with legitimate national economic development aspirations and political processes. This implies the adaptation of financial governance to established norms of (democratic) accountability and distributional fairness associated with contrasting forms of national capitalist development.

The chapter first develops a theoretical framework for understanding the normative importance of these two prerequisites. It then analyses the contemporary global financial order in their light, referring to the

Public interest, diversity and financial governance   289

empirical and conceptual contributions in this volume. It concludes by discussing policy implications.

Normative underpinnings for global financial order

The legitimacy of governance derives from shared norms closely associated with the responsiveness and eventual accountability of policy-makers to a suitable range of their constituencies: legitimacy is about satisfying enough of the people enough of the time. Achieving this is difficult enough at the national level where a defined community may develop shared norms over time, and where lines of accountability are relatively well institutionalised and understood. Over time, the legitimacy of governance grows less dependent on 'specific' support or short-term performance; a reserve of 'diffuse' support builds up so that legitimacy can survive poor performance in the short run (Easton 1965: 265, 273).

This is more difficult to achieve at the global level. As cross-border financial and monetary integration intensifies, the effectiveness of domestic governance is undermined, presenting it with new legitimacy challenges. While global governance may be a solution (Zürn 2004: 286), legitimacy here is fragile: the sense of political community is weak, responsiveness and accountability are underdeveloped, and citizens and constituencies may be poorly represented and distant from policy-making processes – meaning diffuse support will likely be in short supply.

The legitimacy of global governance might be enhanced if states and transnational actors were accountable to the broad publics on whose lives their decisions have an impact (Keohane 2002) and if outcomes eventually corresponded to widely shared norms. Those in authority must to some degree *represent* the interests of the ruled. If they do not, an accountability gap emerges. The impact of this gap within global governance can be better understood by distinguishing the *input* and *output* sides or phases of legitimacy (Scharpf 1999; Wolf 2004) as set out in this volume's Introduction.

Broader legitimacy is underpinned by an uneasy relationship between the input and output phases: if the policy output is perceived as legitimate, the process which produces it may matter less while consistently poor outcomes (e.g. financial crisis) may undermine an otherwise legitimate process. Consistently poor results despite a legitimate process may undermine diffuse legitimacy, whether or not policy-makers can meaningfully influence the circumstances in which they operate. That said, an inclusive (democratic) process with input from those who bear the costs of decisions is more likely to lead to acceptance of poor results over time. A combination of legitimacy on both the input and output sides is most likely to strengthen diffuse support. In particular, more representative and transparent input will more likely lead to output perceived as legitimate. This is because input-side interaction is closely linked to how community and accountability are defined; a sense of community is strengthened over time as inclusive processes heighten the chance of outcomes which better correspond to an accepted set of norms around particular issues.

This uneasy input-output side relationship may be enhanced by a third or accountability 'phase' of legitimacy: the enhanced (democratic) accountability of global policy processes *and* outcomes to a broad range of constituencies outside the narrow, often technical, policy communities which currently participate in policy and regulatory processes. Accountability here implies an ex-post function wherein 'some actors have the right to hold other actors to a set of standards, to judge whether they have fulfilled their responsibilities in light of these standards, and to impose sanctions if they determine that these responsibilities have not been met' (Grant and Keohane 2005: 29). More effective accountability across the institutional layers of financial governance would lead to a more thorough assessment of outcomes and their distributional impact. Ultimately, accountability should function so as to facilitate the inclusion of new and wider constituencies as participants in the input phase as these constituencies find themselves affected (adversely) by the output phase. When institutions of governance are both more inclusive and responsible for their impact, their problem-solving capacities may improve and their policy output is likely to satisfy a broader range of interests. There is then a circular relationship among these three phases of legitimacy, where problems or shifts in one phase may lead to ongoing pressure for change in one or both of the others. Input, output and accountability, while analytically distinct, are intertwined with the legitimacy of global governance in a close causal relationship.

Strengthening the input-side legitimacy of global financial governance is an important point of departure for improving the political underpinnings of the global financial order. This implies sound *representation* of the diversity of interests affected by decision-making in the defined (if rather diverse) community, in this case of states and societies at various levels of development within the global financial architecture. Better representation is thus one way to enhance input legitimacy. This entails recognising various *principles* of representation available to institutions of governance and which, depending on the context, may conflict with or complement each other.

The most obvious principle is one person, one vote (unwieldy in a global context), or one member (state), one vote. But (state) members of institutions may be of differing economic and political import, leading to the principle of representing members differentially according to e.g. wealth, power, population or territory. That some members contribute more resources to institutions than others, voluntarily or according to the rules, gives rise to the 'shareholder principle' of representation – a principle in conflict with one member, one vote. Yet another principle is the representation of those most affected by decisions, e.g. the users of services by monopoly providers – in this case, debtors to the IFIs. A derivation of this is interest-based or 'corporatist' representation where important and identifiable groups in the community are represented on the basis of their common interest vis-à-vis other competing constituencies. Finally one may invoke the principle of minority representation where the purpose is to compensate the weak and to grant them a formal role in decision-making.[1] Processes which systematically exclude may be legitimate to the broad majority of the community but can be prone to serious breakdown if coherent minorities rebel. The most important point here is that most systems of governance at the national or international level employ a mix of these principles depending on the context.

Turning to the output side, political communities assess outcomes in a variety of ways depending on their shared beliefs. Some norms may conflict openly with others, rendering trade-offs necessary; other norms may more easily overlap. In relation to global financial governance, some may prefer stability, others risk. Long-run development and growth may be an accepted norm, perhaps rendered more difficult by preferences for social justice and reasonable distributional outcomes, or risk. One point is certain: claims to legitimacy are stronger in more coherent political communities. If outcomes are persistently unacceptable to a wide spectrum of the global or regional community involved in multilevel arrangements, then these mechanisms of governance will quickly be depleted of any accumulated legitimacy. The stakes may be high. Local or national communities may assert their claims more vigorously, leading to a competitive decentralisation of governance which further undermines the capacity of national authorities either to cope with the problems of global integration or to commit to global governance, reformed or otherwise (Hiscox and Lake 2002; Garrett and Rodden 2003). Financial instability does not respect borders while

---

[1] Doorenspleet, Renske 2001. 'The Fourth Wave of Democratisation', unpublished Ph.D. dissertation, Leiden University.

292   *Geoffrey R. D. Underhill and Xiaoke Zhang*

uncoordinated or competing national solutions may make things worse – as they have in the past.

Extrapolating to the current state of global financial governance, the input, output and accountability elements of legitimacy are all highly problematic in the international financial architecture and are based on norms at variance with the political and economic imperatives of developing and emerging market countries in an era of transition to democracy (and in some cases of developed countries as well). Key aspects of international financial policy-making have become anchored in a discourse of de-politicised market-facilitating technocracy that increasingly deviates from the range of norms compatible with a robust system of (democratic) accountability, a situation which largely reflects the preferences of the alliance between public and private financiers in the developed economies.

Public interest, national diversity and global finance

On the basis of the theoretical points developed in the preceding section, this section demonstrates why an effective and legitimate governance of global finance should be predicated upon a politically sustainable balance between private actors and public authorities and upon the compatibility of the global financial architecture with, and accountability to, contrasting forms of national capitalist development.

Public interest, private power and political legitimacy

The efficient and legitimate functioning of a market-based financial system is predicated on a sound definition of the collective or public interest in relation to the interests of private financial market agents, a public-private balance appropriate to and compatible with the imperatives of (national) economic and political development. There is little basis for the claim that the governance of the system should reside completely in the private domain of the market. Financial transactions in many developed, developing and emerging market countries are largely in the hands of private firms. However, the functioning and impact of the financial and monetary system so affects wider development and distributional outcomes that there is a clear case for considering its governance as part of the public domain (Underhill 1997b, 2000).

Yet global financial integration and its architecture have bolstered the position of relatively unaccountable private market actors. These private actors participate in a narrow and relatively closed policy community, a situation approximating policy capture (Underhill 1995;

Underhill and Zhang 2008). This trend – part of a broader reconfiguration of the role of states as both promoters of market-based global integration and managers of its consequences – does not imply that states are in retreat or could not implement alternative options. With financial globalisation has come a change in the balance of power between public authority and private interests and an accompanying transformation in the notion of the public interest that defines the financial order, posing problems to input and output legitimacy and to accountability.

Against the backdrop of financial globalisation, private market actors have gained a stronger voice within the policy process, often at the expense of broader sets of interests. Public authorities have often responded by adopting market-based approaches to regulation, supervision and corporate risk management where private firms are responsible for risk management through complex mathematical models implemented under the approval of supervisory agencies (e.g. Basel Committee 2006a).[2] Crucial information and expertise for the process remains the proprietary domain of firms which supervisors admit they cannot match. In a highly competitive environment, state agencies also seek to improve market opportunities for national players by granting them greater freedom in product innovation and business expansion. This relative disarming of public authorities implies that private interests increasingly define supervisory criteria (see Chapter 6 on Basel II) and that crucial aspects of public policy – the safety and stability of the financial system – are dominated by the preferences of private market-makers who stand to benefit most. Allowing those with a pecuniary interest in lowering the costs of supervision to define the system is surely a flawed public policy process on both the input and output sides, and there appears to have been a very low level of accountability until the crisis struck.

Perhaps more important is how demands for these new forms of governance initially emerged and were adopted as policy. Financial firms and their associations have close and relatively exclusive relationships with regulatory agencies, with frequent delegation of oversight to self-regulatory processes. Most often statutorily independent from politicians and other state institutions, regulatory agencies are highly responsive to the preferences of private financiers, their main domestic political constituency. In fulfilling their regulatory and supervisory functions, they draw much of their legitimacy, and work in close communion with, private financial firms. Regulators also collaborate with

---

[2] Some analysts cast serious doubts on whether market-based supervisory methods can lead to stability at all; e.g. see Persaud 2000.

294   *Geoffrey R. D. Underhill and Xiaoke Zhang*

national firms to adopt policies that promote competitiveness in the transnational market place.

Close public-private ties are further reinforced by common professional norms, the specialised and technical nature of expertise in the financial sector, and the shared need to maintain public confidence in the financial system itself. These symbiotic relations, prevalent across the G7 leading economies (Baker 2005b), allow private interests to influence strongly the nature of monetary and financial governance and the potential to capture policy-making and regulatory processes. Clear definition of the public interest distinct from the particularistic claims of private market actors has thus become increasingly difficult (Underhill 1995, 1997b, 2000).

The same policy preferences are visible within international cooperative regimes and IFIs, indicating that G7 governments have generally backed the preferences of their corporate sectors (Baker 2005b) in an increasingly transnational policy community. Baker's chapter in this volume has shown how narrowness of debate led to market-oriented reforms being promulgated in the G20, while Chapter 6 outlined how market-based supervision promoted by the Group of Thirty, a public-private think-tank (Tsingou 2003), was developed by the Basel Committee. Cooperative institutions of global financial governance such as the Basel Committee and the International Organisation of Securities Commissions (IOSCO) are characterised not only by exclusive policy communities, but also by virtual separation from accountable political processes (Underhill 1995, 1997b), a problem further exacerbated by frequent recourse to self-regulation. As a result, the transnational financial system is increasingly regulated by agencies constituting regimes that are more responsive to private interests than providers of collective goods (Cerny 1996: 96–9; Porter 1999).[3]

A wealth of evidence indicates that crucial multilateral IFIs such as the IMF are part of this constellation of interests (Wade 1998; Stiglitz 2002). Private institutional investors have attempted to shape the investment environment in emerging market economies by pressing these countries to adopt policy frameworks favourable to their interests (Maxfield 1998; Porter 1999). As Walter showed in Chapter 5, there is a strong push to adopt international standards promoting transparency although it must be noted that these standards are in practice often only implemented haphazardly. This pressure is often reinforced by 'advice'

---

[3] Oatley and Nabors (1998) document how the original Basel Accord was created to respond to the rent-seeking demands of private financial firms in leading industrial nations.

Public interest, diversity and financial governance 295

from the IFIs, especially the IMF, often during crises when emerging market economies are most vulnerable to external pressure. Developing country governments have found it increasingly difficult to deviate from the policy preferences of international financial firms, no matter how important particular policies may be for resolving their individual problems of economic development and socio-political stability.

The emerging system of financial governance across national and global levels is thus flawed in important ways in terms of input-side legitimacy. The guardians governing the monetary and financial order have become relatively isolated from the traditional mechanisms of (democratic) accountability and control as well as from the influence of broader social constituencies. The point here is not that there should be no private sector involvement in financial governance. Private involvement in managing financial policy can improve the transparency of the public and private sectors, foster better risk assessment and limit moral hazard (IMF 2001b), thus facilitating the operation of a market-based system. However, encouraging private sector involvement is problematic if it fails to represent broader social constituencies and aligns notions of the public interest with reducing risks and losses for those who profit most from financial markets.[4] This is precisely what appears to have occurred in the sub-prime crisis.

The output side of legitimacy is likewise flawed. Financial crisis and the difficult policy environment affecting developing countries (and now the developed world as well) has been one of the principal results of global financial integration. Decisions made within unaccountable policy processes have increased cross-border integration and 'marketisation' of economic policy-making, benefiting private market interests at the expense of broader publics and further affecting the capacity of especially developing countries to shape their political economies in line with democratic preferences.

Recognised output-side policy failures originally lay behind the G7/G10/IFI reforms of the global financial architecture. But if the current crisis is anything to go by, the reforms have proven less than effective. Neither the input nor the output sides have changed, with little done to alleviate the legitimacy deficit. In this sense, the existing architecture for governing global finance has been overly responsive to private sector preferences. Focusing narrowly on the technical aspects of private involvement but neglecting its normative ramifications, current patterns of financial governance are unlikely to achieve a sustainable and

---

[4] Furthermore, as de Jong and van der Veer demonstrate in this volume, private sector involvement in IMF debt workout was not to be found where it was to be expected.

296   Geoffrey R. D. Underhill and Xiaoke Zhang

legitimate balance between public interests and private gain. The crisis has made the problem worse as failed bankers retreated into retirement with obscenely substantial severance packages while taxpayers facing unemployment paid for the rescue. It remains to be seen whether the post-crisis reform process will correct these deficiencies, but at the time of writing there was already substantial evidence of a serious fight-back by the financial services industry against a range of robust reform proposals.

Structural pressures, national diversity and distributive justice

A second crucial prerequisite for the legitimate governance of global finance lies with the compatibility of the financial architecture with national development processes and with distributive justice and social stability. States, however, have been increasingly unable to defend the norms and institutions that history has, for better or worse, conferred upon them and with which citizens understandably identify. Here there is a clear and important distinction between developed economies, to which Mosley's 'room to move' (2003) clearly applies, and (especially poor) developing countries, as encapsulated by the notion of 'original sin'.[5]

Volatile capital flows constitute increased pressure to adopt norms and standards compatible to the global architecture; a major plank in the reform process was the promulgation of a range of 'global' standards in the domains of macroeconomic policy, financial stability, accounting and corporate governance (see Chapter 5 by Walter). Convergence on these standards – which can prove destabilising to already weak political economies – does not take place overnight. It takes considerable time to develop administrative and political capacities to implement such changes successfully, and with possible unintended consequences (Caprio *et al.* 2001).

Regulatory change in financial systems – a process which does not take place in a political vacuum – is an obvious source of convergence. First and foremost, US and European financial institutions have long been active in lobbying for deregulation and aggressive in securing diplomatic support to gain access to relatively closed developing country markets.[6] As states seek to attract capital and develop their financial sectors, external pressures may also translate into new domestic

---

[5] See Eichengreen and Hausmann 2005.

[6] This sort of pressure was greatly enhanced by the advent of and eventual conclusion of the WTO agreement on the liberalisation of trade in financial services (Dobson and Jacquet 1998).

Public interest, diversity and financial governance

regulatory preferences as domestic interest coalitions internalise external norms and demand an end to forms of financial repression closely linked to a history of successful development and political stability. As domestic regulators find their national firms involved in international transactions, they are drawn into international cooperative institutions such as the Basel Committee and IOSCO, where the preferences of developed G10 political economies have prevailed over smaller and developing countries (Porter 1999, 2002). The full effect of broadening the membership of these bodies (e.g. Basel Committee and Financial Stability Board) to include G20 members-plus remains to be seen but is certainly to be welcomed.

This pressure has led to the acceptance and promotion of cross-border market-oriented practices in financial governance, whether appropriate for developing countries or not (e.g. the risk of financial globalisation traps, see Chapter 4 by Cassimon, Demetriades and Van Campenhout). If these pressures emanating from G7 treasuries (Baker 2005b) were to be sustained, one might expect national financial systems to increasingly resemble each other over time. Given that many successful developing economies have based their policies on systems characterised by financial repression, liberalisation may involve repetition of the serious risks seen in the outbreak of financial crises in many emerging market countries (Kahler 1998; Zhang 2002).

While regulatory reforms conforming to global standards have precipitated changes in financial systems,[7] the impact of global financial structures on state policy capacity/space and on patterns of corporate behaviour and governance is also important for convergence. If the transnational integration of financial markets constrains the autonomy of state policy preferences in relation to domestic imperatives, it encourages states to make national policies and markets more favourable to foreign financial institutions seeking an environment similar to that at home. This results in domestic reforms aimed at convergence on the norms of the global financial architecture.

Corporate governance and behaviour, as an integral part of any political economy, is closely linked to the nature of national financial systems and the relationships between the financial sector, producer firms, labour market practices and the state. In other words, differences in financial systems and corporate governance are central to what makes different models of capitalism different. Changes in the financial system may unravel these relationships to yield transformations in

---

[7] Though with unintended consequences as demonstrated by Zhang and by Walter in this volume.

corporate governance, new (global) links between finance and industry, altered ties between labour and employers, and thus change in the
distinguishing features of economic development models. The rapid
transformation of systems characterised by financial repression can
produce instability and crisis as well as convergence, further disturbing
the social and political fabric that previously underpinned them.

As inducements to adopt harmonising rules and standards, the IMF
has given a central role to two major instruments of external influence –
conditionality and policy surveillance.[8] The official consensus promotes
structural reforms consisting of transparent macroeconomic policies,
open financial markets, arms-length bank-industry ties, 'shareholder
model' corporate governance and market-led industrial adjustment
strategies. These norms are argued to be of universal relevance despite
national historical differences in financial and economic systems.

While there has been increased pressure for policy harmonisation,
the convergence of economic models is far from inevitable (see chapters by Klagsbrunn and Zhang in this volume), and this is part of the
argument here. Patterns of policy-making, financial systems and corporate practices are deeply embedded in the fabric of local legal, social
and economic institutions, still defined nationally for the most part.
Variations among national forms of capitalism persist as each local
economy continues to refract external market and political constraints
in its own way. Local constituencies will resist and may be successful
in a number of ways, leaving room for the preservation of distinctive
national policies and structures (Crouch and Streeck 1997; Schmidt
2002). Historically, few paths to capitalist development have converged
for long. Where the tensions between harmonising liberal market structures and local contexts and institutions become overwhelming, capitalist development and a market-based society may prove politically
unsustainable or simply ineffectual. This lies behind both the phenomenon of 'mock compliance' referred to by Walter (in Chapter 5) and the
unintended consequences of national reforms as analysed by Zhang (in
Chapter 11).

Convergence to market-oriented practices and institutions has a
significant distributional impact: it may be beneficial in an aggregate
and long-term sense, but involves important short-term costs for more
vulnerable players. The strengthening of monetary authorities, capital
markets and regulatory harmonisation may favour private financiers
over industrialists and workers, mobile asset holders over immobile

---

[8] The pros and cons of these instruments are examined at length in Kapur and Webb
2000.

Public interest, diversity and financial governance 299

factors of production and the rich over the poor. The resultant accentuation of (potentially already intolerable) economic inequalities under the impact of globalisation may alienate substantial segments of the population and generate growing social and political instabilities in developing and emerging market countries. The 'backlash' against Washington-based IFIs in Asia and Latin America over the past decade well illustrates this process.

Furthermore, the pattern of welfare gains and losses for various social constituencies poses a serious challenge to existing national mechanisms for income distribution, favouring policies against inflation over policies for lower unemployment and other social welfare benefits. Efforts to increase central bank autonomy in many emerging markets over the 1990s and associated tight monetary regimes made it difficult for governments to create new jobs; it was the poor in general and unskilled workers in particular who suffered most from rising unemployment (Stallings and Peres 2000; Stiglitz 2000: 4–5).

Cross-country econometric studies have shown that income generated by the liberalisation and development of capital markets in developing countries tends to accrue almost completely to the top 25 per cent of the population at the expense of middle- and low-income social groups (Das and Mohapatra 2003). The perverse redistributive effects of institutional reforms may then undermine political stability and thus growth prospects in developing and emerging market countries. Important empirical studies have shown that those developing countries that were able to maintain high growth rates in the postwar period established effective political systems to manage social conflicts associated with market-oriented reforms and provided adequate social insurance to the poor and vulnerable (Alesina and Rodrik 1994; Rodrik 1998a). In both developed and developing countries, complex political and institutional systems have emerged over time to manage distributional conflicts with varying degrees of success. To the extent that these systems have contributed to socio-political stability and the legitimacy of national governments, constant adjustment to liberal market pressures can sap governments of their political credibility and undermine established patterns of legitimacy in democratic societies.

If convergence is indeed what makes cross-border financial markets work better, then the norms and practices and the outcomes on which it is based need to be perceived as legitimate. The input-side flaws of the current global financial architecture often produce outcomes that conflict with a range of norms of domestic governance; this means that global norms are shared only narrowly, undermining the effectiveness of – and perhaps the desire for – international cooperation

300 *Geoffrey R. D. Underhill and Xiaoke Zhang*

to resolve inevitable collective action problems. Scant attention to the clash between structural pressures and national differences reflects the current regime's efforts to overhaul often deeply embedded institutions in many developing countries. In the wake of the Asian crisis, a number of neoclassical economists breathed a sigh of relief that these once successful exceptions to economic orthodoxy had finally met their come-uppance. The new architecture was, for some, a means to alter long-standing systems of economic development that often proved impenetrable to western corporate entities. Yet the post-crisis effect was the withdrawal of Asian and some Latin American countries from the purview of the IMF through the build-up of reserves, signalling the illegitimacy of a key institution of global financial and monetary governance.

Conclusion and policy implications

The contemporary financial architecture manifests shortcomings on both the input and output sides of legitimacy. Input from emerging market and developing economies has been marginal, yielding financial governance in considerable tension with the interests of these countries as well as some social constituencies in developed countries. The architecture leaves insufficient 'policy space' (Rodrik 2007) for domestic democratic imperatives and choice in terms of national development trajectories.

The accountability 'phase' is similarly deficient: global policy processes are at best answerable to the most powerful states and are more responsive to private preferences than to most developing states. The combination of responsiveness to private interests and the influence wielded by the IFIs and institutions such as the Basel Committee, added to which their lack of external accountability, has undermined both the efficiency and legitimacy of their rules and policies. While some scholars claim that the growth of supranational, private and technical authority in the process of global governance is positive for democracy (Slaughter 2000; Porter 2002), considerable doubt remains.

The analysis presented in this chapter implies that effective and responsible financial governance requires a politically sustainable balance between public authority and private power, and that this should be an explicit concern of the global financial architecture's reform. The ongoing potential for capture analysed in the public choice literature and the empirical evidence of policy capture provided in this volume suggest that a clear definition of the public interest distinct from the particularistic claims of private market actors is the key to

Public interest, diversity and financial governance 301

ensuring the predominance of the public good in the financial system. Maintaining strong public oversight and control over private agents implies effective subordination of private financial firms to democratic institutions and processes across levels of governance. This implies representing a sufficiently broad range of public constituencies on the input side of the policy process in the first place.

This involves examining the policy-making autonomy of regulatory agencies from national to global levels. Where autonomous public agencies – such as financial supervisors with delegated mandates – maintain close interactive ties to private financial firms and associations prone to rent-seeking, governments should establish effective monitoring mechanisms to ensure accountability to representatives of the electorate (Campos and Root 1996: 153–71; Haggard 1999). The power of private actors and potential for capture in situations of delegated authority should also be counterbalanced by including a broader range of social groups in public policy processes and by fashioning more inclusive state-society relations (Biddle and Milnor 1997; Evans 1997). To ensure the responsiveness of the next wave of architectural reforms to the countries and peoples most affected by them, key regional and international financial institutions should also actively engage with transnational social forces (Held 1995; Woods 2001).

The policy implication once again is that input legitimacy could be substantially enhanced through better and broader representation based on a *range* of principles, thus increasing the likelihood of embedding a more acceptable spectrum of norms in global financial governance. To cite a specific example, representation in the Bretton Woods Institutions is arguably based almost entirely on the not-very-democratic shareholder principle: who pays the piper calls the tune. Even on this principle, a range of developing countries are grossly and systematically *under*-represented and a range of (particularly European) developed countries are considerably *over*-represented.[9] Recent but modest reforms to the quota system have only slightly improved the situation.

Yet other principles of representation could be included in the system which go beyond recent and rather limited rebalancing of quotas and vote shares between developed and developing countries. At their founding, Bretton Woods Institutions member countries had proportionately larger 'basic votes' representing one-member-one-vote/population

---

[9] In terms of purchasing power parity, transition plus developing countries constitute the same share of world GDP as the G7, yet the G7 still has well over half of the IMF votes (Buira 2005a). It should be noted that crucial standard-setting bodies like the Basel Committee are far less representative than even the Bretton Woods Institutions, until 2009 excluding non-G10 countries altogether.

302   *Geoffrey R. D. Underhill and Xiaoke Zhang*

elements in their votes, but quota increases have since augmented the shareholder principle. Basic votes could again be strengthened in relative terms, while an emphasis on population would enhance the voice of citizens of developing and transition countries who represent some 84 per cent of the world's population (Buira 2005a). The representation of 'users' on the Board could augment input from societies with an ongoing adjustment programme; a broader range of 'corporatist' social partners from across the membership could also be represented. Finally, no political community is arguably legitimate without serious protections for minorities; this 'minority' is also the most consistent 'user' and 'debtor'. The poorest, mostly African economies subject to almost continuous IMF programmes since the 1960s could receive enhanced representation on the basis of the minority rights principle.

Introducing a broad mix of these enhanced modes of representation, alongside developing greater political and administrative resources at regional and global levels, is part of what is now known as 'cosmopolitan democracy'. By pooling sovereignty through cooperative financial governance – and thus attenuating the raw exercise of state and private corporate power – the principles of 'cosmopolitan democracy' can begin to address the legitimacy deficit while helping individual states deal with the consequences of financial globalisation.[10] This of course is easier said than done, and would encounter the opposition of transnational corporate interests. Equally important, cooperative governance and the required abrogation of national prerogatives may be the most difficult hurdle (especially for the strong) in the development of (democratic) institutions of accountability at regional and global levels. These difficulties, however, do not diminish the potential advantages of a more representative and legitimate process and potentially more legitimate output. The sub-prime crisis has shown that developed countries and their publics can also be victims, and has further highlighted the need for improved cross-border supervisory cooperation.

The G20 process and the Financial Stability Forum (now also G20 based and renamed the Financial Stability Board), in which only a dozen emerging market countries are included, have yet arguably to produce genuine results to address the central concerns of the majority of poor developing countries. It is not yet clear precisely who will be represented on the input side. The next wave of financial architecture reforms is likely to have wide and lasting effects. The greater participation of developing

[10] Cosmopolitan democracy, as a regional and global solution to the democratic deficit caused by economic globalisation, is elaborated in Held (1995: 267–82) and Bohman (1999).

countries and their societies is indispensable for their governments to justify the economic and social costs of structural reforms and to create incentives for adopting international standards and practices within national political economies. In order for the reform agenda to become more legitimate and therefore more achievable, developing countries and broader publics in the developed world will have to be given a major say in the setting of the agenda. So far the input of the corporate sector does not appear particularly diminished.

Conclusion: whither global financial governance after the crisis?

Daniel Mügge, Jasper Blom and Geoffrey R. D. Underhill

For global finance, the year 2008 may prove to be a watershed. The collapse of Lehman Brothers on 15 September of that year brought the global financial system to the brink of meltdown, and much of the world has been experiencing the deepest recession for more than half a century. Only the timely intervention of public authorities prevented a rerun of the 1930s depression. A consensus formed around the unsurprising conclusion that global financial governance was in need of reform – both to ensure a more effective and coordinated crisis response and to prevent a rerun in the future. At least *ex ante*, the London G20 Summit in April 2009 and the Philadelphia follow-up held in the autumn of 2009 were hailed as stepping stones to an overhaul of the global financial architecture. Many observers saw an opportunity for wholesale reform, which had been so conspicuously absent after the crises of the late 1990s and early 2000s, as Helleiner and Pagliari have argued in Chapter 2.

The speed and drama of the crisis have meant that the contributions to this volume ran the risk of obsolescence before they could be published. The crisis might well have ushered in sufficiently dramatic change as to relegate many of the institutions, norms and practices analysed in this book to the dustbin of history. It is therefore somewhat surprising that we find much of pre-crisis financial governance largely intact in early 2010, and much of the analysis in this volume appears to be of continuing relevance. Public finances and private financial institutions have been seriously shaken up. The G20 gained prominence; the Financial Stability Forum turned into the Financial Stability Board (with expanded membership); and the IMF was saved from oblivion by rescue packages for Iceland, many Eastern European states, now Greece, and a tripling of its lending resources. Modifications to the Basel II Capital Accord were proposed alongside many temporary, ad hoc measures and the committee's membership was also considerably expanded. Yet the architectural edifice analysed and indeed much criticised in these chapters still stands – for better or worse. The scholarly

Conclusion: whither financial governance?

efforts of our contributors remain valid and have lost none of their pertinence. The credit crunch will remain a defining moment in financial history, even if only because of the very real economic and social consequences which are still coming to light. What then might the scholarship and analytical framework of this volume add to our understanding of the crisis, and what do they imply for the future evolution of financial governance? These two questions stand central in this conclusion. Underpinning these questions lies a deeper debate which must also take place. The issue has for too long remained inadequately addressed: for what and for whom is a global financial system in the first place? Whose interests in the broad range of financial system stakeholders, many of whom are now financing the excessive risks taken by the financial sector, should predominate?

Financial governance design, legitimacy and the credit crisis

One core theme of this volume has been the link between input and output legitimacy in financial governance, laid out in the Introduction and in the chapter by Underhill and Zhang. Both sides of legitimacy deserve our attention because they are interrelated complements, not substitutes. This is true from a normative perspective, in which the distributive consequences of financial markets and their governance necessitate representation of different stakeholders in rule-making. Equally important, several contributions to this volume have shown that an uneven representation of stakeholders in global financial governance renders it less effective than it might otherwise be. As Walter has argued, the intended targets of putatively global rules may choose to implement them selectively – and thereby defeat the goal of global coherence – or seek out regional alternatives, as in Dieter's discussion. As Baker showed, limited representation may lead to 'skewed argument pools', also reducing the effectiveness of proposed solutions.

We believe that arguments about the importance of input and output aspects of legitimacy also help us understand the origins of the crisis. It is widely acknowledged that financial supervision and regulation was deficient, particularly in the USA and Europe, and allowed financial institutions to pursue strategies that were unsustainable and produced significant negative externalities. This rather problematic policy output, we argue, can be traced to highly exclusionary input into the global financial governance policy process. Limited patterns of interest representation were successfully translated into putatively universal standards which were clearly, at least temporarily, better for some than

306   *Daniel Mügge* et al.

for others. The input side was a part of the problem and now needs to become part of the solution.

Skewed input was evident on at least three levels. First, through the dominance of G10 and G7 representatives in bodies such as the FSF/B or Basel Committee, but also the International Accounting Standards Board or the IMF, global financial governance has reflected the perspectives and interests of the major financial centres although the greater proportion of the global system consists of developing economies with rather different needs and interests. The longstanding emphasis of the IMF on capital account liberalisation is a case in point, and this policy conflicts with the findings of Cassimon *et al.* in Chapter 4. In more general terms, global rules were pervaded by a sense that a mix of the US and British financial market models could serve as a template for the rest of the world. For developing countries, this entailed the internationalisation and marketisation of the financial sector despite the observation that emerging market success had most often been associated with systems characterised by financial repression. Emerging markets were encouraged to strengthen capital markets as a source of corporate investment. And in developed countries with divergent financial market traditions, this template encouraged an internationalisation of the financial sector and a constant search and enlarged scope for 'innovative' banking activities to boost results – often translating into the impenetrable derivative transactions that in the end proved fatal to so many banks. In line with the argument of Germain's chapter, global financial governance showed too little regard for national idiosyncrasies and needs. Instead, by encouraging standardised reform processes, they augmented the vulnerability of many countries to a crisis that was triggered by one sub-segment of the US mortgage market.

Second, private interests disproportionately affected rule-making and global arrangements for cross-border financial supervision. Whether this takes the form of club-like decision-making centred on a shared public-private vision of financial markets, as in the case of international capital requirements (see the chapter by Claessens and Underhill) or outright self-regulation, financial institutions across the board have enjoyed privileged access to policy-making that has too often tilted rules in their favour, while proving disadvantageous to other stakeholders, particularly where bail-outs are concerned. Private financial institutions also and often have been able to keep at bay regulation that might have enhanced systemic stability but imposed unwelcome costs upon their business models – the absence of credit derivatives regulation is one prominent example. This applied even to the domain of money laundering (Chapter 9 by Tsingou) where the goals of the

Conclusion: whither financial governance? 307

criminal justice system supposedly predominate yet the regime functions poorly so as to favour the smooth functioning of international financial markets. Without claiming that the crisis is simply a matter of regulatory capture, it is clear that input-side deficiencies generated policy outcomes with consequences that were both unintended and deleterious to the interest of the public.

Finally, the search for 'optimal' policy design often placed governance in the hands of a relatively narrow group of technocrats. They too often failed to heed either the needs of diverse groups of stakeholders beyond financial firms or to take note of the many critical assessments of market-led approaches to financial governance that emerged from scholarly analysis and practitioners alike. This theme is spelled out most clearly in Baker's contribution. Input legitimacy is thus not only a question of giving stakeholders a chance to articulate and respond to the material stakes that they have in financial governance. It also means ensuring that the policy debate actively seeks out rather than excludes plurality of understanding and critical analysis. Taking these three points together, it is clear that skewed governance structures were far from trivial aspects of the onset of crisis.

A further theme running through the volume is crucial to understanding the origins of the recent meltdown: the crises of the late 1990s and early 2000s appeared initially to trigger a thorough review of global financial rules. After the Asian and the LTCM crisis, international consultations buzzed with talk of a genuinely new international financial architecture. Proposals included a sovereign debt-restructuring mechanism, a departure from the traditional debt-workout conditionality of the IMF, and about potential constraints on cross-border capital flows and their pro-cyclicality. As Helleiner and Pagliari argue, however, the years after the Argentine default of 2001/2 were marked by complacency rather than reform. The surprising rebound of South-East Asian economies and the rapid global growth fuelled by cheap US credit and growing macroeconomic imbalances after the bursting of the 'dot com' bubble diminished the perceived urgency of serious reform. Policymakers and the financial sector had allegedly discovered something 'new', the benign and sustainable context of the 'Great Moderation'. While scholarly discussion and warnings of potential instability persisted, the years before the crisis were in practice characterised by inaction. As Charles Kindleberger had convincingly argued as far back as 1982, the public authorities of the principal financial centres could live with crises as long as the costs were borne by emerging market economies and confidence remained that crisis would fall short of striking at the core of the system. In short, the 2002–7 period of calm was an

308   *Daniel Mügge* et al.

opportunity for reform which regulators now know with hindsight was largely missed at their own peril and that of the public.

Implications for future financial governance

On the one hand, if the process of reform were to lose momentum (for which at time of writing there was some anecdotal but inconclusive evidence), this implies that the failure to undertake a meaningful overhaul of financial governance in the pre-crisis decade threatens to repeat itself. Reminding ourselves of the 'complacent' early 2000s may make dispiriting reading. On the other hand, that complacency was evidently misplaced and several chapters in this volume clearly argue that if a globally integrated financial system is to survive, more and better and indeed more multilevel governance characterised by regional and global-level cooperation and institutions is clearly necessary. Those who continued with a lonely insistence on the need for change after the last bout of crises have now been vindicated. The second half of this conclusion therefore draws together the insights into a future financial governance that emerge from the analyses in this volume's contributions. Clearly not just any sort of change will do, but change which respects a range of parameters identified in the chapters. They can be summarised under three headings: a recalibration of the balance between national autonomy and comprehensiveness of global rules, inclusiveness of governance, and the need for proactive reform.

Balance between national and international

The weaker countries, now including Greece, are already pointing the way. The state of public finance has become an evolving source of difficulty. The public purse has so far absorbed much of the impact of the crisis and done much good in the process, the consequence being that government debt has increased at an unprecedented rate around the world. One way or another the debt will require some combination of repayment and/or workout. The contrasting routes that governments may consider for achieving this goal – for example muddling through, inflation, protectionism or capital controls – may well endanger much that is good in the liberal economic order we know. Reforms should therefore focus on equipping governments with 'policy space', ensuring they have the flexibility to respond to their specific circumstances going forward; but without undermining the positive dimensions of financial openness and access to international capital itself, as had happened in the early 1930s. Germain's analysis suggests that sustainable global financial

Conclusion: whither financial governance? 309

governance should not be one watertight set of rules, but a much looser framework of cooperation that consciously acknowledges the needs and legitimacy of national idiosyncrasies. Such an order would come much closer to what Keynes had in mind when negotiating Bretton Woods: a financial and monetary regime that bolsters rather than constrains governments' ability to make financial policy in the public interest – an arrangement that Ruggie famously labelled 'embedded liberalism'.

Establishing policy space and room for idiosyncrasy also seems appropriate in relation to what we know about national regulatory behaviour in practice and its inevitable need to respond to domestic political imperatives. The chapters by Klagsbrunn and by Zhang explicitly compared how respective pairs of countries fared in this respect. These analyses indicate that the constraints that global regulatory initiatives impose on developing countries in particular could be looser and the outcome no worse, and they may be less stringent in practice than their critics sometimes suggest or, indeed, their proponents would seem to hope. The financial system evolution of Taiwan and Malaysia bears the clear imprint of a balance among crucial national stakeholders in financial system design and their respective preferences. In more dire straits, Brazil and Argentina chose divergent paths to deal with mounting debt and exchange rate difficulties. What these cases also highlight, however, is that there is a gap between the patchwork that financial governance is in practice and international institutions' professed ambition of a single set of globally applicable standards. As Walter shows, these two may be correlated: the lofty goals involved in achieving and enforcing a single set of rules spurs countries to seek out national routes while avoiding blatant non-compliance. National dynamics take over where pressures for convergence cannot easily be accommodated. Arguably, such a situation is at least as challenging to overall system stability as one in which countries are encouraged to make transparent choices about the regimes they want to implement, cognisant of both domestic consequences and global market reactions.

Consciously building 'national room for manoeuvre' into the global financial regime goes further than simply acknowledging the practical limits of imposing and policing a single set of standards. It also means recognising and respecting the needs of developing countries in global financial system design. The chapter by Cassimon, Demetriades and Van Campenhout shows that in particular the needs of the poorest economies may not be well served by the theoretical assumption that a standardised form of financial openness is beneficial for all. We need to build governance on the basis of the evidence and the problems which we observe in practice. This means we must stop adapting evidence to

310   *Daniel Mügge* et al.

particular theoretical models which misunderstood the period of the 'Great Moderation' and have persistently overstated the tendency of a 'governance light' and market-based financial order to produce outcomes characterised by stability and efficiency, and this largely because these arguments served the interests of a few private stakeholders who dominated the input side.

Poor countries and all emerging markets need long-term capital from outside to develop. The volatility of capital flows (in as well as out) to emerging markets over the past two decades was clearly suboptimal in this respect, and has left countries vulnerable in times of international crisis. The challenge is to develop mechanisms that smooth out the cyclical nature of capital flows, for example through GDP-indexed or local-currency bonds, as Ocampo and Griffith-Jones argue. Building such a counter cyclical framework for global capital flows is a challenge, but the claim that there are no alternatives to the current order lacks credibility in view of historical precedents. A successful and legitimate system of global financial governance must be sufficiently flexible to accommodate economies at different levels of development and with different internal dynamics. The vision of a relatively seamless cross-border market functioning on the basis of transparency, information and relatively uniform standards is one that has failed. A far more subtle and differentiated vision which nonetheless does provide global mechanisms of coordination where dictated by global interdependencies is now required.

Indeed, one alternative that has repeatedly been discussed includes the creation of regional institutions to provide capital and buffer countries against the vagaries of volatile capital flows. Asian countries have done so through the various initiatives discussed by Dieter, but other examples come to mind as well, such as the controversial Banco del Sur set up in 2007 on the initiative of Venezuela's Hugo Chávez. These initiatives have stopped short of seriously threatening the global framework of regulations and institutions, and the reasons that the contributors provide for such limitations are likely to hold in the future, too. In East Asia for example, a potential rivalry between China and Japan for financial leadership remains unresolved for the time being. As Walter points out, the leeway that countries have in fact enjoyed to tailor global standards to their own demands and thus feign compliance has decreased the incentives to develop full-blown regional alternatives. Most importantly, however, regional arrangements are likely to remain imperfect substitutes for effective global arrangements though if well-designed they may nonetheless prove complementary. Even with successful regional arrangements, the contemporary financial order also exhibits seriously global patterns of integration and imbalances,

Conclusion: whither financial governance? 311

so better governance will need to be a multi-layered governance. This must emerge in such a way that there is a sensible functional differentiation among the layers, but that they emerge in such a way that coordination across levels is achievable. The growing and massive OECD country deficits are mirrored in the self-insurance reserves of China and other emerging market surplus economies, and these imbalances were not insignificant contributors to the emergence of the credit crunch. Such problems cannot be solved on the regional level, which means that institutions of global financial governance, the G20 and the IMF in particular, also require attention and reinforcement. It goes without saying that their legitimacy also requires enhancement. The difficulties involved here should not be underestimated.

Global inclusiveness

To establish a global financial regime that provides adequate policy space for dealing with national idiosyncrasies and regional initiatives, international leaders must take more seriously the concerns of poor countries and emerging markets and the problems of exclusion and poverty faced by many of their citizens and give them real voice in the restructuring of global financial governance. Several chapters in this volume (Helleiner and Pagliari, Klagsbrunn, Dieter, Walter) have documented an almost cynical stance towards global institutions that had emerged particularly in Asia and Latin America over the past decade. If scepticism towards these standards has not translated into active opposition, then that is largely because of (unintended) loopholes that global rules have contained in practice. A global financial order that manages to close the gap between excessive intrusiveness of global standards on the one hand and poor implementation on the other will thus have to convince countries outside the major western financial centres that global governance has something to offer them. The perspectives of developing countries and emerging markets will need to be taken seriously, even if they deviate from the consensus that has emerged in western-dominated institutions.

At first sight, this call for a strengthening of global governance might seem to contradict the emphasis on less intrusive global rules which expand the policy space available to national governments, yet these should be seen as two sides of the same coin. The absolute bottom line is avoiding a retreat towards competing national solutions and maintaining ongoing incentives and adequate rewards for international cooperation. As argued above, the excessive intrusiveness and purported universalism of pre-crisis standards was a direct consequence of

312   *Daniel Mügge* et al.

the narrowness of input into rule-setting. Broadening input may thus strengthen the legitimacy of global agreements, while at the same time decreasing the chance the agreed rules prove as inappropriate as for example Basel II, thus in turn ultimately enhancing the effectiveness of an emerging multilevel pattern of governance.

This volume has also consistently argued that the poorest countries and their citizens have specific, separate needs from the rest. Young's chapter on microcredit and microfinance dealt with the special needs and place of the poor as a marginal element of the financial system and raised a number of important questions concerning the ways in which the poor may be integrated into the broader, global order. Poor economies also have special needs in the context of the system. As Cassimon, Demetriades and Van Campenhout have shown, financial openness works for those with well-functioning political institutions and a certain level of economic development, but it may be a trap for others. To be sure, investment and developing strong financial systems are central to the successful development of these countries and to poverty relief (see once again Young's chapter on microcredit and finance). Yet realising this potential requires open acknowledgement that market mechanisms alone are insufficient to deliver the necessary public goods. Developing countries should be encouraged to develop domestic institutions facilitating the achievement of financial development goals, and a more comfortable place for poor countries in the international financial architecture should be created. For example, Claessens and Underhill show how Basel II has been likely to increase borrowing costs for developing countries. If the ownership of global financial governance is to be extended to a broader range of countries, their preferences should feature among the criteria used to establish standards in the first place.

De Jong and van der Veer suggest a similar line of reasoning for the capital needs of countries that have experienced macroeconomic and debt problems and sought the help of the IMF. They show that government-sponsored financial flows to countries in post-crisis situations do not necessarily have a 'catalytic effect' on private capital flows aimed at jump-starting the latter. Policy conclusions that follow from their analysis could vary from a stronger emphasis of ex ante crisis prevention and more orderly crisis resolution, for example through a kind of sovereign debt-restructuring mechanism, to an acknowledgement that publicly funded financial support may play a bigger role in post-crisis situations than has so far seemed compatible with a market-led global financial system. These lessons are indeed the more important now that many countries are once again turning to the IMF for help.

Conclusion: whither financial governance? 313

It remains to be seen how the growing relative influence of the EU in global financial governance, as analysed by Posner, will play out in this regard. This more equal relationship between both parties is clearly good for European interests in terms of the outcome. It also may create opportunities for emerging market third parties in global financial governance, as both the EU and the USA may need to seek allies for the policies they wish to promote. In other words, EU strength gained through the development of regional layers of governance – if it survives its internal debt crisis – may push global governance in the direction of the truly multilateral affair that we have argued it should be.

In sum and to repeat a now familiar story in this volume, making the global financial order more inclusive on the input side should boost its legitimacy *and* the effectiveness of the output. This entails a 'mainstreaming' of divergent policy goals, including economic development objectives, into international architectural reform debates. It will not only mean rethinking the rules that should apply to developing countries and emerging markets, but also those in the developed world, which in one way or another will continue to be the main source of capital for the former. For example, Claessens, Cassimon and Van Campenhout show how the effectiveness of aid varies widely with the quality of institutions in the donor countries itself. Whether such aid – often indispensable in cases where private markets will not provide necessary capital – achieves its aims is thus not only a function of conditions in the receiving country, but also in the countries that supply it. Also in this case, reform will be necessary if the global financial system is to deliver on its promises.

Proactive stance towards reform

The final conclusion to emerge from the different contributions to this volume is the need for a forward-looking approach to financial governance reform – a plea that comes at a time when the appearance of 'green shoots' in the economy implies that complacency may be setting in once again. Governments have taken an equity position in the financial sector and are running massive deficits to offset much of the shock generated by the failure of systemically important banks. In combination with the costs of social safety nets in times of economic trouble, these deficits effectively postpone much of the pain. While it is clearly important to address the public policy deficiencies that have led to the crisis, we also need to look forward and anticipate where trouble might emerge next. Internationally incompatible macroeconomic policies to deal with unsustainable public debt loads are one prime contender. Work on a coordinated 'exit strategy' away from massive and unsustainable

314   *Daniel Mügge* et al.

public intervention needs to accelerate at the very least so as to avoid the self-reinforcing downwards spiral caused by the often inadvertent beggar-thy-neighbour policies of the early 1930s. Once again, enhancing inclusiveness on the input side of the policy process should increase the chance of effectively identifying the next or potential source of trouble early on in the debate about the next phase of crisis response The 'castigation of the weak' approach adopted in the eurozone augurs poorly.

A proactive stance towards reform requires above all much political will. Hard choices have to be made among competing policy priorities, and hard choices about rather uneven playing fields perhaps (unintentionally) made worse by public intervention. Equally important, entrenched private interests will have to be confronted if global financial governance is to be put on a more effective, legitimate and sustainable path. Tsingou's chapter on the contemporary anti-money laundering regime is telling in this regard: irrespective of the feasibility of controlling illicit flows and the imperatives of the criminal justice system, the money laundering regime has been largely symbolic as policy-makers were unable to impose on private interests the price that effective oversight would have entailed. There is a real danger going forward that similar patterns of symbolic policy reform – whether aimed and/or misdirected at hedge funds, executive bonuses, tax havens or short selling – might be adopted to satisfy public calls for reform and to breed complacency while trouble continues to brew underneath.

In short, now is the time to apply the analyses presented in this volume to the task of reform. The authors in the preceding chapters have shown where weaknesses lie and they provide important arguments about what should be done. It is up to our democratically elected representatives and the agencies of government to take up the challenge, now that the crisis has opened a window of opportunity for a fundamental rethink of the global financial architecture. The time for action is now, before the reform momentum weakens again, as it has so often done before.

This closing invocation to action still leaves unaddressed one question posed at the beginning of this conclusion: in whose interest? For whom and for what ends should the reform of financial governance be undertaken? We all need finance if the economy is to function, yet the interests of depositors versus their bankers, of small savers and retail investors versus wholesale traders and investment firms, of trading and manufacturing enterprise versus the financial sector, of poor versus rich, of small versus large business, and of different sorts of financial institutions all diverge in important ways beyond the vague requirement

Conclusion: whither financial governance?

of a functioning and stable financial order however defined. The risk appetites and needs of these different stakeholders vary considerably.

So whose notion of financial order and governance should prevail and underpin the process of reform? One point however should be easy to establish and should orient any future discussion or decision-making on the matter: the crisis and its management have made it clear that citizens, most of whom are far from privileged, have become and will remain the guarantors of the risks taken by financiers with other people's money. As long as this is the case, then the interests of this broad public should be front and centre in any system of financial markets and its governance. The accountability trail must much more pointedly lead to them. Their needs are on the whole modest: access to long-term savings and investment opportunities to offset the risks and potential uncertainties of the future, characterised by safety and soundness, stability, regularity of return and relative simplicity. Our financial order should first and foremost serve these needs because these are the very people on whose modest resources financiers and the economy in general ultimately rely when they take risks that may or may not pay off, the end costs of which are potentially collectively to be borne. Public provision of the necessary collective goods and legal and institutional support is central to these needs. If finance requires complexity and complex hedging of risks with financial exotica, this activity must take place in ways which are compatible with the broader and mostly simpler needs of this wide range of 'publics', spread as they are across a range of poor, emerging market and developed economies.

References

ABA Banking Journal 2003. 'Being Good is Just the Beginning', June, pp. 35–57.

ACB (America's Community Bankers) 2003. Submission to the Basel Committee re Third Consultative Paper.

Acemoglu, D., S. Johnson and J. Robinson 2001. 'The Colonial Origins of Comparative Development: An Empirical Investigation', *American Economic Review* 91: 1369–1401.

2004. 'Institutions as the Fundamental Cause of Long-Run Growth', NBER Working Paper 10481. National Bureau of Economic Research, Inc.

Acemoglu, D., S. Johnson, J. Robinson and Y. Thaicharoen 2003. 'Institutional Causes, Macroeconomic Symptoms: Volatility, Crises and Growth', *Journal of Monetary Economics* 50(1): 49–123.

Aggarwal, V. K. 1985. *Liberal Protectionism: The International Politics of Organized Textile Trade.* Berkeley: University of California Press.

Ahamed, L. 2009. *Lords of Finance. The Bankers who Broke the World.* London: Penguin.

Alesina, A. and D. Rodrik 1994. 'Distributive Politics and Economic Growth', *Quarterly Journal of Economics* 109(2): 465–90.

Alesina, A. and D. Dollar 2000. 'Who Gives Foreign Aid to Whom and Why?', *Journal of Economic Growth* 5(1): 33–63.

Alesina, A. and B. Weder 2002. 'Do Corrupt Governments Receive Less Foreign Aid?', *American Economic Review* 92(4): 1126–37.

Alfaro, L., S. Kalemli-Ozcan and V. Volosovych 2005a. 'Capital Flows in a Globalized World: The Role of Policies and Institutions', NBER Working Papers 11696, National Bureau of Economic Research, Inc.

2005b. 'Why Doesn't Capital Flow from Rich to Poor Countries? An Empirical Investigation', NBER Working Papers 11901, National Bureau of Economic Research, Inc.

Alix, M. J. 2004. Testimony, 22 June. US House of Representatives Financial Services Committee.

Allen, F. and D. Gale 2000. *Comparing Financial Systems.* Cambridge: MIT Press.

Amoore, L. and M. de Goede 2005. 'Governance, Risk and Dataveillance in the War on Terror', *Crime, Law and Social Change* 43: 149–73.

Amsden, A. H. and W. Chu 2003. *Beyond Late Development.* Cambridge: MIT Press.

References 317

Andreas, P. and E. Nadelmann 2006. *Policing the Globe: Criminalisation and Crime Control in International Relations.* New York: Oxford University Press.

Andrews, D. M., C. R. Henning and L.W. Pauly (eds.) 2002. *Governing the World's Money.* Ithaca: Cornell University Press.

Andrianova, S., P. Demetriades and A. Shortland 2008. 'Government Ownership of Banks, Institutions and Financial Development', *Journal of Development Economics* 85: 218–52.

Armijo, L. E. 2001. 'The Political Geography of World Financial Reform: Who Wants What and Why?' *Global Governance* 7: 379–96.

Arner, D., Lejot, P. and W. Wang 2009. 'Assessing East Asian Financial Cooperation and Integration', Asian Institute of International Financial Law, Working Paper No. 5, March.

ASEAN+3 2008. Joint Ministerial Statement of the 11th ASEAN Plus Three ASEAN Ministers Meeting, Madrid, Spain, 4 May.

ASX (Australian Stock Exchange) 2003. *International Share Ownership.* Sydney: ASX.

Baker, A. 2005. 'The Three-Dimensional Governance of Macroeconomic Policy in Advanced Capitalist States', in Baker, Hudson, and Woodward (eds.), pp. 102–29.

The Group of Seven Finance Ministries, Central Banks, and Global Financial Governance. London: Routledge.

2008. 'Financial Crises and US Treasury Policy: The Institutional and Ideational Basis of American Capability', in J. Robertson (ed.) *Politics and Power After Financial Crises: Reassessing Foreign Opportunism in Emerging Markets.* London: Palgrave, pp. 31–51.

2009. 'Deliberative Equality and the Transgovernmental Politics of the Global Financial Architecture', *Global Governance* 15(2): 195–218.

Baker, A., D. Hudson and R. Woodward (eds.) 2005. *Governing Financial Globalization.* London: Routledge.

Bakker, I. 2007. 'Financing for Gender Equality and the Empowerment of Women: Paradoxes and Possibilities', Division for the Advancement of Women, Expert Group Meeting on Financing for Gender Equality and the Empowerment of Women, Oslo, September, EGM/FFGE/2007/BP.1.

Bakker, I. and S. Gill 2003. 'Global Political Economy and Social Reproduction', in Bakker and Gill (eds.) *Power, Production and Social Reproduction.* Basingstoke: Palgrave Macmillan.

Balderston, T. 1989. 'War Finance and Inflation in Britain and Germany, 1914–1918', *Economic History Review* 42(2): 222–44.

Baltagi, B., P. Demetriades and S. H. Law 2009. 'Financial Development and Openness: Evidence from Panel Data', *Journal of Development Economics,* 89(2): 285–96.

Banco Central do Brasil 2004. *Annual Report.*

2005. *Annual Report.*

Banker, The 2003. 'Money Laundry Monitor', October.

Barth, J. R., G. Caprio, Jr. and R. Levine 2007. Banking Regulation and Supervision Database, World Bank, www.go.worldbank.org/SNUS W978P0.

318   References

Basel Committee 1993. *The Supervisory Treatment of Market Risks*, consultative paper. Basel: BIS, April.

1995a. *Proposal to Issue a Supplement to the Basel Capital Accord to Cover Market Risks*. Basel: BIS, April.

1995b. *An Internal Model-Based Approach to Market Risk Capital Requirements*. Basel: BIS, April.

1996. *Amendment to the Capital Accord to Incorporate Market Risks*. Basel: BIS, January.

1999. *A New Capital Adequacy Framework* (Basel: BIS, June).

2001a. 'Customer Due Diligence by Banks', consultative document. Basel: BIS.

2001b. *Potential Modifications to the Committee's Proposals*, consultative document. Basel: BIS, November.

2003. *Overview of the New Basel Capital Accord*, consultative document. Basel: BIS, April.

2006a. *Basel II: International Convergence of Capital Measurement and Capital Standards: A Revised Framework – Comprehensive Version*. Basel: BIS, June.

2006b. *Core Principles for Effective Banking Supervision*. Basel: BIS, October.

2006c. *Results of the Fifth Quantitative Impact Study* (QIS 5), Basel: BIS.

Battellino, R. 2004. 'Recent Developments in Asian Bond Markets', Address to the 17th Australasian Banking & Finance Conference, Sydney, 15 December.

Bayoumi, T., B. Eichengreen and P. Mauro 2000. 'On Regional Monetary Arrangements for ASEAN', *Journal of the Japanese and International Economies* 14(2): 121–48.

Beck, T. 2007. *A New Database on Financial Development and Structure*. Washington, DC: World Bank.

Benelli, R. 2003. 'Do IMF-Supported Programs Boost Private Capital Inflows? The Role of Program Size and Policy Adjustment', IMF Working Paper 03/231.

Benería, L. 2003. *Gender, Development, and Globalization. Economics as if All People Mattered*. New York/London: Routledge.

Bergsten, F. and R. Henning 1996. *Global Economic Leadership and the Group of Seven*. Washington, DC: Institute of International Economics.

Berthélemy, J.-C. and A. Tichit 2004. 'Bilateral Donors Aid Allocation Decisions: A Three–Dimensional Panel Analysis', *International Review of Economics and Finance* 13(3): 253–74.

Best, J. 2003. 'From the Top-Down: The New Financial Architecture and the Re-embedding of Global Finance', *New Political Economy* 8(3): 363–84.

Bhagwati, J. 1972. 'Amount and Aid Sharing', in R. Frank, J. Bhagwati, R. Shaw and H. Malmgren (eds.) *Assisting Development Countries*. New York: Preager Publishers for Overseas Development Council.

1998. 'The Capital Myth', *Foreign Affairs* 77–3: 7–12.

Biddle, J. and V. Milnor 1997. 'Economic Governance in Turkey', in S. Maxfield and B. R. Schneider (eds.) *Business and State in Developing Countries*. Ithaca: Cornell University Press, pp. 277–309.

References

Biersteker, T. 2002. 'Targeting Terrorist Finances: The New Challenges of Financial Market Globalisation', in Ken Booth and Tim Dunne (eds.) *Worlds in Collision*. Basingstoke: Palgrave, pp. 74–84.

Bird, G. and D. Rowlands 2000a. 'The Catalysing Role of Policy-Based Lending by the IMF and the World Bank: Fact or Fiction?', *Journal of International Development* 12: 951–73.

2000b. 'Do the Multilaterals Catalyse Other Capital Flows? A Case Study Analysis', *Third World Quarterly* 21–3: 483–503.

2002. 'Do IMF Programmes Have a Catalytic Effect on Other International Capital Flows?', *Oxford Development Studies* 30–3: 229–49.

Birdsall, N., S. Claessens and I. Diwan 2003. 'Policy Selectivity Foregone: Debt and Donor Behavior in Africa', *World Bank Economic Review* 17: 409–35.

BIS (Bank for International Settlements) 2005. *75th Annual Report*. Basel: BIS.

Block, F. 1977. *The Origins of International Economic Disorder*. Berkeley: University of California Press.

Blustein, P. 2001. *The Chastening*. New York: Public Affairs.

2005. *And the Money Kept Rolling In (and Out)*. New York: Public Affairs.

BNM (Bank Negara Malaysia) various issues. *Quarterly Bulletin*. Kuala Lumpur: BNM.

1994. *Money and Banking in Malaysia*. Kuala Lumpur: BNM.

1996. *Annual Report*. Kuala Lumpur: BNM.

2002. *Annual Report*. Kuala Lumpur: BNM.

2003. *Annual Report*. Kuala Lumpur: BNM.

2004. *Annual Report*. Kuala Lumpur: BNM.

2006. *Financial Stability and Payment Systems*. Kuala Lumpur: BNM.

Bohman, J. 1999. 'International Regimes and Democratic Governance', *International Affairs* 75(3): 499–513.

2006. 'Deliberative Democracy and the Epistemic Benefits of Diversity', *Episteme* 3(3): 175–90.

Bordo, M., A. Mody and N. Oomes 2004. 'Keeping Capital Flowing: The Role of the IMF', *International Finance* 7(3): 421–50.

Bordo, M., B. Eichengreen, D. Klingebiel and M. S. Martínez-Peria 2001. 'Is the Crisis Problem Growing More Severe?', *Economic Policy* 32: 51–82.

Borensztein, E. and P. Mauro 2004. 'The Case for GDP-Indexed Bonds', *Economic Policy* 19(38): 165–216.

Börn, K. E. 1977/1983. *A History of International Banking in the 19th and 20th Centuries*, trans. V. R. Berghan. Oxford: Berg Press.

Boughton, J. M. 1997. 'From Suez to Tequila: The IMF as Crisis Manager', IMF Working Paper 97/90.

Braudel, F. 1979/1982. *Civilization and Capitalism, 15th to 18th Centuries, Volume 2: The Wheels of Commerce*, trans. Sian Reynolds. London: Collins/ Fontana.

Brigg, M. 2006. 'Disciplining the Development Subject: Neoliberal Power and Governance through Microcredit', in J. L. Fernando (ed.) *Microfinance: Perils and Prospects*. London/New York: Routledge, pp.64–88.

Brown, W. 1940. *The International Gold Standard Re-interpreted*. Cambridge: NBER.

320 References

Brown, G. 2001. Speech to the Federal Reserve Bank of New York, 16 November.

Brown, R. P. C. and T. J. Bulman 2006. 'The Evolving Roles of the Clubs in the Management of International Debt', *International Journal of Social Economics* 33(1): 11–32.

Bryant, R. 2003. *Turbulent Waters: Cross-border Finance and International Governance*. Washington, DC: Brookings Institution Press.

Buira, A. 2005a. 'The IMF at Sixty', in Buira (ed.) *The IMF and the World Bank at Sixty*. New York: Anthem Press for the G24 Research Programme.

2005b. 'Financial Crises and International Cooperation', briefing note prepared for 'The Orderly Resolution of Financial Crises: A G20-led Initiative', 29–30 January, Mexico.

Burnside, C. and D. Dollar 2000. 'Aid, Policies and Growth', *American Economic Review* 90(4): 847–68.

Cady, J. 2005. 'Does SDDS Subscription Reduce Borrowing Costs for Emerging Market Economies?', IMF Staff Papers 52:3.

Cai, K. G. 2003. 'The ASEAN-China Free Trade Agreement and East Asian Regional Grouping', *Contemporary Southeast Asia* 25(3): 387–404.

Calvo, G. and E. Talvi 2004. 'Sudden Stop, Financial Factors and Economic Collapse: A View from the Latin American Frontlines', paper presented at the 'Universal Forum for Cultures', Barcelona, September.

Calvo, G. A., L. Leiderman and C. M. Reinhart 1993. 'Capital Inflows and Real Exchange Rate Appreciation in Latin America, the Role of External Factors', *IMF Staff Papers*, 40(1).

Camdessus, M. 1995. 'The IMF and the Challenges of Globalization: The Fund's Evolving Approach to its Constant Mission: The Case of Mexico', address at the Zurich Economics Society, 14 November.

Campos, E. and H. Root 1996. *The Key to the Asian Miracle*. Washington, DC: Brookings Institution Press.

Campos, R. C. 2003. 'Embracing International Business in the Post-Enron Era', speech at the Centre for European Policy Studies, Brussels, 11 June.

2006. 'Regulatory Role of Exchanges and International Implications of Demutualization', speech, Armonk, 10 March.

Caprio, G., P. Honohan and J. Stiglitz (eds.) 2001. *Financial Liberalisation*. Cambridge University Press.

Cassimon, D. and B. Van Campenhout 2008. 'Multiple Equilibria in the Dynamics of Financial Globalization', University of Antwerp, IOB, mimeo.

Cassis, Y. 1987. *City Bankers, 1890–1914*, trans. Margaret Rocques. Cambridge University Press.

Cassou, D., A. García Herrero and L. Molina 2006. 'What Kind of Capital Flows Does the IMF Catalyze and When?', *Documentos de Trabajo* 0617, Bank of Spain.

Castellano, M. 2000. 'East Asian Monetary Union: More Than Just Talk?', *Japan Economic Institute Report 12A*.

CBC (Central Bank of China) various issues. *Financial Statistics Monthly*. Taipei: CBC.

References 321

CEPD (Council for Economic Planning and Development) 2005. *Privatisation of SOEs in Taiwan.* Taipei: CEPD.

Cerny, P. G. (ed.) 1993. *Finance and World Politics: Markets, Regimes and States in the Post-Hegemonic Era.* Brookfield: Edward Elgar.

Cerny, P. G. 1995. 'Globalization and the Changing Logic of Collective Action', *International Organization* 49(4): 595–625.

1996. 'International Finance and the Erosion of State Policy Capacity', in Philip Gummet (ed.) *Globalisation and Public Policy.* Cheltenham: Edward Elgar, pp. 83–104.

Chandler, L. 1958. *Benjamin Strong: Central Banker.* Washington, DC: Brookings Institution Press.

Chang, S.-J. 2006. *Business Groups in East Asia.* Oxford University Press.

Chao, C.-M. 2002. 'The Republic of China's Foreign Relations', in B. J. Dickson and C.-M. Chao (eds.) *Assessing the Lee Teng-Hui Legacy in Taiwan's Politics.* New York: M. E. Sharpe, pp. 177–203.

Chauvin, N. and A. Kraay 2007. 'Who Gets Debt Relief?', *Journal of the European Economic Association* 5(2–3): 333–42.

Cheah, K. G. 2005. 'Corporate Governance in Malaysia: Issues and Challenges', in Ho Khai Leong (ed.) *Reforming Corporate Governance in Southeast Asia.* Singapore: Institute of Southeast Asian Studies, pp. 85–101.

Chen, C.-H. 2005. 'Taiwan's Burgeoning Budget Deficit', *Asian Survey* 45(3): 383–96.

Chen, N.-K. and H.-J. Wang 2005. 'Financial Crisis and the Effects on Bank Credits', manuscript, Department of Economics, National Taiwan University.

Chin, K. F. and K. S. Jomo 2001. 'Financial Reform and Crisis in Malaysia', in Masayoshi Tsurumi (ed.) *Financial Big Bang in Asia.* Aldershot: Ashgate, pp. 225–49.

Chinn, M. D. and H. Ito 2006. 'What Matters for Financial Development? Capital Controls, Institutions and Interactions', *Journal of Development Economics* 81(1): 163–92.

Chow, P. C. 2005. 'Financial Restructuring and Corporate Governance in Korea and Taiwan after 1997', in *The Newly Emerging Asian Order and the Korean Peninsula*, Joint US-Korea Academic Studies 15. Seoul: Korean Economic Institute, pp. 77–101.

Christofides, C., C. Mulder and A. Tiffin 2003. 'The Link Between Adherence to International Standards of Good Practice, Foreign Exchange Spreads, and Ratings', IMF Working Paper WP/03/74.

Chung, D.-K. and B. Eichengreen 2007. 'Exchange Rate Arrangements for Emerging Asia', in Chung and Eichengreen (eds.) *Toward an Asian Exchange Rate Regime.* Washington, DC: Brookings Institution Press, pp. 1–21.

Chwieroth, J. 2007. 'Neoliberal Economists and Capital Account Liberalization in Emerging Markets', *International Organization* 61: 443–63.

Claessens, S. 2003, *The International Financial Architecture: What is News(s)?* Inaugural Lecture, Amsterdam: Vossiuspers.

322 References

Claessens, S. and G. Embrechts 2003, 'Basel II, Sovereign Ratings and Transfer Risk: External versus Internal Ratings', paper presented at the conference 'Basel II: An Economic Assessment', BIS, 17–18 May 2002.

Claessens, S., D. Cassimon and B. Van Campenhout 2007. 'Empirical Evidence on the New International Aid Architecture', IMF Working Paper 07/277, Washington, DC.

Claessens, S., G. R. D. Underhill and X. Zhang 2008. 'The Political Economy of Basel II: The Costs for Poor Countries', *The World Economy* 31(3): 313–44.

Clarke, S. V. O. 1967. *Central Bank Cooperation: 1924–1931*. Federal Reserve Bank of New York.

Clavin, P. 1996. *The Failure of Economic Diplomacy: Britain, Germany, France and the United States, 1931–1936*. London: Macmillan.

Clay, H. 1957. *Lord Norman*. London: Macmillan & Co.

CLSA Emerging Markets 2005. *CG Watch 2005: Corporate Governance in Asia*, CLSA Emerging Markets, in collaboration with the Asian Corporate Governance Association.

Cohen, B. J. 2003. 'Capital Controls: Why Do Governments Hesitate?', in L. Armijo (ed.) *Debating the Global Financial Architecture*. New York: SUNY Press, pp. 93–117.

Coleman, W. D. 1996. *Financial Services, Globalization, and Domestic Policy Change*. Basingstoke: Palgrave Macmillan.

Coleman, W. D. and G. R. D. Underhill 1995. 'Globalization, Regionalism and the Regulation of Securities Markets', *Journal of European Public Policy* 2(3): 488–513.

Collier, P. and J. Dehn 2001. 'Aid, Shocks and Growth', World Bank Policy Research Working Paper 2688.

Commonwealth Secretariat 2007. 'Microfinance and Innovative Financing for Gender Equality: Approaches, Challenges and Strategies', 8th Commonwealth Women's Affairs Ministers Meeting, Kampala, 11–14 June, WAMM(07)11.

Cordella, T. and E. L. Yeyati 2005. 'A (New) Country Insurance Facility', IMF Working Paper 05/23.

Corsetti, G., P. Pesenti and N. Roubini 1998. 'Paper Tigers? A Model of the Asian Crisis', NBER Working Paper 6783, October.

Cox, C. 2007a. 'Chairman's Address to the SEC Roundtable on IFRS', speech, Washington, DC, 6 March.

2007b. 'Re-Thinking Regulation in the Era of Global Securities Markets', speech, Coronado, 24 January.

Croall, H. 2003. 'Combating Financial Crime: Regulatory versus Crime Control Approaches', *Journal of Financial Crime* 11(1): 45–55.

Crouch, C. and W. Streeck (eds.) 1997. *Political Economy of Modern Capitalism: Mapping Convergence and Diversity*. London: Sage.

Culpepper, R. 2003. 'Systemic Reform at a Standstill: A Flock of "Gs" in Search of Global Financial Stability' in: Berry and Indart (eds.) 2000. *Critical Issues in International Financial Reform*, New Jersey: Transaction Publishers, pp. 203–36.

References

Cutler, C. A., V. Haufler and T. Porter (eds.) 1999. *Private Authority and International Affairs*. Albany: State University of New York Press.

Dahl, R. 1994. 'A Democratic Dilemma: System Effectiveness Versus Citizen Participation', *Political Science Quarterly* 109(1): 23–34.

Daily Telegraph, 13 September 2007. 'Alistair Darling Signals End of Easy Money'.

Daley-Harris, S. 2006. *Microcredit Summit Campaign Report 2006*. Washington, DC: The Microcredit Summit Campaign.

2009. *State of the Microcredit Summit Campaign Report 2009*. Washington, DC: The Microcredit Summit Campaign.

Dam, K. W. and H. S. Scott 2004. Statement on the US-EU Financial Markets Dialogue, Committee on Financial Services, US House of Representatives, Washington, DC.

Das, M. and S. Mohapatra 2003. 'Income Inequality', *Journal of Empirical Finance* 10(2): 217–48.

Dayaratna-Banda, O. and J. Whalley 2007. 'Regional Monetary Arrangements in ASEAN+3 as Insurance through Reserve Accumulation and Swaps', CIGI Working Paper 22.

de Brouwer, G. 2002. 'The IMF and East Asia: A Changing Regional Financial Architecture', *Pacific Economic Papers* 324.

2005. 'Monetary and Financial Integration in Asia: Empirical Evidence and Issues', mimeo, March 2005.

de Goede, M. 2003. 'Hawala Discourses and the War on Terrorist Finance', *Environment and Planning D: Society and Space* 21: 513–32.

de Koker, L. 2006. 'Money Laundering Control and Suppression of Financing Terrorism: Some Thoughts on the Impact of Customer Due Diligence Measures on Financial Exclusion', *Journal of Financial Crime* 13(1): 26–50.

Delonis, R. 2004. 'International Financial Standards and Codes: Mandatory Regulation Without Representation', *International Law and Politics* 36(2–3): 563–634.

Demetriades, P. O. and K. Hussein 1996. 'Does Financial Development Cause Economic Growth? Time-series Evidence from 16 Countries', *Journal of Development Economics* 51: 387–411.

Demetriades, P. O. and K. B. Luintel 1997. 'The Direct Costs of Financial Repression: Evidence from India', *Review of Economics and Statistics* 79: 311–20.

2001. 'Financial Restraints in the South Korean Miracle', *Journal of Development Economics* 64: 459–79.

Demetriades, P. O. and S. H. Law 2006. 'Finance, Institutions and Economic Development', *International Journal of Finance & Economics* 11: 245–60.

Demetriades, P. O, J. Du, S. Girma and C. Xu 2008. 'Does the Chinese Banking System Promote the Growth of Firms?', World Economy and Finance Working Paper WEF0036.

Demirgüç-Kunt, A. and R. Levine 2001. 'Bank-Based and Market-Based Financial Systems', in Demirgüç-Kunt and Levine (eds.) *Financial Structure and Economic Growth*. Cambridge: MIT Press, pp. 81–140.

324 References

Deutsche Bank Research 2007. 'Microfinance: An Emerging Investment Opportunity'.

Dieter, H. 2000. 'Monetary Regionalism: Regional Integration without Financial Crises', University of Warwick, Centre for the Study of Globalisation and Regionalisation Working Paper 52/00.

2001. 'East Asia's Puzzling Regionalism', *Far Eastern Economic Review*, 12 July, p. 29.

2005. *Die Zukunft der Globalisierung. Zwischen Krise und Neugestaltung*, Baden-Baden: Nomos-Verlagsgesellschaft.

2006. 'The Limited Utility of Bilateral Free Trade Agreements', *Journal of Australian Political Economy* 58: 94–113.

2007. 'Transnational Production Networks in the Automobile Industry and the Function of Trade-Facilitating Measures', Notre Europe (Paris) Studies and Research 58/2007.

2009. 'Global Economic Governance: Is the Multilateral Regulation of International Trade and Finance a Basket Case?', Business and Politics, III/2009 (in print).

Dieter, H. and R. Higgott 1998. 'Verlierer Japan, Gewinner China? Außenpolitische Konsequenzen der Asienkrise', *Internationale Politik* 53(10): 45–52.

2003. 'Exploring Alternative Theories of Economic Regionalism: From Trade to Finance in Asian Co-operation?', *Review of International Political Economy* 10(3): 430–55.

Dieter, H. and C. Silva-Garbade 2004. 'Das Ende des Höhenflugs? Krisenpotentiale in der amerikanischen Ökonomie und Konsequenzen für die Weltwirtschaft', SWP-Studie 49.

Dimson, E. and P. Marsh 1994. *The Debate on International Capital Requirements: Evidence on Equity Position Risk for UK Securities Firms*, London: City Research Project, London Business School, February.

Dinan, D. 2002. Testimony, 22 May. US House of Representatives Committee on Financial Services.

Dobson, W. and P. Jacquet 1998. *Financial Services Liberalization in the WTO*. Washington, DC: IIE.

Dodd, R. and S. Spiegel 2005. 'Up from Sin: A Portfolio Approach to Financial Salvation', in Buira (ed.) *The IMF and the World Bank at Sixty*. London: Anthem Press, pp. 85–115.

Dodd, R. and S. Griffith-Jones 2007. 'Report on Derivatives Markets: Stabilizing or Speculative Impact on Chile and a Comparison with Brazil', ECLAC.

Dollar, D. and V. Levin 2006. 'The Increasing Selectivity of Foreign Aid, 1984–2003', *World Development* 34(2): 2034–46.

Donaghy, M. and M. Clarke 2003. 'Are Offshore Financial Centres the Product of Global Markets? A Sociological Response', *Economy and Society* 32(3): 381–409.

Drummond, I. M. 1979. *London, Washington and the Management of the Franc, 1936–1939*, Princeton Studies in International Finance 45. Princeton University Press.

References

325

1981. *The Floating Pound and the Sterling Area: 1931–1939*. Cambridge University Press.

Dudley, L. and C. Montmarquette 1976. 'A Model of the Supply of Bilateral Foreign Aid', *American Economic Review* 66(11): 132–42.

Duffy, R. 2000. 'Shadow Players: Ecotourism Development, Corruption and State Politics in Belize', *Third World Quarterly* 21(3): 549–65.

Easterly, W. 2003. 'Can Foreign Aid Buy Growth?', *Journal of Economic Perspectives* 17(3): 23–48.

2007. 'Are Aid Agencies Improving?', *Economic Policy* 22(52): 633–78.

Easton, D. 1965. *A Systems Analysis of Political Life*. New York: John Wiley & Sons.

Economist, The. 14 December 2002. 'The Needle in the Haystack'.

3 November 2005. 'The Hidden Wealth of the Poor'.

Edwards, M. 2006. 'Signalling Credibility? The IMF and Catalytic Finance', *Journal of International Relations and Development* 9(1): 27–52.

Eichengreen, B. 1992. *Golden Fetters*. Oxford University Press.

1996. *Globalizing Capital*. Princeton University Press.

1999. *Toward a New International Financial Architecture: A Practical Post-Asia Agenda*. Washington, DC: Institute for International Economics.

2004. 'Global Imbalances and the Lessons of Bretton Woods', NBER Working Paper 10497.

2007. 'Parallel Processes? Monetary Integration in Europe and in Asia', in Chung and Eichengreen (eds.) *Toward an Asian Exchange Rate Regime*. Washington, DC: Brookings Institution Press, pp. 137–56.

Eichengreen, B. and T. Bayoumi 1999. 'Is Asia an Optimum Currency Area? Can It Become One? Regional, Global and Historical Perspectives on Asian Monetary Relations', in Collignon, Pisani-Ferry and Park (eds.) *Exchange Rate Policies in Emerging Asian Countries*. London: Routledge, pp. 347–66.

Eichengreen, B. and A. Mody 2001. 'Bail-ins, Bailouts, and Borrowing Costs', IMF Staff Papers 47, pp. 155–87.

Eichengreen, B. and R. Hausmann (eds.) 2005. *Other People's Money: Debt Denomination and Financial Instability in Emerging Market Economies*. University of Chicago Press.

Eichengreen, B., R. Hausman and U. Panizza 2003. 'Currency Mismatches, Debt Intolerance and Original Sin: Why They are Not the Same and Why They Matter', NBER Working Paper 10036.

Eichengreen, B., K. Kletzer and A. Mody 2006. 'The IMF in a World of Private Capital Markets', *Journal of Banking and Finance* 30: 1335–57.

Economist Intelligence Unit. 2000. *Country Report Taiwan*, November.

Elson, D. 2006. *Budgeting for Women's Rights: Monitoring Government Budgets for Compliance with CEDAW*. New York: UNIFEM.

European Commission 1995. *Accounting Harmonisation*, COM95 (508) EN.

1999. *Financial Services Action Plan*, COM (1999) 232.

2005. *White Paper: Financial Services Policy 2005–2010*, Com (2005) 177.

2006a. *Single Market in Financial Services Progress Report, 2004–2005*, SEC (2006) 17.

2006b. Comments on Proposed Rule: Termination of a Foreign Private Issuer's Registration of a Class of Securities Under Section 12 (g) and

326 References

Duty to File Reports Under Section 15 (d) of the Securities Exchange Act of 1934, 1 March, Brussels.

2007. *First Report to the European Securities Committee and to the European Parliament on Convergence between IFRS and Third Country National GAAPs*, SEC (2007) 968 or COM (2007) 405 Final.

EU-US Coalition 2005. The Transatlantic Dialogue in Financial Services: the Case for Regulatory Simplification and Trading Efficiency, London.

Evans, P. 1997. 'State Structures', in Maxfield and Schneider (eds.) *Business and State in Developing Countries*. Ithaca: Cornell University Press, pp. 63–87.

Feis, H. 1930/1964. *Europe the World's Banker*. New York: Augustus M. Kelley.

Felker, G. 2001. 'The Politics of Industrial Investment Policy Reform in Malaysia and Thailand', in K. S. Jomo (ed.) *Southeast Asia's Industrialization*. Basingstoke: Palgrave, pp. 129–82.

Fernández de Lis, S., J. Martínez and J. Saurina 2001. 'Credit Growth, Problem Loans and Credit Risk Provisioning in Spain', BIS Papers 1: 310–30.

Fernando, J. L. 2006. 'Introduction: Microcredit and Empowerment of Women: Blurring the Boundary between Development and Capitalism', in Fernando (ed.) *Microfinance: Perils and Prospects*. London/New York: Routledge.

Financial Times 13 February 2006 'Doing Good and Making a Profit', p. 10.

28 September 2006. 'Women are the Hidden Engine of World Growth', p. 11.

4 January 2008. '$6.5bn of CDOs Face Ratings Downgrades'.

25 January 2008. 'Gates Pushes "Creative Capitalism"', p. 4.

29 May 2008. 'Who Rates the Ratings Agencies?'.

4 June 2008. 'Rating Agencies Agree to Change Charges'.

23 March 2009. 'Buzz Around India's Maturing Microfinance Sector Quietens', p. 8.

Fishkin, J. 1995. *The Voice of the People*. New Haven: Yale University Press.

Fitch Ratings 2002. 'Korean Banks' Asset Quality – Fact or Fiction?', March.

FitzGerald, V. 2004. 'Global Financial Information, Compliance Incentives and Terrorist Funding', *European Journal of Political Economy* 20(2): 387–401.

Flandreau, M. 1997. 'Central Bank Cooperation in Historical Perspective: A Sceptical View', *Economic History Review* 50(4): 735–63.

Flandreau, M., C.-L. Holtfrerich and H. James (eds.) 2003. *International Financial History in the 20th Century*. Cambridge University Press.

Franke, J. and V. Potthoff 1997. Comment Letter from Deutsche Börse AG (34–38672), SEC File No. S7-16-97, Washington, DC.

French-Davis, R. 2001. *Financial Crises in 'Successful' Emerging Economies*. Washington, DC: Brookings Institution Press and ECLAC.

Frenkel, M. and L. Menkhoff 2000. *Stabile Weltfinanzen? Die debate um eine neue internationale Finanzarchitektur*, Springer.

FSI (Financial Stability Institute) 2004. 'Implementation of the New Capital Adequacy Framework in non-Basel Committee Member Countries,' Occasional Paper no. 4 (Basel: BIS, July).

2000a. *Report of the Working Group on Highly Leveraged Institutions (HLIs)*. Basel: Financial Stability Forum. 5 April.

References

2000b. *Report of the Follow-Up Group on Incentives to Foster Implementation of Standards*. Basel: Financial Stability Forum.

2007. *Update of the FSF Report on Highly Leveraged Institutions*. Basel: Financial Stability Forum. 19 May.

FSS (Financial Supervisory Service, Korea) 2002. *Financial Supervisory System in Korea*. Seoul: FSS.

G7 2003. G7 Finance Ministers and Central Bank Governors' Statement, 12 April, Washington, DC.

G20 2003. Globalization: The Role of Institution Building in the Financial Sector – Report to Ministers and Governors, G20 Discussion Paper.

2004. Summary Transcript G20 Workshop on Developing Strong Domestic Financial Markets, 26–7 April.

Galbraith, J. K. 1995. *Money: Whence it Came and Where it Went*. London: Penguin.

GAO 2004. *Financial Regulation*, GAO-05-61. Washington, DC: US Government Accountability Office.

2006. *Sarbanes-Oxley Act*, GAO-06-361. Washington, DC: US Government Accountability Office.

Garrett, G. and J. Rodden 2003. 'Globalization and Fiscal Decentralization', in M. Kahler and D. Lake (eds.) *Governance in a Global Economy*. Princeton University Press, pp. 87–109.

Garten, H. A. 1997. 'Financial Reform, the United States and the New World Order in International Finance', in G. R. D. Underhill (ed.) 1997. *The New World Order in International Finance*. Basingstoke: Macmillan. pp. 294–312.

Geiger, H. and O. Wuensch 2007. 'The Fight Against Money Laundering: An Economic Analysis of a Cost-Benefit Paradox', *Journal of Money Laundering Control* 10(1): 91–105.

Germain, R. 1997. *The International Organization of Credit*. Cambridge University Press.

2001. 'Global Financial Governance and the Problem of Inclusion', *Global Governance* 7: 411–426.

2004. 'Globalizing Accountability within the International Organization of Credit: Financial Governance and the Public Sphere', *Global Society* 18(3): 217–42.

2007. 'Global Finance, Risk and Governance', *Global Society* 21(1): 71–93.

Ghosh, A., T. Lane, M. Schulze-Ghattas, A. Bulíř, J. Hamann and A. Mourmouras 2002. 'IMF-Supported Programs in Capital Account Crises', Occasional Paper 210. Washington, SC: IMF.

Gilbert, E. and E. Helleiner (eds.) 1999. *Nation-States and Money*. London: Routledge.

Gill, S. 2003. *Power and Resistance in the New World Order*. Basingstoke: Palgrave Macmillan.

Giradin, E. 2004. 'Methods of Information Exchange and Surveillance for Regional Financial Co-operation', in Asian Development Bank (ed.) *Monetary and Financial Integration in East Asia Vol. 2*. New York: Palgrave Macmillan, pp. 331–63.

Glennerster, R. and Y. Shin 2003. 'Is Transparency Good For You, and Can the IMF Help?', IMF Working Paper WP/03/132.

328 References

Goetz, A. M. and R. Sen Gupta 1996. 'Who Takes the Credit? Gender, Power, and Control Over Loan Use in Rural Credit Programmes in Bangladesh', *World Development* 24(1): 45–63.

Goldstein, J. 1993. *Ideas, Institutions, and American Trade Policy.* Ithaca/London: Cornell University Press.

Gomez, E. T. 2002. 'Political Business in Malaysia', in E. T. Gomez (ed.) *Political Business in East Asia.* London: Routledge.

2004a. 'Governance, Affirmative Action and Enterprise Development', in E. T. Gomez (ed.) *The State of Malaysia.* London: RoutledgeCurzon.

2004b. 'Paradoxes of Governance: Ownership and Control of Corporate Malaysia', in F. A. Gul and J. S. L. Tsui (eds.) *The Governance of East Asian Corporations: Post Asian Financial Crisis.* Houndmills and New York: Palgrave Macmillan, pp. 117–37.

Gomez, E. T. and K. S. Jomo 1997. *Malaysia's Political Economy.* Cambridge University Press.

Goodhart, C. and A. Persaud 2008. 'A Proposal for How to Avoid the Next Crash', *Financial Times*, 30 January, p.7.

Goodmann, P. 2006. 'Microfinance Investment Funds: Objectives, Players, Potential', in I. Matthäus-Maier and J. D. von Pischke (eds.) *Microfinance Investment Funds. Leveraging Private Capital for Economic Growth and Poverty Reduction.* Berlin/Heidelberg: Springer.

Gourevitch, P. A. and J. Shinn 2005. *Political Power and Corporate Control.* Princeton University Press.

Grabel, I. 2003. 'Ideology, Power and the Independent Monetary Institutions in Emerging Markets', in J. Kirshner (ed.) *Monetary Orders: Ambiguous Economics, Ubiquitous Politics.* Ithaca: Cornell University Press, pp. 25–40.

Grant, R. W. and R. O. Keohane 2005. 'Accountability and Abuses of Power in World Politics', *American Political Science Review* 99(1), February, 29–43.

Green, R. and T. Torgerson 2007. 'Are High Foreign Exchange Reserves in Emerging Markets a Blessing or a Burden?', Department of the Treasury, Office of International Affairs Occasional Paper 6.

Griffith-Jones, S. and J. A. Ocampo 2003. *What Progress on International Financial Reform? Why so Limited?* Stockholm: Expert Group on Development Issues.

Griffith-Jones, S. and A. T. Fuzzo de Lima 2006. 'Mitigating the Risks of Investing in Developing Countries: Currency-Related Guarantee Instruments for Infrastructure', in I. Kaul and P. Conceicao (eds.) *The New Public Finance: Responding to Global Challenges.* New York: Oxford University Press.

Griffith-Jones, S. and K. Sharma 2006. 'GDP-Indexed Bonds: Making It Happen', DESA Working Paper 21.

Griffith-Jones, S. and J. A. Ocampo 2008. 'Compensatory Financing for Shocks: What Changes are Needed? Initiative for Policy Dialogue.

Griffith-Jones, S. and A. Persaud 2008. *The Pro-Cyclical Impact of Basel II on Emerging Markets and its Political Economy.* New York: Oxford University Press.

References

Griffith-Jones, S., M. A. Segoviano and S. Spratt 2003. 'CPE and the Developing World', submission to the Basel Committee on Banking Supervision.

Griffith-Jones, S. *et al.* (2002a). 'The Onward March of Basel II: Can the Interests of Developing Countries be Protected?', Globalisation and Poverty Research paper for conference sponsored by the Commonwealth Secretariat, the Commonwealth Business Council and the World Bank, London, 3 July.

(2002b). 'Basel II and Developing Countries: Diversification and Portfolio Effects', Institute for Development Studies, University of Sussex, December.

Group of Thirty (G30) 1997. *Global Institutions, National Supervision, and Systemic Risk,* Washington, DC: Group of Thirty/Study Group Report.

Group of 24 . 2005. *Communiqué,* 23 September.

Guo, C.-T., S.-M. Chen and Z.-H. Huang 2000. 'Money Up for Grabs? The Impact of Democratisation on Taiwan's Financial System', in Chu Yun-Han and Bau Tzong-Ho (eds.) *Democratic Transition and Economic Conflicts.* Taipei: Laureate Book, pp. 75–111.

Haggard, S. 1999. 'Governance and Growth', *Asia-Pacific Economic Literature* 13(2): 30–42.

2000. *The Political Economy of the Asian Financial Crisis.* Washington, DC: Institute for International Economics.

Hall, R. B. 2003. 'The Discursive Demolition of the Asian Development Model', *International Studies Quarterly* 47: 71–99.

2008. *Central Banking as Global Governance: Constructing Financial Credibility,* Cambridge University Press.

Hamilton, D. S. and J. P. Quinlin 2006. *The Transatlantic Economy 2006.* Washington, DC: Center for Transatlantic Relations.

Hamilton-Hart, N. 2002. *Asian States, Asian Bankers: Central Banking in Southeast Asia.* Ithaca and London: Cornell University Press.

Hanak, I. 2000. '"Working Her Way Out of Poverty": Micro-credit Programmes' Undelivered Promises in Poverty Alleviation', *Journal für Entwicklungspolitik* 3: 303–28.

Hansen, B. E. 2000. 'Sample Splitting and Threshold Estimation', *Econometria* 63(3): 575–603.

Hansmann, H. and R. H. Kraakman 2000. 'The End of History for Corporate Law', Yale Law and Economics Working Paper 235.

Hausmann, R. and U. Panizza 2003. 'On the Determinants of Original Sin: An Empirical Investigation', *Journal of International Money and Finance* 22: 957–90.

Hegarty, J., F. Gielen and A. C. Hirata Barros 2004. 'Implementation of International Accounting and Auditing Standards: Lessons Learned from the World Bank's Accounting and Auditing ROSC Program', World Bank.

Held, D. 1995. *Democracy and the Global Order.* Stanford University Press.

Helleiner, E. 1994. *States and the Re-emergence of Global Finance.* Ithaca: Cornell University Press.

330 References

2003. *The Making of National Money*. Ithaca: Cornell University Press.

2005. 'The Strange Story of Bush and the Argentine Debt Crisis', *Third World Quarterly* 26(6): 951–69.

2009a. 'The Geopolitics of Sovereign Wealth Funds: An Introduction', *Geopolitics*, 14(2): 300–4.

2009b. 'Filling a Hole in Global Financial Governance? The Politics of Regulating Sovereign Debt Restructuring', in W. Mattli and N. Woods (eds.) *The Politics of Global Regulation*. Princeton University Press.

Helleiner, E. and B. Momani 2008. 'Slipping into Obscurity? Crisis and Reform at the IMF', in A. Alexandroff (ed.) *Can the World Be Governed? Possibilities for Effective Multilateralism*. Waterloo: Wilfrid Laurier University Press.

Henning, C. R. 1994. *Currencies and Politics in the United States, Germany and Japan*. Washington, DC: Institute for International Economics.

Herr, H. 1997. 'The International Monetary System and Domestic Economic Policy', in D. J. Forsyth and T. Notermans (eds.) *Regime Changes: Macroeconomic Policy and Financial Regulation in Europe from the 1930s to the 1990s*. Providence: Berghahn, pp. 124–68.

Hirschman, A. O. 1980/1945. *National Power and the Structure of Foreign Trade*. Berkeley: University of California Press.

Hiscox, M. and D. Lake 2002. 'Democracy, Federalism, and the Size of States', unpublished manuscript, University of California San Diego.

Ho, D. E. 2002. 'Compliance and International Soft Law: Why do Countries Implement the Basel Accord?', *Journal of International Economic Law* 5(3): 647–88.

Hodges, M. 1998. What Future for the Summits? Concluding panel remarks at the Annual pre-summit conference of the University of Toronto G8 Research Group, 13 May.

Hollis, A. and A. Sweetman 1998. 'Micro-credit: What Can We Learn from the Past?', *World Development* 26(10): 1875–7.

Hveem, H. 2006. 'Explaining the Regional Phenomenon in an Era of Globalization', in R. Stubbs and G. R. D. Underhill (eds.) *Political Economy and the Changing Global Order*. Oxford University Press, 294–305.

ID (Investor Digest), Kuala Lumpur.

IIF 1993. Report of the Working Group on Capital Adequacy. Washington DC: IIF.

1998. *Recommendations for Revising the Regulatory Capital Rules for Credit Risk*, Report of the Working Group on Capital Adequacy. Washington, DC: IIF, March.

2003. *Corporate Governance in Korea: An Investor Perspective*. Washington, DC: IIF Equity Advisory Group Task Force Report.

2006a. *Principles for Stable Capital Flows and Fair Debt Restructuring in Emerging Markets*. Washington, DC: IIF.

2006b. *Principles for Stable Capital Flows and Fair Debt Restructuring in Emerging Markets*, Report on Implementation by the Principles Consultative Group. Washington, DC: IIF.

2006c. *Investor Relations: An Approach to Effective Communication and Enhanced Transparency – Update of Key Borrowing Countries*. Washington, DC: IIF.

References 331

2008. *Capital Flows to Emerging Market Economies.* Washington, DC: IIF.

IMF 2001a. *Involving the Private Sector in the Resolution of Financial Crises – Restructuring International Sovereign Bonds.* Washington, DC: IMF.

2001b. *Reforming the International Financial Architecture: Progress through 2000.* Washington, DC: IMF.

2003a. *The IMF and Recent Capital Account Crises: Indonesia, Korea, Brazil.* Washington, DC: IMF.

2003b. 'IMF Approves US$12.55 Billion Three-Year Stand-By Credit for Argentina', Press Release 03/160, 15 October.

2003c. *Republic of Korea: Financial System Stability Assessment,* IMF Country Report 03/81.

2004a. *Fund-Supported Programs – Objectives and Outcomes.* Washington, DC: IMF.

2004b. *Evaluation Report: The IMF and Argentina, 1991–2001.* Washington, DC: IMF.

2004c. 'Assessing Sustainability', document presented to the Executive Board, 28 May.

2005a. *The Managing Director's Report on the Fund's Medium-Term Strategy,* document presented to the International Monetary and Financial Committee, 15 September.

2005b. 'Contingent Financing', in *IMF Survey,* April.

2005c. 'Evaluation of PRGF', document presented to the Executive Board, July.

IMF, Independent Evaluation Office 2005d. *Report on the Evaluation of the IMF's Approach to Capital Account Liberalization,* Washington, DC .

IMF 2007. *United States: 2007 Article IV Consultation – Staff Report; Staff Statement; and Public Information Notice on the Executive Board Discussion,* IMF Country Report 07/264.

2008a. *Global Financial Stability Report, April 2008.* Washington, DC: IMF.

2008b. *IMF Executive Board Recommends Reforms to Overhaul Quota and Voice,* Press release 08/64. Washington, DC: IMF.

Jabko, N. 2006. *Playing the Market: A Political Strategy for Uniting Europe, 1985–2005.* Ithaca: Cornell University Press.

Jeanneau, S. and C. E. Tovar 2006. 'Domestic Bond Markets in Latin America: Achievements and Challenges', *BIS Quarterly Review,* June, pp. 51–64.

Johnson, S. and T. Mitton 2003. 'Cronyism and Capital Controls', *Journal of Financial Economics* 67(3): 351–82.

Johnston, R. B. and J. Abbott 2005. 'Placing Bankers in the Front Line', *Journal of Money Laundering Control* 8(3): 215–19.

Jomo, K. S. 2003. *M Way: Mahathir's Economic Legacy.* Kuala Lumpur: Forum.

2004. 'Were Malaysia's Capital Controls Effective?', in K. S. Jomo (ed.) *After the Storm.* Singapore University Press, pp. 173–203.

Jones, K. P. 1977. 'Discord and Collaboration: Choosing an Agent General for Reparations', *Diplomatic History* 1(2): 118–39.

Kahler, M. (ed.) 1998. *Capital Flows and Financial Crises.* Ithaca: Cornell University Press.

332 References

Kaminsky, G.L., C.M. Reinhart and C.A. Végh. 2004. 'When it rains, it pours. Pro-cyclical capital flows and macroeconomic policies.' NBER working paper 10780.

Kaplan, E. and D. Rodrik 2001. 'Did the Malaysian Capital Controls Work?', paper presented at the Conference on Currency Crisis in Emerging Markets, National Bureau of Economic Research, Washington, DC, 11–13 January.

Kapstein, E. B. 1989. 'Resolving the Regulator's Dilemma: International Coordination of Banking Regulation', *International Organization* 43(2): 323–47.

Kapur, D. and R. Webb 2000. 'Governance-related Conditionalities of the International Financial Institutions', *G-24 Discussion* Paper 6. Geneva: UNCTAD.

Kaufmann, D., A. Kraay and M. Mastruzzi 2004. 'Governance Matters III: Governance Indicators for 1996, 1998, 2000 and 2002', *World Bank Economic Review* 18(2): 253–87.

2007. 'Governance Matters VI: Aggregate and Individual Governance Indicators 1996–2006', World Bank Policy Research Working Paper no. 4280, July. See also www.govindicators.org.

Kaul, I. 2000. 'Die Debatte über die Entwicklungsfinanzierung damals und heute', in F. Nuscheler (ed.) *Entwicklung und Frieden im Zeichen der Globalisierung.* Bonn: Bundeszentrale für politische Bildung.

Kawai, M. 2007. 'Dollar, Yen, or Renminbi Bloc?', in Chung and Eichengreen (eds.) *Toward an Asian Exchange Rate Regime.* Washington, DC: Brookings Institution Press, pp. 90–120.

Kenen, P. B. 2001. *The International Financial Architecture: What's New? What's Missing?* Washington, DC: Institute for International Economics.

Keohane, R. O. 1984. *After Hegemony: Cooperation and Discord in the World Political Economy.* Princeton University Press.

2002. 'Global Governance and Democratic Accountability', Miliband Lectures, London School of Economics.

Kerrison, O. 2004. 'Bolkestein's Bid for Compromise on Derivatives Fails', *The Accountant* 3.

Kharas, H. 2008. 'The New Reality of Aid', mimeo, Brookings, Wolfensohn Center for Development.

Khoo, B. T. 2000. 'Unfinished Crises', in *Southeast Asian Affairs 2000.* Singapore: Institute of Southeast Asian Studies, pp. 165–83.

Killick, T. 1995. *IMF Programmes in Developing Countries. Design and Impact.* London: Routledge.

Kindleberger, C. 1973. *The World in Depression.* Berkeley: University of California Press.

1978. *Manias, Panics, and Crashes.* New York: Basic Books.

Kindleberger, C. (ed.) 1982. *Financial Crises: Theory, History, and Policy.* Cambridge University Press.

Kindleberger, C. 1984/1993. *A History of Finance in Western Europe*, 2nd edn. Oxford University Press.

King, R. G. and R. Levine 1993. 'Finance and Growth: Schumpeter Might be Right', *Quarterly Journal of Economics* 108: 717–37.

References

Klein, M. W. 2005. 'Capital Account Liberalization, Institutional Quality and Economic Growth: Theory and Evidence', *NBER Working Papers* 11112, National Bureau of Economic Research.

Kohsaka, A. 2004. 'A Fundamental Scope for Regional Financial Cooperation in East Asia', *Journal of Asian Economics* 15(5): 911–37.

KPMG 2007. *Global Anti-Money Laundering Survey.*

Krasner, S. D. 1991. 'Global Communications and National Power: Life on the Pareto Frontier', *World Politics* 43: 336–66.

Krueger, A. O. 2001. 'International Financial Architecture for 2002: A New Approach to Sovereign Debt Restructuring', address given at the national economists' club annual members dinner, Washington, DC, 26 November.

    2002. *A New Approach to Sovereign Debt Restructuring.* Washington, DC: IMF.

Kuziemko, I. and E. Werker 2006. 'How Much is a Seat on the Security Council Worth? Foreign Aid and Bribery at the United Nations', *Journal of Political Economy* 14: 905–30.

Lackritz, M. E. 2005. Testimony, 16 June, US House of Representatives Financial Services Committee.

Lamfalussy, A. 2001. *Final Report of the Committee of Wise Men on the Regulation of European Securities Markets.* Brussels.

Lane, P. R. and G. M. Milesi-Ferretti 2001. 'The External Wealth of Nations: Measures of Foreign Assets and Liabilities for Industrial and Developing Countries', *Journal of International Economics* 55(2): 263–94.

    2006. 'The External Wealth of Nations Mark II: Revised and Extended Estimates of Foreign Assets and Liabilities, 1970–2004', The Institute for International Integration Studies, Discussion Paper Series, no. 126.

Langley, P. 2002. *World Financial Orders.* London: Routledge.

La Porta, R., F. Lopez-de-Silanes and A. Shleifer 1998. 'Corporate Ownership Around the World', Harvard Institute of Economic Research Paper 1840.

    2002. 'Government Ownership of Banks', *Journal of Finance* 57(1): 265–301.

La Porta, R., F. Lopez-de-Silanes, A. Shleifer and R. W. Vishny 1997. 'Legal Determinants of External Finance', *Journal of Finance* 52: 1131–50.

Laurence, H. 2001. *Money Rules: The New Politics of Finance in Britain and Japan.* Ithaca: Cornell University Press.

Lele, P. P. & M. M. Siems 2007. 'Shareholder Protection: A Leximetric Approach', *Journal of Corporate Law Studies* 7: 17–50.

Levi, M. and M. Maguire 2004. 'Reducing and Preventing Organised Crime: An Evidence-based Critique', *Crime, Law and Social Change* 41: 397–469.

Levin, M. 2002. 'The Prospects for Offshore Financial Centres in Europe', CEPS Research Reports 29.

Levine, R. 2002. 'Bank-Based or Market-Based Financial Systems: Which is Better?', *Journal of Financial Intermediation* 11(4): 398–428.

Little, I. and D. Clifford 1965. *International Aid.* London: Allen & Unwin.

Liu, L. S. 1997. 'Law and Political Economy of Capital Market Regulation in the Republic of China on Taiwan', *Law and Policy in International Business* 28(3): 813–56.

334 References

Lowe, P. 2002. 'Credit Risk Measurement and Procyclicality', Bank for International Settlements Working Paper, 116.

Lucarelli, B. 2005. 'Microcredit: A Cautionary Tale', *Journal of Contemporary Asia* 35(1): 78–86.

Lucas, R. E. J. 1990. 'Why Doesn't Capital Flow from Rich to Poor Countries?', *American Economic Review* 80(2): 92–6.

Lütz, S. 1998. 'The Revival of the Nation-State? Stock Exchange Regulation in an Era of Globalized Financial Markets', *Journal of European Public Policy* 5(1): 153–68.

MacIntyre, A. 2003. *The Power of Institutions: Political Architecture and Governance*. Ithaca: Cornell University Press.

Mahathir, M. 2003. 'Why Capital Controls', in K. S. Jomo (ed.) *M Way: Mahathir's Economic Legacy*. Kuala Lumpur: Forum, pp. 201–8.

Mahbubani, K. 2008. *The New Asian Hemisphere: The Irresistible Shift of Global Power to the East*. New York: Public Affairs.

Marfán, M. 2005. 'Fiscal Policy, Efficacy and Private Deficits: A Macroeconomic Approach', in J. A. Ocampo (ed.) *Beyond Reforms: Structural Dynamics and Macroeconomic Vulnerability*. Palo Alto: Stanford University Press and ECLAC, pp. 161–88.

Martinez-Diaz, L. 2009. 'The G20 After Eight Years: How Effective a Vehicle for Developing Country Influence?' in Martinez-Diaz and Woods (eds.) *Networks of Influence? Developing Countries in a Networked Global Order*, Oxford University Press, 39–62.

Matin, I., D. Hulme and S. Rutherford 2002. 'Finance for the Poor: From Microcredit to Microfinancial Services', *Journal of International Development* 14: 273–94.

Matsuyama, K. 2008. 'Poverty Traps', in S. N. Durlauf and L. E. Blume (eds.), *The New Palgrave Dictionary of Economics*, online edition. Palgrave Macmillan.

Matthäus-Maier, I. and J. D. von Pischke (eds.) 2006. *Microfinance Investment Funds. Leveraging Private Capital for Economic Growth and Poverty Reduction*. Berlin: Springer.

Maxfield, S. 1998. 'Understanding the Political Implications of Financial Internationalisation in Emerging Market Countries', *World Development* 26(7): pp. 1201–19.

Mayoux, L. 2000. 'From Access to Empowerment: Widening the Debate on Gender and Sustainable Micro-finance', *Journal für Entwicklungspolitik* 16(3): 247–73.

2002. 'Women's Empowerment versus Sustainability? Towards a New Paradigm in Micro-finance Programmes', in B. Lemire, R. Pearson and G. Campbell (eds.), *Women and Credit: Researching the Past, Refiguring the Future*. Berg, pp. 245–70.

MB (Malaysian Business), Kuala Lumpur.

McDowell, J. and G. Novis 2001. 'The Consequences of Money Laundering and Financial Crime', *Economic Perspectives* 6(2): 6–8.

McGillivray, M. 2004. 'Descriptive and Prescriptive Analyses of Aid Allocation: Approaches, Issues, and Consequences', *International Review of Economics and Finance* 13: 275–92.

References   335

McKinlay, R. and R. Little 1977. 'A Foreign Policy Model of U.S. Bilateral Aid Allocation', *World Politics* 30(1): 58–86.

McKinnon, R. 1993. *The Order of Economic Liberalization: Financial Control in the Transition to a Market Economy*. Baltimore: John Hopkins University Press.

McNeil, W. C. 1986. *American Money and the Weimar Republic*. New York: Columbia University Press.

Milner, A. 2003. 'Asia-Pacific Perceptions of the Financial Crisis: Lessons and Affirmations', *Contemporary Southeast Asia* 25(2): 284–305.

Minsky, H. P. 1982. *Can 'It' Happen Again?: Essays on Instability and Finance*. Armonk: M. E. Sharpe.

Mitchell, D. 2003. 'US Government Agencies Confirm that Low-Tax Jurisdictions are not Money Laundering Havens', *Journal of Financial Crime* 11(2): 127–33.

MiX (Microfinance Information eXchange) 2007. *The MicroBanking Bulletin* 14 (Spring).

Mody, A. and D. Saravia 2006. 'Catalyzing Capital Flows: Do IMF-Supported Programs Work as Commitment Devices?', *The Economic Journal* 116: 843–67.

Moggridge, D. E. 1972. *British Monetary Policy: 1924–1931*. Cambridge University Press.

Mohammed, A. A. 2003. 'Implementing Standards and Codes through the BWIs: An Overview of the Developing-Country Perspective', in B. Schneider (ed.) *The Road to International Financial Stability*. Basingstoke: Palgrave Macmillan, pp. 62–86.

Molenaers, N. and R. Renard 2008. 'Policy Dialogue under the New Aid Approach: Which Role for Medium-sized Donors? Theoretical Reflections and Views from the Field', IOB Discussion Paper, 2008.05.

Moody's Investor Services 2008a. 'Korean Banks: Funding Difficulties Set to Ease in Second Half, While Ratings to Remain Stable', January.

2008b. *Bank Credit Research: Weekly Ratings List*, 5 May.

Moran, M. 1986. *The Politics of Banking*. London: Macmillan (2nd edn.).

1991. *The Politics of the Financial Services Revolution: The USA, UK and Japan*. New York: St. Martin's Press.

Morduch, J. 1999. 'The Microfinance Promise', *Journal of Economic Literature* 37: 1569–1614.

2000. 'The Microfinance Schism', *World Development* 28(4): 617–29.

Morris, C. 2008. *The Trillion Dollar Meltdown*. New York: Public Affairs.

Morris, S. and H. S. Shin 2006. 'Catalytic Finance: When Does It Work?', *Journal of International Economics* 70(1): 161–77.

Mosley, L. 2003. *Global Capital and National Governments*. Cambridge University Press.

Mügge, D. 2006. 'Private-Public Puzzles: Inter-firm Competition and Transnational Private Regulation', *New Political Economy* 11(2): 177–20.

2010. 'Limits of Legitimacy and the Primacy of Politics in Financial Governance', *Review of International Political Economy* (forthcoming).

Mundell, R. A. 1961. 'A Theory of Optimum Currency Areas', *American Economic Review* 51: 657–65.

References

Naim, M. 1999. 'Fads and Fashion in Economic Reforms: Washington Consensus or Washington Confusion?', paper at IMF Conference on Second Generation Reforms, Washington, DC, 26 October.

2002. 'The Washington Consensus: A Damaged Brand', *Financial Times* 28 October.

Nam, S.-W. and I. C. Nam 2004. *Corporate Governance in Asia: Recent Evidence from Indonesia, Republic of Korea, Malaysia and Thailand*. Tokyo: Asian Development Bank Institute.

Navias, M. 2002. 'Finance Warfare and International Terrorism', in L. Freedman (ed.) *Superterrorism: Policy Responses*. Oxford: Blackwell, pp. 57–79.

Naylor, R. T. 1999. 'Wash-Out: A Critique of Follow-the-Money Methods in Crime Control Policy', *Crime, Law and Social Change* 32: 1–57.

Neal, L. 1979. 'The Economics and Finance of Bilateral Clearing Arrangements: Germany 1934–38', *Economic History Review* 32(3): 391–404.

New York Times, The. 2008. 'Obama Reviewing Bush's Use of Executive Powers', 10 November.

Nicolaisen, D. T. 2004. 'The Future of Standard Setting for Public Companies', speech, American Accounting Association Annual Meeting, Orlando, 10 August.

Nikomborirak, D. 2004. 'Problems of Corporate Governance Reform in Thailand', in F. A. Gul and J. S. L. Tsui (eds.) *The Governance of East Asian Corporations: Post Asian Financial Crisis*. Houndmills and New York: Palgrave Macmillan, pp. 216–35.

Noble, G. W. 1997. 'From Island Factory to Asian Center', Working Paper 1997/5, Department of International Relations, Australian National University.

Nooruddin, I. and J. W. Simmons 2006. 'The Politics of Hard Choices: IMF Programs and Government Spending', *International Organization* 60: 1001–33.

Nourse, T. H. 2001. 'The Missing Parts of Microfinance: Services for Consumption and Insurance', *SAIS Review* 21(1): 61–9.

NST (New Strait Times), Kuala Lumpur.

Nutter, F. W. 2005. Testimony, 16 June, US House of Representatives Committee on Financial Services.

Oatley, T. and R. Nabors 1998. 'Redistributive Cooperation: Market Failure, Wealth Transfers, and the Basel Accord', *International Organization* 52(1): 35–54.

Ocampo, J. A. 2005. 'A Broad View of Macroeconomic Stability', DESA Working Paper 1.

Ocampo, J. A., J. Kregel and S. Griffith-Jones 2007. *International Finance and Development*. London/New York: Zed Books.

OECD 1969. 'Development Assistance: Efforts and Policies of the Members of the Developing Assistance Committee', Review.

2004. *Principles of Corporate Governance*. Paris: OECD.

2007. *Aid Effectiveness: 2006 Survey on Monitoring the Paris Declaration. Overview of the Results*. Paris: OECD.

References 337

Ooi, K. B. 2008. *Lost in Transition: Malaysia under Abdullah*. Singapore: Institute of Southeast Asian Studies.

Park, Y. C. and Y. Wang 2005. 'The Chiang Mai Initiative and Beyond', *The World Economy* 28(1): 91–101.

Passas, N. 2006. 'Setting Global CFT Standards: A Critique and Suggestions', *Journal of Money Laundering Control* 9(3): 281–92.

Pauly, L. W. 1997. *Who Elected the Bankers?* Ithaca: Cornell University Press.

 2002. 'Global Finance, Political Authority, and the Problem of Legitimisation', in R. B. Hall and T. Biersteker (eds.) *The Emergence of Private Authority in Global Governance*. Cambridge University Press, pp.76–90.

 2008. 'Financial Crisis Management in Europe and Beyond', *Contributions to Political Economy* 27(1): 73–89.

Persaud, A. 2000. 'Sending the Herd Off the Cliff Edge', *The Journal of Risk Finance* 2(1): 59–65.

 2002. 'The New Capital Accord from Basel', Gresham College Lecture, 3 October 2002.

Pieth, M. 2006. 'Multistakeholder Initiatives to Combat Money Laundering and Bribery', Basel Institute on Governance Working Paper 02.

Pieth, M. and G. Aiolfi 2003. 'The Private Sector Becomes Active: The Wolfsberg Process', *Journal of Financial Crime* 10(4): 359–65.

Pilbeam, K. 2001. 'Economic Fundamentals and Exchange Rate Movements', *International Review of Applied Economics* 15(1): 55–64.

Polanyi, K. 1944/1957. *The Great Transformation*. Boston: Beacon Press.

Pomfret, R. 2005. 'Sequencing Trade and Monetary Integration: Issues and Application to Asia', *Journal of Asian Economics* 16: 105–24.

Porter, T. 1999. 'The Transnational Agenda for Financial Regulation in Developing Countries', in L. E. Armijo (ed.) *Financial Globalisation and Democracy in Emerging Markets*. London: Macmillan, pp. 91–116.

 2002. 'Multilevel Governance and Democracy in Global Financial Governance', paper presented at 'Globalisation, Multilevel Governance and Democracy', Queen's University, Kingston, 3–4 May.

 2003. 'Technical Collaboration and Political Conflict in the Emerging Regime for International Financial Regulation', *Review of International Political Economy*, 109(3): 520–51.

Posner, E. 2005. 'Sources of Institutional Change: The Supranational Origins of Europe's New Stock Markets', *World Politics* 58: 1–40.

 2007. 'Financial Transformation in the European Union', in S. Meunier and K. McNamara (eds.) *Making History: European Integration and Institutional Change at Fifty*. Oxford University Press, pp. 139–56.

 2009. *The Origins of Europe's New Stock Markets*. Cambridge: Harvard University Press.

Prasad, E., R. Rajan and A. Subramanian 2006. 'Foreign Capital and Economic Growth', Research Department Working Paper, IMF, 30 August.

Prasad, E., K. Rogoff, S.-J. Wei and M. A. Kose 2003. 'Effects of Financial Globalization on Developing Countries: Some Empirical Evidence', IMF Occasional Paper 220.

338 References

Quaglia, L. 2007. 'The Politics of Financial Regulation and Supervision in the European Union', *European Journal of Political Research* 46(2): 269–90.

Qudrat-I Elahi, Khandakar and M. Lutfor Rahmann 2006. 'Micro-credit and Micro-finance: Functional and Conceptual Differences', *Development in Practice* 16(5): 477–8.

Radelet, S. 2006. 'A Primer on Foreign Aid', Center for Global Development, Working Paper 92, Washington, DC.

Rahn, R. 2003. 'Follow the Money: Confusion at Treasury', The Cato Institute.

Rajan, R. and L. Zingales 2003. 'The Great Reversals: The Politics of Financial Development in the Twentieth Century', *Journal of Financial Economics* 69: 5–50.

Rajan, R. and R. Siregar 2004. 'Centralized Reserve Pooling for the ASEAN+3 Countries', in Asian Development Bank (ed.) *Monetary and Financial Integration in East Asia Vol. 2*. New York: Palgrave Macmillan, pp. 285–329.

Rankin, K. N. 2002. 'Social Capital, Microfinance, and the Politics of Development', *Feminist Economics* 8(1): 1–24.

Rapkin, D. 2001. 'The United States, Japan, and the Power to Bloc: The APEC and AMF Cases', *The Pacific Review* 14(3): 373–410.

Ratha, D., S. Mohapatra and S. Plaza 2008. 'Beyond Aid: New Sources and Innovative Mechanisms for Financing Development in Sub-Saharan Africa', World Bank Policy Research Working Paper, 4609.

Raustiala, K. and A.-M. Slaughter 2002. 'International Law, International Relations and Compliance', in W. Carlsnaes, T. Risse and B. A. Simmons (eds.) *The Handbook of International Relations*. Thousand Oaks: Sage, pp. 538–58.

Reinhart, C. and K. Rogoff 2002. 'The Modern History of Exchange Rate Arrangements: A Reinterpretation', NBER Working Paper 8963.

2008. 'This Time is Different: A Panoramic View of Eight Centuries of Financial Crises', NBER Working Paper 13882, March.

Reisen, H. 2001. 'Will Basel II Contribute to Convergence in International Capital Flows?' OECD Development Centre, Paris, 2001.

Renard, R. 2006. 'The Cracks in the New Aid Paradigm', IOB Discussion Paper 2006/01, IOB/University of Antwerp.

Reuter, P. and E. Truman 2004. *Chasing Dirty Money: The Fight Against Money Laundering*. Washington, DC: Institute for International Economics.

Reuters 2008. 'U.S. Rejected IMF's Banking Supervision: IMF Chief', 10 April.

Richardson, J. (ed.) 1982. *Policy Styles in Western Europe*. Winchester: Allen & Unwin.

Rieffel, L. 2003. *Restructuring Sovereign Debt: The Case for Ad Hoc Machinery*. Washington, DC: Brookings Institution Press.

Rioja, F. and N. Valev 2004. 'Does One Size Fit All? A Re-examination of the Finance and Growth Relationship', *Journal of Development Economics* 74: 429–47.

Risse, T. 2004. 'Transnational Governance and Legitimacy', in A. Benz and Y. Papadopoulos (eds.) *Governance and Democracy*. London: Routledge, pp. 79–119.

References

Robertson, J. 2007. 'Reconsidering American Interests in Emerging Market Crises: An Unanticipated Outcome to the Asian Financial Crisis', *Review of International Political Economy* 14(2): 276–305.

Robinson, M. 2001. *The Microfinance Revolution*. New York: Open Society Press.

Rodan, G. 2004. *Transparency and Authoritarian Rule in Southeast Asia*. London: RoutledgeCurzon.

Rodrik, D. 1995. 'Why Is There Multilateral Lending', NBER Working Paper 5160. Cambridge: National Bureau of Economic Research.

1998a. 'Globalisation, Social Conflict and Economic Growth', *The World Economy* 21(2): 143–58.

1998b. 'Who Needs Capital-Account Convertibility', Technical Report 207, Princeton University.

1999. 'Governing the Global Economy', paper presented to the Brookings Institution Trade Policy Forum Conference on Governing in a Global Economy, Washington, DC, 15–16 April.

2006. 'The Social Cost of Foreign Exchange Reserves', NBER Working Paper 11952.

2007. 'How to Save Globalization from its Cheerleaders', *Journal of International Trade and Diplomacy* 1(2): 1–33.

Rodrik, D. and A. Velasco 2000. 'Short-Term Capital Flows', in *Proceedings of the Annual World Bank Conference on Development Economics 1999*. Washington, DC: World Bank, pp. 59–90.

Rodrik, D. and A. Subramanian 2009. 'Why Did Financial Globalization Disappoint', IMF Staff Papers.

Rogoff, K., M. A. Kose, E. Prasad and S. J. Wei 2006. 'Financial Globalization: A Reappraisal', IMF Working Paper 06/189.

Ronit, K. and V. Schneider 1999. 'Global Governance Through Private Organizations', *Governance* 12(3): 243–66.

Roodman, D. 2005. 'An Index of Donor Performance', Center for Global Development Working Paper 67, Washington, DC.

Ross, S. 2004. Testimony, 13 May, US House of Representatives Committee on Financial Services.

Rubio-Marquez, V. 2009. 'The G20: A Practitioner's Perspective', in Martinez-Diaz and Woods (eds.) *Networks of Influence: Developing Countries in a Networked Global Order*, Oxford University Press, pp. 19–38.

Ruggie, J. G. 1982. 'International Regimes, Transactions and Change: Embedded Liberalism in the Postwar Order', *International Organization* 369(2): 379–405.

Russell, E. D. 2008. *New Deal Banking Reform and Keynesian Welfare State Capitalism*. London: Routledge.

Ryou, J.-W. and Y. Wang 2003. 'Monetary Cooperation in Asia: Major Issues and Future Prospects', Study Forum on Monetary Cooperation in East Asia workshop paper.

Sakakibara, E. 2003. 'Asian Cooperation and the End of Pax Americana', in J. J. Teunissen and M. Teunissen (eds.) *Financial Stabilty and Growth in Emerging Economies. The Role of the Financial Sector*. The Hague: Fondad, pp. 227–44.

340 References

Scharpf, F. 1997. *Games Real Actors Play*. Boulder: Westview.
1999. *Governing Europe: Effective and Democratic?* Oxford University Press.
Schmidt, R. and A. Winkler 2000. 'Building Financial Institutions in Developing Countries', *Journal für Entwicklungspolitik* 16(3): 329–46.
Schmidt, V. 2002. *The Futures of European Capitalism*. Oxford University Press.
Schneider, B. 2003. 'Implications of Implementing Standards and Codes: A Developing Country Perspective', in B. Schneider (ed.) *The Road to International Financial Stability*. Basingstoke: Palgrave Macmillan, pp. 15–61.
Schwartz, H. 2009. *Subprime Nation: American Power, Global Capital, and the Housing Bubble*. Ithaca: Cornell University Press
Schwartz, R. A. 1996. 'Equity Trading II', in B. Steil (ed.) *The European Equity Markets*. London and Copenhagen: ECMI and RIIA, pp. 59–80.
Scott, H. S. and P. A. Wellons 1996. 'Financing Capital Market Intermediaries', in Scott and Wellons (eds.) *Financing Capital Market Intermediaries in East and Southeast Asia*. The Hague: Kluwer Law, pp. 1–49.
Scully, N. D. 1997. 'Micro-credit No Panacea for Poor Women', mimeo, www.gdrc.org/icm/wind/micro.html.
SEC 1997. *Report on Promoting Global Pre-eminence of American Securities Markets*. Washington, DC: SEC.
2003. Part III: 17 Cfr Part 240; Supervised Investment Bank Holding Companies; Proposed Rules. *Federal Register* 68(215).
2004. *2004–2009 Strategic Plan*. Washington, DC: SEC.
2005. 'Chairman Donaldson Meets with EU Internal Market Commissioner McCreevy', Press Release 2005–6.
2007. 'SEC, Euronext Regulators Sign Regulatory Cooperation Arrangement', Press Release 2007–8, 25 January.
Seibel, H. D. 2005. 'Does History Matter? The Old and the New World of Microfinance in Europe and Asia', paper presented at 'From Moneylenders to Microfinance', Asia Research Institute, National University of Singapore, October.
Semkow, B. W. 1994. *Taiwan's Capital Market Reform*. Oxford: Clarendon.
Serrano, M. and P. Kenny 2003. 'The International Regulation of Money Laundering', *Global Governance* 9: 433–9.
Shambaugh, D. 2004. 'China Engages Asia', *International Security* 29(3): 64–99.
Sharman, J. 2006a. *Havens in a Storm: The Struggle for Global Tax Regulation*. Ithaca: Cornell University Press.
2006b. 'Developmental Implications of Anti-Money Laundering and Taxation Regulations', paper prepared for the Commonwealth Secretariat.
Shea, J.-D. 1995. 'Financial Development and Policies in Taipei, China', in S. N. Zahid (ed.) *Financial Sector Development in Asia*. Manila: Asian Development Bank, pp. 81–161.
Shelton, D. (ed.) 2003. *Commitment and Compliance: The Role of Non-Binding Norms in the International Legal System*. New York: Oxford University Press.

References 341

Shen, Z.-H. 2005. 'Launching the Second Financial Reform', *Taiwan Economic Forum* 3(4): 1–25.

Shi, Y. and Y.-D. Chen 2003. 'The Development of a Multidimensional Financial System', *CBC Quarterly* 25(4): 23–9.

Shin, K. and Y. Wang 2002. 'Monetary Integration Ahead of Trade Integration in East Asia?', paper presented at 'Linkages in East Asia: Implications for Currency Regimes and Policy Dialogue', 23–4 September, Seoul.

Shirono, K. 2007. 'Real Effects of Common Currencies in East Asia', IMF Working Paper 07/166.

SIA 2004. 'US Securities Industry Urges SEC, EU to Forge Framework to Achieve Regulatory "Convergence"', Press Release, 7 April.

Simmons, B. 1993. 'Why Innovate? Founding the Bank for International Settlements', *World Politics* 45(3): 361–405.

2001. 'The International Politics of Harmonization: The Case of Capital Market Regulation', *International Organization* 55(3): 589–620.

Singer, D. A. 2004. 'Capital Rules: The Domestic Politics of International Regulatory Harmonization', *International Organization* 58(3): 531–65.

2007. *Regulating Capital: Setting Standards for the International Financial System*. Ithaca: Cornell University Press.

Slaughter, A.-M. 2000. 'Governing the Economy through Government Networks', in M. Byers (ed.) *The Role of Law in International Politics*. Oxford University Press, pp. 177–205.

2004. *A New World Order*. Princeton University Press.

Smith, R. and I. Walter 2003. *Global Banking*. Oxford University Press (2nd edn.).

Sobel, A. C. 1994. *Domestic Choices, International Markets*. University of Chicago Press.

Soederberg, S. 2003. 'The Promotion of "Anglo-American" Corporate Governance in the South: Who Benefits from the New International Standard?', *Third World Quarterly* 24(1): 7–27.

Soederberg, S., G. Menz and P. G. Cerny (eds.) 2005. *Internalizing Globalization: The Rise of Neoliberalism and the Decline of National Varieties of Capitalism*. London: Palgrave Macmillan.

Sohn, I. 2005. 'Asian Financial Cooperation: The Problem of Legitimacy in Global Financial Governance', *International Studies Quarterly* 11: 487–504.

Soros, G. 2008. *The New Paradigm For Financial Markets: The Credit Crisis of 2008 and What it Means*. Public Affairs: New York.

Stallings, B. and W. Peres 2000. *Growth, Employment, and Equity*. Washington, DC: Brookings Institution Press.

Standard & Poor's 2004a. 'Corporate Governance Disclosures in Thailand: A Study of SET50 Companies', Joint report by S&P and Corporate Governance and Financial Reporting Centre, NUS Business School, Singapore.

2004b. 'Corporate Governance Disclosures in Malaysia', Joint report by S&P and Corporate Governance and Financial Reporting Centre, NUS Business School, Singapore.

342 References

2004c. 'Country Governance Study: Korea', March.

2004d. 'Corporate Governance Disclosures in Singapore', Joint report by S&P and Corporate Governance and Financial Reporting Centre, NUS Business School, Singapore.

Steil, B. 1996. *The European Equity Markets*. London and Copenhagen: RIIA and ECMI.

1998. *Regional Financial Market Integration: Learning from the European Experience*. London: Royal Institute of International Affairs.

Stevenson, A. E. 2004. 'Regional Financial Cooperation in Asia', *Journal of Asian Economics* 15(5): 837–41.

Stiglitz, J. 2000. 'Capital Market Liberalisation, Economic Growth, and Instability', *World Development* 28(6): 1075–86.

2002. *Globalization and Its Discontents*. London: Penguin.

2003. 'Whither Reform? Toward a New Agenda for Latin America', *CEPAL Review* 80: 7–38.

2005. 'Finance for Development', in M. Ayoen and D. Ross (eds.) *Development Dilemmas: The Methods and Political Ethics of Growth Policy*. New York: Routledge.

Story, J. and I. Walter. 1997. *Political Economy of Financial Integration in Europe: The Battle of the Systems*. Cambridge: MIT Press.

Strange, S. 1994. *States and Markets*. London: Pinter Publishers (2nd edn.).

1998. *Mad Money*. Oxford: Blackwell.

Studwell, J. 2007. *Asian Godfathers: Money and Power in Hong Kong and South-East Asia*. London: Profile Books.

Sundberg, M. and A. Gelb 2006. 'Making Aid Work', *Finance and Development*, IMF, Washington, DC, 14–17.

Sunstein, C. 2002. 'The Law of Group Polarization', *The Journal of Political Philosophy* 10(2): 175–95.

Tafara, E. 2004. Testimony, 13 May, US House of Representatives Committee on Financial Services.

Tafara, E. and R. J. Peterson 2007. 'A Blueprint for Cross-Border Access to U.S. Investors: A New International Framework', *Harvard International Law Journal* 48(1): 31–68.

Taylor, J. 2007. *Global Financial Warriors*. New York: W. W. Norton.

Thirkell-White, B. 2004. 'The International Monetary Fund and Civil Society', *New Political Economy* 9(2): 251–70.

2007. 'International Financial Architecture and the Limits of Neoliberal Hegemony', *New Political Economy* 12(1): 19–41.

Thomas, B. 1967. 'The Historical Record of International Capital Movements to 1913', in J. Adler (ed.) *Capital Movements and Economic Development*. London: Whurr Publishers.

TianXia (Commonwealth), Taipei.

Tirole, J. 2002. *Financial Crises, Liquidity, and the International Monetary System*. Princeton University Press.

Toniolo, G. (with P. Clement) 2005. *Central Bank Cooperation at the Bank for International Settlements: 1930–1973*. Cambridge University Press.

Torres, H. 2007. 'Reforming the IMF: Why its Legitimacy is at Stake', *Journal of International Economic Law* 10(3): 443–60.

References 343

Tourk, K. 2004. 'The Political Economy of East Asian Economic Integration', *Journal of Asian Economics* 15: 843–88.

Trumbull, W. and H. Wall 1994. 'Estimating Aid-Allocation Criteria with Panel Data', *Economic Journal* 104: 876–82.

Tsingou, E. 2003. 'Transnational Policy Communities and Financial Governance', CSGR Working Paper 111/03, University of Warwick.

2007. 'Transnational Private Governance and the Basel Process', in J. Graz and A. Nölke (eds.) *Transnational Private Governance and its Limits*. London: Routledge, pp. 58–68.

United Nations (UN) 1999. 'Towards a New International Financial Architecture', Report of the Task Force of the Executive Committee on Economic and Social Affairs of the United Nations, New York, 21 January.

2002. *Monterrey Consensus*. New York: UN.

UNCDF 2006. *Building Inclusive Financial Sectors for Development*. New York: UN.

Underhill, G. R. D. 1995. 'Keeping Governments out of Politics: Transnational Securities Markets, Regulatory Co-operation, and Political Legitimacy', *Review of International Studies* 21(3): 251–78.

1997a. 'The Making of the European Financial Area: Global Market Integration and the EU Single Market for Financial Services', in Underhill (ed.) *The New World Order in International Finance*. New York: St. Martin's Press, pp. 101–23.

1997b. 'Private Markets and Public Responsibility in a Global System', in Underhill (ed.) *The New World Order in International Finance*. New York: St. Martin's Press, pp. 17–49.

2000. 'The Public Good versus Private Interests in the Global Financial and Monetary System', *International Comparative and Corporate Law Journal* 2(3): 335–59.

2007. *Global Financial Architecture, Legitimacy, and Representation: Voice for Emerging Markets*, GARNET Policy Brief 3, GARNET/CERI Institut d'Etudes Politiques.

Underhill, G. R. D. and X. Zhang (eds.) 2003. *International Financial Governance Under Stress*. Cambridge University Press.

Underhill, G. R. D. and X. Zhang 2008. 'Setting the Rules: Private Power, Political Underpinnings, and Legitimacy in Global Monetary and Financial Governance', *International Affairs* 84(3): 535–54.

Unger, B. 2007. *The Scale and Impacts of Money Laundering*. Cheltenham: Edward Elgar.

US ITA (International Trade Administration) 2003. 'Issue and Decision Memorandum for the Final Determination in the Countervailing Duty Investigation of Dynamic Random Access Memory Semiconductors from the Republic of Korea', C580–851.

US Senate 1999. 'Private Banking and Money Laundering: A Case Study of Opportunities and Vulnerabilities', hearings before the Permanent Subcommittee on Investigations of the Committee on Governmental Affairs, US Senate, 9 and 10 November. Washington, DC: US Government Printing Office.

References

2001. 'Role of US Correspondent Banking in International Money Laundering', hearings before the Permanent Subcommittee on Investigations of the Committee on Governmental Affairs, volume 1 of 5, US Senate, 1, 2 and 6 March. Washington, DC: US Government Printing Office.

van der Veer, K. J. M. and E. de Jong 2007. 'Paris Club Involvement: Helping or Harming IMF's Attempts to Catalyse Private Capital?', mimeo, Radboud University Nijmegen.

Véron, N. 2007. 'Is Europe Ready for a Banking Crisis?', Bruegel Policy Brief 3.

Vetterlein, A. 2007. 'Economic Growth, Poverty Reduction, and the Role of Social Policies: The Evolution of the World Bank's Social Development Approach', *Global Governance* 13(4): 513–33.

Visconti, R. M. 2009. 'Post-Recession Survival: Evolution at Play?', *Microfinance Insights*, Mar/Apr: 54.

Vitale, A. 2001. 'US Banking: An Industry's View on Money Laundering', *Economic Perspectives* 6(2).

Vitols, S. and T. Kenyon 2004. Corporate Governance in Germany and the United States, presentation, AICGS/The Johns Hopkins University seminar, Washington, DC, 23 April.

Vogel, D. 1995. *Trading Up: Consumer and Environmental Regulation in a Global Economy*. Cambridge: Harvard University Press.

Vogel, S. K. 1996. *Freer Markets, More Rules: Regulatory Reform in Advanced Industrial Countries*. Ithaca: Cornell University Press.

Vreeland, J. 2003. *The IMF and Economic Development*. Cambridge University Press.

Wade, R. 1998. 'The Asian Crisis', *New Left Review* 228: 3–23.

2004. 'Is Globalization Reducing Poverty and Inequality?' *World Development* 32(4): 567–89.

2007. 'A New Global Financial Architecture?' *New Left Review* 46: 113–29.

Wade, R. and F. Veneroso 1998. 'The Asian Crisis: The High Debt Model versus the Wall Street-Treasury-IMF Complex', *New Left Review* 228: 3–22.

Wall, H. J. 1995. 'The Allocation of Official Development Assistance', *Journal of Policy Modelling* 13(3): 307–14.

Walter, A. 2006. 'From Developmental to Regulatory State? Japan's New Financial Regulatory System', *The Pacific Review* 19(4): 405–28.

2008. *Governing Finance: East Asia's Adoption of International Standards*. Ithaca: Cornell University Press.

Wang, Y. 2004. 'Financial Cooperation and Integration in East Asia', *Journal of Asian Economics* 15: 939–55.

Wang, Z.-H. 1996. *Who Rules Taiwan?* Taipei: Chuliu Book.

Webb, M. 2005. 'The Group of Seven and Global Macroeconomic Governance', in R. Stubbs and G. Underhill (eds.) *Political Economy and the Changing Global Order*. Oxford University Press, pp. 158–69.

Weber, H. 2002. 'The Imposition of a Global Development Architecture: The Example of Microcredit', *Review of International Studies* 28: 537–55.

2004. 'The New Economy and Social Risk: Banking on the Poor?', *Review of International Political Economy* 11(2): 356–86.

References   345

2006. 'The Global Political Economy of Microfinance and Poverty Reduction: Locating Local "Livelihoods" in Political Analysis', in J. L. Fernando (ed.) *Microfinance: Perils and Prospects*. London/New York: Routledge, pp. 43–63.

Weder, B. and M. Wedow 2002. 'Will Basel II Affect International Capital Flows to Emerging Markets?' OECD Development Centre Technical Paper 199, October.

Wei, S. J. 2006. 'Connecting Two Views on Financial Globalization: Can We Make Further Progress?', *Journal of the Japanese and International Economies* 20(4): 459–81.

White, H. and M. McGillivray 1995. 'How Well is Aid Allocated? Descriptive Measures of Aid Allocation: A Survey of Methodology and Results', *Development and Change* 26(1): 163–83.

White, W. 2006. 'Pro-Cyclicality in the Financial System: Do We Need a New Macrofinancial Stabilization Framework?', BIS Working Paper 193.

Williams, D. 1963. 'London and the 1931 Financial Crisis', *Economic History Review* 15(3): 513–28.

Williamson, J. 2002. 'Did the Washington Consensus Fail?', speech at Institute for International Economics, Washington, DC, 6 November.

2004. 'A Short History of the Washington Consensus', paper at the conference 'From the Washington Consensus towards a New Global Governance', Barcelona, 24–5 September.

Wolf, K. D. 2004. 'Private Actors and the Legitimacy of Governance Beyond the State', in A. Benz and Y. Papaopoulos (eds.) *Governance and Democracy*. London: Routledge, pp. 200–7.

Wolf, M. 2008. *Fixing Global Finance*. Baltimore: John Hopkins University Press.

Woo, W. T. and L.-Y. Liu 1994. 'Taiwan's Persistent Trade Surpluses', in J. D. Aberbach, D. Dollar and K. L. Sokoloff (eds.) *The Role of the State in Taiwan's Development*. New York: M. E. Sharpe, pp. 90–112.

Wood, D. 2005. *Governing Global Banking: the Basel Committee and the Politics of Financial Globalisation*. Aldershot: Ashgate Publishing.

Woods, N. 2001. 'Making the IMF and the World Bank More Accountable', *International Affairs* 77(1): 83–100.

World Bank 1998. *Assessing Aid: What Works, What Doesn't, and Why*. Oxford University Press.

2001. *World Development Report 2000/2001: Attacking Poverty*. Oxford University Press.

2004. *Report on the Observance of Standards and Codes: Republic of Korea, Accounting and Auditing*. Washington, DC: World Bank.

2005. *Report on the Observance of Standards and Codes (ROSC): Corporate Governance Country Assessment, Thailand*. Washington, DC: World Bank.

2006a. *Global Development Finance 2006*. Washington, DC: World Bank.

2006b. *Gender Equality as Smart Economics: A World Bank Group Gender Action Plan (Fiscal years 2007–10)*.

346 References

World Economic Forum (ed. Peter K. Cornelius) 2003. *The Global Competitiveness Report 2002–2003*. New York: Oxford University Press.

Wu, X.-L. 2003. 'The Road to Liberalization', *Taiwan Economic Forum* 1(7): 39–61.

Wu, Y.-S. 2002. 'Taiwan in 2001', *Asian Survey* 42(1): 29–38.

Ye, M.-F. 2005. 'Taiwan's Financial Reforms', *Taiwan Economic Forum* 3(7): 23–47.

Young, B. 2003. 'Financial Crises and Social Reproduction: Asia, Argentina and Brazil', in I. Bakker and S. Gill (eds.) *Power, Production and Social Reproduction*. Basingstoke: Palgrave Macmillan.

2008. 'Die Globale Politische Ökonomie der Mikrofinanzprogramme. Ideeller Institutionalismus als Erklärungsansatz für den Wandel der Normen in der Entwicklungsfinanzierung', in *Zeitschrift für Internationale Beziehungen* 2/2008: 187–208.

Zakaria, F. 2005. 'Does the Future Belong to China?', *Newsweek*, 9 May.

Zhang, X. 2002. 'Domestic institutions, liberalization patterns, and uneven crises in Korea and Taiwan', *Pacific Review* 15(3): 409–41.

2003a. 'Political Structures and Financial Liberalisation in Pre-Crisis East Asia', *Studies in Comparative International Development* 38(1): 64–92.

2003b. *The Changing Politics of Finance in Korea and Thailand*. London: Routledge.

Zürn, M. 2004. 'Global Governance and Legitimacy Problems', *Government and Opposition* 39(2): 260–87.

Index

ABF, *see* Asian Bond Fund
ABMI, *see* Asian Bond Market Initiative
accountability, 13, 25, 27, 41, 62, 117, 169, 176, 288–95, 300–2, *see also* legitimacy
accounting, 48, 98, 101–2, 230–7, *see also* International Accounting Standards; US Generally Accepted Accounting Principles
Advanced Internal Ratings Based approach, 119–27
Agent General for Reparations Payments, 34–5
aid, 76, 86, 89–90, 150–71, 249, 286
allocation/conditionality, 150, 152, 155–61, 165–8, 170
architecture, 150–6, 168–71, 256–61
delivery, 162–5, 169, 256
donor countries, 19, 159, 165–9
see also Millennium Development Goals; Paris Declaration on Aid Effectiveness
AMF, *see* Asian Monetary Fund
anti-money laundering, *see* money laundering
apex policy forums, 58–73
Argentina, 20, 45, 50, 187–203
see also Latin America
ASEAN, *see* Association of Southeast Asian Nations
ASEAN+3, 246–7, 250, 254
Association of Southeast Asian Nations (ASEAN), 244–50
Asia, 4, 21, 44–5, 51–2, 56, 264, 310–1
international financial standards, 95–112
financial transformation, 204–19
regional cooperation, 241–55
see also ASEAN+3; Association of Southeast Asian Nations; Chiang Mai Initiative; China; Japan; financial crises
Asian Bond Fund (ABF), 243, 252–3

Asian Bond Market Initiative (ABMI), 252–3
Asian Monetary Fund (AMF), 43, 52, 248
auditing/auditors, 47, 98–100, 108, 176, 229, 231–2, 234

Badawi, Abdullah, 214
bailing in, *see* private sector; catalytic approach
Baker, Andrew, 17, 58–73, 294, 307
Bank Financial Strength Rating (BFSR), 109
see also Moody's
Bank for International Settlements (BIS), 34–6
Basel Capital Accord
1996 Market Risk Accord, 114, 116
Basel I, 97–8, 103, 278
Basel II, 18, 48, 55–6, 113–33, 278–80, 304, 312
Basel Committee (BC), 14–6, 51, 113–123, 131–2, 277, 279–80, 294, 300
Basel Core Principles (BCP), 97, 100, 107
BCP, *see* Basel Core Principles
Berry, Nancy, 266–7
Best, Jacqueline, 38–9
best practices, *see* standards and codes
BFSR, *see* Bank Financial Strength Rating
BIS, *see* Bank for International Settlements
Blom, Jasper, 1 –22, 304–15
bond markets, 252–4, 271, 282
boom-bust cycles, 271, 273–5, 278, 283
Brazil, 20, 187–203, *see also* Latin America
Bretton Woods 7, 14, 16, 33, 36, 301, 309

CACs, *see* collective action clauses
Campenhout, Björn Van, 74–91, 150–71
capital account
crises/ volatility, 272–5, 284–5
liberalisation/ openness, 31–2, 63–4, 72–6, 79–82, 89, 216, 275, 284, 306

347

348　Index

capital adequacy, 97, 108, 112–3, 116, 119, 122–4, 279–80
capital mobility, 4, 7–8, 25–6, 32, 37, 40, 74
capital to risk-weighted asset ratios (CARs), 101, 109
capture, *see* policy capture; regulatory capture
Cassimon, Danny, 74–91, 150–71
catalytic approach, 134–42, 147–8
CCL, *see* Contingent Credit Line
CDI, *see* Commitment to Development Index
CDOs, *see* Collateralised Debt Obligations
central banks, 12, 105, 284
　cooperation, 35, 44, 244, 253
　history, 26, 29–33, 36, 38, 40
　see also apex policy forums
CFF, *see* Compensatory Financial Facility
CFT, *see* Combat the Financing of Terrorism
Chiang Mai Initiative (CMI), 21, 52, 245–50
China, 64, 190, 240, 246–51
Claessens, Stijn, 113–33, 150–71
CMI, *see* Chiang Mai Initiative
Collateralised Debt Obligations (CDOs), 125
Collective Action Clauses (CACs), 3, 10, 45–7, 51, 65, 281
collective action problems, 9, 15, 300
Combat the Financing of Terrorism (CFT), 180–6
Commitment to Development Index (CDI), 164, 166–8
comparability of treatment, 136–7, 143–8
　see also Paris Club
Compensatory Financial Facility (CFF), 285
compliance, 53, 95–112, 206, 309–10
　anti-money laundering, 172–3, 176, 179–80, 182–3, 185
　Basel II, 121, 126
　formal, 97–8, 102–3, 106–8
　mock, 18, 51, 96–100, 102, 104–9, 111
　substantive, 96–7, 99, 102–107, 110
　see also regulatory forbearance; surveillance
conditionality, 9, 50, 54, 89, 152, 258, 285
contagion, 16, 46, 130, 243, 251, 273, 283–6
Contingent Credit Line (CCL), 284
convergence
　financial systems, 6, 8, 84–8, 204–5, 214, 297–300
　regulatory, 9, 18, 95–112, 230, 239, 296

corporate governance,
　reform, 44, 99–102, 106, 213–4
　national diversity, 102, 107, 110, 204–5, 207, 214, 218, 297–8
counter-cyclicality, 89, 112, 125, 268, 270–86, 307, 310
Country Policy and Institutional Assessment (CPIA), 158–61, 169–71
credit rating agencies, 48, 55–6, 108–10, 119–30, 200, 213, 252
　see also Moody's; Standard and Poor's
currencies, 188
　common, 40, 241, 244–5, 250–1
　parallel, 251
　pegs, 194, 250-1
　see also exchange rate; US dollar; euro
cyclicality, 22, 55, 169, 270–8, 281–2, 286, 307
　Basel II, 18–9, 114–5, 118–21, 124–5, 127, 129–32, 277–80
　see also boom-bust cycles; counter-cyclicality; systemic risk

DAC, *see* Development Assistance Committee
Dawes Plan, 34
debt
　bilateral, 143–8
　catalytic approach to workout, 134–49
　Latin America, 187–203
　reduction/relief, 46, 144–6, 148, 151, 154, 156–8, 160, 170
　restructuring, 45, 47, 51, 136, 143–7
　sovereign, 30, 39, 52, 65, 134–49, 187–203, 281–2, 308–9, 313
　see also heavily indebted poor countries; Multilateral Debt Reduction Initiative; Paris Club; Sovereign Debt Restructuring Mechanism
default, 17, 20, 45–7, 119, 144, 158, 187, 191, 199, 202, 281
deliberation, 58–73
Demetriades, Panicos, 74–91, 309, 312
Democratic Progressive Party (DPP), 209, 216–7
developing countries, *see* emerging markets; Heavily Indebted Poor Countries
development, institutional preconditions, 74–84
Development Assistance Committee (DAC), 86–7
derivatives, 3, 7, 55, 274–6, 306
　see also Collateralised Debt Obligations
Dieter, Heribert, 21, 241–55, 310
distributive justice, 296–300

Index

349

donor countries, *see* aid
DPP, *see* Democratic Progressive Party

ECAs, *see* export credit agencies
ECU, *see* European Currency Unit
EFFs, *see* Extended Fund Facilities
Eichengreen, Barry, 11, 33, 35, 244, 251, 275
embedded liberalism, 26
EMEAP, *see* Executives' Meeting of East Asia and Pacific Central Banks
emergency financing, 284
emerging markets
 integration into global finance, 9, 16, 42–3, 50–3, 55, 95–112, 204–19, 306
 foreign debt, 11, 20, 187–203
 growing influence, 2, 5, 10, 17, 40–1, 43, 47, 50–3, 72, 135, 313
 volatility, 1–3, 11, 42, 125, 272–6, 284, 295, 297, 299, 310
 see also developing countries, financial crises; G20; legitimacy; policy space
ERMs, *see* Exchange Rate Mechanisms
ERs, *see* external ratings
ESF, *see* Exogenous Shocks Facility
euro, 226, 241, 250–1
European Commission, 182, 226–30, 232–3, 237, 239
European Currency Unit (ECU), 251
European Union (EU), 21, 40, 47–8, 121–3, 182, 244, 313
 transatlantic financial regulation, 223–40
 see also European Commission; Financial Services Action Plan; Markets in Financial Instruments Directive
EWN Mark II databases, 86
Exchange of Securities Dealing and Automated Quotation, 214
exchange rate
 foreign debt, 20, 191–7
 pegs, 193, 249–51
 regional cooperation, 242–52
 stabilization, 31–3, 243, 249–52, 254, 276
 volatility, 3, 8, 243, 245, 254, 269
 see also currencies
Executives' Meeting of East Asia and Pacific Central Banks (EMEAP), 252–4
Exogenous Shocks Facility (ESF), 285–6
export credit agencies (ECAs), 283
Extended Fund Facilities (EFFs), 138–9, 142, 145–6
external ratings (ERs), 123, 127–31

FASB, *see* Financial Accounting Standards Board

FATF, *see* Financial Action Task Force
FBI, *see* Federal Bureau of Investigation
FCD, *see* Financial Conglomerates Directive
FCL, *see* Flexible Credit Line
Federal Bureau of Investigation (FBI), 180
Federal Reserve, 33, 254
Federation of European Securities Exchanges (FESE), 233
FESE, *see* Federation of European Securities Exchanges
financial architecture, 1–4, 17, 75–6, 272
 apex policy forums, 58–73
 Basel II, 113–33
 legitimacy, 6, 12, 136, 270–1, 287–303, 312–3
 reform, 9, 12, 14, 18, 46, 135, 147–8, 243, 257, 271, 286–8, 295, 297, 300–4, 307–15
 see also new international financial architecture
Financial Accounting Standards Board (FASB), 232
Financial Action Task Force (FATF), 173–84
Financial Conglomerates Directive (FCD), 231, 236
financial crises
 Asian Crisis, 2, 50–3, 104–5, 125, 215–6, 241–52, 275
 Great Depression, 32–3, 35, 39
 Peso Crisis, 9, 115, 196
 Latin American Debt Crisis, 187–203
 Sub-prime Crisis, 120, 124–6, 133, 203, 241, 287, 295, 302
financial repression, 297–8, 306
Financial Sector Assessment Programme (FSAP), 44, 51, 53, 67, 98–100, 104
Financial Sector Masterplan (FSM), 213–4
Financial Services Action Plan (FSAP), 226–8
Financial Stability Board (FSB), 2, 14, 16, 57, 60–2, 69, 115, 297, 302, 304
 see also Financial Stability Forum
Financial Stability Forum (FSF), 2, 14, 44, 47, 302
 see also Financial Stability Board
Flandreau, Marc, 29
Flexible Credit Line (FCL), 284–5
forbearance, *see* regulatory forbearance
foreign reserves, *see* reserves
forward-looking provisions, 277–9
Foundation Internal Ratings Based approach, 119, 121–2, 125

350   Index

Framework for Advancing Transatlantic Economic Integration, 229
France, 29, 33–4, 157, 182
FSAP, *see* Financial Sector Assessment Programme; Financial Services Action Plan
FSF, *see* Financial Stability Forum
FSM, *see* Financial Sector Masterplan

G7, 2, 9, 16–7, 42–8, 50–65, 67, 69, 95–6, 178, 223, 294–7, 301, 306
G10, 2, 9–10, 15–7, 45, 60, 74, 113–4, 297, 306
G20, 2, 14–5, 44, 47, 55–65, 67–9, 72, 99, 112–4, 121, 203, 240, 302, 304, 311
GDP-indexed bonds, 280–2
Germain, Randall, 17, 25–41, 308–9
Germany, 29, 31, 34, 54, 157, 184, 262
Gold Standard, 29, 32–3, 36
Grameen Bank, 263–4
Griffith-Jones, Stephany, 21–2, 89, 124, 169, 270–86
Group of Thirty (G30), 117–8, 294
guarantee facilities, 283

hawala remittance system, 185
Heavily Indebted Poor Countries (HIPCs), 144, 158, 160
Heavily Indebted Poor Countries (HIPC) Initiative, 157, 160
hedge funds, 47, 55, 276, 314
hegemony, 103, 104, 225, 231, 240, 248
Helleiner, Eric, 42–57
herd behaviour, 11, 124, 130, 273
HIPC, *see* Heavily Indebted Poor Countries
hyperinflation, *see* inflation
Hyundai, 100

IAASB, *see* International Auditing and Assurance Standards Board
IAS, *see* International Accounting Standards
IASB, *see* International Accounting Standards Board
Ibrahim, Anwar, 211–2
ICRG, *see* International Country Risk Guide
IFF, *see* International Finance Facility
IFIs, *see* International Financial Institutions
IFRS, *see* International Financial Reporting Standards
IIF, *see* Institute of International Finance
IMF, *see* International Monetary Fund

indexed bonds, *see* GDP-indexed bonds
inflation, 7–8, 11, 34, 86, 193, 195, 198, 299
initial endowment hypothesis, 79
innovation
    institutional, 2, 15, 26, 30–8
    financial, 7, 121, 132, 252, 281, 293, 306
Institute of International Finance (IIF), 10, 14, 47, 63, 68, 116–18
interest rates, 30, 187–8, 192–8, 258, 262, 275
internal ratings (IRs), 118, 127–31
Internal Ratings Based (IRB) approaches, 119, 121–24, 127
    see also Advanced Internal Ratings Based approaches; Foundation Internal Ratings Based approaches
internal risk management, *see* risk management
International Accounting Standards (IAS), 97, 230
International Accounting Standards Board (IASB), 14, 47, 55–7, 97, 229, 306
International Auditing and Assurance Standards Board (IAASB), 47
International Country Risk Guide (ICRG), 77, 87
International Finance Facility (IFF), 259
international financial architecture, *see* financial architecture; new international financial architecture
International Financial Institutions (IFIs), 4, 11, 13, 20, 74, 95, 103–6, 294–5, 299–300
    see also IMF, World Bank
International Financial Reporting Standards (IFRS), 97–8, 102–3, 107, 232–3, 237
International Monetary Fund (IMF)
    catalytic effect, 19, 89, 134–49
    conditionality, 50–1, 105, 187–9, 195
    counter-cyclicality, 277, 283–6
    legitimacy, 9–10, 50, 52–3, 105, 135, 147, 241, 258, 294–5, 300
    reform of, 16, 54, 271, 285–6, 300–2
    see also Extended Fund Facilities; Poverty Reduction and Growth Facilities; Reports on the Observance of Standards and Codes; Sovereign Debt Restructuring Mechanism; Special Data Dissemination Standard; Stand-By Arrangements; surveillance
interwar period, 25–41
IRB, *see* Internal Ratings Based approach

Index

IRs, *see* internal ratings

Japan, 43, 52, 56, 101, 108–9, 161, 245–55
Jong, Eelke de, 19, 89, 134–49, 312

KKM indices, 167–8
Klagsbrunn, Victor Hugo, 20, 187–203
KLSE, *see* Kuala Lumpur Stock Exchange
KMT, *see* Nationalist Party or Kuomintang
Kuala Lumpur Stock Exchange (KLSE), 211, 214

Lamfalussy Process, 227–8
Langley, Paul, 28
Latin America, 4, 13, 31, 45, 52–3, 187–203, 299, 311
  see also financial crises
legal origins hypothesis, 78
legitimacy, 1–2, 5–7, 12–22, 44, 135–6, 155, 254–5, 258, 260, 269, 286, 287–315
  anti-money laundering regime, 172–3, 177–9, 186
  apex policy forums, 59–73
  financial architecture, 6, 12, 14, 136, 270–1, 287–303, 312–3
  input/inclusiveness, 5–6, 12–7, 22, 56–7, 70–3, 76, 95, 205, 224, 242, 254, 260, 268, 270, 286, 287–95, 300–1, 305–15
  International Monetary Fund, 9–10, 50, 52–3, 105, 135, 147, 241, 258, 294–5, 300
  output/effectiveness, 5–6, 11–3, 22, 56, 76, 89, 95–6, 136, 155, 241, 255, 268, 270, 286, 287–95, 300, 305–15
  regionalism, 1, 2, 13, 15–6, 33, 38, 226, 254, 291, 301–2, 310–1, 313
  see also accountability; policy space; private sector
liberalisation, 7, 20, 38, 195–6, 204–8, 239, 275, 297, 299
  see also capital account; financial repression
limited argument pools, 65–7, 70
liquidity, 30, 138, 188, 212, 243, 247, 266, 271–2, 282–6
loan classification, 100–1
local currency bonds, 278, 282, 286, 310
Long Term Capital Management, 46

Mahathir, Mohamad, 211–4
market discipline, 48, 67, 119–21, 126, 132
Markets in Financial Instruments Directive (MiFID), 235, 238

MDBs, *see* multilateral development banks
MDGs, *see* Millennium Development Goals
MDRI, *see* Multilateral Debt Reduction Initiative
MERCOSUR, 192, 203
Mexico, 9–10, 42–5, 51, 110, 135–6, 143, 191, 196, 281, 285
microcredit/microfinance, 21, 256–69, 312
MiFID, *see* Markets in Financial Instruments Directive
Millennium Development Goals (MDGs), 151, 259, 264, 269
minority shareholders, 101, 105–6, 108, 110
mock compliance, *see* compliance
money laundering, 46, 99, 172–86, 306, 314
money service businesses (MSBs), 185
Moody's, 48, 109–10, 119, 125, 127–9, 133
  see also Bank Financial Strength Ratings
MSBs, *see* money service businesses
Mügge, Daniel, 1–22, 304–15
Multilateral Debt Reduction Initiative (MDRI), 158
multilateral development banks (MDBs), 16, 282–3

Nationalist Party or Kuomintang (KMT), 209
NCCTs, *see* Non-Cooperative Countries and Territories
new international financial architecture (NIFA), 2, 17, 39, 42–4, 46, 50, 53–6, 111, 133, 204, 218, 307
  Basel II, 115–20
  see also financial architecture
NGOs, *see* non-governmental organisations
NIFA, *see* new international financial architecture; financial architecture
non-compliance, *see* compliance
Non-Cooperative Countries and Territories (NCCTs), 174, 178–9, 181–2
non-governmental organisations (NGOs), 151, 155, 260–8
non-performing loans (NPLs), 100–1
NPLs, *see* non-performing loans

Ocampo, José Antonio, 21–2, 169, 270–86
OECD, *see* Organisation for Economic Cooperation and Development
Organisation for Economic Cooperation and Development (OECD), 98, 115, 172
  see also Development Assistance Committee; Principles of Corporate Governance

352 Index

Office of Foreign Assets Control (OFAC), 181
original sin, 11, 296
offshore finance, 19, 172–3, 182–6, 211, 276

Pagliari, Stefano, 17, 42–57, 62, 307
Pan-Asia Bond Index Fund (PAIF), 253
Paris Club, 19, 134–49, 198
  see also comparability of treatment
Paris Declaration (PD) on Aid Effectiveness, 19, 151, 155–6, 163–5, 167–8, 259
PCAOB, *see* Public Company Accounting Oversight Board
PCG, *see* Principles of Corporate Governance
PD, *see* Paris Declaration on Aid Effectiveness
Polanyi, Karl, 26, 28, 41
policy capture, 6, 13, 49, 68–9, 114, 118, 131, 270–1, 292, 294, 300
  see also regulatory capture; private sector
policy space, 6, 20, 25, 76, 89–90, 96, 111–2, 134, 151, 155, 187, 204, 218–9, 256, 258, 268–9, 270–2, 278, 286, 288, 300, 308–11
  see also legitimacy
Posner, Elliot, 20, 223–40
poverty, 14, 21, 76, 84, 156–60, 256–64, 268–9, 285–6, 311–2
  see also developing countries; Heavily Indebted Poor Countries
Poverty Reduction and Growth Facilities (PRGFs), 142–8, 285–6
Poverty Reduction Strategy Papers (PRSPs), 151, 155, 160, 259
PRGFs, *see* Poverty Reduction and Growth Facilities
Principles of Corporate Governance (PCG), 97–8
private sector
  bailing in, 19, 45–6, 90, 134–5, 138, 143–8
  compliance, 51, 98–107, 175–6, 182
  lobbying/influence, 3, 10, 12, 46–7, 68–9, 97, 114, 116–8, 135, 180, 202, 207–8
  legitimacy, 50, 292–6
  see also catalytic approach; comparability of treatment; Institute of International Finance; policy capture; regulatory capture
pro-cyclicality, *see* cyclicality
projection bias, 139–41
property rights, 77–8, 82–3, 85

PRSPs, *see* Poverty Reduction Strategy Papers
Public Company Accounting Oversight Board (PCAOB), 229, 232

Raiffeisen system, 261–2
rating agencies, *see* credit rating agencies
regionalism
  financial/monetary cooperation, 21, 241–55
  legitimacy, 1, 2, 13, 15–6, 33, 38, 226, 291, 301–2, 310–1, 313
  see also ASEAN+3; Association of Southeast Asian Nations; European Union; MERCOSUR; transatlantic financial regulation
regulation, 1, 37, 47–50, 55, 294, 296–7, 306
  anti-money laundering, 172–86
  Basel II, 48, 113–33
  counter-cyclical, 270–86
  international standards/convergence, 95–112
  national diversity/divergence, 18, 50, 86, 108–10, 208, 296–7
  prudential, 44, 68, 72, 125, 275–80
  self-regulation/deregulation, 8, 26, 37, 55, 116, 179, 216–7, 293–4, 296, 306
  transatlantic cooperation, 223–40
  see also compliance; convergence; financial architecture; new international financial architecture; regulatory capture; regulatory forbearance; standards and codes
regulatory capture, 49, 118, 126, 238, 294, 301, 307
  see also policy capture; private sector
regulatory convergence, *see* convergence
regulatory forbearance, 96–97, 99–101, 106–7, 109, 112
  see also compliance
relationship banking, 121–2
Reports on the Observance of Standards and Codes (ROSCs), 2, 44, 51, 53–4, 66–7
repression, *see* financial repression
reserves
  accumulation, 4, 51–2, 56, 191, 197–9, 202, 243–7, 254, 271, 276, 300, 311
  pooling, 245–7, 253
  see also liquidity
risk management, 118–122, 124, 126, 131–2, 273, 282, 293
  see also systemic risk
ROSCs, *see* Reports on the Observance of Standards and Codes

Index

353

Ruggie, John, 26, 39, 309
Russia, 40, 46, 63, 178, 193, 196, 271

Sarbanes-Oxley Act, 46, 231–4
SBAs, *see* Stand-By Arrangements
SDDS, *see* Special Data Dissemination Standard
Scharpf, Fritz, 5
SDRM, *see* Sovereign Debt Restructuring Mechanism
sectoralisation, 31
Securities and Exchange Commission (SEC), 31, 228–39
Securities Industry Association (SIA), 236
securitization, 3, 7, 37, 55, 132, 266, 282
sequencing, 64, 242, 244–5
Shambaugh, David, 248
SIA, *see* Securities Industry Association
sovereign wealth funds, 3, 52, 271
Small and Medium-sized Enterprises (SMEs), 122–3
SOEs, *see* State-Owned Enterprises
Sovereign Debt Restructuring Mechanism (SDRM), 3, 10, 46–7, 51, 61, 65, 135, 143
Special Data Dissemination Standard (SDDS), 43, 97–9, 102–3, 107
Stability and Growth Pact, 281
Standard and Poor's, 48, 119, 125, 127–9, 131
standards and codes, 9, 18, 43–4, 46–8, 50–1, 53, 56, 65–8, 95–6
Stand-By Arrangements (SBAs), 142–3, 145–6, 148
State-Owned Enterprises (SOEs), 209, 217
stock markets/exchanges
  emerging markets, 197, 204–18
  regulation of, 48, 229–38
  see also Kuala Lumpur Stock Exchange; Taipei Stock Exchange
substantive compliance, *see* compliance
supervision, 44, 48, 102, 113–5, 118–20, 131, 227, 231, 267, 275–6, 278–9, 293–4, 305–6
  see also Basel Core Principles; risk management
Supplemental Reserve Facility, 284
surveillance, 16, 44, 67, 242, 249–52, 298
  see also transparency
systemic risk, 3, 18, 117, 120–7, 131–3, 276

Taipei Stock Exchange (TSE), 214–17
terrorism, financing of, 180–1
Thailand, 100–5, 108–112, 249–50, 253

trade, 30, 32, 79, 86, 105, 158, 189–93, 196–7, 242–5, 248–9, 273, 285–6
transatlantic financial regulation, 20–1, 223–40
transparency, 2, 8, 19, 39, 43–7, 66–9, 103–6, 126, 156, 168–9, 181–2, 213, 272, 294–5
TSE, *see* Taipei Stock Exchange
Tsingou, Eleni, 172–86, 314

Underhill, Geoffrey, 1–22, 52, 113–33, 287–315
United Kingdom (UK), 30–1, 67, 69, 95, 161, 177, 182, 225, 254
United Malay National Organisation (UMNO), 209, 211–4
United Nations (UN), 65, 72, 144, 157, 174–5, 184, 259
United States (US), 4, 16, 21, 27, 30–1, 33, 37, 48–9, 53, 63, 67–8, 95, 103–4, 122, 161, 196, 241, 247, 249, 254, 273, 277, 305–7, 311
  transatlantic financial regulation, 223-40
  global anti-money laundering regime, 172–86
  see also Federal Reserve; Federal Bureau of Investigation; financial crises; Securities and Exchange Commission; US dollar; US Generally Accepted Accounting Principles; US Treasury; Wall Street; Washington Consensus
US dollar, 3–4, 33, 192–4, 198–9, 249–51, 253
US GAAP, *see US* Generally Accepted Accounting Principles
US Generally Accepted Accounting Principles (US GAAP), 230, 232–3, 236–7
US Treasury, 30, 45, 50, 68–9, 228–9, 236

Value at Risk (VaR) models, 119, 132
Visconti, Roberto Moro, 266
volatility
  exchange rate, 3, 8, 11, 243, 245, 254, 269
  external financing, 127, 129–30, 272–4, 284–6, 310
  systemic, 2, 10, 75, 80, 82, 88–9, 121, 130, 254, 269, 275–8
  see also boom-bust cycles; cyclicality; systemic risk
Volcker, Paul, 117–18

Wall Street, 1, 67, 69, 236
Walter, Andrew, 18, 51, 95–112, 126, 206, 294, 309–10

354   Index

Washington Consensus, 20, 74, 151, 152, 188–9, 194–7, 258
Wolfsberg Group of Banks, 182–3
World Bank, 44, 51, 60, 66, 138, 151, 258–9, 281–2
see also Country Policy and Institutional Assessment; Financial Sector Assessment Programme; Reports on the Observance of Standards and Codes

Young, Brigitte, 21, 256–69, 312
Yunus, Muhammad, 260, 263

Zhang, Xiaoke, 20, 111, 204–19, 287–303

For EU product safety concerns, contact us at Calle de José Abascal, 56–1°, 28003 Madrid, Spain or eugpsr@cambridge.org.

www.ingramcontent.com/pod-product-compliance
Ingram Content Group UK Ltd.
Pitfield, Milton Keynes, MK11 3LW, UK
UKHW020926110825
461507UK00029B/195